Film, Form, and Culture

Film, Form, and Culture (fourth edition) offers a lively introduction to both the formal and cultural aspects of film. With extensive analysis of films past and present, this textbook explores film from part to whole: from the smallest unit of the shot to the way shots are edited together to create narrative. It then examines those narratives (both fiction and non-fiction) as stories and genres that speak to the culture of their time and our perceptions of them today.

Composition, editing, genres (such as the gangster film, the Western, science fiction, and melodrama) are analyzed alongside numerous images to illustrate the discussion. Chapters on the individuals who make films—the production designer, cinematographer, editor, composer, producer, director, and actor—illustrate the collaborative nature of filmmaking.

This new edition includes:

- An expanded discussion of the digital "revolution" in filmmaking: exploring the movement from celluloid to digital recording and editing of images, as well as the use of CGI
- A new chapter on international cinema covering filmmaking from Italy to Mumbai, offering students a broader understanding of cinema on a worldwide scale
- A new chapter on film acting that uses images to create a small catalogue of gestures and expressions that are recognizable in film after film
- Expanded content coverage and in-depth analysis throughout, including a visual analysis of a scene from Christopher Nolan's *The Dark Knight*
- An expanded chapter on the cultural contexts of film summarizing the theories of cultural and media studies, concluding with a comparative analysis of Alfred Hitchcock's *Vertigo* and Judd Apatow's *This is 40*
- Over 260 images, many in color, creating a visual index to the discussion of films and filmmaking
- Updated suggestions for further reading and viewing at the end of each chapter, and an expanded glossary of terms.

Additional resources for students and teachers can also be found on the companion website (www.routledge.com/cw/kolker), which includes extension activities, additional case studies and links to useful websites.

This textbook is an invaluable and exciting resource for students beginning film studies at undergraduate level.

Robert P. Kolker is Professor Emeritus at the University of Maryland, College Park, USA. He is the author/editor of several books on film including *The Cultures of American Film* (2014), *The Oxford Handbook of Film and Media Studies* (2008), *A Cinema of Loneliness*, 4th edition (2011) and *The Altering Eye* (1983 and 2009).

Praise for this edition

"Kolker's lucid, accessible style gives this book a pace and energy that sets it apart. Among the many introductory film textbooks, *Film, Form, and Culture* captures the reader's attention at first glance, and holds it throughout."

Robert Burgoyne, *Professor of Film Studies, University of St Andrews*

"*Film, Form, and Culture* is a thoughtful, ambitious, and thorough introductory textbook that is also an absolute pleasure to read. Put simply, this richly illustrated book makes it easy to understand how to take film seriously. It is scaled to a manageable size and scope for classroom use, providing a comprehensive set of tools and skills with which to approach the study of film. Kolker introduces his reader to film and art history, theories of representation, genres and international cinemas, and the vocabulary with which to discuss moving images. True to its title, the book provides a framework with which to understand and engage with the way that form and culture interact through the medium of film. Kolker pulls off a rare feat with *Film, Form, and Culture*: he has provided teachers at any level with a readable and immensely useful book that is also rigorously intellectual. I have used earlier editions of *Film, Form and Culture* in my introductory film classes and I'm delighted to now be able to use this updated edition. This is a fantastic introductory book by one of the field's foremost thinkers that will be appreciated by anyone wishing to better understand what makes films tick."

Marsha Gordon, *Associate Professor, Film Studies, North Carolina State University*

"Robert Kolker is both a brilliant analyst of film and a great teacher. He manages to explain and use complex concepts in limpid prose, and his effortless blend of textual and contextual approaches to cinema is a model to us all."

Toby Miller, *Professor of Journalism, Media and Cultural Studies, Cardiff University*

"Robert Kolker's *Film, Form, and Culture* (4th edition) is a lucidly written textbook for undergraduate students who are beginning their film and media studies programs. Kolker takes the readers on a tantalizing journey in which they will encounter film language, grammar, history, theory and the broader issues of culture and ideology. The book does not get bogged down in jargon and theoretical trapeze walks. Its purpose is to teach students to unpack the artifice of cinema by learning the analytical tools to take the scenes apart and then figuring out how the audience puts them all together. The students will also learn the fact that film developed all over the world, almost at the same time, and form and style have been evolving ever since in different cultural contexts to render a rich body of work for all to see."

Manjunath Pendakur, *Professor, School of Communication and Multimedia Studies, Florida Atlantic University*

Film, Form, and Culture

Fourth Edition

ROBERT P. KOLKER

LONDON AND NEW YORK

First published by McGraw-Hill Higher Education 1999
Second edition published 2002
Third edition published 2006

This fourth edition published 2016
by Routledge
2 Park Square, Milton Park, Abingdon, Oxon OX14 4RN

and by Routledge
711 Third Avenue, New York, NY 10017

Routledge is an imprint of the Taylor & Francis Group, an informa business

British Library Cataloguing-in-Publication Data
A catalogue record for this book is available from the British Library

Library of Congress Cataloging-in-Publication Data
Kolker, Robert Phillip.
Film, form, and culture / Robert P. Kolker. — 4th edition.
pages cm
Includes bibliographical references and index.
1. Motion pictures. 2. Culture in motion pictures. I. Title.
PN1994.K573 2015
791.43—dc23
2015004360

ISBN: 978-1-138-84571-8 (hbk)
ISBN: 978-1-138-84572-5 (pbk)
ISBN: 978-1-315-72802-5 (ebk)

Typeset in Bembo and Frutiger
by Florence Production Ltd, Stoodleigh, Devon, UK

Printed and bound in the United States of America by Sheridan Books, Inc. (a Sheridan Group Company).

Contents

List of illustrations xiii
Preface xxi
Acknowledgments xxii

Introduction **1**

1 Image and reality **9**

Images, the real, and history 9
The "truth" of the image 10
Natural Born Killers and the objectivity of the image 15
The urge to represent "reality" 17
Perspective and the pleasures of tricking the eye 17
Photography and reality 19
Manipulation of the image 21
Reality as image 22
From the photographic to the cinematic image 23
Moving images 23
Acknowledgments 26
Further reading 26
Suggestions for further viewing 27
Note 27

2 Formal structures: how films tell their stories **29**

The image, the world, and the film studio 29
From image to narrative 29
The economics of the image 32
The system develops: Buster Keaton and Charlie Chaplin 33

The growth of corporate filmmaking 35
The classical Hollywood style 36
Casablanca 36
Entertainment and invisibility 39
Fabricating the image 39
The whole and its parts 45
Making the parts invisible 47
Story, plot, and narration 48
Jaws 48
Convention and consciousness 50
Further reading 51
Suggestions for further viewing 52
Note 52

3 The building blocks of film I: the shot 53

The shot 53
The long take 53
The Magnificent Ambersons 54
Touch of Evil 55
Rope, Russian Ark, and *Birdman* 55
Goodfellas 56
How composition works 57
Composition in early cinema 58
D. W. Griffith 58
The Unchanging Sea 58
The Musketeers of Pig Alley 61
The size of the frame 61
Wide screen 62
Anamorphic and "flat" wide-screen processes 63
Loss of standards 64
The studios and the shot 65
Mise-en-scène 66
Lighting 67
Color 69
Vertigo 71
Red Desert 73
The mise-en-scène of German Expressionism 73
Expressionist mise-en-scène in the United States 74
Orson Welles and the reinvention of mise-en-scène 75
Deep focus and the long take 76
Citizen Kane 76
The Hitchcock mise-en-scène 81
Psycho 81
Working against the rules 81
Further reading 84
Suggestions for further viewing 84
Notes 84

4 **The building blocks of film II: the cut** **85**

Editing and the classic Hollywood style 85
The Great Train Robbery 87
The development of continuity cutting 89
Griffith and cutting 90
The Lonedale Operator 90
2001: A Space Odyssey 92
Shot/reverse shot 92
Point of view 95
Sight lines 95
The 180-degree rule 96
Psycho and the shot/reverse shot 97
Convention, culture, resistance 99
Gender 102
Coding 102
Responses to conventional cutting 103
Eisensteinian montage 104
Battleship Potemkin 105
Eisenstein and Oliver Stone 107
The narrative of the classical style 107
Working creatively within and against conventions 108
Further reading 109
Suggestions for further viewing 109
Notes 110

5 **The storytellers of film I** **111**

Collaboration as creativity 113
Creative craftspeople 114
Cinematographer 114
Editor 116
Production designer 117
Special effects and CGI 119
Sound designers 122
Composer 123
Screenwriter 126
Producer 129
Further reading 131
Suggestions for further viewing 132
Notes 133

6 **The storytellers of film II: acting** **135**

Methods of performance 135
Delsarte 136
The Method 137
Cultures of acting 139

How screen acting works: the gaze and the gesture 142
Eyes Wide Shut and *Vertigo* 142
Celebrity 146
Further reading 146
Suggestions for further viewing 147
Notes 147

7 The storytellers of film III: the director 149

The producer as director 149
European origins of the auteur 150
France and the French New Wave 150
The auteur theory 151
Andrew Sarris and the three principles: competence, style, vision 151
Robert Altman 156
Martin Scorsese 157
Stanley Kubrick 163
Alfred Hitchcock 165
Women auteurs 167
Alice Guy-Blaché and Lois Weber 167
Dorothy Arzner 168
Ida Lupino 169
Women filmmakers today 171
Kathryn Bigelow 171
African American filmmakers 173
Spike Lee 173
Tyler Perry 174
Julie Dash 174
Auteurism today 176
Christopher Nolan 176
What is the director? 178
Further reading 179
Suggestions for further viewing 180
Notes 180

8 International cinema 181

Early influences 181
Neorealism 182
Bicycle Thieves and *Rome, Open City* 183
Neorealism's influence 186
Italian cinema after neorealism 187
Federico Fellini and Michelangelo Antonioni 187
Bernardo Bertolucci 189
The New Wave 190
François Truffaut and Jean-Luc Godard 191
The new German cinema 194
Wim Wenders 194

Werner Herzog 195
Rainer Werner Fassbinder 197
Chantal Akerman 199
Jeanne Dielman 199
Film in Asia 200
Japan and Yasujiro Ozu 200
Hong Kong and Wong Kar-wai 202
Bollywood 203
Satyagraha 203
The Lunchbox 204
European cinema today 205
Jean-Pierre and Luc Dardenne 205
Michael Haneke 205
Film culture 208
Further reading 209
Suggestions for further viewing 209
Notes 210

9 The stories told by film I 213

The stories we want to see 213
It's a Wonderful Life 213
Closure 214
Dominant fictions 214
Narrative constraints 215
Censorship 216
Genre 217
Subgenres 217
Generic origins 218
Generic patterns: the gangster film 220
Genre and narrative economy 222
Documentary 223
Newsreels and television 223
Early masters of the documentary 224
Dziga Vertov and Esther Shub 224
Robert Flaherty 225
Pare Lorentz 226
Leni Riefenstahl 228
John Grierson and the British documentary movement 229
World War II 230
Cinéma vérité 231
David and Albert Maysles 231
Michael Moore 232
Errol Morris 233
The genres of fiction films 234
The Western 235
The Western landscape 235

The obstacle to westward expansion 236
The Western star and the Western director 236
Stagecoach 237
Fort Apache and *The Man Who Shot Liberty Valence* 238
The Searchers 239
The Western after the 1950s 240
The Wild Bunch, Little Big Man, McCabe and Mrs. Miller 240
Science fiction and horror 242
Fritz Lang's *Metropolis* 243
Science fiction in the 1950s and beyond 243
The Day the Earth Stood Still 244
The Thing from Another World 245
Forbidden Planet 245
Alien, Blade Runner, and *Dark City* 247
2001: A Space Odyssey 249
The post-apocalyptic world and zombies 250
Further reading 252
Suggestions for further viewing 253
Notes 255

10 The stories told by film II 257

Film noir 257
Expressionist roots of noir 258
Hard-boiled fiction 258
The Maltese Falcon 259
Murder, My Sweet, Double Indemnity, Scarlet Street 259
Anthony Mann 261
Noir's climax 262
In a Lonely Place 262
The Wrong Man 263
Kiss Me Deadly 263
Touch of Evil 264
Noir's rebirth 265
Melodrama 266
Broken Blossoms 267
Now, Voyager 271
Casablanca 275
Contemporary melodrama 276
The Fault in Our Stars 276
Flight 276
Brokeback Mountain 276
One genre, two countries, three directors 278
All That Heaven Allows, Ali: Fear Eats the Soul, Far From Heaven 278
The filmmakers 278
Rainer Werner Fassbinder 278
Douglas Sirk 278

Todd Haynes 279
The common thread 280
All That Heaven Allows and *Far From Heaven* 280
Race 282
Gender 283
Ali: Fear Eats the Soul 285
The influence of Bertolt Brecht 286
The gaze 287
Fassbinder's narrative 288
Happiness is not always fun 289
Genre resilience 289
Further reading 290
Suggestions for further viewing 290
Notes 291

11 Film as cultural practice 293

Film in the realm of culture 293
Culture as text 294
Subcultures 295
Media and cultures 295
The new Web 298
Theories of culture 299
The Frankfurt school 299
The critique of American popular culture 300
High culture, masscult, and midcult 301
Walter Benjamin and the age of mechanical reproduction 302
The aura of state intervention 304
The Birmingham School of Cultural Studies 305
Reception and negotiation 306
Judgment and values 307
Intertextuality and postmodernism 308
Cultural criticism applied to *Vertigo* and *This is 40* 309
The cultural–technological mix: film, television, digital 310
Judd Apatow and the digital 312
The actor's persona: James Stewart and the Apatow boys and women 312
James Stewart 312
The Apatow stock company 313
Vertigo and the culture of the 1950s 315
The Kinsey Reports 316
This is 40 and the culture of the early 2000s 317
The vulnerable male in film 319
Film, form, and culture 321
Modernity, modernism, the postmodern 323
Formal structures 324
Conclusion 325

Further reading 327
Suggestions for further viewing 328
Notes 329

Glossary 331
Index 340

Illustrations

1.1 Quentin Tarantino destroys the Nazis in a movie house (*Inglourious Basterds*, 2009) 10

1.2 The green screen—a production still from Tim Burton's *Alice in Wonderland* (2010) 11

1.3 René Magritte's *The Treachery of Images* (*This is Not a Pipe*), 1929. Los Angeles County Museum of Art (LACMA). © 2015. Digital Image Museum Associates/ LACMA/Art Resource NY/Scala, Florence 12

1.4–1.5 Oliver Stone interrogates the reliability of the image (*JFK*, 1991) 14

1.6–1.7 Stone imitates the video of the 1991 police beating of Rodney King (*Natural Born Killers,* 1994) 16

1.8 Perspective in painting illustrated by Fra Carnavale's *The Annunciation* (*c.* 1445–1450). Courtesy National Gallery of Art, Washington 18

1.9 The camera obscura, used by painters in the seventeenth and eighteenth centuries 19

1.10 A zoopraxiscope made by the late nineteenth-century visual inventor, Eadweard Muybridge 25

2.1 Early eroticism from Thomas Edison's studio. *The Kiss* (William Heise, 1896) 31

2.2 Auguste and Louis Lumière's *Arrival of a Train at La Ciotat Station* (1896) 31

2.3 Georges Méliès, the magician, creates trick shots in *A Trip to the Moon* (1902) 31

2.4 A house falls on Buster Keaton (Charles Reisner, Buster Keaton, *Steamboat Bill, Jr.*, 1928) 34

2.5–2.10 The long introduction to Rick at the beginning of *Casablanca* (Michael Curtiz, 1942) 38

2.11 Example of a layered composition using matte paintings in *Casablanca* 40
2.12 The lyricism of artificiality. F. W. Murnau's *Sunrise* (1927) 41
2.13 The digital mise-en-scène in James Gunn's *Guardians of The Galaxy* (2014) 42
2.14 The immediacy of location shooting. Satyajit Ray's *The World of Apu* (1959) 44
2.15 Life on the streets. Martin Scorsese's *Mean Streets* (1973) 44
2.16 The illusion of characters in space. Alfonso Cuarón's *Gravity* (2013) 45
2.17 Changing nature to fit the mise-en-scène. Michelangelo Antonioni's *Blow-Up* (1966) 46
2.18–2.21 Steven Spielberg manipulates point of view in *Jaws* (1975) 49
2.22–2.23 Spielberg zooms in one direction and tracks in the other (*Jaws*) 50
3.1 A moment from the almost four minute static take in Orson Welles's *The Magnificent Ambersons* (1942) 54
3.2 A slice from the over three minute moving camera beginning Welles's *Touch of Evil* (1958) 55
3.3 The dynamics of the Copacabana shot in Scorsese's *Goodfellas* (1990) 56
3.4 A still image from the tracking shot through the record boutique in Stanley Kubrick's *A Clockwork Orange* (1971) 57
3.5–3.7 Demonstrating the 90-degree position of the camera (John Crowley, *Closed Circuit*, 2013) 59
3.8 The off-center placement of characters in D. W. Griffith's *The Unchanging Sea* (1910) 60
3.9 Griffith's use of close-up in *The Musketeers of Pig Alley* (1912) 60
3.10 An example of an iris shot from D. W. Griffith's *The Birth of a Nation* (1915) 62
3.11 An anamorphic wide-screen composition in *The Railway Man* (Jonathan Teplitzky, 2013) 64
3.12 An example of shallow focus in *Grand Hotel* (Edmund Goulding, 1932) 65
3.13–3.14 Unmasking the Joker in Christopher Nolan's *The Dark Knight* (2008) 66
3.15–3.17 Examples of three-point lighting 67
3.18–3.19 High-key and low-key lighting in *The Public Enemy* (William Wellman, 1931) 68
3.20 The exotic mise-en-scène in Josef von Sternberg's *Shanghai Express* (1932) 68
3.21 The face withdraws into darkness in Mervyn LeRoy's *I Am a Fugitive from a Chain Gang* (1932) 68
3.22 An example of early two-color Technicolor in Buster Keaton's *Seven Chances* (1925) 69
3.23 The subtle use of grayscale in Pawel Pawlikowski's Polish film *Ida* (2013) 70
3.24 The walls glow red in Hitchcock's *Vertigo* (1958) 71
3.25 The passionate red becomes a sickly green when Madeleine appears to return from the dead in *Vertigo* 71
3.26 The color scheme in Stanley Kubrick's *Eyes Wide Shut* (1999) 72

3.27 David Fincher emphasizes the horizontal line and a dark mise-en-scène in *Seven* (1995) 72

3.28 The use of color in Michelangelo Antonioni's *Red Desert* (1964) 73

3.29 *The Cabinet of Dr. Caligari* (Robert Wiene, 1920) 74

3.30 *The Bride of Frankenstein* (James Whale, 1935) 74

3.31–3.32 Expressionist mise-en-scène and the imaginary city in F. W. Murnau's *Sunrise* (1927) 75

3.33 Putting the main character in darkness (Orson Welles, *Citizen Kane*, 1941) 76

3.34–3.35 Deep focus in *Citizen Kane* 78

3.36–3.40 Annotated sequence from *Citizen Kane* 79

3.41 A low angle shot from *Citizen Kane* 80

3.42–3.46 Demonstration of the abstract patterns underlying the compositions of Hitchcock's *Psycho* (1960) 82

3.47 A Hitchcock high angle shot from *Psycho* 82

3.48 A symmetrical composition from Stanley Kubrick's *The Shining* (1980) 83

3.49 A figure in the Midwestern landscape in Alexander Payne's *Nebraska* (2013) 83

4.1 Example of a flashback dissolve from *Casablanca* (Michael Curtiz, 1941) 86

4.2–4.5 Editing in *The Great Train Robbery* (Edwin S. Porter, 1903) 88

4.6 Shooting directly at the camera (*The Great Train Robbery*) 88

4.7 Scorsese's allusion to this shot in *Goodfellas* (1990) 88

4.8–4.13 Continuity cutting in D. W. Griffith's *The Lonedale Operator* (1911) 91

4.14–4.15 Stanley Kubrick cuts from bone to spaceship in *2001: A Space Odyssey* (1968) 92

4.16–4.21 Over-the-shoulder editing in Alfred Hitchcock's *North by Northwest* (1959) 94

4.22 Diagram illustrating the 180-degree rule 96

4.23–4.24 Kubrick breaks the 180-degree rule in *The Shining* (1980) 97

4.25–4.29 Point-of-view–shot/reverse shot editing in Hitchcock's *Psycho* (1960) 98

4.30–4.33 Non-continuity editing in Sergei Eisenstein's *Battleship Potemkin* (1925) 106

4.34 Oliver Stone plays a variation on Eisenstein's techniques in *Nixon* (1995) 107

5.1 Travis Bickle, "You talkin' to me?" (Martin Scorsese, *Taxi Driver*, 1976) 112

5.2 Lighting used by cinematographer Robert Richardson in *Django Unchained* (Quentin Tarantino, 2012) 116

5.3–5.4 Comparison of production design in two versions of *The Great Gatsby*—Jack Clayton, 1974 and Baz Lurman, 2013 119

5.5–5.7 CGI creation of characters Rocket and Groot in *Guardians of the Galaxy* (James Gunn, 2014) 121

5.8 Image of a 35-mm film frame with soundtrack 123

5.9 Sergei Eisenstein's chart of music and image for his film *Alexander Nevsky* (1938) 126
6.1–6.2 Chart of eye movements from a nineteenth-century actor's guide 137
6.3 James Dean in *Rebel Without a Cause* (Nicholas Ray, 1955) 138
6.4 Marlon Brando in *On the Waterfront* (Elia Kazan, 1954) 138
6.5 Brando in *The Godfather* (Francis Ford Coppola, 1972) 138
6.6 Marilyn Monroe in *The Seven Year Itch* (Billy Wilder, 1955) 140
6.7 Meryl Streep in *The Devil Wears Prada* (David Frankel, 2006) 140
6.8 Samuel Jackson in *Django Unchained* (Quentin Tarantino, 2012) 140
6.9 Charlie Chaplin in *The Gold Rush* (Chaplin, 1925) 141
6.10 Buster Keaton in *The General* (Keaton, Clyde Bruckman, 1926) 141
6.11 Contemporary comic actors in *This is the End* (Evan Goldberg, Seth Rogen, 2013) 141
6.12 Jeffrey Wright in *The Hunger Games: Catching Fire* (Francis Lawrence, 2013) 141
6.13 Philip Seymour Hoffman, Catherine Keener and Christopher Walken in *A Late Quartet* (Yaron Zilberman, 2012) 142
6.14 Madeleine looks away in fear in *Vertigo* (Alfred Hitchcock, 1958) 143
6.15 Alice looks distracted in *Eyes Wide Shut* (Stanley Kubrick, 1999) 143
6.16 The averted gaze in *The Girl and Her Trust* (D. W. Griffith, 1910) 143
6.17 An expression of fear in *The Girl and Her Trust* 143
6.18 Fear expressed in *Scream* (Wes Craven, 1996) 144
6.19 Rage expressed by actor Lee J. Cobb in *12 Angry Men* (Sidney Lumet, 1957) 144
6.20 Malice on the face of Woody Harrelson in *Out of the Furnace* (Scott Cooper, 2013) 144
6.21 Wistful look by Judi Dench in *Philomena* (Stephen Frears, 2013) 144
6.22 Troubled frustration, posed by Tom Hanks in *Saving Mr. Banks* (John Lee Hancock, 2013) 144
6.23 Faces of psychosis: Norman Bates in *Psycho* (Alfred Hitchcock, 1960) 145
6.24 Private Pyle in *Full Metal Jacket* (Stanley Kubrick, 1987) 145
6.25 Jesse Eisenberg plays two versions of himself in *The Double* (Richard Ayoade, 2013) 145
6.26 Romantic comedy: actors Juliette Binoche and Clive Owen in *Words and Pictures* (Fred Schepisi, 2013) 145
6.27 The look of love lost. Nimrat Kaur in *The Lunchbox* (Ritesh Batra, 2013) 145
7.1 Low angle shot from Orson Welles's *Touch of Evil* (1958) 153
7.2 High angle shot from *Touch of Evil* 153
7.3 The Ford landscape of Monument Valley in *The Searchers* (1956) 154
7.4 The cramped, cold spaces of Robert Altman's *McCabe and Mrs. Miller* (1971) 155
7.5 Actor Matthew Modine dressed as a clown in Robert Altman's *Short Cuts* (1993) 157

7.6 Jake La Motta takes a punch in Martin Scorsese's *Raging Bull* (1980) 159

7.7 Taking apart the HAL 2000 computer in Stanley Kubrick's *2001: A Space Odyssey* (1968) 164

7.8 Norman Bates in a threatening shot from Hitchcock's *Psycho* (1960) 165

7.9–7.13 How mise-en-scène relates narrative information in Hitchcock's *Vertigo* (1958) 166

7.14 An actress talks back to her audience in Dorothy Arzner's *Dance, Girl, Dance* (1940) 168

7.15 Men held hostage in Ida Lupino's *The Hitch-Hiker* (1953) 169

7.16 An explosives expert in Kathryn Bigelow's *The Hurt Locker* (2008) 172

7.17 A happy moment in Spike Lee's *Red Hook Summer* (2012) 173

7.18 The former slave and voice of history in Julie Dash's *Daughters of the Dust* (1991) 175

7.19–7.24 Analysis of a scene from Christopher Nolan's *The Dark Knight* (2008) 177

8.1 Ricci (Lamberto Maggiorani), putting up a poster, sees his bicycle stolen in Vittorio De Sica's *Bicycle Thieves* (1948) 184

8.2 The death of Pina in Roberto Rossellini's *Rome, Open City* (1945) 185

8.3 A surreal scene in Federico Fellini's *La strada* (1954) 187

8.4 Fellini in circus mode. *8½* (1963) 188

8.5 Marlon Brando in Bernardo Bertolucci's *Last Tango in Paris* (1972) 189

8.6 The freeze frame that ends François Truffaut's *The 400 Blows* (1959) 191

8.7 The jump cut in Jean-Luc Godard's *Breathless* (1960) 192

8.8 Godard's post-apocalyptic *Weekend* (1967) 193

8.9 A shadow play in Wim Wenders' *Kings of the Road* (1976) 195

8.10 Killed for shooting in black and white in Wenders' *The State of Things* (1982) 196

8.11 Aguirre in the solitude of his madness in Werner Herzog's *Aguirre: The Wrath of God* (1972) 197

8.12 The fanciful mise-en-scène of Rainer Werner Fassbinder's *The Bitter Tears of Petra von Kant* (1972) 198

8.13 Chantal Akerman's passive camera gaze in *Jeanne Dielman, 23 Quai du Commerce, 1080 Bruxelles* (1975) 200

8.14 The "tatami" position in Yasujiro Ozu's *Tokyo Story* (1953) 201

8.15 Martial arts in the rain. Wong Kar-wai's *The Grandmaster* (2013) 202

8.16 A political demonstration in Prakash Jha's *Satyagraha* (2013) 204

8.17 A sudden outburst of violence in Michael Haneke's *Caché* (2005) 207

9.1–9.2 Darkness and redemption in Frank Capra's *It's a Wonderful Life* (1946) 214

9.3 The female hero in *The Hunger Games: Catching Fire* (Francis Lawrence, 2013) 218

9.4 *Little Caesar* (Mervyn LeRoy, 1931) 221

9.5 The end of the lone gangster in Raoul Walsh's *White Heat* (1949) 221

9.6 Gangsterism as a business. Francis Ford Coppola's *The Godfather: Part II* (1974) 221

9.7 The "kino eye." Dziga Vertov's *Man with a Movie Camera* (1929) 225

9.8 Found footage of the Russian Revolution. Esther Shub's *The Fall of the Romanov Dynasty* (1927) 225

9.9 Digging a seal out of the ice in Robert Flaherty's *Nanook of the North* (1922) 226

9.10 Visual poetry in the dustbowl. Pare Lorentz's *The Plow That Broke the Plains* (1936) 227

9.11 A Nazi rally documented by Leni Riefenstahl in *Triumph of the Will* (1935) 228

9.12 George Lucas imitates a shot from *Triumph of the Will* in the first *Star Wars* film (1977) 229

9.13 Mick Jagger in *Gimme Shelter* (David and Albert Maysles, 1970) 232

9.14 Former Secretary of State Robert McNamara in Errol Morris's *The Fog of War* (2003) 233

9.15 The tracking shot that introduces John Wayne in John Ford's *Stagecoach* (1939) 238

9.16 The opening shot of Ford's *The Searchers* (1956) 239

9.17 Hatred and fear in the gaze of Ethan Edwards in Ford's *The Searchers* 239

9.18 The end of the West and the Western. Sam Peckinpah's *The Wild Bunch* (1969) 241

9.19 Visitors from space in Robert Wise's *The Day the Earth Stood Still* (1951) 244

9.20 The electrocution of the vegetable from another planet. *The Thing from Another World* (Christian Nyby, Howard Hawks, 1951) 246

9.21 Robby the Robot in *Forbidden Planet* (Fred Wilcox, 1956) 247

9.22–9.23 "Visionary architecture" in Fritz Lang's *Metropolis* (1927) and Ridley Scott's *Blade Runner* (1982) 248

9.24 The replicant Roy Batty in Ridley Scott's *Blade Runner* (1982) 248

9.25 The Jupiter room at the end of Stanley Kubrick's *2001: A Space Odyssey* (1968) 250

9.26 Computer-generated zombies in *World War Z* (Marc Foster, 2013) 251

10.1 The noir detective in Edward Dmytryk's *Murder, My Sweet* (1944) 260

10.2 Walter Neff and Phyllis Dietrichson killing each other in Billy Wilder's *Double Indemnity* (1944) 260

10.3 A noir image from Anthony Mann's *T-Men* (1947) 261

10.4 The expression of anger and restrained violence in Nicholas Ray's *In a Lonely Place* (1950) 262

10.5 The light of an atomic device hidden in a box in Robert Aldrich's *Kiss Me Deadly* (1955) 263

10.6 The image is alluded to in Quentin Tarantino's *Pulp Fiction* (1994) 263

10.7 The dark mise-en-scène of Orson Welles's *Touch of Evil* (1958) 264

10.8–10.9 Mirror images in D. W. Griffith's *Broken Blossoms* (1919) 269

10.10 Battling Burrows looms out of the frame in *Broken Blossoms* 269

10.11 He takes an axe to the closet where his daughter is hiding 269

10.12 Stanley Kubrick has this scene in mind in *The Shining* (1980) 269

10.13 The melodramatic gaze in *Now, Voyager* (Irving Rapper, 1942) 273

10.14 The face of loss. *Brokeback Mountain* (Ang Lee, 2005) 277

10.15 The 1950s domestic interior in Todd Haynes's *Far From Heaven* (2002) 279

10.16 Spectral light in Douglas Sirk's *All That Heaven Allows* (1955) 281

10.17 Shadows and screens in *All That Heaven Allows* 281

10.18 The lonely image: Cary reflected in the TV screen in *All That Heaven Allows* 282

10.19 Trapped in small rooms. Rainer Werner Fassbinder's *Ali: Fear Eats the Soul* (1974) 285

10.20 Actors staring at the viewer in *Ali: Fear Eats the Soul* 285

10.21 The humiliating gaze in *All That Heaven Allows* 287

10.22 Emmi's family glowers in *Ali: Fear Eats the Soul* 287

10.23–10.24 The racist glare in *Far From Heaven* 288

10.25–10.26 Repression returns like a rhyme. *Ali: Fear Eats the Soul* 288

11.1–11.2 Scottie drives around San Francisco in Alfred Hitchcock's *Vertigo* (1958) 311

11.3 "A miniature Tom Petty." Judd Apatow's *This is 40* (2012) 314

11.4 A screwball comedy couple in Leo McCarey's *The Awful Truth* (1936) 318

11.5 The contemporary screwball couple in *This is 40* 318

11.6 Marlon Brando as Johnny, in tears, in *The Wild One* (Laslo Benedek, 1953) 319

11.7–11.10 Scottie and Midge discuss her love life in *Vertigo* 322

11.11–11.15 Brought in front of the Vice Principal in *This is 40* 325

11.16 –11.20 The complex cutting of shot/reverse shot as Scottie pursues Madeleine in *Vertigo* 326

Preface

The goal of the fourth edition of *Film, Form, and Culture* is to create an introduction to film textbook that provides accessible discussion and examples of the formal structures and cultural contexts of American and—with a new chapter—international cinema. There is expanded discussion of the digital "revolution" in filmmaking: the movement from celluloid to digital recording and editing of images, as well as the all-pervasive use of CGI (computer-generated imagery) that has taken the place of old special effects techniques, often turning films into a peculiar hybrid of live action animations. In addition to the new chapter on international film, there is as well a new chapter on film acting that uses still images to create a small catalogue of gestures and expressions that are recognizable in film after film.

Still images take the place of the DVD that had accompanied the previous editions. Because so many instructors have their own collection of illustrative film clips, it was no longer necessary to include a disk of clips separate from the text. Instead, there are some 265 still images, many in color, that create a visual index to and illustration of the discussion of films and filmmaking. That discussion has itself been expanded to include more references to current movies, including a visual analysis of Christopher Nolan's *The Dark Knight.*

The chapter on the cultural contexts of film is now the concluding chapter of the book and serves not only to introduce students to various cultural interventions in the study of film, but also as an experiment in comparative analysis, looking at two films that might not ordinarily be thought of together, namely Alfred Hitchcock's *Vertigo* and Judd Apatow's *This is 40.*

Throughout the book, chapters have been opened up to more analysis and references to more films, without, however, overwhelming the reader with titles. Each chapter ends with suggestions for further reading and further viewing—a short list of relevant films not mentioned in the chapter itself. There is an expanded glossary of terms.

Robert P. Kolker

Acknowledgments

Many people were involved in the making of the various editions of *Film, Form, and Culture*. I am particularly grateful to Natalie Foster, my editor at Routledge, who saw the value of creating a fourth edition of the book. Her assistant, Sheni Kruger and project editor, Anna Callander, were of invaluable help in the production process.

Many film students, patiently working with me over the years, helped me hone and clarify my ideas. Mike Mashon indirectly provided the name of the book. In its earlier versions, Marsha Gordon did important research on its behalf, and Devin Orgeron helped check out the facts. David and Luke Wyatt read the original manuscript of the first edition, and their comments made it better. Stanley Plumly made me feel better with his encouragement. Other University of Maryland colleagues—particularly Joe Miller, Sharon Gerstel, Elizabeth Loiseaux, Barry Peterson, Jenny Preece, Ben Shneiderman—helped with conversation, ideas, and facts. Jay Telotte and Angela Dalle Vacche at Georgia Tech were endless sources of information and good humor. Patty Zimmerman offered invaluable information on independent women filmmakers. Manjunath Pendakur supplied important information on Indian cinema.

Introduction

Film, Form, and Culture asks you to think seriously about film, as seriously as you would about literature, music, or sports. It's a book about cinematic form and structure, content and contexts, history and business. It will give you some sense of film's history and its place in the greater scheme of things, especially in that envelope of words and deeds, money, art, artifacts, and daily life we live in that is called **culture**.

But why think seriously about film at all? Many people don't. Movies are among those things in our lives that we apparently don't *need* to take seriously. We go to the movies to be entertained, scared, grossed out; to make out, spend time, have something to discuss afterward. We watch a movie or a television show on our tablet or smartphone, or we stream a film or series on Netflix. But we don't often want to think about movies as a serious part of our emotional or intellectual lives, or even treat them with the same intensity we use when we discuss more serious things. Outside of a film studies course, we rarely hear people engaged in a discussion of films that goes much deeper than plot or characters.

Even the people who review movies in print or online are not as serious about their subject as other journalists or bloggers are about sports or music. They make jokes and puns, tell us the plot and whether the characters are believable. Many reviewers, in fact, are often part of the show, a kind of overture to the film we may go to see or stream. They are another part of the entertainment.

The reason that attention must be paid to film is that most of us get our stories—our narratives and myths—from it, or from its close cousin, television. In other words, from the late nineteenth century onward, people have turned to film as entertainment, escape, *and* (however unconsciously) education—as an affirmation of the way they live or think they ought to live their lives. But even if film were "only" entertainment it would be important to find out how it works. Why does it entertain us? What constitutes entertainment? Why do we need to be entertained? And film is part of world politics and national policy. Some governments support filmmakers as a means to express their national culture to the world. Other governments have caused international incidents over film, particularly when copyright and piracy issues were at stake.

Sometimes international policy about film can lead to aesthetic consequences. After the end of World War II, in 1946, for example, a major agreement was drawn up between France and the United States: the Blum–Byrnes Accords. The agreement came about because France was concerned about getting its own films shown on its own screens. The French public wanted American films, most countries still do. The Accords forced France to accept American films in an uneven ratio: it could show sixteen weeks of its own films, thirty-six weeks of anything else. The Accords changed the way the French made films because some filmmakers decided that the best way to meet the quota was to make high-quality films through the adaptation of literary works. Other French filmmakers hated these adaptations and started to experiment with new cinematic forms, resulting in a revolution of filmmaking in the late 1950s that was called the **French New Wave**. The result, in turn, was a change in film form all over the world.

More recently, near the end of 2014, Sony Pictures was set to distribute a film called *The Interview* (Evan Goldberg, Seth Rogen),[1] a comic satire of sorts that involved the assassination of North Korea's leader, Kim Jong-un. North Korea, a paranoid state at the best of times, took exception and launched a massive attack on Sony's computer servers, releasing personal emails and threatening violent retaliation if the film were released. The media relished the unpleasant remarks about actors and executives contained in the emails; theaters refused to show the film. Sony withdrew it, ready to accept a huge financial loss, until the President of the United States stepped in and urged the company not to fold in the face of North Korea's threats. Sony put the film into limited release and streamed it on various online sites, recouping if not their losses, at least something to show on the books. If the Blum–Byrnes Accords changed the aesthetics of French cinema many years ago, *The Interview* may have an economic effect, potentially changing the way films are distributed.

The business of film ripples through the economy, the policies, and the technology of the world at large to this very day. Media mergers have created a confluence of various delivery systems—film, digital video, print, music, and the Internet—that make film as we now understand it a different form and kind of entertainment. To take just one example: in 1915, Universal Pictures was one of the earliest studios to be established in Hollywood. It was famous in the 1930s for a series of horror films such as *Frankenstein* (James Whale) and *Dracula* (Tod Browning), both made in 1931. The sequels still continue. In 1964, Universal opened a theme park with rides based on its popular films. Meanwhile, the National Broadcasting Company (NBC) founded in 1926 by the Radio Corporation of America (RCA) became one of the nation's premier broadcasting companies, which now also runs a number of cable companies, like USA, MSNBC, and CNBC. In 2004, NBC and Universal merged under the ownership of General Electric and a French company, Vivendi. Comcast, the cable company, bought this amalgam in 2011. In 2013, Comcast tried and failed to buy the cable company Time Warner, an independent company that was originally the result of a merger between the one-time magazine giant, Time Inc. and Warner Bros., one of the most prominent studios in Hollywood. Though the acquisition failed, it indicated how the carriers of television and the Internet want to provide content as well.

It may be fruitless to bemoan the monopolies of media. There is little to be done besides recognizing that all nations, our own included, understand the power of film and television to influence their people, to propagandize values and ideologies, to make money from content and its distribution. Film may be a bargaining chip in foreign policy, always an economic commodity, sometimes the subject of the politician's wrath at home (as when candidates for office rail against the evil moral influence of "liberal" Hollywood, while Hollywood stars become politicians and influence our lives even more). Therefore, film becomes the subject of study in many different kinds of academic courses in which its power and complexity are acknowledged and analyzed. We will talk some about the politics and the business, because film is big business and its creation, its form, and its content are about power, the core of politics. But mostly we will talk about the form—the way films are put together so that we, as viewers, understand what they are attempting to tell us—and the content of film. We will come to all of this from the perspective of textuality—studying the film itself and how all its parts work—and find out how film, its production and reception, its place in our culture, makes up a large, coherent construction of meaningful and interrelated elements that we can analyze—a text that we can read.

Let's go back for a moment to our straw men, the film reviewers. The first thing almost any reviewer does is talk about (usually summarize) the film's plot. *Citizen Kane* (Orson Welles, 1941): "Charlie Kane is an unhappy newspaper man. His wife leaves him, and he loses all his friends." "*2001: A Space Odyssey* (Stanley Kubrick, 1968) opens with a number of shots of animals out on the desert. Then one tribe of apes attacks another until, in the middle of the night, one of the tribes discovers this strange monolith in the middle of their camp. There isn't much dialogue, but the apes look real enough."

What film reviews almost always evade is one of the few realities of film itself, that it is an artificial construct, something made in a particular way for specific purposes, and that the plot or story of a film is a function of this construction, not necessarily its first principle. In other words, and as we'll see in more detail as we go along, the formal elements of film—the **shot** and the **cut**, for example—are unique to film. They are the basic forms of its construction—along with lighting, camera movement, music, sound, acting—and they themselves were and are determined by things going on in the overall development of film throughout its history and the development of the culture that filmmaking is one part of. When I speak of film as "artificial," I don't mean it's false; I'm using the term in its root sense, made by art or, often in the case of film, by craft. Film is an artifice, and it becomes an artifact, made in specific ways, using specific tools, fashioned to produce and create specific effects (one of which is the plot, which we sometimes do have to revert to for convenience and to make a point about a movie) with the aim of pleasing the audience who pays to see it. Film reviewers and most everyday discussions of film try to ignore the artificial, constructed aspect of film—its form—and instead talk about it as pure story—which is the outcome most filmmakers want. The characters of its story become, somehow, "realistic," as if they might "really" exist rather than result from the way the film itself puts meaning together.

There is no doubt that filmmakers and the development of film form early in the last century play a role in this deception. Many filmmakers assume that most viewers are not interested in the construction principles of their work and have accomplished a remarkable feat, making the structure of their films invisible. In other words, one reason we don't pay attention to the form and structure of film is that the form and structure of film disappear behind the very story and characters they produce. This is a great act of prestidigitation and one of the main reasons film has become so popular. Movies have achieved a presence of being, an emotional immediacy that seems unmediated—simply there, without a history, without apparatus, without anything actually between us except the story.

In the discussion that follows, we will explain, analyze, and demystify this apparent act of magic. As we come to understand that film has a complex and flexible form and that story and characters are created by that form, we will become more comfortable with the notion of film as something carefully and seriously *made*. From that point we will be able to move on and understand that the making has a history and the history has a number of parts and branches. One branch—the largest—is the commercial narrative cinema of Hollywood, the major subject of our study. There are a number of national cinemas, some of them, like India's, almost as large as America's, and with a growing influence outside the nation's borders. Still another is a more experimental cinema—often found in Europe, Asia, Africa, the Middle East, and Latin America but occasionally cropping up in the United States—which explores and experiments with the potentials of film form in the way a good novelist or poet or computer programmer explores her language in order to create new meanings, new structures of thought and feeling. We will look into film made in other countries in Chapter 8.

Understanding film history will help us to understand the conventions of form and content. Clearly, films change over the course of time: they and their makers have a history, as we do, as the culture does. Visual structure, acting styles, story content, the way films *look*—all seem different now than ten or a hundred years ago. But, in many ways, these changes are only superficial. It would be only a small exaggeration to say that, with a few important exceptions, the structure of film and the stories and characters created by that structure have remained mostly unchanged, or have changed in only a gradual way, during the course of film history. With the introduction of the digital, technical methods have indeed changed, and many aspects of style, including acting styles, have changed; but by and large the stories film tells and the ways it tells them follow a continuum almost from the very first images shown to the public. And yet film is always publicizing its uniqueness and originality. "For the first time on the screen . . ." was a popular publicity phrase in the 1940s and 1950s. "The funniest," "most unique," "unlike anything you've ever seen," "the best film," and "you've never seen anything like it" remain useful nonsense phrases for film advertisements. In truth, every commercial, theatrical film is in one way or another like every other commercial, theatrical film, and all are consciously created to be that way. In order to get a film made in Hollywood, an agent or a producer or a studio head has to be convinced that the film you have in mind is "just like" some other film "only different." Watch the first half-hour of Robert Altman's *The Player* (1992) for a hilarious representation of what "pitching a story" to a Hollywood producer is like, and see Albert Brooks's *The Muse* (1999), Spike Jonze's *Adaptation* (2002), or even Ben Affleck's *Argo* (2012) for an ironic fantasy about the search for an original film idea.

"Just like . . . only different" is the engine that drives film. Hollywood cinema in particular is based upon the conventions of genre, the *kinds* of stories, told with styles and cinematic elements, drawing upon conventions that are repeated with major and minor variations throughout the history of the genre. Through genres, films are influenced by history and, very rarely, influence history in return. Genres, as we will see in Chapters 9 and 10, are complex contractual events drawn between the filmmaker and the film viewer. We go to a horror film or a thriller, a romantic comedy or a science fiction movie, a Western or a **melodrama** with certain expectations that the film must meet. If it doesn't meet them, we will be disappointed and probably will not like the film. If a film masquerading as a genre turns out to attack or make fun of it, interesting things can happen. If other historical and cultural events are in sync with the attack or the parody, it is possible that the genre may wither and all but disappear.

This happened to the Western in the late 1960s and early 1970s. Three moving and disturbing films that questioned the historical and formal elements of the Western—Sam Peckinpah's *The Wild Bunch* (1969), Arthur Penn's *Little Big Man* (1970), and Robert Altman's *McCabe and Mrs. Miller* (1971)—echoed the negative response to the Vietnam War and some profound questions about American imperial interests and the myths of "manifest destiny" to bring the

Western down from its enormous popularity, a point from which it has barely recovered. These days, the Western is most likely to be a commentary on the genre rather than a repetition of it, or absorbed into other genres, like science fiction (Jon Favreau's 2011 film, *Cowboys and Aliens*). Among the more interesting recent Westerns are those that use the genre as something like a cover for other investigations of character, history, and gender, such as Maggie Greenwald's *The Ballad of Little Jo* (1993), Jim Jarmusch's *Dead Man* (1995), and Gore Verbinski's *The Lone Ranger* (2013), a serio-comic take on a character who first appeared on radio and then on early television. Interestingly this and *Dead Man* both star Johnny Depp. *The Lone Ranger* was widely panned and was a commercial failure, though in fact it is an interesting and amusing play on many of the lost conventions of the Western.

Even though they approach parody and strain credulity, the near epidemic of comic book inspired action heroes doesn't seem to garner a negative response, and most of them—the Spider-Man, Batman, and X-Men franchises—are extremely popular. The troubled superhero has rapidly become a convention that every male spectator, dreaming of power and knowing how little he has, has accepted as a desirable fantasy. Power and doubt have become attractive character traits, providing entertaining outlets for our own insecurities.

Stereotypes, the expected character, the unsurprising story, the hoped-for conclusion, the invisible style are all part of our contract with the movies, what filmmakers believe and hope we demand of them. Such demands are certainly not restricted to movies alone: in television, pop music, news reporting, and politics, we tend to be most comfortable with what we've most often heard. We are wary of the new. Our popular culture is, more often than not, an act of affirming already held ideas, of defining, delimiting, and limiting what we accept as the real. The "new" is either quickly absorbed by convention or ignored.

The worst thing we can say about a film is that it is "unrealistic." "The characters weren't real." "The story didn't strike me as being real." Reality is always our last resort. If someone thinks we're not being serious, we're told to "face reality." If our ideas are half-baked, overly narcissistic, or even just silly, we're told to "get real!" If we are college teachers or adolescents, we're told we'll find things different "in the real world." Reality can be a threat, the thing we're not facing, not in, or not dealing with. But it can also be a verbal gesture of approbation. "That was so real." And, of course, it's the greatest compliment we can give a film, even though—and this is the great paradox—in our media-wise world, we know deep down that what we are seeing has very, very little to do with reality—a fact proved by our superheroes.

In truth, "reality," like all other aspects of culture, is not something out there, existing apart from us. Reality is an agreement we make with ourselves and between ourselves and the rest of the culture about what we will call real. Maybe, as some people have argued, the only dependable definition of reality is that it is something a lot of people agree on. This is not to say that there aren't actual, "real" things in the world. Natural processes, states of matter (heat, cold, the relative solidity of physical things), the fact that, in temperate climates, plant life dies off in the fall and returns in the spring—these constitute a "reality," perhaps because they happen without our presence. But no matter what natural events and processes occur, they have little meaning without human interpretation, without our speaking about them within the contexts of our lives and our culture, without our giving them names and meanings.

We find films realistic because we have learned certain kinds of responses, gestures, attitudes from them; and when we see these gestures or feel these responses again in a film or a television show, we assume they are real, because we've felt them and seen them before. We've probably even imitated them. (Where do we learn the way to kiss someone? From the movies.) This is reality as an infinite loop, a recursion through various emotional and visual constructs, culturally approved, indeed culturally mandated, that we assume to be "real" because we see them over and over again, absorb them, and, for better or worse, live them. In an important sense, like films themselves, "reality" is made up of repetition and assent.

Here is where the reality factor is joined with genre, history, culture, convention, and the invisible structure of film that we talked about earlier. What we call "realistic" in film is, more often than not, only the familiar. The familiar is what we experience often, comfortably, clearly, as if it were always there. When we approve of the reality of a film, or accept fantasy as a given, we are really affirming our comfort with it, our desire to accept what we see. Desire—simply wanting to see the familiar or a twist on the familiar and receive pleasure from the seeing—is an important idea, because filmgoers aren't fools. No one literally believes what they see on the screen; we all desire and in a certain sense covet, and in a greater sense *want*, what we see, despite what we know about its probability or, more likely, its improbability. We respond with a desire that things could be like this or, simply, that we might want to inhabit a world or a character that looks and behaves like the one on the screen. We want to share, or just *have* the same feelings that the characters up there are having. We want to accept them uncritically, respond emotionally. Our culture keeps telling us over and over that emotions don't lie. If we feel it, it must be so.

In the discussion that follows, we will steer our way through the thickets of desire and try to find why we want so much from movies and how the movies deliver what they and we think we want—or in some cases don't. By examining form and the ways in which our responses are culturally determined, we will attempt to look at our responses in order to understand what we are really getting when we ask for realism, why we should be asking for it at all, and why our expectations keep changing. Remember that many of the most popular films—science fiction and superhero action films, for example—are fantasies; and more and more of them are based on comic books! Horror films and horror film parodies are fantasies that now openly depend on the viewers' understanding of horror film conventions and enjoyment of the ability to laugh at them. The film is proof that "reality" is not a given, but chosen.

Culture is another important idea in this book. Chapter 11 will cover in detail what the study of culture, and popular culture in particular, is and how our very ideas about culture keep changing, almost as much as the culture that's being studied. But since we will use the term before then, let me begin to introduce it here.

Culture is the sum total of the intricate ways we relate to ourselves, our peers, our community, our country, world, and universe. It is made up of the minutiae of our daily lives: from the toothpaste we use, and the fact we use toothpaste at all, to the music we like; the websites we visit; the political ideas we hold; our gender; the image we have of ourselves; the ways we interact on social media; the models we want to emulate. Culture is more than ourselves, because our selves are formed by a variety of influences and agreements. So culture is also made up of the general ideological components, the web of beliefs and things we take for granted in the society we live in. Politics, law, religion, art, entertainment are all part of our culture: they form its ideological engine, the forces of assent, the values, images, and ideas we agree to embrace and follow or struggle against.

We will use culture here in a broad sense, perhaps close to what the French think about when they worry about their culture being at stake because of the influx and popularity of American movies. In our definition, culture doesn't mean "high-toned" or refer only to works of high art that are supposed to be good for us. Rather, culture is the complex totality of our daily lives and acts. Culture is the form and content of our selves in relation to our community, our country, our social and economic class, our entertainments, our politics and economics. Culture is the way we act out ideology.

Ideology is the way we agree to see ourselves, to behave, and to create the values of our lives. Ideology and culture are intertwined. When I decide to act calmly or angrily in a difficult situation, my reaction is determined by ideological and cultural demands of appropriate behavior. In this case it is determined by my gender, which culture forms in the course of my upbringing. Men are "supposed" to react strongly, if not violently, while women "should" be more passive, without an aggressiveness that would be perfectly acceptable in male behavior. Much of our culture calls "nerdy" or "gay" any behavior that is intellectually driven and outside the norm. But "norms" are not created naturally. They are made by the ideological assent we give to—in this instance—what kind of behavior or personality type is considered "normal." Who determines the norm? We all do to the extent to which we assent to ideological and cultural givens. If we suddenly, as a culture, agreed that intellectual work was as meaningful and "manly" as physical work—athletics, for example—the ideological engine might shift gears and "nerds" would become as heroic as jocks. The cultural response to gayness is already shifting in a positive direction, though only sometimes reflected in our films.

The givens of ideology are actually created over the course of time and are changeable. For example, in older films, women were seen as needing to be saved by a heroic male, a reflection of the ideologies and culture of the time. Today, we often see and cheer in film a strong female character. Contemporary horror films are a good example of the newly seen power of women over destructive forces, while contemporary action films often question male heroics, even while celebrating them.

Of course, when we speak of culture, it might be more accurate to think of cultures. Neither culture nor ideology is singular or monolithic. Let's move from film for a moment and take popular music as an example of how complex culture can be and how it can move in many directions. Hip-hop and rap emerged from African American popular culture in the 1970s and 1990s. Rap moved from the streets to the recording studios and into the wider population by the mid-1990s, and then separated into a number of strands. One strand, Gangsta Rap, became a way for male African American teenagers to express anger at middle-class white society. But its language of violence and misogyny also disturbed parts of African American culture and signified class and economic divisions within that culture. It brought down the wrath of some of the white establishment as well. Rap as a whole quickly transcended the music world into the larger cultural arena where art, industry, politics, and promotion are intertwined. It became sound, fashion, aggression, record sales, movie deals, murders, police busts, highway noise, and big business. Attraction for many and irritant to some, rap became a phenomenon of the culture, a practice of one subculture (a term used to define one active part of the entire culture) and a representation of all of the culture.

The point is that culture is made up of expressions and intersections, representations, images, sounds, and stories, almost always influenced or even formed by gender, race, and economics. It is local and global, moving and changing, depending upon the needs of individuals and groups. It can be as peaceful as family churchgoing or as violent as young men beating each other up in imitation of David Fincher's 1999 film, *Fight Club*.

In *Film, Form, and Culture*, we will look closely at all the contexts of film (with some references to television and digital media): where it fits in the culture, what constitutes its popularity, and why popularity is sometimes used to condemn it.

Finally, a word about the films we will discuss. We will be thinking about and analyzing theatrical, narrative, fiction film—films that tell stories that are meant to be seen by relatively large numbers of people—and will discuss documentary films because, with the success of Michael Moore's *Fahrenheit 9/11* (2004), this genre has gained a renewed popularity. We will talk a lot about American film, because that is the dominant cinema around the world. But there are other very important and very wonderful cinemas and individual filmmakers outside Hollywood, many of whom make their films in response to Hollywood. We will, therefore, also address world cinema, the roles it plays, its individual filmmakers and their films.

But doing all this raises a problem. What particular films should we discuss? Within the context of a book, it is impossible to mention (not to say analyze) everyone's favorites, or to deal with films that everyone has seen or wants to see. Adding to the problem is that there is not really an established canon in film studies as there is in literature. Of course, there are great films. Everyone agrees that *Citizen Kane* is among the most important films ever made, and we will discuss it here. But every film scholar and film teacher, like every filmgoer, has his or her favorites. I am no exception. The choice of films I discuss and analyze is often very subjective. I've tried to follow the principle of part for whole. Rather than drown you in names and titles (though I am guilty of occasionally opening the spigot), my hope is that the analyses of the films I do discuss can provide tools for thinking, talking, and writing about other films; and that each discussion of film, genre, or larger theoretic principles will serve as a template for work on other films, other genres, and other related interests. This is one reason that a few filmmakers are referred to a number of times in different contexts and why there is a short list of suggested viewing that follows each chapter and that contains titles not mentioned in the chapter itself.

One more word on the selection of films. Because film has a history, I have included many older films, even (especially) black and white films. Black and white was the norm—the reality and the mark of realism!—before the late 1960s. My hope is that you will want to see the films referred to and get a sense of how wonderful they were and still are.

No matter what the film, you will be asked to connect things and to refuse to believe that the experience of any one thing exists in isolation from any other experience. This book therefore invites you to look at the movies, and, by extension and example, television and the tablet or smartphone screen, as one item in the enormous palette of your own experience and the wider experiences of the culture we all belong to. It invites you to think of a film narrative as seriously as a literary narrative and to understand that the array of images and stories, beliefs and prejudices, love and rejection, peace and violence that we learn about in literature we can learn in very different ways from film. In effect, this book is about the end of film innocence; it is an invitation to discover a world in which nothing is simple, nothing is "just there," and nothing can be dismissed without, at least, your being conscious that dismissal has consequences.

NOTE

1 The convention of naming a film is title followed by director and year of release.

CHAPTER 1

Image and reality

IMAGES, THE REAL, AND HISTORY

Quentin Tarantino's *Inglourious Basterds* (2009) ends with a glorious fantasy. In the mid-1940s, a group of American army Nazi hunters manages to herd Adolf Hitler and his high command into a movie theater and incinerate them. No such thing happened in "real life" and in the life of the film's making, no one was actually burned and blown up. But Tarantino revels in the notion that in cinema revenge can be made to appear real and certainly emotionally satisfying. In *Inglourious Basterds* and again in *Django Unchained* (2012) he revises history and creates moving images of the revenge against history: film, he thinks, can allow us to fantasize the undoing of monstrous wrongs committed against Jews in one case and African American slaves in another. There is a violent naiveté in these films, a trust that the images and the stories they tell will make us somehow feel better about the past. They recreate not events that occurred, but events we somehow wish had occurred, though not until we have seen them in the films. There is a circuitry of memory and desire at work in which the films call upon a memory (itself based only on what we have already read and learned about, or seen in other films) and then create and satisfy a desire to adjust that memory for the better.

The reverse happens when we consider science fiction films, whose images and **narratives** create a projection of the future, memories of things to come. The images of science fiction represent nothing but the imagination of their makers—the **director,** the **production designer**, the digital effects team—which in turn move us as viewers into a state of awe. As much as film set in the past or the present, we insist on the reality of the images in films set in the future, even when they are created on a computer. Arthur C. Clarke, the science fiction writer who co-wrote *2001: A Space Odyssey* (1968) with Stanley Kubrick—a film made without digital

FIGURE 1.1 Quentin Tarantino destroys the Nazis in a movie house in his wish fulfillment revenge film, *Inglourious Basterds* (2009)

effects—said that, if a science fiction film were to be more realistic than this, it would have to be shot on **location**. As if believing this joke, and turning it upside down, some conspiracy theorists claim that the first landing of a man on the moon in 1969 was a fake, created in a studio by, of course, Stanley Kubrick. Not to be undone, in 1977, Peter Hyams made *Capricorn One* about a faked Mars landing.

The truth of all this is that all fiction film images are lies. Any fiction is. What I mean is that, when films pretend to show us "reality," they are in fact only showing a representation of reality, a simulacrum. When they show us fantasy—think of James Cameron's *Avatar* (2009)—they try to immerse us so completely in their fictional world that we tend not to question the artifice that made it. This becomes all the more interesting given that the supplementary materials on DVDs show us the methods by which the images that make up the fictional worlds are created. We desire the illusion even when we know it is an illusion.

And always have. All films, from the earliest artifacts at the turn of the twentieth century to the present, have used a variety of special effects to create their images. One of the methods of filmmaking was and still is to build a **shot** in layers and put in more visual information after initial photography with the actors is over. These days, many shots are made against a **green screen**. The background is then digitally added in postproduction. All films today, whether they are shot on film or digitally, are transferred to digital files, called the **digital intermediate**, where a **digital colorist** works with the director and the **director of photography** to manipulate the image. We will return to the question of digital effects in the next chapter.

THE "TRUTH" OF THE IMAGE

There is a curious cliché that says pictures don't lie. This is part of that greater cliché that says seeing is believing. Somehow a thing seen directly—or through a visual representation like a painting, a photograph, or a film—brings us closer to some actual reality. Words are too obviously not things themselves; words are made-up sounds, developed throughout the life of a culture, represented by made-up letters, put together in a contrived grammar that everyone in a culture uses to communicate through a decision that the particular words will refer to particular things.

FIGURE 1.2 This still from the production of Tim Burton's *Alice in Wonderland* (2010) is a good indication of modern filmmaking methods in which computers play as much of a role as the camera. You can just see the actors in the distance. Everything that's green will be filled in by CGI

Language is clearly cultural and not natural: it is human made and accepted with some variations throughout a particular culture. Every English speaker understands what the word "food" refers to, even though the particular kind of food that comes to mind to each individual may vary. More abstract words, like "cool," may have a range of meanings that keep changing. But seeing the image of a thing seems to bring us something very close to the thing itself—to "reality." Things that are *seen* appear to be and even feel as if they are unmediated; that is, they seem to be conveyed directly to us, not conveyed indirectly. Nothing stands in their way. They are true.

But, in fact, an image, whether photographed, painted, or digitized, is not the thing itself. This is something humorously recognized by the Belgian surrealist painter, René Magritte, in his painting of a pipe. The painting is called "The Treachery of Images" and bears the words (in French), "This is Not a Pipe." Indeed, it is not. Like all images, it is a representation of a mediated transmission, a painting in this instance mediating the idea of a pipe. But any image, composed and lit, painted on canvas, pushed through the camera lens onto a silver nitrate surface or by means of binary code onto the chip of a digital camera, may appear to be the thing itself, though, in reality, it is only its image. And even when we acknowledge the intervention of optics, chemistry, computer science, and the human hand and eye of the photographer in the recording and developing of the photographic image, we still haven't considered all the **mediation** that goes on. An image of the thing is not the thing. The subject of a photograph is not neutral: the subject—a person or a thing—is first chosen to be a subject, and then poses or is posed for the camera, often assuming a camera-ready attitude dictated by the culture (smiling, for example). Even a subject caught unawares by the camera has been changed by the very act of having been caught unawares. In the act of being captured on film, a subject who may be unaware of the presence of a camera is frozen in photographic time and space, turned into an image, made into something she wasn't when the camera snapped her picture.

FIGURE 1.3 The surrealist painter René Magritte made it clear that an image is only an image. *The Treachery of Images*, also known as *This is Not a Pipe*, was made in 1929. © 2015. Digital Image Museum Associates/LACMA/Art Resource NY/Scala, Florence

The natural object—a landscape, for example—is marked by the fact of its being chosen, as well as by the time of day during which it is photographed, the way the photographer composes it for shooting, chooses an appropriate lens, and manipulates the quality of light, first with the camera and then in the darkroom or, more likely, in Photoshop.

Here is a core issue for everything discussed in this book. We may wish to perceive "the thing itself," but it is a wish impossible to come true. Whether in a photograph, or the series of photographs that make up a movie, or the electronic scanning of objects that create a television image, or based on a computer's binary code; whether on the page, from someone's own mouth, or from a teacher and her textbook: what we see, hear, read, and know is mediated by other things, other perceptions. These days, given the ubiquity of smartphones with video recording capability, all kinds of events are recorded, and put on the Web, often making it to television news. Beatings, killings, and other atrocities from around the world are recorded and broadcast. "We have not been able to independently verify these images" are the words that are usually spoken when such images are put on the air. As powerful and appalling such images might be, they are not the thing itself—the proof itself. Images are unverifiable and often ideologically fraught. Even, perhaps especially, **documentary** films raise questions of veracity and authenticity. A documentary is supposed to look at its subjects as they "really" are. But more and more, as we will see in Chapter 9, documentaries are subjective renderings of their directors' view of the world. But even if we simply let a camera run untended on a street corner, the result would be an image of the world, not the world itself.

The artificiality of the image is a hard concept to accept, because evidence seems to go against it. "Seeing is believing." The image looks too much like the thing. Unlike words, which obviously interpret or mediate experience ("let me describe what happened," we say, and then give a verbal interpretation of what we've seen, like summarizing the plot of a movie), images appear to be present and immediate: there, whole, and real. Of course we know they are not exactly the thing itself. A picture of a cat is no more a cat than the word "cat." It just looks more like a cat than the word "cat" sounds like one. Animals believe the image—notice how a dog perks up when it sees a dog on television! Even "in reality" when we look at something out in the world, we aren't seeing the thing itself either but an image of it, in fact two images, focused upside down by the lens of each of our eyes onto their retina, righted and merged by the brain to create the sensation of an object in space. The point, again, is that everything we do is mediated, and everything we see is some kind of representation. We *choose* how close to reality—which is itself something built upon complex, often unconscious, but always learned agreements we have made with our culture—an image might be. Often, having made the choice, we revel in it, because the image seems to be delivering the thing itself to our eyes. Yet, when it comes to special effects movies, we are delighted to learn how the illusions were created to appear so *real*!

Images entrance us because they provide a powerful illusion of owning reality. If we can photograph reality or paint or copy it, we have exercised an important kind of magical power. This power is clear in the linguistic tracings of "image": "imagination," "imaginary," and "imagining" are all related to "image" and indicate how the taking, making, or thinking of a picture is an integral part of understanding. Through the image we can approach, understand, and play with the material of the external world in ways that both humanize it and make it our own. The image allows us to maintain a real connection with the external world, a solid, visual connection.

We love to look and see. It's part of our curiosity about the world and our desire to know. There's even an erotic component to our desire to see, which films depend on so much that critics have adopted a term for it: **scopophilia**, the love of looking. The term is slightly more benign than "voyeurism," the act of looking at a person who is unaware of our look, but it is still erotically charged. We love to look and we especially love to look at pictures of people and things, and often we do it to satisfy a variety of desires. We take and look at photographs, make videos, and create digital images; we do it as amateurs, often allowing the camera to be our intermediary amidst the chaos of real events, or we enjoy the work of professionals. Images are our memory, the basis of our stories, our artistic expression, our advertising, and our journalism. Images have become an integral part of popular music since MTV, and they are, of course, the core of movies.

We so believe in the presence and reality of images that we may take them at face value. They are, we often think, exactly what they are (or what someone tells us they are). Journalism and politics are infamous for doing this: picking out some aspect of an event, editorializing on a public figure by choosing a particularly unflattering pose, and then manipulating and describing it to present only one part, one perspective of the event itself—all the easier now with digital manipulation. Television news, by concentrating endlessly on murder and violence, uses images of a small part of what is in the world, which, in their selection and repetition, may convince some that this is what most of the world is about. In *JFK* (1991), a film that imagines—through

FIGURES 1.4–1.5 By means of lighting, mixing color and black and white film stock, documentary and reenactments, Oliver Stone asks the viewer to interrogate the reality and reliability of the image in an attempt to pierce the mystery of John F. Kennedy's assassination. These stills come from the sequence in which Jim Garrison (Kevin Costner) tests the single shooter theory of the assassination. *JFK* (1991)

an onslaught of images—alternative explanations of the assassination of the thirty-fifth President, the director Oliver Stone is at pains to make sure we understand that seeing is *not* believing, that the images given us by the media, molded by politics, make us think that we are seeing what is, but may, actually, not be.

We invest images with emotion and meaning; we may forget that they are images—mediations—and create a kind of short circuit: if the image of a thing is close enough to the thing itself, perhaps we may be in some danger of neglecting the thing itself—those events actually going on in the world—and merely believe the image. The emotions we attach to an image or to the images that make up a film can be simply set in motion by the images themselves, and we can ignore the origin as well as the formal properties—the composition, what is chosen to be in the shot and how these elements are arranged in the **frame**; **editing**, the placement of the shot in relation to other shots; the lighting—all the imaginative things that went into the making of a single image or a motion picture. We can cut ourselves off from the events that made the image possible—the material of the external world, the computer, and the various acts of illusion making—and make that short circuit, accepting the cliché that pictures never lie. If pictures never lie and are worth a thousand words, they must be dependable, true and, if not the thing itself, at least a suitable substitute.

NATURAL BORN KILLERS AND THE OBJECTIVITY OF THE IMAGE

Natural Born Killers, directed by Oliver Stone in 1994, is a mad, hallucinatory film about a couple of mass murderers. There is a **scene** in which the homicidal Mickey (the male part of the couple, Mickey and Mallory, played by Woody Harrelson and Juliette Lewis) is caught by the police in front of a drugstore. The media are present: television is capturing Mickey's capture in a fiction film that represents the capture of a criminal. The police get Mickey on the ground and viciously beat him with their clubs. The camera assumes a position at some distance from the action, observing it.

In 1991, the Los Angeles police pulled an African American, Rodney King, from his car and viciously beat him. A bystander videotaped the beating, which was shown over and over again on television news, seen by millions of people (this was before YouTube). It appeared to be an eloquent example of how a simple image can communicate a violent truth. Or so everybody thought. But when the police who took part in the beating were first brought to trial, their lawyers used the videotape as evidence against the prosecution. The defense lawyers turned themselves into a parody of film scholars, teaching the jury how they should read the images in a way that was favorable to the defense. They showed the tape in slow motion, backwards and forwards, frame by frame. They instructed the jury in the methods of close visual analysis, and they used their analysis to prove to the jury that they weren't seeing what they thought they were. What was really on the videotape, the defense said, was an offender violently resisting arrest. The jury, perhaps predisposed against the victim in the first place, believed it. (After a violent uprising by the African American community in Los Angeles, the Federal Government brought a civil rights suit that resulted in two of the officers found guilty and a large cash settlement for King.)

The Rodney King videotape contained an image of an event, taken without the knowledge of those who were participating in it, which is the closest image making can get to objective recording, an argument used by documentary filmmakers, who try to maintain the illusion that their images are closer to objective reality than those made by fiction filmmakers. But, as Stone shows, such footage is not "objective": it exists because of the economics of video recording, the relative cheapness and ubiquity of amateur equipment; the willingness of an onlooker with a camera to turn it on as the beating was in progress, rather than do something to stop the beating; the willingness of television news programs to show over and over again any kind of novel, violent imagery they can find. The footage exists not merely because there was someone there to tape it, but because on the other end there was a desire of people to watch it and use it. Today, such footage would "go viral" on the Internet (like the police choking to death an African American man in New York in 2014), and, with almost everyone having video capability in their smartphones, and the omnipresence of surveillance cameras, there is considerably more of its kind.

Stone re-creates the images of the King beating, this time with all the expensive, professional apparatus available to Hollywood filmmaking, and he turns it into an ironic commentary. Just as with the original footage, where we felt sympathy for the victim of a vicious beating, here we

FIGURES 1.6–1.7 This shot from Stone's 1994 film *Natural Born Killers* imitates the infamous video of the Rodney King beating by police in 1991

feel sympathy for the trapped and beaten Mickey. But in the fiction of *Natural Born Killers*, Mickey is a vicious, psychotic killer who needs capturing. He is, at the same time, something of a sympathetic figure. The reference to the "actual" Rodney King footage serves, therefore, to complicate our response and to make us wonder about how objective images can actually be. In many ways, Stone is expanding the experiment he began in *JFK*, a film that is not only about a presidential assassination but also about how images and the history they try to create can be read in multiple ways.

What about the "objectivity" of the image itself? Anyone who took to heart the cliché "seeing is believing" saw, in the King video, a man being beaten by the police, in the fuzzy gray wash of an underexposed, amateur videotape taken at night. The trial lawyers, however, who analyzed the image from their own perspective in their desire to debunk the evidence in order to free their clients, proved to a jury—willing to believe them—that they didn't quite see a man being beaten but an aggressive person the police were trying to restrain. The evidence held in those images was a matter of political and racial conviction, not of any self-evident "truth." In Oliver Stone's re-creation, the police are brutally restraining a brutal, aggressive person, an absurd, amoral killer. The image is a complete fabrication, done in the studio or in a carefully controlled location. Most likely the actor, Woody Harrelson, isn't even in the shot, replaced by a double. There is, in a sense, nothing there, only a studio or location fabrication of an image within a narrative fiction, fully exaggerated as representatives from television news (including Japanese television, with an excited commentator whose remarks are translated through subtitles) look on, make their images, make comments, while the **soundtrack** is filled with the music of Carl Orff's *Carmina Burana*. The re-creation is, as I said, twisted with irony, begging us to provide a more complex reaction than we might have given to the original King videotape or the trial lawyers' interpretation of it.

Stone asks us to think about the construction of images, something that few films attempt to do because their value is built upon our desire not to ask what images are made of and what they might really mean, or, in the case of special effects movies, to wonder at the realism of the fake. We love to look; movies love to show us things. Maybe we don't want to know what we're looking at and want to simply enjoy the illusion, or enjoy the illusion even knowing how it was created. In the case of *Natural Born Killers* Stone's ironies were lost on many people, who found the film too violent. Unwilling to decipher the complex visual structure of the film and understand what that structure was trying to say—that images of violence are manufactured to play upon our desire to see and enjoy violence at a safe distance—they took the images too literally and were repelled. They believed what they saw.

All of which leads us to the central question of this chapter: When we look at an image, and especially when we look at the images that make up a movie, what do we see? What's there, what do we think is there, and what do we want to be there? We can begin an answer by turning very briefly to the development of painting and photography, because film is so much an extension of the latter and borrows many effects from the former.

THE URGE TO REPRESENT "REALITY"

People painted before they wrote. Cave paintings are among the earliest artifacts we have of prehistoric civilizations: an outline of a hand, a deer, images of the human figure and the naturalized world, even sculptures of animals, things caught and seen and then, in the case of the deer, eaten. There is elemental magic in these early images, the kind of magic that says if you own a part of or representation of a thing, you have power over that thing. In this case, the "thing" is nature itself. These early cave paintings show that humans wanted imaginative control over the natural world and wanted to make permanent representations of it. The painted image, in different ways in different cultures, came to express not merely seeing but an interpretation and a desire to own what is seen. Painting, along with storytelling, grew from the same urge to interpret and control the world—to give it a human and humanized shape. "Primitive" art is simple and direct. Painting moved from the primitive in interesting ways.

PERSPECTIVE AND THE PLEASURES OF TRICKING THE EYE

"Primitive" art is never, of course, simple and direct, not even primitive, but seems that way because of the major changes that occurred as painting moved from a desire to capture the world through simple images to a scientific and technology-driven desire to remanufacture images of the world for the viewer's pleasure. We must understand that, no matter what a painting represents (or, in the case of abstract painting, doesn't represent), it is an interpretation of something seen that has been executed by the artist's hand and imagination. A painting is pigment on canvas articulated through a combination of color, shape, volume, and spatial organization. The way space is organized and the subject represented in a painting is very specific to a given culture and time, though it also bears traces of a particular artist's style and personality. Perspective, for example—the illusion of depth on a two-dimensional surface—is hardly a universal way of organizing space on canvas and did not always exist. Traditional Asian painting has never used it. Western painting didn't use it until the early fifteenth century. It was developed by the Florentine architect Filippo Brunelleschi (1377–1446) and the painter Masaccio (1401–1428). Perspective is based on mathematical principles of linear convergence, the way lines can be drawn so they appear to vanish at a single point in space.

People have theorized that perspective was invented for ideological and cultural reasons, because it allowed the wealthy patrons who sponsored artists to be given a privileged place in viewing the canvas. That is, perspective allowed the viewer a sense of ownership, a sense of standing before a space that was made for his gaze. He stood outside the painting, occupying a position that seemed to be at the convergence of an imaginary set of lines that opened into the canvas and then appeared to converge again behind the canvas. These "vanishing lines" created

FIGURE 1.8 This painting of the Annunciation by Fra Carnavale (*c.* 1445–1450) clearly demonstrates how perspective was used in early painting. As if discovering a new way of seeing, the painter exaggerates the vanishing point twice: once in the foreground of the picture plane and again through the archway at the rear of the painting. By looking at the way the perspective lines move outward, you can get an idea of how the painting opens out to embrace the viewer. Courtesy National Gallery of Art, Washington

the illusion that the space of the painting completed the patron's gaze—indeed any viewer's gaze. The double convergence creates an important effect, for if sight lines converge toward the back of the image on the canvas, they also converge in the imaginary space in front of the canvas, a space that is filled by the controlling look of the spectator. This phenomenon would have tremendous repercussions in the development of film in the twentieth century.

By the neoclassical period (from the late seventeenth century to the mid-eighteenth in most of Europe) the ideological thrust of painting was to be as "true" to the natural world as possible. Interpretation and inspiration were, in theory at least, subordinated to imitation and to the capturing of the image, to reproducing it, proclaiming that nature could be taken and owned whole by the imagination. Many artists approached the imitation of nature through technology. The camera obscura came to prominence in the seventeenth century: a box with a pinhole through which light could pass, it projected an upside-down image on its opposite side. A painter would enter the box and literally trace the image of the outside world that was reflected through the pinhole. Another version of this contraption, called a "Claude Glass," after the admired French landscape painter Claude Lorrain (1600–1682), was also put to use by painters. It had a convex

FIGURE 1.9 The camera obscura, used by painters in the seventeenth and eighteenth centuries to reflect an image of the outside world that they could then copy

black mirror that concentrated an image of the landscape that could be painted over or copied. The Dutch painter Jan Vermeer (1632–1675) may have created his paintings using the lighting and imaging effects that were created by the camera obscura as well as lenses and mirrors. A fascinating movie about this, *Tim's Vermeer* (2013), was made by the magicians Penn and Teller.

PHOTOGRAPHY AND REALITY

The camera obscura was a sort of prephotographic device, designed to make possible the urge to capture the real world with as little apparent mediation as possible, even while using the optical technologies of the day. Photography was invented in the nineteenth century out of experiments that, like those involving perspective, were both scientific and aesthetic. At its most basic, photography is a chemical process, during which a light-sensitive material is altered when exposed to light. When this altered material is chemically treated, the exposed particles wash away, creating transparent or translucent spaces where the light fell. The negative image (light for dark) is reversed during printing. The chemistry hasn't changed very much since the middle of the nineteenth century, though the optics have, and faster, more light-sensitive film stock was developed that made nighttime shooting possible. Now, digital imaging has pretty much rendered chemical processing obsolete. The aesthetics and ideology of photographic mediation are a different matter. Despite the technologies of image production, photography became and remains a major factor in the ways we observe and perceive the world around us.

The great French film theorist André Bazin speaks about the inevitability of photography. What he means is that art has always been motivated to capture and maintain the reality of the world, to hold its images eternally. Photography is the climax of that desire because, Bazin believes, it is the first art in which, at the exact instant during which the image is transferred to film, the human hand is not involved. For Bazin, the taking of a photograph is a pure, objective act. He puns in French on the word *objectif*, which means both "objective" and "lens." Bazin was deeply committed to the concept of film and photography as the arts of the real, but he was also aware that the reality of film and photography was "artificial," made by art. He was intrigued by the paradox. He was well aware that in the seemingly automatic passing of a thing to its image, some human intervention always occurs. So, even though the image passes through the lens to the film or image sensor in the camera without the intervention of the human hand, that intervention has already occurred. It happens in the crafting of the lens and the chemical manufacture of the light-sensitive film emulsion or the technology of the digital sensor, by the photographer who chooses a particular lens and a particular shutter or film speed for a particular shot, in the way the photographer lights and composes the shot. Every photographer is a composer: think of the basic, practically universal gesture of an amateur picture taker, waving her arm to signal people in front of the lens to move closer together, to get in the frame. Think of the ramifications if this photographer purposively moved the camera slightly to the right to remove one member of the party from the frame or Photoshopped another figure into the picture. The professional photographer and the photographer as artist make more elaborate preparations for a shot and, after the shot is composed and taken, manipulate the image in the darkroom or, more likely, on the computer screen. They reframe and crop, alter the exposure so the image is darker or lighter. They play with color, make substitutions. They make the image their own.[1]

When photography came along in the nineteenth century, painting was put in crisis. The photograph, it seemed, did the work of imitating nature better than the painter ever could. Some painters made pragmatic use of the invention. There were Impressionist painters who used a photograph in place of the model or landscape they were painting. But by and large, the photograph was a challenge to painting and was one cause of painting's moving away from direct representation and reproduction to the abstract painting of the twentieth century. Since photographs did such a good job of representing things as they existed in the world, painters were freed to look inward and represent things as they were in their imagination, rendering emotion in the color, volume, line, and spatial configurations native to the painter's art.

Photography was not wholly responsible for the development of abstract painting, which emerged in concert with other movements both in the world and in the aesthetics of the late nineteenth and early twentieth century, movements that began to call attention to form and away from an apparently simple representation of "reality." The very inventions of the age—photography, movies, railroads, the telephone—along with the coming apart of old political alliances and traditional class and family connections pushed artists to embrace new forms that would speak to the changes in the old concepts of space and time, of religious and political allegiances. The stresses of modernity in culture led to the beginnings of modernism in the arts. The important point here is that photography introduced to modern culture another form of image making, of visual representation, one apparently more "real" than painting because it seemed to capture an image of the world out there and bring it, framed, composed, and contained, before our eyes. It is almost as if the photograph could stop the confusing rush of the modern world.

When we look at the family photo album, we don't ask how the images were constructed and what the construction is saying about the subject of the photograph. We don't wonder why the photographer chose to be outside the frame, behind the camera, or to time the shutter and leap into the picture; we may not question why one aunt is not smiling, or why some relatives have been cut out of the composition, or why father is way in the back, barely visible. We desire to see and feel something through the image. So we look at the images and feel nostalgia or joy or pain about the family represented in the photographs. We indulge ourselves with a "selfie," which does allow the photographer to be present in the representation of a slightly distorted moment.

However, when the image is not transparently clear, when the photograph is of something unrecognizable, or the painting is abstract, or an **avant-garde** film denies recognizable plot, our first question is, "What is this about?" We want our images to be transparent, to seem to relate some kind of story that we understand, to allow us to look through them to the meanings they seem to convey. They exist to transmit the real world to our eyes and to trigger emotional response.

MANIPULATION OF THE IMAGE

During its relatively brief existence, photography has taken on many culturally and economically determined forms. In the very early days, in order to overcome a perceived inferiority to painting, photographers adopted a painterly style. Some of them hand-colored their work (as did many early makers of silent film), after composing a figure or landscape in poses or compositions similar to those used by the Impressionist painters. As photography found its independent path, many other styles emerged, all of them depending upon some kind of manipulation of the image during the picture-making process. These included the creation of "abstract" photographs, images that reveal only patterns, shapes, and volume. This style flourished in the 1920s at the same time that Dadaist and Surrealist artists incorporated the photographic image into their work. During this period, the photographer Man Ray created abstract patterns by putting actual objects directly onto photographic paper and exposing them to light. The resulting "rayograms" parody Bazin's notion of the objective lens. Here there is no lens and the "real" is turned into the abstract. When, again in the 1920s, photography became more common in journalism and advertising, manipulation of the image became extreme. Removed from the status of art—with all its implications of personal style, subjective vision, and revelation—the photograph became a tool for representing specific commercial and political points of view with the purpose of selling commodities and focusing opinions. Shifting from a cultural realm of style and ideological determination in which individual expression counted strongly, photography became part of another, a corporate style in which the image of a politician making a speech, or a group of strikers in a menacing posture, or a woman assuming a conventional pose of seduction while wearing a particular brand of makeup or clothing has specific designs on the viewer and asks for specific responses, to make a political point or show a hamburger in the best light—especially when the hamburger is painted, sprayed, lit, and in general "styled" to make it look the best it can.

Images like these are obviously determined by external, cultural, economic, and political needs. But the image in the cause of economics and politics is different from the image in the cause of art only in its purpose. All images, all stories, all creations made by people have designs, in all senses of the term. The particular designs of journalism and advertising photography are narrow and focused, wanting the viewer to respond with a political action, hatred for the opposition candidate, putting money into circulation by purchasing a product, in a word, buying into something—an attitude, idea, commodity, or ideology. This kind of photography does not primarily imitate, reveal, or show. Rather, it exhorts, cajoles, and manipulates. It exploits fully the one abiding reality of representation and mediation: a call for some kind of response from the viewer. Something does indeed come between the thing itself and the image. In the case of the work of art, that "something" is a form and structure that ask of us an emotional and intellectual response meant to help us understand the artist and the way she understands the world. In the case of the journalistic, advertising, or political image, that something is a form and structure that ask us to agree to the general values of our culture and the various commodities it creates, to form an opinion, to spend money or cast a vote. In the case of movies, form and structure ask us to respond to many of these same requests simultaneously.

REALITY AS IMAGE

The argument of this book is that reality is always a mutually agreed upon social construct, a more or less common consensus about what is out there and what it all means to most people. Our shared ideas of truth, beauty, morality, sexuality, politics, and religion; the ways we interpret the world and make decisions on how we act in it are determined by a complex process of education, class, gender, assimilation, acculturation, and assent that begins at birth.

It is a cliché that human beings are out of touch with nature, and that more than a few of us are out of touch with reality. The fact is, even when we are in touch, it's not with some given natural world or some objective, existing reality. Being in touch with nature means acting upon a learned response to the natural world. In fact, responding with awe in the face of natural beauty dates back only to the early eighteenth century and became a major cultural event only in the nineteenth. Before the late seventeenth century, people in Western Europe did not pay much attention to nature's grandeur; they were not moved by it nor did they care much to contemplate it. A mountain range was something in the way. A complex shift in sociological and aesthetic responses occurred in the early eighteenth century and can be traced in its development through travel literature and then in poetry, fiction, and philosophy. By the mid-eighteenth century, wild, mountainous landscapes became the site of grand, overwhelming emotional response. The mountains had not, themselves, changed; cultural response had. The "Sublime," the effect of being transported before nature's wildness and in front of representations of that wildness in painting and poetry, was born. With it came nineteenth-century romanticism and attitudes toward the natural world that remain with us still.

Reality is not an objective, geophysical phenomenon like a mountain. Reality is always something said or understood about the world. The physical world is "there," but reality is always a polymorphous, shifting complex of mediations, a kind of multifaceted lens, constructed by the changing attitudes and desires of a culture. Consider how difficult it has been to give voice—to give reality—to the changes in nature due to global warming. Reality is a complex image of the world that many of us choose to agree to. The photographic and cinematic image is one of the ways we use this "lens" (here in a quite literal sense) to interpret the complexities of the world. Reality becomes a kind of cultural baseline upon which we can build a variety of responses. One response is a feeling of security. We feel safe in front of something that strikes us as "real" or realistic. Another response is to dismiss someone who doesn't seem to be operating from this same base. We bless something (a film, a painting, a novel, a political program, a way of life) with the name of realism if it comforts us with something we desire or are familiar with, or have been told we should desire or be familiar with. We are asked or we ask someone to face reality when we or someone else acts in unfamiliar ways. We say "that's not realistic" to dismiss someone or something that does not fit into our range of beliefs, hopes, or desires. "Get real," we say. "Get a life."

So, when the critic André Bazin said that the history of art is equal to the history of people's desire to save an image of the real world, he quickly modified this idea by saying that the desire to capture reality is in fact the desire "to give significant expression to the world." In that phrase "significant expression" lies the key. It's not the world we see in the image but its significant, mediated expression. For Bazin, such expression becomes very significant in photography and film because of the apparent lack of interference from a human agent. This is a peculiar paradox. The image is a significant expression of the real world; it almost is the real world because its image is formed without human interference. Recall Bazin's theory that, at the instant of transferring the image to the film, the photograph occurs without human intervention. As we have seen, this theory has a kernel of truth but is deeply compromised by all the manipulation that goes on before and after the image is actually made (and even while the image is being made, because lenses are not neutral). Out of the paradox come many of our confusions over what the photographic and cinematic image actually is and actually does.

FROM THE PHOTOGRAPHIC TO THE CINEMATIC IMAGE

The alleged reality of the cinematic image is, in reality, a mechanical or digital event. In a sense, film itself is a reality machine. Time and space—the coordinates of Western art, story, and life—were represented by the vertical strip of images that travels through the projector. Twenty-four photographs, or frames, flew past the projector lens each second. A simple, very nineteenth-century mechanical process pulled the filmstrip down, one frame at a time, while a shutter in the shape of a Maltese cross opened and closed the lens so that each frame was projected on the screen in its turn. Today, digital recording and projection have largely taken the place of the filmstrip and its projection. Instead of twenty-four photographs a second, light is transformed into binary digits that record and project images at twenty-four or more frames a second. In either case, the resulting illusion is extraordinary. Because of a cognitive desire to attach the events of one image to the next, and thanks to perceptual optics that cause our eyes to see images fused together above a certain rate of flicker, the series of stills or the interlaced frames projected on the screen by digital projection is interpreted by our brains as a continuous flow. Space and time appear unified and ongoing.

MOVING IMAGES

The search for "reality" in photographic images moved with some speed in the nineteenth century when it joined with the invention (or, more appropriately, the inventions) of cinema. Before the very late nineteenth century, the moving image and the photograph developed along separate lines. Projections of painted images, by machines called magic lanterns, had been around since the seventeenth century. Various devices that created an illusion of figures in motion, or the sense of moving images in a large space surrounding the viewer—devices with wonderful names like zoetropes, phenakistoscopes, thaumatropes, cycloramas, and panoramic views—had been around since the eighteenth century and reached their apogee in the nineteenth. These were mostly toys or sideshows that in various ways placed painted images in progressively different positions of movement on the inside of a revolving drum. By peering through slits in the side of the turning drum, or—in the case of cycloramas—standing in front of an unrolling canvas, the figures or painted landscapes seemed to elide into each other in a semblance of continuous motion.

Magic lanterns, zoetropes, and photography intersected in the late nineteenth century in a quasi-scientific way through the work of two photographers, Eadweard Muybridge and Etienne-Jules Marey. Muybridge was born in England and did much of his work in America. Marey was French. In their work, the nineteenth-century curiosity about mechanical invention, industry, and the ways in which both could overcome the limitations of time and space met and pointed to the development of movies: a time and space machine that rivaled the locomotive and the telegraph.

Muybridge and Marey photographed human and animal movements in ways that analyzed the motion into its component parts. Marey actually used a gunlike photographic mechanism to "shoot" his photographs (and the terms "shooting a picture" and a "shot" originate from that machine). With its aura of scientific investigation, their work situates one branch of photography in that tradition of Western culture that seeks to analyze and quantify nature. It very roughly duplicates the discovery and implementation of perspective in painting during the fourteenth century; both are part of the larger movement to comprehend, own, and control the natural world, to become the visual owner of the image, even enter it imaginatively. With the advent of film, science and technology and imagination merged to make the reality machine.

Leland Stanford, a former governor of California, who liked both horses and science, invited Eadweard Muybridge to help him settle a wager concerning whether or not at one point in a horse's gallop all four hoofs leave the ground. Muybridge proved that they do by taking a series of photographs at high speeds. Muybridge and Stanford went on to publish photographs of animals in motion in *Scientific American.* Muybridge parlayed this into a career of public lectures in which he demonstrated his analytic series of shots of animals—as well as naked people—in motion. He published a version of his work in 1887, the eleven-volume *Animal Locomotion.* Marey had published his animal locomotion studies, called *La machine animale*, in France in 1873. Muybridge further combined his analytic photographs with the old kinetoscope-zoetrope toy to create an illusion of movement of his animals and people and, by 1881, he was projecting them on a wall to a large audience. Scientific investigation, commerce, and spectacle merged in the projected image.

The image was becoming a commodity. The rapidity of this event was accelerated during the last decade of the nineteenth century when Thomas Alva Edison's employee, William K. L. Dickson, developed a way to record moving images on a kinetograph and show them on a kinetoscope. Edison had wanted to make moving images as an accompaniment for his phonograph, but, because he did not have the means of amplifying sound, decided to concentrate on the image alone, thereby holding back the development of sound film for almost thirty years. The work of Edison's company in the late nineteenth century led to a slow but steady proliferation of moving images in peep shows, in which "flip cards" or a film loop was viewed through a viewer in a machine; in nickelodeons, where working-class people paid a nickel to go into a small room and see a short film projected on a sheet; and finally by the 1920s in the movie palaces built as part of the successful attempt of moviemakers to create a "respectable" middle-class audience for their images. By the late 1920s, in an economic slump, the movie studios revived Edison's original notion of synchronizing image to sound and made "talking pictures" to the delight of audiences and a resulting rise in box office receipts.

The steady progression from the individual photographers, inventors, and entrepreneurs who developed the moving image up to the film studios, which were actually large-scale factory operations that mass-produced these images, may seem, at first, a big leap, but it took less than twenty-five years.

FIGURE 1.10 Eadweard Muybridge made this version of the zoopraxiscope, showing athletes boxing. When spun around in the appropriate contraption, the figures seem to be moving (c. 1893)

The immediate and almost instantaneous emergence around the world of movies as a popular commercial art was just slightly in advance of the great boom of popular culture that would take place in the 1920s. Film's invention came with the great nineteenth-century technologies that included telegraphy and the railroads. Its beginnings coincided with the growing influence of newspapers. It completed its growth as a mass medium in the 1920s, at the same time as radio, and each shared in the other's popularity, radio shows often consisting of spoken versions of film. In the end, film infiltrated the imagination more than any other nineteenth-century invention because it told stories with images. It also made its storytellers rich.

The popularity of movies was so great that, soon after 1900, demand for films exceeded supply. Various theater-owner entrepreneurs on the East Coast, most of them immigrants from Eastern Europe, who had engaged in wholesale and retail selling before entering the business of film exhibition, decided that the best way to supply their theaters with product was to manufacture it themselves. They would make the images they needed to sell. They fought with Edison, who attempted to control the patents on his motion picture machines and who sometimes employed thugs to beat up the filmmakers and take their equipment away, constituting what film historians call the "patent wars" of 1910 to 1913. The filmmakers went to California to escape Edison's reach, settled in Los Angeles, and rather quickly established their own tightly knit companies that by the 1920s had evolved into the studios that centralized all facets of motion picture production and exist, if only in name—Warner Bros., MGM, Paramount, Universal, Columbia, RKO—to this day.

In the history of film, the first quarter of the twentieth century was a particularly active period of creativity on all levels and in many countries: the development of film's visual narrative structure; the creation, the buying and the selling of studios and human talent; the invention of the star system; the integration of the entire production and distribution of images through theaters owned by the studios, which guaranteed that the studios had an automatic outlet for their products. This is—in very compressed form that we will open up in the following chapters—the history of production that moved from an individual, director-based activity into a huge industrial operation headed by an executive who delegated individual films to **producers** and peopled by an enormous in-house staff of writers, directors, composers, designers, electricians, actors, and other craftspeople.

The speed of the process by which moviemaking developed into commerce was driven by the willingness of audiences to look and look and look and want to see more and more. Movies supplied a visual imagination and narrative flow for the culture at large. They extended basic stories of popular culture—stories of sexuality and romance, captivity and release, family and heroism, individualism and community—into visual worlds that were immediately comprehensible, almost tactile, *there*, in front of the viewers' eyes. In the movies, time and space appeared as if intact. Human figures moved and had emotions. Life seemed to be occurring. The moving image was a vibrant, story-generating, meaning-generating thing. More than literature, painting, or the photograph, moving images eloquently expressed what many, almost most, of the people across economic and social classes wanted to hear and see. That what they were hearing and seeing was an illusion in every respect did not matter. It might, in fact, have contributed to film's popularity. Seeing and feeling in the secure knowledge that no obvious consequences are involved is an important aspect of our response to any aesthetic experience. The moving image was a particular attraction to everyone who wanted to see more, feel more, and do it in the safe embrace of an irresistible story. It still is, despite the changes in the technologies of the image and viewing habits that have occurred over the last decade. For many, the screens are smaller. For those who stream television series, "binge viewing" of a Netflix series becomes a way to create one's own movie. But the changes in technologies, formats, and viewing habits don't change the central fact that we love to watch.

In the following chapters, we will analyze the endurance of the desire to see and how the desire is created and maintained. We will examine the elements of image, motion, story, creator, and creation, and the culture they and we inhabit. We will examine how and why moving images work and speculate about why we respond to them. In the course of that examination, we will try to account for a great number of kinds of films and filmmakers, and film viewers, too.

ACKNOWLEDGMENTS

Professor Sharon Gerstel of the University of Maryland supplied information about the history of perspective. Professor Elizabeth Loizeaux of the University of Maryland offered ideas about the camera obscura.

FURTHER READING

Some of the best analysis of the use of digital imagery in filmmaking is by Lev Manovich, *The Language of New Media* (Cambridge, MA: MIT Press, 2003).

For a good study of the changes that are occurring with digital cinematography and projection, see D. N. Rodowick, *The Virtual Life of Film* (Cambridge, MA: Harvard University Press, 2007).

Basic resources for information on the way we perceive image and reality include Rudolf

Arnheim, *Art and Visual Perception* (Berkeley and Los Angeles: University of California Press, 1974) and E. H. Gombrich, *Art and Illusion* (London: Phaidon, 1977).

Linda Williams' *Figures of Desire: A Theory and Analysis of Surrealist Film* (Berkeley, University of California Press, 1992) extends the discussion of surrealist painting and its influence on film.

A detailed study of the image is provided by Jacques Aumont, *The Image*, trans. Claire Pajackowska (London: British Film Institute, 1997).

Erwin Panofsky's *Perspective as Symbolic Form*, trans. Christopher S. Wood (New York: Zone Books, 1991), is a good source for the theory of perspective.

Michel Foucault's essay "Las Meninas" argues the theory of perspective as a means of owning the space of a painting. It is in *The Order of Things* (New York: Vintage Books, 1994). This is an invaluable book for understanding the theories of reality and the moving image.

See also Bill Nichols, *Ideology and the Image* (Bloomington: Indiana University Press, 1981).

For an emotional and theoretical discussion of photography, see Roland Barthes, *Camera Lucida: Reflections on Photography*, trans. Richard Howard (New York: Hill and Wang, 1981).

A classic work on the Sublime in literature is M. S. Abrams, *The Mirror and the Lamp: Romantic Theory and the Critical Tradition* (New York: Oxford University Press, 1985). But Robert Macfarlane's *Mountains of the Mind* (New York: Pantheon, 2003), told from a mountain climber's perspective, also relates the history of the perception of mountains.

Material on early movie machines, Marey, Muybridge, and Edison can be found in Charles Musser, *The Emergence of Cinema: The American Screen to 1907, History of the American Cinema*, vol. 1 (Berkeley, Los Angeles, and London: University of California Press, 1990). This volume is an excellent source for the development of early cinema.

For Etienne-Jules Marey, see Marta Braun, *Picturing Time: The Work of Etienne-Jules Marey (1830–1904)* (Chicago: University of Chicago Press, 1992).

David A. Cook's *A History of Narrative Film* 4th ed. (New York: W. W. Norton & Company, 2003) and Kristin Thompson and David Bordwell's *Film History: An Introduction* 3rd ed. (New York: McGraw-Hill, 2009) are good sources for information about the development of film as art and industry.

Anne Friedberg, *Window Shopping: Cinema and the Postmodern* (Los Angeles and Berkeley: University of California Press, 1993) offers a good reading of nineteenth-century technology and the development of mass media.

SUGGESTIONS FOR FURTHER VIEWING

Un chien Andalou (Luis Buñuel and Salvador Dali, 1929). An early surrealist film that plays with temporality and our expectations of the realistic image.

Barry Lyndon (Stanley Kubrick, 1975) slows tempo and creates painterly images.

The Draughtsman's Contract (Peter Greenaway, 1982) is in part a visual meditation on composing painterly images.

Cave of Forgotten Dreams (Werner Herzog, 2010) is an enchanted documentary about cave paintings in Southern France.

NOTE

1 The references to and quotations from André Bazin are from *What Is Cinema?* vol. I, trans. Hugh Gray (Los Angeles and Berkeley: University of California Press, 1968), p. 12.

CHAPTER 2

Formal structures

How films tell their stories

THE IMAGE, THE WORLD, AND THE FILM STUDIO

The evolution of the photographic image into the moving **narrative** image is itself a narrative of the making and comprehension of illusions. It is a narrative that runs almost as smoothly as a good Hollywood film. And it is a narrative that is tightly linked to the economic history of filmmaking. Almost from the beginning, filmmaking and moneymaking went hand in hand, one determining the other. Filmmakers, from very early on, understood on an intuitive level that images were profoundly desirable and manipulable. They knew that by their manipulating the image, the image in turn would manipulate how and what people saw and the way they responded to what they saw. This would in its turn create the desire to see more images and to pay to see more. As sophisticated as the Renaissance painters, who plotted the sight lines in their paintings to create the illusion of depth and presence, filmmakers could plot all aspects of the image for very similar purposes. Sight lines, plot lines, character, spectator positioning—how an ideal viewer is literally created by the images and the narrative going on up on the screen—all are planned to reduce the sense of distance between spectator and image and to optimize an illusion of participation.

FROM IMAGE TO NARRATIVE

Let us take a moment and stay with the early development of the moving image and its stories in order to more easily understand the structuring of illusions and the formation of conventions—those structures of form and content that, once invented, are used over and over again. This chapter will start with an examination of how image and narrative structure were formed and then move into a discussion of how that form and its variations were perpetuated throughout the history of film. We need to understand the formation of image and story and then go on to its meanings.

Moving-picture viewing and projection was developed almost at the same time in the United States, France, England, Germany, and other countries around the world. In 1888, Eadweard Muybridge, the photographer, visited Thomas Alva Edison, the inventor. Muybridge urged Edison to combine Muybridge's image projector, the zoopraxiscope, with Edison's phonograph. In 1889, Edison met Etienne-Jules Marey, who had developed a moving-image filmstrip in Paris. In 1891, Thomas Edison's assistant, William K. L. Dickson, demonstrated a viewing machine in which could be seen a smoothly moving image of a man—Dickson himself. In France, in 1895, Auguste and Louis Lumière projected a short film they had made of workers leaving their factory. The French magician Georges Méliès, who had watched the films of the Lumière brothers, projected his first film in 1896.[1]

The Edison Company's early attempts at filmmaking were of single, staged events: a co-worker sneezing, a couple kissing—the erotic image emerging in cinema at its very start. The Lumière brothers shot events going on in the world: their workers leaving their factory, a train arriving at a station. But they soon began staging incidents: a child squirting a gardener with a water hose, brother Auguste feeding his baby. The magician, Méliès, on the other hand, worked largely inside his studio, mocking up images, creating trick **shots** on film. He showed people disappearing in the middle of a **scene**, people underwater, men traveling to the moon. Before distributing the finished film, Méliès had his factory workers hand-paint each **frame**, creating an illusion of color—a technique common among many filmmakers.

This greatly reduced history may give a faulty impression. While we know the history of Edison's work, as well as what was happening in France and in other countries where inventions similar to Edison's were appearing at the end of the nineteenth century, it grows increasingly difficult to develop a coherent history of film's very rapid early development after this point. It is especially hard to say who was the "first" to do anything for the simple reason that approximately three-quarters of all films made during the **silent era** (roughly 1893–1927) are lost. But the Lumière brothers, Méliès, and the Edison factory do provide us with models for certain lines of development in film, lines by no means straight or uncomplicated. What they developed leads to a notion—a theory, actually—that three fundamental conventions of filmmaking emerged from their work. From the Edison factory came both the Hollywood **studio system**, with its division of labor, and, eventually, the **classical Hollywood** or **classical narrative style**, based on character and action. The Lumières pointed the direction to the **documentary**, to film's power to record events that would occur anyway, even if the camera were not present (we will talk in some detail about documentary filmmaking in Chapter 9). From Georges Méliès' magic trick films came the cinema of fantasy, of science fiction and the wondrous voyage, which would, of course, become an important part of Hollywood filmmaking.

Another, much later, French filmmaker, Jean-Luc Godard, who throughout his career as critic and **director** from the 1950s to the present has been interrogating the nature of the film and television image, came to a different conclusion. He suggested (through a character in his 1967 film, *La Chinoise*) that the Lumière brothers, those presumed documentarians and makers of ***actualités***—events filmed as they were happening, events that *would* be happening even if the camera weren't there—did not in fact give us documentaries of late nineteenth-century Parisian life. From the prospect of a century, Godard suggests that what the Lumières really made

FIGURE 2.1 Early eroticism from Thomas Edison's studio. *The Kiss* (William Heise, 1896)

FIGURE 2.2 The camera setup in Auguste and Louis Lumière's *Arrival of a Train at La Ciotat Station* (1896) emphasizes the vanishing line, giving perspective to the shot

FIGURE 2.3 Georges Méliès, the magician, creates trick shots in *A Trip to the Moon* (1902). The rocket, having returned from the moon, falls into a fantasy ocean

constitutes our fantasy images of what Paris looked like in the late nineteenth century. Their images constitute the imaginary, the shared image fantasy, of the way things were, through the images of film. Méliès, Godard suggests, seems to be the documentarian of the fantasies of late nineteenth-century, middle-class France.

This is a neat turning of things on their heads. More than an intellectual puzzle, Godard's proposition gets to the root of the question of the image. Just because the Lumière brothers turned their cameras on events in the street or a railway station does not make them recorders of things as they were. We know that they set up many of their shots in advance. They composed their images carefully, often employing the fundamentals of perspective invented during the Renaissance. Because Méliès made trick shots in his studio does not make him a mere fantasist. Each was involved in different kinds of early cinematic mediation, of putting on the screen images that were not about reality but about different ways of constructing reality cinematically, different ways of seeing and interpreting the world. The same is true of the work of the Edison factory. Edison's film inventor, William K. L. Dickson, made moving images that, like the French, moved people's imaginations, all the while working toward the commercial exploitation of his inventions. The work of the Edison factory prefigures the Hollywood process in which film is a commodity that demonstrates the imagination's ability to create images that are eloquent and moving and that can be manufactured for profit.

Ultimately, cinema did not evolve simply into two or three separate paths, but into various branches, growing out of basic impulses, almost never pure, to see, manipulate, and represent the world in images. "Documentary" and "fiction" intertwine in curious ways, especially in the **genre** of "**docudrama**" in which fiction and history are mixed in ways that historicize the former and fictionalize the latter (Ava DuVernay's 2014 film about the civil rights movement, *Selma*, for example). Film sees the world from a variety of perspectives, which often intersect. Whatever the origin of the moving image—whether it is a recording of what is already there in the world or made up in the studio—imagination, culture, ideology, and economics intervene. They mediate and form what we finally see on the screen; we, as viewers, mediate in turn, interpreting the images to make them meaningful to us.

THE ECONOMICS OF THE IMAGE

As cinema developed, the impulses of the Lumière brothers, Méliès, and Edison were joined in intriguing ways. From the Edison factory came the economic impulse, the urge to treat the image as commodity, to own it, rent it, sell it, profit from it. This quickly led to the burgeoning of nickelodeons and the **producers** who made films, the film exchanges and distributors that fed them product, and by the early teens, film studios and movie houses. From the Lumière brothers came the urge to reveal, to present an image of what appears to be the world as it is, but always turns out to be the world as it is seen in a particular way in film and the other visual arts. They also sold and profited from their images. From Méliès came a sense of the image as the space of fantasy, the origins of science fiction cinema; he also developed a concept and methods of image fabrication that finally came to form the basis of American film production, part of its economy of manufacture. Méliès also sold his images and profited from them.

The work of Méliès was about control, crafting every element of the image, putting it together, element by element, for specific effect. Where Auguste and Louis Lumière allowed a certain serendipity to occur when they exposed motion picture film to the outside world, Méliès arranged and accounted for each element in the shot. Working in the studio, using **stop action** (shutting off the camera, removing or putting something in the scene, then starting the camera, so the person or object seemed to pop into or out of view), working with miniatures, painted backdrops, and then hand-coloring the film, he and his factory allowed nothing to occur by chance and little of the outside world to intrude. Even though legend has it that the first stop-action event in a Méliès film occurred by accident, in fact the elements of his image making were calculated, created, and circulated by the filmmaker and seen by the viewer in a closed accounting system in which nothing appeared by chance. This was to prove to be the future of the Hollywood system of image making where "reality" is a product manufactured in the studio and economy means not only the calculation of profit and loss but the entire circulation of imagination, production, distribution, and exhibition, each calculated to create the maximum return of emotion and grosses at the box office. We cannot understand film, American film in particular, without understanding this complex economic system. And we cannot understand the economic system without understanding the formal and thematic systems of the films themselves.

THE SYSTEM DEVELOPS: BUSTER KEATON AND CHARLIE CHAPLIN

As an example of the way these various threads became woven into the kinds of films we watch today, I want to remain in the early history of cinema for a moment and concentrate on two comic filmmakers, Buster Keaton and Charlie Chaplin, whose films and working methods remain a model for current film.

Before the studio system, filmmakers experimented with different attitudes toward the external world and the economics of the image. Many filmed outdoors, where light was available and backgrounds were ready-made. Much of the pleasure of watching the films of the silent comedian Buster Keaton, for example, comes from seeing images of the world of early twentieth-century America go by. This world is not foregrounded, however. Keaton's images are not documentary, not about chance, but rather about his body in flight, running, falling, endangered, engineered into precarious situations. One of the great moments in silent film comedy comes in Keaton's *Steamboat Bill, Jr.* (Charles Reisner, Buster Keaton, 1928). Keaton stands in the midst of a terrific storm and the facade of a house behind him suddenly falls. It is a full-sized house, or at least the front of one, towering over the still figure of Keaton. When it falls, the sense of his fragility is marked. He will be crushed. But the engineering of the trick is such that when the facade of the house falls straight over him, the cutout of the window in the middle of the top floor neatly falls around his body. He stands stock-still without a flinch, and then runs away.

The essential physicality of this stunt is unthinkable in any other medium because none other, not even live theater, could create the illusion of the thereness of the actor's body and the house falling on him within a space that is so obviously in the world. Only film can make things look "real" by means of fabricating and composing reality out of a trick occurring in the way it configures, and we perceive, space. In the case of the Keaton gag, the two-dimensionality of the image (like all images, film has no depth, so things can be hidden, angles and points of view can trick our eye, depth and volume can be manufactured), the obvious weight of the building (which was, in fact, a set and probably extremely light), the presence of the body, that figure in a landscape that film depends upon like no medium other than painting, make the stunt startling, funny, and in the peculiar manner of film, "real."

Manipulated, used, and also there, the human figure and the landscape are part of the **mise-en-scène** of a film by Keaton or any other great physical comedian, including the much maligned Jerry Lewis. Mise-en-scène—originally a theatrical term that literally means "put in the scene"—is an element of any film, comic or not, and refers to the way space is organized and perceived in a film, including the way figure and background are composed. Mise-en-scène also includes lighting and movement, the use of black and white or color, the distance between camera and figure—everything that happens within the frame, including the frame itself. In almost any Keaton film we see Buster and the streets, curbs, houses, cars, and people around him. Space is used generously; it is open and wide and many things occur in the frame other than the main action. Keaton himself becomes one of the many elements that occur within that space. At any time, any one of these elements may be called upon to become a prop for a gag or a stunt. As in the case

FIGURE 2.4 A house falls on Buster Keaton. *Steamboat Bill, Jr.* (Charles Reisner, Buster Keaton, 1928). See also Figures 3.22 and 6.10

of the house facade in *Steamboat Bill, Jr.*, parts of the world may be built specifically for the gag. But even the apparently spontaneous appearance of people and streets in a Keaton film is part of its preconceived presence, its mise-en-scène. Our response to Keaton's images is—as Jean-Luc Godard said of the Lumière brothers—the response of our fantasy of what the world might have looked like. Even in Keaton, we do not see the world itself. We see its image. Its visual memory. And that remains strong enough, present enough to surprise and delight us.

Keaton's great rival in silent comedy, Charlie Chaplin, worked somewhat closer to Méliès' method of studio shooting. Chaplin had less use for the outside world than did Keaton. He worked almost exclusively in the studio and reduced the mise-en-scène to himself. The main signifying element in a Chaplin film is Chaplin. He might indeed engineer a complex gag, as when he gets caught in the gears of an elaborate machine in *Modern Times*. (*Modern Times* is a post-silent film made in 1936, but Chaplin doesn't talk.) Constructed in the studio, the process of the gag highlights Chaplin and his combat with the guts of the machine rather than the mad confluence of physical structure and the body as in Keaton and the falling house.

Foregrounding his own persona and making that persona, the Tramp, a representation of character, attitude, and sentiment, a figure onto which the viewer could overlay his or her own desires, vulnerabilities, and feelings of social or economic inadequacy, Chaplin could demand that focus be kept on his body. Here he was quite unlike either the Lumière brothers or Méliès and closer, perhaps, to the tradition of Edison. The latter foregrounded characters and faces in his early films; Méliès and the Lumière brothers worked with a larger mise-en-scène in which human figures were often only one element of many. For them, the moving image represented intersections between subject, foreground, and background. For Méliès, those intersections were crafted together in the studio, parts of them literally by hand, whereas Chaplin's studio work uses little of the potential sleight of hand (or eye) offered by the camera, by paintings, and by trick shots (perhaps with the exception of his 1925 film *The Gold Rush*, which does use trick shots of Charlie in the snow). His was the cinema of personality, of the star (see Figure 6.9).

The different styles of Keaton and Chaplin represent, in a sense, the next level in the culture of the image, in the processes of cinematic representation and the transition from film as craft to film as commodity. Their work also puts another turn on our investigation of the reality of the image. As comedians, the images they made and the stories they told exaggerated the world and the place of the human figure in it. Though both filmmakers indulged in the comic movements of falls and chases, pursuits and being hit by blunt instruments, their styles were quite different. Keaton saw his cinematic world as a place for combat between his body and the physical things of the world. Chaplin saw his as a site of sentimental triumph, of the cleverness of the "little guy," conquering odds and winning the heart of a simple woman. Image making for him provided the vehicle to carry his character of the Tramp through misadventures to redemption and the triumph over class, from despair to a measure of self-possession. He wanted all this to take place in a world whose presence was immediate and apparently unmediated. He wanted his audience's hearts.

But we can find a delightful paradox when we compare Chaplin with Keaton that makes the parallels with Méliès even more interesting. As much as he liked to work his gags in the middle of the ongoing, outside world, Keaton, like Méliès, also understood how he could manipulate the components of the shot to best effect. Keaton liked to make the artificiality of the image part of the joke of his films. In *The Play House* (1921), Keaton plays with multiple exposure, performing an entire vaudeville act by himself, with himself as every member of the audience. In *Sherlock, Jr.* (1924), Keaton is a movie projectionist who dreams himself into the screen, into the image, and is overcome by its conjuries. Scenes change, the weather changes, the flow of images confuses him and causes him to take pratfalls.

This **sequence** in *Sherlock, Jr.* is among the great statements and admissions of how artificial the film image actually is. Keaton, in all his films, is either doing or being undone by things that happen around him. Objects and people in the image conspire; Buster flees and then cleverly gets the better of them. In *Sherlock, Jr.*, he is conspired against by the very medium in which he works. The image itself turns against him. Chaplin, however, appears as the master of the image and intends to subdue it to his comic persona. He tends to battle people more than things, as Keaton does, or use things for simple, heart-tugging comic effect, as when he sticks a fork in two rolls and makes them perform a ballet or delicately eats his shoe in *The Gold Rush* (1925).

THE GROWTH OF CORPORATE FILMMAKING

Together, Chaplin and Keaton indicate what is happening as filmmaking grows to industrial proportions and, in the course of that growth, reconciles or fudges the boundaries between illusion, realism, audience response, and corporate need. Both very independent filmmakers, their styles reflected and incorporated the complex, sometimes contradictory parts of art and commerce that would form filmmaking both in America and abroad. Even their professional careers pointed to the directions in which filmmaking moved in the 1920s.

Late in the 1920s, Keaton, who successfully operated his own production company, signed with MGM, already one of the giants among film studios. By doing so, by signing with a studio that developed and promoted the **producer system** in which the director had only a small role, Keaton lost much of his creative control and creative edge. The films he made for MGM were not as good as his previous independent work, and he disappeared into obscurity until rediscovered in the 1960s. Earlier, in 1919, Charlie Chaplin, together with two of the biggest stars of the silent period, Douglas Fairbanks and Mary Pickford, along with D. W. Griffith, the great film director, formed United Artists. They first formed the company for their own films, but as financial problems grew, and the actors and directors turned control over to an important management figure in the early studio days, Joseph Schenck, United Artists became a major studio, though one that acted as a financing and distribution, rather than a production company. Artists' control of the means and economics of production may have been short lived, and it never quite came back, but the origins of United Artists did indicate that some in early Hollywood understood the direction filmmaking was moving in.

Chaplin and Keaton were used by the Hollywood system in different ways. Chaplin's privileging of his own star presence, making his figure the sentimental focus of a studio-bound construction in which everything is made in order to foreground the star and his story, became, in fact, the dominant mode in American filmmaking. Becoming part owner—with two other big movie stars and a pioneering director—of a studio, Chaplin further helped the studio system to come into dominance. (Ironically, later in his life, during the U.S. government's and the film studios' anticommunist purges in the 1950s, Chaplin's career and reputation were all but ruined.) Keaton's individual talent was swallowed by the studio system. Later in his life, after the old studio system collapsed, Keaton emerged from oblivion and re-entered film and television, a rediscovered comic talent. Within the studios, the image that represented the world outside was subdued to the image of the world made within the studio's confines. The image made in the studio became, in turn, subdued to the attractiveness of story, star, and, always, economics. Mediated by story and star, and by the viewer's willingness to see what the story asked her to see, the image became "realistic." That is, it became transparent, invisible. It became the classical Hollywood style.

THE CLASSICAL HOLLYWOOD STYLE

Casablanca

In order to understand where all this led to, I will start by leaping ahead in time with an example of a film that remains, so many years after its creation in 1942, not only popular, but whose very dialogue has burrowed into the ordinary discourse: "Play it again, Sam"—not, in fact, the exact line spoken in the film—is known by everyone. "Here's looking at you, kid" and "I am shocked, shocked . . ." are among other bits of dialogue that have exited the film and entered everyday life. I want to re-enter the film and look at it as an example of a near perfect studio production. This will allow us to begin investigating some of the basic formal structures of film that we will continue to expand upon throughout the book.

Warner Bros., the studio that made *Casablanca*, was established by Albert, Sam, Harry, and Jack Warner in 1923 in order, as was the case with so many other studios, to maintain a steady supply of films for their distribution business. They made their fortune in the 1920s with a series of movies starring a dog named Rin Tin Tin, and they made film history by producing the first part-talking sound feature film, *The Jazz Singer*, in 1927. By the 1930s, Warner Bros. was turning out **melodramas** and, especially, gangster and detective films. Like all the other studios—MGM, Paramount, Universal, 20th Century Fox, RKO, Columbia (United Artists was a distribution rather than a production company)—it was run as a closed, self-sufficient filmmaking factory, whose stars and creative staff were under strict contract. Michael Curtiz directed *Casablanca*. A Hungarian by birth, he never gained a strong grasp of English, but did have a remarkable talent for action films and melodramas. Humphrey Bogart, the male lead of *Casablanca*, had been largely relegated to playing cheap hoods in the 1930s, but achieved something of a breakout as detective Sam Spade in John Huston's *The Maltese Falcon* in 1941. *Casablanca* was his first major romantic role. With the exception of Ingrid Bergman, the film's co-star, the rest of the cast were Warner Bros. stock players, recognizable to any moviegoer of the time. As would the look and the form of the film's storytelling be.

The film begins by introducing its contemporary audience to the history of the moment they would be familiar with: the war in Europe; the occupation of France; the refugees streaming into

Morocco. A resistance fighter is shot by the police. Various bystanders await anxiously word of their safe passage out of the country. A plane arrives carrying the Nazi Major Strasser (Conrad Veidt), who then, in a long **tracking shot**, walks with police captain Renault (Claude Rains), talking about the murder of the Resistance fighters and about Rick's, the nightclub owned by the Bogart character. "Everybody comes to Rick's," Renault tells Strasser. This seven-minute-long opening sequence serves an important function beyond introducing us to the lesser characters of the film and filling in some contemporary history. The sequence draws us into the narrative flow, removing any sense of separation from the film that is getting started. It intrigues us, supplies a certain amount of suspense, and urges us forward, most especially to see Rick. The publicity and reviews for the film would have prepared a contemporary viewer for Bogart's appearance, and even today, the legend of the film will make a new viewer eager to see Rick.

Casablanca holds off revealing its star for as long as possible. Expectation is heightened, and the gaze is teased. The gaze, the way a character looks at another character or at an object, is of fundamental importance to the Hollywood **continuity style**, and we will have reason to return to it often. Right here, at the beginning of *Casablanca*, our gaze is held in suspension: What are we about to see? Who is Rick and what will he look like? Like everyone else, will we come to Rick's? From the left to right tracking shot of Strasser and Renault, the film **dissolves** to a nighttime shot. A spotlight moves across the scene of people entering a doorway, over which is a sign reading "Rick's Café Américain." In case we miss it, there is a **close-up** of the sign. The camera moves down from the sign and tracks toward the door with the other customers, entering the café as if we were given permission to see its interior.

There is a **cut**, and the camera begins a right to left tracking shot along the interior of Rick's. The movement of a waiter, carrying a tray of drinks in the middle of the shot, serves as the point of focus for the movement of the camera until it comes to Sam (Dooley Wilson), Rick's confidant and pianist–singer for the café. At this point, the camera tracks forward so we can enjoy Sam's music, which has been playing on the **soundtrack** all along. At this point there is another cut, and the camera **pans** quickly to two men at a table, one worrying that he will never get out of Casablanca. Another cut brings us to a woman who is trying to sell her diamonds. The cuts to various other customers, worrying over their lives, continue until the camera picks up the waiter again and resumes its right to left movement, pausing once at the bar and then cutting again to observe the café's maître d' entering Rick's inner sanctum. Will we get a view of him now? Not quite. There are shots of women at various tables, turning their eyes as if gazing at someone. One of them asks the waiter if Rick would sit with them. The answer is "never," even if the invitation comes from the head of the second largest bank in Amsterdam. "The leading banker in Amsterdam is now the pastry chef in our kitchen . . . and his father is the bellboy."

But we are getting close, closer than any of the other customers. A waiter brings a bill from one of the customers for an advance of money to Rick's table to sign, and Rick's hand briefly enters the frame. There is a cut to that hand signing it. Another cut brings our gaze to the table where Rick is sitting. We see his hand and part of his midsection. On the table are the tools of his life and trade: the signed advance, a cigarette resting on an ashtray, an empty cocktail glass, a chessboard. Rick's hand passes the check to the waiter out of the **frame**. He touches a pawn on the chess board, reaches for his cigarette, and as he brings it to his lips, the camera finally pans up to reveal Bogart/Rick, pulling back slightly as he tinkers with his chess pieces.

FIGURE 2.5 Holding off expectations. The audience want to see Rick. The filmmakers retard that expectation while seamlessly moving toward him. "Everybody comes to Rick's," Captain Renault (Claude Rains) tells Major Strasser (Conrad Veidt) as they move left to right

FIGURE 2.6 That evening, people (and the viewer) enter Rick's Café Américain

FIGURE 2.7 Inside the Café, the camera tracks right to left, picking up Sam (Dooley Wilson) and cutting to the tables of various characters desperate to leave town

FIGURE 2.8 In Rick's inner sanctum, privileged customers gaze at him, hoping for an audience

FIGURE 2.9 We get close to Rick and gaze at the objects on his desk

FIGURE 2.10 Finally, the camera tilts up, revealing Rick (Humphrey Bogart). *Casablanca* (Michael Curtiz, 1942)

ENTERTAINMENT AND INVISIBILITY

I elaborate the first ten minutes of *Casablanca* as a way to understand how the Hollywood style works to entice and invite us into story and character. The **edits** and camera movements that become obvious on close analysis are invisible to us as casual viewers. Because we go to the movies for entertainment, and moviemakers believe that entertainment means unobstructed access to story and character, they allow us to be entertained by rendering the forms of their story invisible. In a sense, they don't want us so much to look as to feel our way into the film's story and therefore have created an elaborate set of conventions that were developed from the earliest days of filmmaking. These conventions not only allow the viewer to be comforted by the unobtrusiveness of form, but also allow filmmakers to work as expeditiously and cheaply as possible. If "entertainment" is the byword for the audience, "budget and schedule" were the bywords for the studios and remain in effect in the **post-studio period**. In what follows, we will take apart the components of the filmmaking and film viewing process to show how they work.

FABRICATING THE IMAGE

Let's first repeat and then elaborate on some basic principles. What you see when you look at a movie is not what is actually there. What you are actually seeing on the movie screen is the reflection of a strong beam of light sent through a moving ribbon of plastic or translated from digital code. The screen reflects the projected images back to you, and you interpret them as objects and figures, still or in motion. This means of projecting and perceiving moving images has not changed much since the late nineteenth century, when it was invented. Newer digital technologies make the process more complicated. The original images still pass as light through a lens, but rather than create an analogue image on a filmstrip, they are transformed into the ones and zeros of binary code, which are then reconverted to light and projected on a white screen or by illuminating the diodes on the screen of an LCD television, computer, or phone. Aside from the problem of screen size, however, the results are the same.

Our perception of cinematic narratives is an illusion, made up of fragmentary elements of light and shadow, pieced together and then interpreted as coherent, ongoing wholes. The studios that make the films were pieced together from a number of small moviemaking and movie distributing businesses in the 1910s and 1920s. Self-contained filmmaking "factories", with employees who included everyone from writers, directors, and actors to set decorators and electricians, the studios created an economy of the visible, an organized, rationalized, commodity-driven form of production that depended upon the manufacture of a film out of various pieces, each one made by a different group of people in the studio hierarchy. The finished product depended upon the audience's willingness to interpret and decode those pieces, reading and responding to the stories they told—stories that often went beyond the film itself into celebrity narratives and, these days, "makings of," relating the behind-the-scenes events of the filmmaking process.

In order to accomplish the manufacture of up to two films a week during the peak years of studio production, from the late 1920s through the early 1950s, the studios had to streamline production processes. They followed essential manufacturing processes, begun in the 1920s, by dividing up the work. At the top, the studio boss in Hollywood communicated with his financial officers in New York, who, by controlling the money, actually held the reins of the studio. The studio head in Hollywood settled on the stars and properties (books, plays, scripts) that were handed along to the producers. The producers, in collaboration with the studio head, in turn assigned writers, a director, and other crewmembers to the film. By the time shooting was begun, everyone's role was laid out: shots were sketched on **storyboards**, sets were built, the script, usually the product of many hands, was largely finished (*Casablanca* was an unusual case because the script was being written as it was filmed). The work of making the film was and remains largely a process of executing a plan in precise, piecemeal fashion, so well determined as to allow as few mistakes, as few time and cost overruns, as possible We will look in detail at the various people involved in the process in Chapters 5, 6, and 7.

Part of the planning involves creating the images themselves as a staging process. Very often, a shot—which is any length of an unedited, or uncut, piece of exposed film (a close-up, or a long tracking movement of the camera, as in the sequence in which Strasser and Renault walk from the airport, for example)—is actually put together bit by bit over a course of time, with many different hands contributing to the construction process. In studio filmmaking very few of the various elements of a shot—the human figures, the background, foreground, sky, scenery, buildings—need to be present at any one time in its creation. The economics of the image require that the studio break the shot elements into the smallest, most manageable units, just as they break the entire production process down into manageable units. Everything that can be done indoors is. Whole sets or parts of them are put together on a sound stage or on the back lot. It's not possible to put up tall buildings in a studio, but it is possible to build

FIGURE 2.11 This early shot from *Casablanca* is a layered composition in which the various elements (mostly painted) have been added at various times to construct the finished image

the lower part of a building facade and compose the shot so that the character is standing in front of a structure that appears to be large because we are inclined to want to imagine a whole even though we see only a part. In any given shot, if more of the building needs to appear, it can be added in the special effects studio, or painted on glass and put in front of the camera. Because we are looking at a two-dimensional image, perspective can be used to fool our sense of depth.

Great detail can be suggested by simple means. An early scene showing the city of Casablanca was filmed on the Warner Bros.' back lot, with the minaret of the mosque and the buildings, sky, and ocean in the background created by models and paint. A swamp is a difficult place to shoot in, but a mound of dirt, a pool of water, some vegetation strewn carefully about, combined with careful lighting and **composition**, will convey the appropriate image. The swamp sequence in the German director F. W. Murnau's American film *Sunrise* (1927), with a spotlight standing in for the moon and the camera gracefully moving around the characters on a movie set, remains one of the most lyrical shots in the history of film, despite its utter artificiality.

FIGURE 2.12 The lyricism of artificiality. Within the studio, filmmakers can pool resources to create images that suggest more than they show. Here the idea of the moon and some water and vegetation has a lyrical effect and feeling of foreboding. This image is the end of a long, complex tracking shot that brings the Man (George O'Brien) and the Woman from the City (Margaret Livingston) together in F. W. Murnau's *Sunrise* (1927). See also Figures 3.31 and 3.32

FIGURE 2.13 Flying through an alien landscape in *Guardians of the Galaxy* (James Gunn, 2014). This is an excellent example of the digital mise-en-scène, very much an animation as opposed to live action

Going to sea to shoot a film is an expensive and tactically difficult proposition. It is cheaper to send a **second unit** crew out to shoot some boats in the ocean and then do the rest in the studio. A large tank of water with a skillfully built model boat can substitute for the full-scale event out in the vagaries of the natural world. A set of the captain's deck constructed on hydraulic lifts that rocks back and forth will serve for the dialogue shots in which the characters need to be seen talking. For added realism, the set can be placed in front of a large movie screen with a projector behind it. On the screen, a film of waves and stormy sky shot by the second unit or taken from the studio library of stock shots can be projected while the dialogue scene is being shot. In *Titanic* (1997), James Cameron had most of the ship created digitally. *All is Lost* (J. C. Chandor, 2013), a fascinating film with actor Robert Redford the sole character, finding himself stranded in the middle of the ocean, uses a volley of digital effects combined with **location** shooting to provide complex and harrowing visuals. The imaginary Old Testament world of Darren Aronofsky's *Noah* (2014) is almost entirely a digital creation, as are the alien worlds of *Guardians of the Galaxy* (James Gunn, 2014).

Rear-screen projection is the most common means studios used—and still use—for scenes shot in moving cars. A cutout model of a car is put in front of the screen, the driver and passenger sit and deliver their dialogue, and the street is projected on the screen behind them. In older studio films, rear-screen projection would sometimes be used to show two people simply walking down a street. The actors would be put on a treadmill and simulate walking. Again, this is all done to provide as much visual detail as possible without having to put more in the shot at any one time than is absolutely necessary.

There are relatively straightforward image manipulations, like rear-screen projections. More complicated are the paintings, models, mattes, or computer-generated images of backgrounds and foregrounds that, well executed and well lit and integrated with the human figures in the frame, give the illusion of a complex and articulated world. The paintings, the models, and the actors need not be in the same place at the same time. A process called a blue or green screen **matte** or traveling matte allows the parts of the shot to be photographed in front of a blue or green screen. The various shots that will eventually make up one completed shot are projected one after the other through an **optical printer**, which is simply a projector and camera that can be carefully calibrated and synchronized with each other. The blue or green color is dropped out, the components of the shot merge, resulting in an image of illusory wholeness, even of illusory motion when the matte shot includes a figure in motion: Superman flying, Spider-Man swinging across buildings, the SAC bomber flying over Arctic wastes in *Dr. Strangelove* (1964)—indeed almost any sequence in which a figure or object is foregrounded in front of a complicated background.

We usually think of such highly wrought special effects in relation to action or science fiction films, and we take a special pleasure in seeing the results of "f/x." We enjoy the reality effect of such shots while acknowledging their artificiality. But the fact is that all Hollywood studio films, no matter what their genre, use special effects much of the time.

And it is an old tradition. In 1903, Edwin S. Porter made a short film called *The Great Train Robbery.* An early Western and among the first films in which the story shifts back and forth between narrative sequences, it contains a scene in a railroad car where the scenery going by outside is actually processed in—taken at another time and then matched with the set of the railroad car through either rear-screen projection or optical printing. The difference between this sequence and a film by Georges Méliès is that the trickery is not supposed to be noticed. It is not meant to be part of the visible appeal of the film. This peculiar **process shot**—as rear-screen projections or matte shots are called—is a forerunner of all those shots of people driving their cars in front of movie screens showing images of passing roads and streets, or people walking up roads whose surroundings have been painted or computed and matted into the image long after the actors have gone on to other films (see Figures 1.2 and 4.3).

Are there shots in films in which everything we see was present when the shot was made? Certainly. Some small-budget independent films shoot entirely on location. And the immediacy of the image is part of the appeal of documentary films in which the camera observes, with a minimum of intrusion, a sequence of events that might have occurred had the camera not been there. The documentary filmmaker looks for or tries to re-create a whole ongoing event, and we will examine this work in Chapter 9.

The post-World War II Italian **neorealist** movement was based on making films in the street, observing people in their surroundings with an immediacy that was powerful and sometimes shocking. Hollywood took immediate notice. In the late 1940s and early 1950s, American films used some exterior, on-location shooting, especially in low-budget gangster films. American theatrical films in the 1960s and 1970s, responding to yet another European innovation, the films of the **French New Wave**, tended to move away from the synthetic image, at least for a while. Sequences in cars were actually shot in cars moving along the street. Crews spent more time at locations, with actors and their surroundings present at the same time within the shot as the shot was taken. Historically, in European cinema, there has been almost as much dependence on constructing an image from component parts as there is in American filmmaking. (We will look closely at European and other national cinemas in Chapter 8.) But abroad and at home, there have been and continue to be a few, mostly independent filmmakers willing to go outside the studio and shoot in the world. When that happens—in the streets and countryside of Calcutta in Satyajit Ray's Apu trilogy (*Pather Panchali*, 1955; *Aparajito*, 1956; *The World of Apu*, 1959); in the post-World War II ruins of Rome in Roberto Rossellini's *Rome, Open City* (1945); or in the streets of New York in so many American gangster films of the 1950s, and in Martin Scorsese's early work—the image and our relationship to it change. The reality effect becomes even stronger, and the sense of seeing a world as it might actually exist makes the image stronger. For these filmmakers, both European and American, the response to the closed and secure world

FIGURE 2.14 Shot on location in Calcutta, Satyajit Ray's *The World of Apu* (1959) is the last of a trilogy of films (including *Pather Panchali*, 1955 and *Aparajito*, 1956) in which a culture is explored by seeing characters in their landscape

FIGURE 2.15 The characters of Martin Scorsese's *Mean Streets* (1973) are defined by their life on the streets. Robert De Niro is Johnny Boy. See also Figures 8.1 and 8.2

generated by the studio is the opportunity of opening into a more detailed, textured, less manageable image of the world outside.

As we have noted, in Hollywood today, the artificial construction of the image has made a major comeback. All the old practices of rear-screen projection, matte work, and other forms of image manufacture are now being done by computer. Through digital manipulation, the image is put together bit by bit. Backgrounds are rendered in three-dimensional graphics programs. Characters are pasted into the middle of crowds, the members of which are digitally duplicated, or on mountaintops, or in outer space. Dinosaurs are graphically rendered and made to leap across a plain as humans look at them; a gigantic spaceship hovers over New York; a huge ocean liner hits an iceberg and sinks; an atomic bomb or a meteor destroys a city; incredible acts of transformation and destruction are possible with no location necessary other than a computer terminal. Anything and anyone can be placed anywhere and made to do anything—even in an apparently simple, "realistic" shot. Even the movement of actors is computer simulated.

Rotoscoping is an old animation technique in which live action characters are converted into cartoon figures. With **computer-generated imagery** (**CGI**), nodes are connected to a stunt person, whose movements are captured by a computer and then combined with live action in which the actual actor's figure and face can be placed on the computer-generated image. Gollum in *The Lord of the Rings Trilogy* (Peter Jackson, 2001, 2002, 2003) is an example of an actor turned into a digital figure (for an example from *Guardians of the Galaxy* see Figure 5.5). Alfonso Cuarón's *Gravity* (2013) uses a complex combination of rotoscoping, wire work (actors or stunt people suspended by wires so they appear to be floating), and other computer-generated effects to create the illusion of characters lost in space. Even the three-dimensional effects of the film were computer-generated.

Digital effects hold true for sound as well as images. Digital sound allows intricate sonic mixes to be made in which every single sound, from footsteps to the human voice, is built and processed to achieve the best effect. The purpose of digital image and sound manipulation is the same as old-fashioned optical work: to save the filmmakers money while achieving the greatest illusion of the real.

FIGURE 2.16 A combination of green screen, wire work, and rotoscoping creates the illusion of characters in space in Alfonso Cuarón's *Gravity* (2013)

Paradoxically, major digital effects are very expensive and time-consuming, but they give the studios the greatest amount of control possible and, like all aspects of the classical Hollywood style, engineer the viewer into the image and then beyond it into the story. With digital effects, there is a seemingly unlimited possibility to substitute spectacle for substance. There are times in the economy of filmmaking when expense is carried for the sake of control, spectacle, and audience pleasure. The more common the use of digital composition, the cheaper it becomes, and as the years pass and digital techniques replace celluloid completely, when all films, no matter how they are shot, are converted to digital files to be color corrected and edited, the old film-making special effects processes will disappear altogether and digital cameras will directly transform the image into the abstractions of binary code, which are processed, CGI effects added, and delivered via digital files to theaters or high-definition television.

THE WHOLE AND ITS PARTS

The construction of shots, including all the choices that go into how many elements will appear in the shot at any one time of its manufacture, and how the shots will be edited together, is a combination of economics and aesthetics. The economy of the image is entwined with the economy of production and the economy of perception. Even while the studios change from independent entities into holdings of large media corporations, while production practices alter to incorporate new technologies, even while some experimentation in form and content is allowed to occur as the culture surrounding filmmaking changes, the basic structures of shot making tend to remain the same. The formal structures, the very substructure of film construction and film viewing, are largely unchanged, or changed so subtly that they are hardly noticeable.

As we have noted, the production process is executed in bits and pieces, from the selection of a story to the writing of a screenplay—often by many hands—to the creation of sets, the direction of scenes, and the **editing** of the scenes into a whole. Film is made in bits and pieces, and that is what we see on the screen: bits and pieces of image and story so cunningly put together that they appear as if they were an ongoing whole. Film acting, for example, is built shot by shot. A performance in a film is not a continuous process as it is on the stage but is put together out of many parts. A film is not shot in sequence, nor is a sequence made completely in one **take**. (For convenience, I use the term "**scene**" as the unit of action or a segment of a story, while a "**sequence**" is a related series of scenes or shots. In many cases, scene and sequence are used interchangeably.) Therefore, an actor has to perform in spurts, in short spasms of emotion, guided by the director and a staff member called the continuity person (or, in older Hollywood parlance, the script girl), whose job is to keep tabs on everything from the hands on a clock that may be in the shot, to the position of a necktie, to a half-completed gesture, to a facial expression or the direction of a gaze that must be held from shot to shot. We will look at film acting in detail in Chapter 6.

Any given part of a film can be made at any time. The middle may be shot first, the third sequence last, the end at the beginning, the next-to-last sequence just before the middle. For example, if a number of scenes throughout a film take place in the same room, it is more economical to shoot all those shots at the same time, rather than leave the set unused and then return to relight or rebuild it. If a high-priced, in-demand actor is involved in a film, it is more economical to shoot all the scenes in which that actor is involved rather than recall the actor to the set again to shoot a scene that will occur later in the narrative. If an actor grows a beard or gains weight in the course of the narrative, then all the scenes in which he has the beard or all the scenes in which he is thin will be shot first because it might take too long for him to grow the beard or gain weight during the course of the production. And if a scene involves the actor looked at from behind or in a long shot, or in a dangerous action sequence, a stand-in will probably be used. If a location—that is, a site, usually out of doors, at a distance from the studio—is involved, all the scenes that take place at that location will be shot together, no matter where or when they appear in the film. There is a story about the making of the film *Blow-Up* (1966),

FIGURE 2.17 Changing nature to fit the mise-en-scène. The park painted green (or so the story goes) in Michelangelo Antonioni's *Blow-Up* (1966). David Hemmings is the photographer

directed by the Italian filmmaker Michelangelo Antonioni. He wished to film in chronological order. Two major parts of the film, one early, the other at the end, take place a day or two apart in the story, in a London park. Actual filming began in spring and concluded in the fall. When director and crew returned to the park for the last sequence, the leaves and grass had changed color. They had to spray them green to re-create the earlier effect. An American filmmaker would have shot all the sequences in the park at one time and worked out the temporal arrangements during the editing process. Or, instead of shooting outside at all, the American filmmaker might have had a tree and some grass put up in the studio, matting in the rest of the environment in the effects lab or, these days, on a computer. If all else failed, the leaves would be recolored digitally.

MAKING THE PARTS INVISIBLE

Creation through bits and pieces is a production procedure, not a reception problem. In other words, as viewers we see fragments, but are not supposed to perceive the fragmentary, stop and start process that filmmaking is. With relatively few and important exceptions, films from all over the world are constructed on a principle of radical self-effacement, rendering their form invisible while causing few economic difficulties during the creative and manufacturing process and no obstacle at all for the viewers during the process of reception. This is made possible through a set of conventions and assumptions by means of which the viewer will accept the illusion of transparency and see the film as an unmediated, ongoing whole, a story played out in front of her eyes. Form and structure, the artifice of the image, and the fragmentary nature of screen acting and editing will all melt away and merge together in apparent wholeness.

This effect is not unique to movies. Recall our discussion of perspective. Although perspective is based on carefully calculated mathematical structures, the result of perspective in painting was to naturalize the image, to give the illusion of three dimensions on a two-dimensional surface and, by so doing, provide a window through which the viewer's gaze could own the contents of the image. Painting presented "content," represented things in the outside world, until late in the nineteenth century. When photography and film took over this job, painting began to represent its own form, to speak about surface, color, form, and texture. When it did, it created obstacles. Looking at abstract art, people keep wanting to know "what is it trying to show?"

Music depends upon its ability to link itself effortlessly to emotional response. Few people understand the mathematical complexities of harmony and counterpoint, know what a hemidemisemiquaver is (a musical note that is one sixty-fourth the length of a whole note), or can explain the sonata form. In the early twentieth century, a group of composers rebelled against the transparency of musical form and wrote atonal music based on the mathematical principles of the twelve-tone scale. They sought less a pathway to emotion than an expression of musical form. Their work demanded knowledge of how music works and attention to something other than the emotions of the sounds. This music was not very easy to listen to or very popular.

Prose writing also has its version of an invisible form. Reading some books requires little attention to the structure of language. The style of the book may ask the reader to concentrate instead on what the writer is saying and what his characters are doing, which correlates with our desire to see what the painting is about or feel the emotions of the music. Those writers who concentrate on form, who foreground the structure of their prose and how it makes meaning—Henry James, James Joyce, Samuel Beckett, Jorge Luis Borges, Toni Morrison, to name a few—become the focus of academic study. In ordinary reading, though, the greatest compliment many will give to a book is that it is a "page turner." The phrase implies the reader moves past page, prose, form, and style into the movement of story and character.

There is no equivalent phrase for film, probably because there are relatively few films that are not the equivalent of "page turners" and because, while we are watching, the "pages," the images, are turned for us. The assumption is that the structure and style of any film will be invisible, allowing the viewer to enter and move into the story and the emotions of the characters. The point is for us to be carried away by plot and the motivations of the characters. Image structure and editing, the way the story is put together, are subservient to the story and the characters' lives, even though they are the forms that create them.

STORY, PLOT, AND NARRATION

Our task, now that we have an inkling of how a film is put together and its parts made invisible (all of which we will examine in greater detail in the following chapters), is to bring the form and structure of film—its means of production, construction, and comprehension—back into consciousness and make them visible again. To start, let's redefine "story." This is what the film tells us, the process of events the characters go through and enact. Plot is the abstract scheme of that story, what we summarize after we've seen the film, what film reviewers give us. Narrative is the actual telling of the story, the way the story is put together, formed, and articulated.

Jaws

Narrative is the structure of the story. Take Steven Spielberg's *Jaws* (1975) as an example. Here's some plot: a great white shark terrorizes a beach town, kills people, and is finally hunted down by three men in a boat. I could elaborate that into something closer to the story, although it would be more description than story and in any case would be my story, derived from the film, because I am giving it narrative structure: Sheriff Brody is pulled from a peaceful domestic life by the intrusion of the terrible creature into the town he has been hired to protect. The shark attacks people, but the elders of the town want it kept quiet so as not to ruin holiday tourist business. There is tension between Brody and the elders, and also uncertainty. Brody has been hired to do the bidding of the town, but he has a moral responsibility to protect the innocent. And so forth.

I could also talk about this in a way that comes closer to the film's narrative: the presence of the shark is indicated by John Williams' music—low, almost staccato chords played on bass fiddles, a mirror of the high staccato strings Bernard Herrmann wrote for Alfred Hitchcock's *Psycho* (1960). When the shark is ready to attack, the film allows us to look as if through the shark's eyes, moving in the water toward its prey. Suspense is further created by playing with the gaze of Sheriff Brody on the beach. He looks and looks at the water. People move in front of him, and he has to bend and rise to see. There are false alarms, and our tension keeps rising. The intercutting of **shot/reverse shot** from Brody (the shot) to what he sees (the **reverse shot**) reaches a climax when Brody finally does see something in the water. At this point, Spielberg uses a device that Alfred Hitchcock developed in *Vertigo* (1958). By combining two movements of the camera—a tracking shot in one direction and a **zoom** in the opposite—he shows Brody as if space were collapsing around him, thereby heightening our awareness of some exciting and terrifying event.

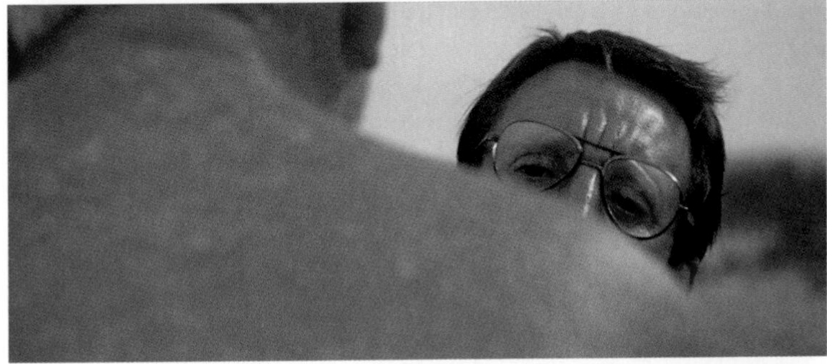

FIGURES 2.18–2.21 On the level of plot, Brody is looking out for the shark. But the structure of this sequence does more than tell us that: it locks our gaze to the character's by alternately looking at him and assuming his own point of view. The result is to create expectation and frustration. Steven Spielberg, *Jaws* (1975)

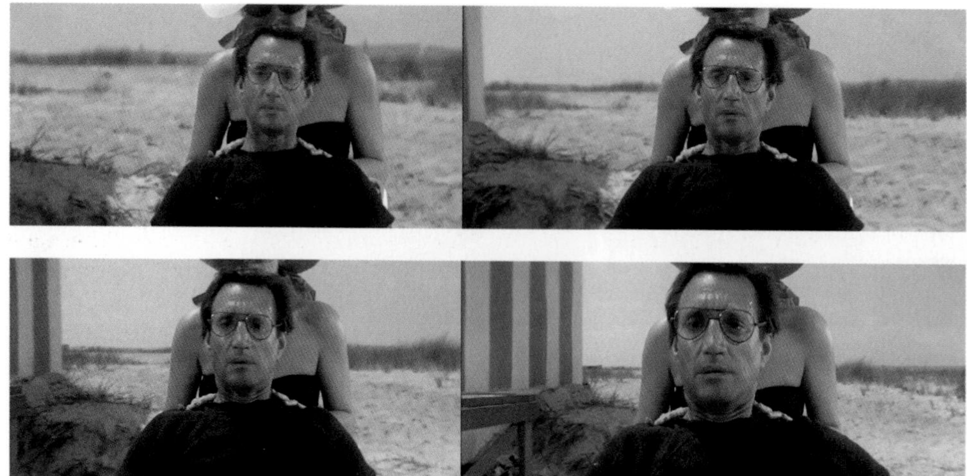

FIGURES 2.22–2.23 By zooming in one direction and tracking in the opposite, Spielberg (imitating a similar setup in Alfred Hitchcock's *Vertigo*, 1958) communicates surprise and fear as space seems to collapse

In this brief analysis, I began by recounting plot and then moved from plot to structure, that is, from content to form, describing some of the ways the narrative is put together to tell us its story. This analysis also puts the structure into a context by revealing that Spielberg didn't invent everything but borrowed and developed some stylistic devices from another filmmaker. The point is that all aspects of a film are based on formal, structural principles and that meaning and emotion as well are always communicated by structure. We see, understand, and feel by the way we are manipulated by the shot and the arrangement of shots edited into a narrative structure that tells a story. Meaning or emotion does not exist without a form to communicate it. We never simply "know" something, or see something, or are told something. When we respond to a film, there is always a formal structure driving that response. The development of that structure occurred intuitively during film's early history, beginning with very short one-reelers that showed one event—a couple kissing, a train entering a station—and within a few years, in films such as *The Great Train Robbery* (1903), directors began combining shots, leading to the long period of experimentation undertaken by D. W. Griffith that led to what we now refer to as the classical Hollywood style.

CONVENTION AND CONSCIOUSNESS

We have come full circle. Our opening analysis of the early sequences of *Casablanca* through its more recent expression in *Jaws* or, for that matter, *Gravity*, demonstrates that the classical Hollywood style forms the basis of almost all American film and has done so since the early 1920s. With the exception of the work of a very few directors who try different means of cinematic expression, and overseas filmmakers who battle against it in order to find their own visual statement, it is the way films make us see. Perhaps the complexities of the classical Hollywood style and the responses to it can be summed up by a notion of unconsciousness and consciousness. The classical style asks that we be unconscious of form and structure but conscious of their effects. That is, most films want us to understand them immediately, directly, without mediation. Filmmakers who wish to explore the language of cinema and make its form and structure expressive in their own right—the way some painters and novelists use the language of their art to draw attention to its own devices—want us to be conscious at all levels. They want us to know when they are cutting and to ask how the editing pattern is creating narrative meaning; to be aware of a camera movement and think about its purpose; to look at the way people and objects are arranged in the frame and not look through that frame as if it were some kind of open window or mirror.

In the end, we have to be conscious of everything in every film. To be lulled by the classical continuity style into a trance of identification with light and shadow on a white screen is pleasurable but not entirely useful. Assenting to the ideology of the invisible may be entertaining, but, in an important way, it is not safe. To look through form and structure does not mean that form and structure have actually disappeared. They are present, working to create the meaning and generate the feelings you experience during a movie. To ignore them means that they and the corporate communities that created them are given permission to continue on their way doing what they want, telling stories that may or may not be beneficial to us in our dealings with the world. But to read them, consciously, analytically, with as much attention as we read those films that do not use the classical style, means that we not only are entertained, but understand why and how we are entertained.

Analyzing the illusory nature of film does not discredit it or diminish the pleasure of watching: quite the contrary. The more you know about what you are and are not seeing, the richer the experience is, and the more reflective. It's exciting to respond emotionally and intellectually to film; to feel the story and understand how that story is being constructed; to see through the images to the characters and their turmoil and at the same time observe and understand what the images themselves are doing. It is possible and important to feel and understand, to synthesize and analyze.

We can extend this process of analysis and synthesis beyond the individual film to the individuals who are responsible for making them and then to a wider context and consider the role of film and other popular forms of entertainment in the culture at large. How do films reflect larger cultural events? Why does the culture support the conventions of storytelling in film and other forms of mass entertainment? Why do films keep telling us the same stories and continue to delight us? Who is doing the telling? To begin doing this, we need to more completely unpack the ideas presented in these opening chapters, to examine the complexities of shot composition and editing, to look even more closely at how the stories are told in order to understand how much work goes into making the form of film invisible.

FURTHER READING

Linda Williams discusses the early development of the image and its relationship to the body in *Hard Core: Power, Pleasure, and the "Frenzy of the Visible"* (Berkeley and Los Angeles: University of California, 1989), pp. 34–57.

A study of Chaplin and his times is Charles J. Maland, *Chaplin and American Culture: The Evolution of a Star Image* (Princeton: Princeton University Press, 1989).

One Keaton film is analyzed in Andrew Horton, ed., *Buster Keaton's Sherlock Jr.* (Cambridge, UK and New York: Cambridge University Press, 1997).

A complete history of United Artists can be found in Tino Balio, *United Artists: The Company Built by the Stars* (Madison: University of Wisconsin Press, 1976).

Douglas Gomery writes *The Studio System: A History* (London: British Film Institute, 2008).

A recent study of the interaction of imagination and corporation is Jerome Christensen's *America's Corporate Art: The Studio Authorship of Hollywood Motion Pictures* (Stanford, California: Stanford University Press, 2012).

Thomas Elsaesser's collection of essays, *Early Cinema: Space, Frame, Narrative* (London: British Film Institute, 1990), is a good source of information on the formation of the early film industry.

The standard work on the classical Hollywood style is David Bordwell, Janet Staiger, Kristin Thompson, *The Classical Hollywood Cinema: Film Style and Mode of Production to 1960* (New York: Columbia University Press, 1985).

Discussion of the computer effects in *Gravity* can be found at http://library.creativecow.net/kaufman_debra/Gravity-3D-Conversion/1 (accessed 19 November 2014).

SUGGESTIONS FOR FURTHER VIEWING

The Kiss (William Heise, 1896) is an example of early eroticism in film.

Workers Leaving the Lumière Factory (Auguste and Louis Lumière, 1895), a "documentary" by the two French pioneers.

Execution of Czolgosz with Panorama of Auburn Prison (Edison, 1901). This film reenacts the execution of the assassin of President William McKinley along with documentary footage of the prison where he was executed.

A Trip to the Moon (Georges Méliès, 1902). The great "magic" film of early cinema and perhaps the first science fiction film.

The Life of an American Fireman (Edwin S. Porter, 1903). Porter was an early experimenter in editing to create a more complex narrative structure.

Intolerance (D. W. Griffith, 1916). Griffith's attempt to respond to the racism of *Birth of a Nation* (1915) is one of the monuments of the silent period, weaving together multiple narratives.

Greed (Erich von Stroheim, 1924) is a response to the sentimentality of Griffith and other silent film directors. An adaptation of Frank Norris's 1899 novel *McTeague*, it was brutally cut by its studio, but remains a powerful film of the pre-sound period.

Grand Hotel (Edmund Goulding, 1932). An excellent example of the MGM high style of the early 1930s.

The Best Years of Our Lives (William Wyler, 1946) is a culmination of 1940s filmmaking, using deep focus and long takes to address the issues of veterans returning home after World War II.

Rear Window (Alfred Hitchcock, 1954). Hitchcock's response to the classical Hollywood style.

The films of Michelangelo Antonioni are good examples of a director who works against the norms of the classical Hollywood style. See especially his trilogy: *L'avventura* (1960), *La notte* (1961), and *L'eclisse* (1962).

NOTE

1 The story of Muybridge and Edison and the information about early projection is from Charles Musser, *The Emergence of Cinema: The American Screen to 1907, History of the American Cinema*, vol. 1 (Berkeley, Los Angeles, and London: University of California Press, 1990), pp. 62–68, 91.

CHAPTER 3

The building blocks of film I

The shot

Analogue or digital, no matter what the format, when we look at a film what we essentially see are images in motion. We have discussed the illusion of image reception, how we see the story the images are telling whole and unbroken. Here I want to talk about those images themselves, what they look like and why, and then, in the next chapter, what happens when they are edited together to tell the story.

THE SHOT

Film form can be reduced to two basic elements, the **shot** and the **cut**, or **edit**, each of which is complex and can be executed in a great variety of ways. A *shot* is any unbroken, unedited length of film. That length can be the entire magazine of film in a 35-mm camera (twenty minutes or more) or the much longer length of a file in a digital camera. A shot can also be made in the editing room when an otherwise unedited length of film has some unwanted material trimmed from either end and is then joined with other shots. The shot is determined by its physical or digital existence as an unbroken entity—or its appearance as such.

THE LONG TAKE

Despite the fact that it may be made up of many parts photographed separately, once fabricated, the shot makes up cinema's unit of internal and physical continuity. That is, the shot is of a physical or digital length. Within the shot itself, space and time are represented as connected and ongoing: the shot composes space and either guides the viewer's eye within that space, or offers a reflective, meditative gaze at the space. What happens in a shot can be as simple as the camera gazing at a character or as complex as a movement in which the camera follows a character across a long and articulated space. Such shots are so rare that many of them can be enumerated throughout the history of film.

The Magnificent Ambersons

In Orson Welles's *The Magnificent Ambersons* (1942), for example, the camera watches for almost four minutes as characters in a darkly lit, turn-of-the-century kitchen talk about the decline of their family and home. This is a classic example of the **long take**, in which the filmmaker allows action to proceed at length without cutting into it. The intensity of the **sequence** grows from the camera's unflinching gaze and the power of the actors' (Tim Holt and Agnes Moorehead) performance—one stuffing his face with strawberry shortcake, the other getting more and more upset. This is a rare moment in film in which a performance, in the usual sense of an ongoing and developing process, is allowed to continue on its own, and Welles's unwillingness to give us any other view, to cut into or away from the action, gives us no option but to watch it unfold.

FIGURE 3.1 This still image is a slice of the almost four minute static take in Orson Welles's *The Magnificent Ambersons* (1942)

FIGURE 3.2 Another slice, this from the over three minute moving camera beginning Welles's *Touch of Evil* (1958). The camera begins on the timer of a bomb being placed in the trunk of the car and then cranes up, tracking across the roofs of buildings to the other side of the border, following the car—and many other characters—until the car explodes

Touch of Evil

Welles's most famous long take is the opening of his 1958 film, *Touch of Evil*. In the course of about three minutes and twenty seconds, his camera races along with a character who runs to place a bomb in the trunk of a car. It follows that car across a narrow border from Mexico to California. The camera executes a remarkable **crane** up as the car drives off, **tracks** on its crane across the rooftops of buildings, settling on the other side of the border as the car drives to the check point. People come by, music blares, the central characters of the film, Mike Vargas and his wife (Charlton Heston and Janet Leigh) walk past the checkpoint, stop, kiss, and the car with the bomb blows up. This is a masterful piece of choreography for camera and actors, where every move has to happen at precisely the right moment or the shot has to be started over again. This is the reason why such long takes are frowned upon by **producers**, who find them expensive and attention-calling, both of which are against the implicit rules of the Hollywood style.

Rope, Russian Ark, and *Birdman*

Alfred Hitchcock experimented with the long take in his 1948 film *Rope*, about two young gay men who kill a friend, put his body in a chest in their living room, and hold a party in an attempt to demonstrate how they could get away with their crime. Restricted to a set made up of just a few rooms, Hitchcock lets his camera roam without cutting (with the exception of two instances) until it runs out of film, at which point it moves behind a character's back or a piece of furniture to allow the film magazine to be changed. The experiment is not a great success, because there is not enough going on in the **frame** to maintain the unblinking gaze at unlovely people at the mercy of two mocking killers.

With digital cinematography, filmmakers are not constrained by reels of film. Alexander Sokurov creates a dramatic example of the long take in *Russian Ark* (2002). The film is a continuous, ninety-six minute take in which the most contradictory thing—a **montage** made without cutting that covers three centuries of Russian history—is created in the halls and galleries of St. Petersburg's Hermitage museum.

More recently, Alejandro González Iñárritu's *Birdman* (2014), a film about acting, identity, transformation, and the mysterious effects of superheroes, is filmed to create the illusion of being made in one continuous take. As with *Rope*, the edits are hidden and the result is a rhythmic slide through the life of an actor in search of his self, a search doomed from the start, but which enables him to fly away, more free, finally, than the camera which pursues him.

Goodfellas

Perhaps the most famous contemporary example of the long take is the Copacabana sequence in Martin Scorsese's *Goodfellas* (1990). Using a **Steadicam** camera—a gyroscopic mechanism that allows the operator to move with the camera strapped to him, creating a steady image—Scorsese follows his characters crossing the street, descending the stairs into the nightclub, moving through the kitchen into the main floor, where a table is prepared for them. They sit and talk, greet other people, until the camera **pans** off to a performer on stage, and, after running for three minutes, the shot ends. This is virtuoso filmmaking, and it depends on the opposite response from us than the long shot in Welles's *The Magnificent Ambersons*. There, we are asked to concentrate on the acting within a long shot where the camera doesn't move. The *Goodfellas*

FIGURE 3.3 The dynamics of the Copacabana shot in Scorsese's *Goodfellas* (1990) is only suggested by a still image. For three minutes, the camera follows Henry (Ray Liotta) and Karen (Lorraine Bracco) from the street, down the stairs, through the kitchen and into the nightclub. (See also Figure 4.7)

FIGURE 3.4 Alex (Malcolm McDowell) is tracked as he moves through the record boutique in Stanley Kubrick's *A Clockwork Orange* (1971)

shot impresses us with its vitality and the dynamics of its movement, an exclamation of the **director's** bravura.

Similarly with Stanley Kubrick. In *A Clockwork Orange* (1971), the central character, Alex (Malcolm McDowell) is a violent dandy who commands our attention through the sheer energy of his physical and verbal presence. At the peak of his power, he walks through the record boutique at a mall. Kubrick's camera precedes Alex in a long **tracking shot**, an electronic version of Beethoven sounding triumphantly on the **soundtrack**. Alex is in full command, the camera and the space it creates giving way before him, his servant.

HOW COMPOSITION WORKS

Static or dynamic, the long take focuses our gaze on the composition of the shot, the arrangement of characters and objects within the screen frame, as opposed to the linear movement from shot to shot that constitutes editing. In most films, shots are very short, perhaps four or six seconds in length, and they tend to be loosely composed, so that we see only what is important to carry the dialogue of the sequence of which the shot is a part. Directors anxious to stay on time and budget will compose quickly, usually framing the characters at eye level, from the knees up, intercutting a **close-up**, keeping the background in **soft focus** (see Figure 3.12). The frame serves as a convenient boundary, holding as much visual information as is necessary for the shot's duration. But many directors are much more conscious of the details of composition, so much so that the elements within the frame express as much meaning as the dialogue.

Composition in early cinema

The miniature computer or smartphone screen is not a recent development. Before projection, the earliest films of the late nineteenth century were peered at through the eyepiece of a viewing machine, invented by the Edison Company, called a kinetoscope. Inside was a continuous loop of a single shot. Even as film began to be projected on a screen in early nickelodeons (so called because they charged a nickel admission), this "primitive" cinema was show without telling: images without a **narrative**. The shots were often of spectacular, erotic, or sometimes disgusting events—Edison's infamous *Electrocuting an Elephant* (1903), for example. It's been called a "Cinema of Attractions." At the early moments of its life, much film depended entirely on the shot: frontal, eye level, offering the viewer something unusual, exciting, even arousing (at least at the time), like Edison's *The Kiss* (see Figure 2.1). It was a kind of representational extension of vaudeville, the music hall entertainments popular through the turn of the nineteenth and into the twentieth centuries. But unlike vaudeville, these early films brought the world close-up and often full of action. "Primitive" perhaps, but as we've seen in the Lumière brothers' *Arrival of a Train at La Ciotat Station* (Figure 2.2), there were also very early attempts to give depth to the image and compose along the lines of Renaissance perspective. And, in fact, once film moved ahead and developed narrative structure, the perspectival line became more and more important.[1]

As they developed, the compositional elements of the early "cinema of attractions" set the pattern for cinema to come. Even today, in most films, the main action is centered, the sight lines of the audience aimed at the middle of the screen where the image is weighted. The peripheries may contain some visual element, even be carefully set and lit to provide the right environment. But the eye will almost always be led to the center, with perspective used to create an illusion of depth. One difference is that today we only rarely see a shot made straight on, 90 degrees to the subject being photographed. Instead, the camera is almost always placed at some angle off the 90-degree axis.

D. W. GRIFFITH

The Unchanging Sea

A pioneer in compositional experimentation in early cinema was D. W. Griffith, best known for *The Birth of a Nation* (1915) and *Intolerance* (1916), two large and controversial works. *The Birth of a Nation* was especially controversial given its racist content. We will look at it more closely in Chapter 9. But these large works were preceded by a kind of apprenticeship at the Biograph Company, from 1908 to 1913, where Griffith turned out in the neighborhood of 500 short narrative films. In the course of this tremendous output, Griffith, like all other filmmakers of the time, taught himself cinema. There were no rules, but plenty of room to experiment, both in Composition and in editing. We'll focus on the first here. Much of the time, Griffith, like most of his contemporaries, used the frontal, eye-level style and, like a classical painter, some perspective, all to the purpose of focusing the viewer's attention on the most important element in the frame, the human figure. But within these constraints, he tried different things, different ways of composing the image. In some instances he would put the characters in a lower corner of the frame, so that the viewer's eye would have to find them out and, even more important, understand them as part of the landscape they were inhabiting. The shot in Figure 3.8 from *The Unchanging Sea* (1910) makes the sea itself the immediate focus of our attention. We don't have to look hard

FIGURES 3.5–3.7 The first two of these three images from the film *Closed Circuit* (John Crowley, 2013) demonstrate the position of the camera placed 90 degrees to the characters (they also demonstrate a rare 180-degree cut, which we will discuss in Chapter 4 and demonstrate again in Figures 4.23 and 4.24). The third image, from the same sequence, has the camera placed in a more traditional angle off the 90-degree axis

FIGURE 3.8 D. W. Griffith in *The Unchanging Sea* (1910) experiments with how the human figure will be seen within the larger composition

FIGURE 3.9 Using the face to accentuate drama in D. W. Griffith's *The Musketeers of Pig Alley* (1912)

to see the characters. They are dark against the light, and in the foreground. But, placing them in the lower left of the frame, Griffith's composition represents an early attempt to make the human figure only one part of the landscape.

The Musketeers of Pig Alley

Griffith is well known for using the close-up to achieve dramatic effect. It became a standard compositional strategy to bring the viewer close to a character and allow that character to communicate an intense reaction to events. Griffith, especially in his later work, used it for intense effect. Earlier, in this famous image from his 1912 Biograph gangster film *The Musketeers of Pig Alley*, Griffith uses the close-up without giving up the environment surrounding the characters. The gangsters are pressed against the wall, moving forward with menace, almost threatening the boundaries of the frame itself.

THE SIZE OF THE FRAME

There are some basic properties of composition that all filmmakers need to consider and film viewers need to be aware of. One of these is the size of the frame itself, the boundaries of where the image will begin and end. In painting and photography, the frame is flexible. A painter can choose a small frame, a large one, the entire ceiling of a chapel, like Michelangelo's dome of the Sistine Chapel, or a gigantic mural, covering many walls, like those of the great Mexican muralist, Diego Rivera. It is hard to get a photograph quite that large, but the photographer too has a choice about the size of the image and therefore how much can be included and where the viewer's eye will be focused. Through cropping and reframing during the developing of the film, or its manipulation on the computer, she can determine the composition as much as she did when the picture was taken. The prime purpose for such framing and composing is to direct the viewer's eye in ways that, for the artist, make the most sense for her vision and the narrative the visuals are telling. All art is about control: the artist controls what is seen in order that the viewer will see it expressed in exactly the way the artist wants it to be seen.

Filmmakers have never quite had the options available to other visual artists. Frame sizes, or, more correctly, the ratio of height to length, were rarely up to the filmmaker. In the silent period, many filmmakers could vary the frame internally, by masking off parts of it, using an **iris shot**, for example—a circular mask that would open out or close down the frame, concentrating on a character or an action without cutting. Even the gauge, or the physical width of the celluloid, varied in the early years, as did the placement of the sprocket holes, by means of which the camera and projector pull down the film strip, exposing one frame after another. But shortly after the coming of sound, a frame size that would incorporate the soundtrack was established as the industry standard, with dimensions of four units wide and three units high. It was called the "standard ratio" and lasted almost thirty years. This was the frame the filmmaker had to work with, and the best thing about it, as with any standard, was that it was dependable. The **director of photography** and the director could compose within that frame with the knowledge that their composition would be faithfully reproduced in the movie theater, where the proportions of the screen were more or less the same as the film image, even though the physical size of the screen varied according to the size of the theater. An example of what standard ratio looked like on the film itself can be seen in Figure 5.8 (see also Figure 3.10).

FIGURE 3.10 An example of the iris shot from a Civil War battle sequence in D. W. Griffith's *The Birth of a Nation* (1915). The red tint was common for violent scenes

Wide screen

All this changed in the 1950s, when film began competing with television for an audience. Rather than working on making better films, studio executives decided that if they offered an enormous image it would give them the competitive edge against the small-screen TV that was drawing audiences away from theaters and keeping them at home. Wide screen was not invented in the 1950s—various experiments had been attempted since the 1920s—but, as with sound, which the studios also experimented with before the famous *Jazz Singer* in 1927, the studios had had no economic need to exploit it. In the 1950s, need emerged, and filmmakers slowly lost their control over the frame. First there was **Cinerama**, a cumbersome process in which the image was captured on three cameras and then projected from three projectors onto a gigantic curved screen—a kind of clumsy precursor of Imax, which originally used only one very large, usually 70-mm gauged film strip (today, even if photographed on film, Imax is usually projected digitally). The seams between the three panels were always visible, but Cinerama was as much a method for foregrounding form as content. Rather than conveying story, as in the **classical Hollywood style**, Cinerama conveyed the size potentials of cinematic exhibition, attempting to create an immersive experience by wrapping the audience within the image. In other words, one went to see and be amazed by Cinerama, not by any story that might be told by this particular form. Except for its size, it was a return to the very earliest beginnings of cinema, with its emphasis on amazing views—an update of early cinema's representation of spectacular events. Only one narrative film, the multi-director *How the West Was Won* (1962), was filmed in the three-strip process, though at least one important film, Stanley Kubrick's *2001: A Space Odyssey* (1968), was shot in single strip, 70-mm Cinerama, creating a huge, curved screen image. This served Kubrick's wish to engulf the viewer with overwhelming images of space travel.

Anamorphic and "flat" wide-screen processes

Cinerama was only the beginning of the end of film frame standards. In 1953, 20th Century Fox introduced a proprietary format that they had originally played with in the 1920s, **CinemaScope.** It was an **anamorphic process**, meaning that, with a special lens on the camera, it squeezed a wide image into a distorted form onto standard 35-mm film. Another lens on the projector unsqueezed the image to a ratio of 1:2.35. CinemaScope introduced distortion on the sides of the frame. For this and other reasons, another anamorphic process, Panavision, slowly took over and the company became the dominant supplier of lenses for anamorphic and other wide-screen processes, which are now the dominant means of framing.

Anamorphic wide screen introduced problems that were multiplied during its first decade. What were filmmakers to do with the enormous width of the CinemaScope/Panavision screen? How could a close-up be made without cutting off the top and bottom of the actor's head? What to do with the space around two characters engaged in an intimate dialogue? A few directors, such as the Japanese filmmaker Akira Kurosawa and the American Robert Altman, took full advantage of the screen width, placing characters and actions at the peripheries, emphasizing the horizontal line. Some directors fought against wide screen. Alfred Hitchcock said it was like looking through a letterbox and never used it (although in *Dial M for Murder*, 1954, he did use one short-lived, recently revived, and again short-lived 1950s process, 3D, with the audience wearing glasses to filter out the double image on the screen to give the illusion of depth). The German director Fritz Lang said that wide-screen processes were good only for photographing snakes and funerals. But such resistance was futile. In the early 1950s all the studios were attempting varieties of screen sizes. To compete with Fox's CinemaScope, Paramount Pictures developed "**VistaVision**." Picking up on a major fad of 1950s music recording and playback, they called it "Motion Picture High Fidelity." And today anamorphic and "flat" (non-anamorphic) wide screen are the industry standards.

VistaVision was originally photographed on reels of 65-mm film running horizontally through the camera. It was then printed down vertically on standard 35 mm, but the width of the image, even though reduced, allowed it to be projected at various ratios. Vista Vision—the aesthetics of which we will discuss again when we analyze Hitchcock's *Vertigo*—was part of the movement toward "flat" ratios. **Flat wide screen** can be made and projected in a number of ways. The film can be matted in the camera—that is, black bars are placed at the top and bottom of the image. Another matte in the projector allows the image to fill a wide screen. Alternatively, and increasingly rarely, a film can be shot "full frame", filling the 35-mm frame. When projected, the film is matted down to wide-screen proportions.

By the mid-1950s, "standard ratio" was finished and all films were composed in one form of wide screen or another: the 1:2.35 ratio of CinemaScope and Panavision or the 1:1.66 or 1:1.85 of flat wide screen. Interestingly, the 1:1.66 ratio goes all the way back to the ancient Greeks, who created it (as the Renaissance would perspective hundreds of years later) mathematically and called it the "golden section" or "golden mean," representing a perfect proportion. It needs to be said as well that, soon after the standard compositional bounds of the screen disappeared, at the time when television went to all color and all films wound up on television, black and white cinematography also disappeared. This, too, will become part of our story.[2]

Loss of standards

These technological shifts, like so much in film production, remove a great deal of control from the filmmaker's hands. Wide screen has made careful composition all but impossible. Videotape very rarely transferred anamorphic wide screen with the black bars necessary to represent the width of the image. Instead a film was "**panned and scanned**," with a lab technician determining what he or she might consider the most important action in the frame—you know that this has happened when a card appears before the movie, stating "this film has been formatted to fit your television," or if a DVD says "full screen." The viewfinders used by directors and **cinematographers** to frame the image for the camera may contain many frame lines: anamorphic and flat wide screen, and television ratio—which is almost square.

Shopping mall movie theaters size their screens not according to the ratios in which the films might be shot, but rather to fit the often small and oddly shaped auditoriums in which they will be exhibited. So, even a film shot in anamorphic wide screen might be cropped at the sides, reducing its width. DVDs, Blu-rays, and flat screen televisions are bringing more and more films to home viewers in something approaching the ratio in which they were shot (16 × 9 is the format for wide screen television). Still, the filmmaker is stymied: the edges of the frame are not dependable. Anything put there might not be seen in a theater or on television.

And if the filmmaker is stymied, so is the film viewer, but this time by choice. During the past years, due to the popularity of tablets and smartphones, screen sizes have shrunk. While more or less retaining a wide screen **aspect ratio**, viewing on the 8″ by 6″ iPad or the 5½″ by 2½″ iPhone screen results in lost detail. Immersion is impossible. The image becomes handheld, something toy-like. Composition, in such viewing conditions, barely matters, and the image is

FIGURE 3.11 This anamorphic wide screen composition from *The Railway Man* (Jonathan Teplitzky, 2013) places the lovers on the extreme left of the frame, emphasizing their place by the sea and drawing our attention to their umbrella that has blown away. Compare this with Figure 3.8

something caught on the fly. With the handheld screen, we substitute convenience for perception, content for form. Or, more accurately, content is reduced to the miniaturization of the image, without detail or depth.

THE STUDIOS AND THE SHOT

Experimentation with compositional effects has continued throughout the history of film and is still going on. But in most cases, in conventional filmmaking, the emphasis remains on the human figure, and this became accentuated in the early sound period, when it was assumed, probably correctly, that people wanted to see the actors talking. The 1930s were the years of **shallow focus**, where the background was often in soft focus, the camera concentrating on brightly lit characters. As always in the history of film, there are no universals. Universal Pictures, using techniques of **German Expressionism** in its extraordinarily popular cycle of Frankenstein and Dracula films during the 1930s, paid much attention to light and dark and the placement of figures within strange surroundings and unusual compositions (see Figure 3.12, and Figures 3.29 and 3.30).

FIGURE 3.12 An example of shallow focus: one of the great stars of the 1930s, Greta Garbo, in *Grand Hotel* (Edmund Goulding, 1932, William H. Daniels, cinematographer). Her face is the major point of the composition. The background is soft, but so is her face. It was common in the 1930s to photograph a female star in soft focus so that no blemishes would be seen. You can just see the key light in Garbo's eyes and clearly see the backlighting on her hair and shoulders and fill lighting in the background (see Figures 3.15–3.17)

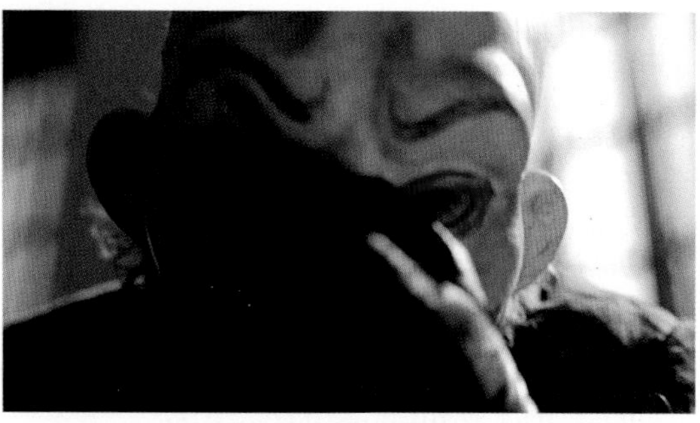

FIGURES 3.13–3.14 Christopher Nolan plays a joke: The Joker is wearing a mask over his face (itself a mask). He removes it to reveal a full face close-up, filling the wide screen frame. *The Dark Knight* (2008)

In the post-studio period, there is, of course, no general studio style. But individual filmmakers often take care in composing their images to create expressive compositions. Despite general loose framing and rapid cutting, Christopher Nolan often takes pains to compose a full and busy frame in his Batman films. Look at two frames from a scene in *The Dark Knight* (2008), where the Joker (Heath Ledger) removes his clown face mask after the bank robbery, revealing his real mask—his grotesque face filling the frame of the wide screen, his menace fully communicated.

MISE-EN-SCÈNE

Composition concerns the way people and objects are arranged within the screen frame. **Mise-en-scène**, to expand on our definition in Chapter 2, refers to all the elements that are the result of the composition. Mise-en-scène encompasses everything that happens in the frame, including the placement of characters in relationship to their surroundings and to other characters, camera position, camera movement, lighting, how grayscale tonalities in a black and white film are used, or color in a color film. Even sound and music might be considered an aspect of mise-en-scène. The term is also evaluative. That is, we can say that a film made with **high-key lighting,** in which everything in the frame is lit evenly, composed with an eye-level camera with little movement, concentrating on the characters, who are placed centrally in the frame, has a kind of negative mise-en-scène that adds little to what we learn from the dialogue or editing. A director who creates a consistent visual atmosphere, who uses black and white or color expressively, moves the camera in relation to the characters, who, in short, creates spaces that express as much about the film as what the characters say is a mise-en-scène director. Such work is relatively rare, because doing all these things requires imagination and time. But strong directors who create a consistent mise-en-scène are present throughout the history of film, and a film with a strong mise-en-scène cannot be mistaken for any other film. Various examples of mise-en-scène are illustrated below.

LIGHTING

The way a film is lit is an important element of mise-en-scène. Without light, there would be no image. But, at the same time, the way a filmmaker uses light and dark, in effect sculpting with light, creates images that can be expressive, beautiful, and eloquent.

We might say that the shallow focus, **high-key** (that is, brightly lit), dialogue-centered films of the 1930s that we discussed earlier define the mise-en-scène of that decade. This lighting technique represented a standard that exists to this day called **three-point lighting**. The character's face is illuminated by a **key light**, the results of which you can see by the glint in a character's eye. **Backlighting** sets the character off from the background, while **fill lighting** accents the character and various elements in the set surrounding the character.

FIGURE 3.15 The key light illuminates the face and eyes

FIGURE 3.16 Backlighting separates the figure from the background

FIGURE 3.17 Fill lighting provides accents around the figure and background

The three-point scheme is a kind of blueprint that can be used and varied by directors and directors of photography for any given film. Even during the 1930s, when the **studio system** was working full throttle, each studio, with its own craftspeople, its own producers, directors, cinematographers, and **production designers**, created its own general lighting style. So, where MGM epitomized the bright, high key, shallow focus that was the general rule of the decade, Warner Brothers often used different compositional strategies, lower lighting, a more mobile camera—especially in the famous Busby Berkeley musicals that not only choreographed dancers and characters, but composed them so that the bodies of the dancers made strange, erotic patterns.

MGM prided itself on the high style: it was the visual lift from the economic and cultural depression of the 1930s. Warner, on the other hand, found itself more comfortable with darker subjects, both thematically and visually. Warner Bros. was the studio of the earliest sound gangster films (Mervyn LeRoy's *Little Caesar* and William Wellman's *The Public Enemy*, both 1931). LeRoy's *I Am a Fugitive from a Chain Gang* (1932) was perhaps the darkest of them all. Condemning the work gang brutalities of Southern jails, the film wrung sympathy for the unjustly accused, not only in its narrative movement, but in its visual treatment that moves from the relatively bright, open compositions that show its central character, James Allen (Paul Muni) at the peak of his powers as an engineer, to the last shot of the film, still among the most chilling, in which light disappears. Allen, escaped again, arranges a furtive meeting with his girlfriend. "How do you live?" she asks. He pulls back into the dark: "I steal."

In all these cases, lighting is used to create a concentration of the viewers' gaze, or to deny it in the case of *I Am a Fugitive from a Chain Gang*. In many instances, lighting and framing, side to side and front to back, may be used to create the needed effect.

FIGURES 3.18–3.19 In *The Public Enemy* (William Wellman, 1931), Warner Bros. could copy the high-key glamor of an MGM film (see Figure 3.12), creating an interestingly layered composition with the glamor star of the day, Jean Harlow, in the foreground, the gangster James Cagney in the middle plane of the image, and the strange statue averting its eyes in the rear. But when the gangster gets his due, Wellman reverts to the dark, rainy streets that foreshadow the film noir style of the 1940s

FIGURE 3.20 In this image from Josef von Sternberg's *Shanghai Express* (1932), we can clearly see a number of 1930s compositional and lighting effects come together. Sternberg and cinematographers Lee Garmes and James Wong Howe put his favorite actress, Marlene Dietrich, in mildly soft focus and at the same time mark the exoticism of the mise-en-scène with the Chinese banner while striping the whole image with dark bands and accentuating the veil across her face

FIGURE 3.21 "I steal . . . ." The final word of Mervyn LeRoy's *I Am a Fugitive from a Chain Gang* (1932). James Allen (Paul Muni) withdraws into the darkness

COLOR

Films have been in color from the very beginning. The earliest films were tinted and toned: gold/yellow for daytime scenes; blue for night; red for scenes of violence. Sometimes, films would be hand-stenciled, the elements in each frame carefully colored. Various processes to capture a more natural color were tried, until **Technicolor** was established. Technicolor actually began in 1917 but it wasn't until 1932 that the "three-color" process was perfected. This was a complicated process that used three strips of black and white negative, filtered so that each would capture one of the primary red, green, and blue colors. The negatives were then literally printed onto the positive in ways that allowed dyes, corresponding to the colors filtered onto the negative, to be transferred to the film. The process was expensive, the equipment huge (if you visit the Smithsonian in Washington, DC, you can see an enormous, old Technicolor camera on display), and the lighting demands enormous. Also, Technicolor was a proprietary process so that each studio had to lease equipment and a Technicolor consultant. The consultant, usually Natalie Kalmus, former wife of the man who owned the process, had a particular idea of what color on the screen should look like: bright, with a tendency to vibrant pastels.

Most of us consider black and white "unrealistic" and color the opposite. However, from the 1930s through the 1950s, exactly the reverse was true. Color was reserved almost exclusively for some musicals and for fantasy films. Black and white was the norm and particularly considered the format for serious films, another phenomenon that allows us to rethink the notion of cinematic

FIGURE 3.22 An example of the early two-color Technicolor process. Buster Keaton's *Seven Chances* (1925)

realism. By the 1960s, when films were ultimately aimed at television, which was becoming all color, black and white cinematography, and the compositional effects that could only be achieved with grayscale, disappeared. So did Technicolor. The expensive three-color process was over by the early 1960s. Eastman Kodak's "monopack" process, in which all the color dyes were embedded in one negative, took over. It was cheaper, and there were no proprietary strings attached. Unfortunately, the color of an Eastman color **release print** was completely unstable. When filmmakers such as Martin Scorsese began complaining in the 1970s that their films turned an irreversible pink in about five years, Kodak made a more stable formula.

Many black and white films demonstrate a subtle gradation of graytones, the result of careful lighting, choice of lenses, and a desire on the part of the director and the director of cinematography to be as expressive as possible in the black and white format. With the universal move to color and the relatively narrow color range of early color television, many filmmakers shot without much thought about using color expressively. But, as always, there were and are exceptions. Alfred Hitchcock, for example, used color to create emotional effect—to express the emotions of his characters and to elicit emotion from his audience.

FIGURE 3.23 Despite the dominance of color cinematography, occasionally a film will be made in black and white, sometimes with startling effect. The careful use of grayscale and lighting makes this image from the Polish film *Ida* (2013) almost painterly (Pawel Pawlikowski, cinematography by Ryszard Lenczewski and Lukasz Zal). See also Figure 3.49

Vertigo

Vertigo (1958), a film about male sexual obsession and the destructive force of delusional romantic longings, uses color to communicate the faulty perceptions of its central character, Scottie (James Stewart). When he first sees the woman he has been asked to follow (who is in fact not the woman he thinks she is), the walls behind her glow a passionate red. When he pursues her, he discovers her in a florist shop. He enters a dark alley, where brown tones dominate. As he opens the door and sees Madeleine (who is really Judy in a masquerade engineered by the real Madeleine's husband), the screen suddenly bursts into color (see Figure 11.16). Near the film's end, when Scottie has transformed Judy back into Madeleine (both played by Kim Novak), the color turns a sickly green, the opposite of the warm red that indicated Scottie's dawning passion. We will return to *Vertigo* again in the last chapter.

FIGURE 3.24 The walls glow red when Scottie (James Stewart) sees and is entranced with Madeleine (Kim Novak) in Alfred Hitchcock's *Vertigo* (1958)

FIGURE 3.25 The passionate red becomes a sickly green when Madeleine appears to return from the dead near the end of *Vertigo*

Hitchcock is certainly not the only director to use color expressively. Stanley Kubrick's last film, *Eyes Wide Shut* (1999), uses blue and gold-yellow lighting throughout the film in order to render an almost painterly effect that pulls the images together. A few directors experimented with flashing or otherwise pre-exposing the film stock so that the image would have uniform color tone, such as the sallow yellow-green that pervades David Fincher's *Seven* (1995), a film notable not only for its color, but for its severe composition. Fincher composes on the horizontal line of the wide screen, emphasizing the compressed, oppressed lives of cops tracking down a serial killer.

FIGURE 3.26 Blue and yellow light, punctuated by green and red: Stanley Kubrick creates a color scheme in *Eyes Wide Shut* (1999)

FIGURE 3.27 David Fincher emphasizes the horizontal line and a dark mise-en-scène in *Seven* (1995)

Red Desert

The Italian director, Michelangelo Antonioni, whose *Blow-Up* (1966) we discussed in the previous chapter, turned color in *Red Desert* (1964) to an even more painterly use so that the film's palette forms the canvas of the almost inarticulate characters' emotions. Like Hitchcock, Antonioni used color expressively, giving it emotional values, those of the characters or those of the film as a large canvas itself on which the director can paint with a varied palette.

In the digital age, directors and cinematographers are told to "shoot down the middle," using as neutral a color palette as possible. Whether shot on film or digitally, during the editing process, the film will exist as digital files and the color will be manipulated in ways not so different from how we manipulate the color of photographs in Photoshop. Note the credits at the end of a film. There will always be credits for the "**digital intermediate**" and often a credit for the **digital colorist**, who works with the director and the director of cinematography to achieve the necessary visual spectrum and tone for the film.

FIGURE 3.28 Color and form become a means to define and even engulf the characters of Michelangelo Antonioni's *Red Desert* (1964)

THE MISE-EN-SCÈNE OF GERMAN EXPRESSIONISM

Bright, high key lighting is the hallmark of much of American film. The play of light and dark, the emphasis on shadow, using light to highlight the dark, has its origins in the films of Germany early in the twentieth century. Born out of the turmoil of the First World War, German Expressionism in film (it was a movement that crossed all artistic disciplines, including literature, painting, and theater) extrapolated perturbed, sometimes psychotic emotional states onto the mise-en-scène itself. To achieve their desired effects, in a film like *The Cabinet of Dr. Caligari* (Robert Wiene, 1920) German Expressionist directors controlled all elements of the composition.

FIGURES 3.29–3.30 An early German Expressionist film, *The Cabinet of Dr. Caligari* (Robert Wiene, 1920), had a major influence on American cinema, as can be seen in this image (right) from James Whale's *The Bride of Frankenstein* (1935) and the images (opposite) from F. W. Murnau's *Sunrise* (1927)

Sets were painted with representations of buildings that were distorted and threatening, streets zigzagged to nowhere; the very shadows cast by lampposts were painted on the set.

Expressionist mise-en-scène in the United States

The influence of German Expressionism has been enormous. While the extreme artificiality did not transfer across the Atlantic, many German directors did, bringing with them a style that, while not entirely new to American filmmakers, did make a lasting impression. German filmmakers, like Fritz Lang, left in the face of Nazi oppression and enjoyed a long career in Hollywood. Earlier, F. W. Murnau, who made the very first Dracula film, *Nosferatu*, in 1922, while still in Germany, was invited by Fox studios to create an "artistic" production. His first American film, *Sunrise* (1927), brought Expressionist techniques to late American silent films. *Sunrise* is a magical work. We've seen in the previous chapter how he could create a mood in the studio with some lights and a moving camera (see Figure 2.12). He could also combine images within one composition and superimpose his characters in fantastic city scenes expressing their happiness or their despair. Murnau used every trick available to filmmakers at the time, even using small people for background figures to force the perspective of his shots. *Sunrise* is a source book of compositional styles, as well as one of the most perfect **melodramas** we have in film.

FIGURES 3.31–3.32 F. W. Murnau's *Sunrise* (1927) used every cinematic trick at the director's disposal. In the country house, the seductive Woman from the City in the background seems to knock everything off kilter in a typical Expressionist shot that distorts spatial expectations. In the second image, multiple exposure and optical printing creates a vision of an imaginary city. See also Figure 2.12

ORSON WELLES AND THE REINVENTION OF MISE-EN-SCÈNE

The Expressionist influence was felt immediately in the United States. The cycle of horror films produced by Universal Studios, beginning in the early 1930s with *Frankenstein* (James Whale, 1931) and *Dracula* (Tod Browning, 1931, photographed by Karl Freund, a German émigré), was marked by the German style: dark, shadowy, and scary. But perhaps the most important and far ranging influence of the movement was on Orson Welles in *Citizen Kane* (1941), a film which forced a rethinking of cinematic composition. Welles came to film from a background in radio and theater. He wanted his visual compositions to have the depth of a theatrical set while at the same time exhibiting the movement and flexibility that was possible in film. He and his cinematographer Gregg Toland used a technique called **deep focus** that had been used only rarely in previous films, and turned it into a compositional imperative. Deep focus, or "depth of field," is a result of camera optics. A lot of light and a very small aperture opening of the camera iris (which translates as a high f-stop) create the effect in which everything from near to far is in focus in the frame. It is hard to do, expensive, and tends to call attention to itself, three reasons why it is rarely used in filmmaking.

There are occasional examples of faked depth of field, in which a special lens is used to focus two spatial planes. You can see it in Martin Scorsese's *Cape Fear* (1991). For *Kane*, Toland had special lenses ground to obtain the effect he wanted but if that failed, he used traditional special effects to achieve something new—placing characters behind a glass painting to achieve forced perspective (on the screen's two-dimensional surface, a painting correctly placed in front of characters will give the impression of the reverse), or other optical tricks to achieve what he and Welles wanted. Remember our earlier discussion about the general rule: build a shot in layers, one element at a time.

FIGURE 3.33 The "Declaration of Principles" sequence from Orson Welles's *Citizen Kane* (1941). Kane is in darkness

But many of the shots in *Kane* are done with most elements present, and the result is astonishing. Welles forces the viewer to look: there are sharply focused characters and items in front, in the middle, in the rear of a given shot, each one demanding attention. Shadow is used to accent a scene in place of light. No longer is the person talking the main focus of the composition. In fact, at a crucial moment in the narrative, when Kane is reading his "Declaration of Principles" for his newspaper—declarations he will quickly forget as he rises to power—he is in total shadow. This may not sound terribly subtle, but it is striking when seen, and it plays a double narrative role by bringing into question Kane's sincerity about his "principles" and foreshadowing a scene, much later in the film, when Kane receives the torn pieces of the declaration from Jed Leland (Joseph Cotton), his one-time friend.

DEEP FOCUS AND THE LONG TAKE

Citizen Kane

Welles played with perspective in *Citizen Kane*, and all his subsequent films, in ways that were not entirely different from what many contemporary painters were doing. Far from the simple vanishing point that the Lumière brothers' cinematographer borrowed from classical painting, Welles, like other visual artists, understood that perspective was a convention—something invented and then naturalized as the only way to represent the "real" world. But, as we have been saying, the "real" is what we or an artist make of the world, and Welles saw the world cinematically as a dark, enigmatic place, where the true character of an individual depended upon who was talking about him. The space the characters inhabit in *Kane* and Welles's subsequent films, was not only dark, in deep focus, but composed in such a way that the perspective lines were out of joint, forcing the eye in a number of directions at once, giving it ownership of nothing.

A visual example of this is shown in Figure 3.34. It takes place early in *Citizen Kane*, when the reporter, Thompson (William Alland), makes his first visit to Kane's second wife, Susan (Dorothy Comingore). She is sullen and silent and Thompson calls his editor. The scene is shot in one very long take, in deep focus, and by the time Thompson enters the phone booth, the composition is divided into a four-paneled layout in which each panel is related to the other. Susan sits in despair in the rear of the left part of the first frame. The waiter is in the center, and Thompson, in silhouette, in the foreground, is on the phone, between the middle and right panels. He's doing the talking and should be the center of attention, but the waiter, in the middle distance, and especially Susan, although in the background, also demand our attention. Where is the perspective of this composition? The answer is that there are not merely two, but many perspective lines, each drawing our eyes in various directions. Figure 3.35 shows some of them.

There is a sequence in *Citizen Kane* that tells us about Kane's childhood, concentrating on the moment when his mother (Agnes Moorehead) signs over his care to the rich Mr. Thatcher (George Coulouris). The sequence concerns the shifting relationships between mother, son, father, and a new patriarchal figure, Thatcher, who will take the son from his parents and introduce him to the world of wealth and personal isolation. Welles describes these relational changes not so much through what the characters say to each other—mother and father argue about who has the right to determine the boy's future—as through the way the camera and characters move through the space of the sequence. The sequence begins with Mrs. Kane looking out of the window and calling to her son, who is playing with his sled in the snow (a sled at the end of the film will be revealed as "Rosebud," Kane's dying word). The camera pulls up and back as Mrs. Kane turns around, and as the camera moves, it reveals a figure to her right. This is the new guardian, Mr. Thatcher. The camera tracks backward in front of them as they move to the other side of the room, talking about signing the papers that will give Thatcher custody of young Charlie Kane. Through most of this, the child outside in the snow, shouting "the union together," remains visible and audible through the window even as the camera moves back. As a result of deep focus and the long backward track of the camera, space expands to the rear of the frame. The small cabin in which all this takes place is expanded into a larger area of psychological change and uprooting, which is underscored by the appearance of the father in the shot.

As Mrs. Kane and Thatcher continue to move toward the opposite end of the room, Mr. Kane is revealed on the left side of the frame. Throughout the shot, he remains always slightly behind his wife as she and Mr. Thatcher approach the table where the papers are. In their movement to the table, the child, still playing outside the window, is sometimes blocked out by his mother or father, but throughout the shot a triangulated dynamic is maintained between the three adults and the child. After withdrawing her gaze from Kane out in the snow, Mrs. Kane transfers it to Thatcher and then looks straight ahead while she moves to the table. Thatcher's and Mr. Kane's gazes remain fixed on Mrs. Kane. She is the pivotal figure, the one making the choice. The two men are dependent upon her actions while the child is separated from her, almost literally pulled away by the visual effect created as the camera moves from the window to the table.

After Mrs. Kane and Thatcher sit down at the table and Mr. Kane comes closer to the two of them, the camera tilts up, causing the father to appear for a moment as a slightly threatening figure—threatening, at least, to those ready to sign away his child. Note that an unusually low camera position often has the effect of making a character loom over the frame in a threatening manner. However, Welles will sometimes use this position ironically to indicate that the imposing figure is about to fall from power. An unusually high camera position diminishes a character.

FIGURES 3.34–3.35 This deep focus shot of Susan Kane in the nightclub while Thompson the reporter is on the phone forces the viewer to visually interrogate the various levels of the picture plane. There are four panels within the composition and to complicate matters even further, perspective lines and eye lines are skewed, as demonstrated by the diagram of the shot

FIGURE 3.36 As the sequence begins, Kane's mother (Agnes Moorehead) is gazing at her son playing in the snow

FIGURE 3.37 As the camera pulls back, it reveals Mr. Thatcher (George Coulouris), who takes Mrs. Kane's gaze away from her son

FIGURE 3.38 The camera continues to pull back, revealing Mr. Kane (Harry Shannon), momentarily eclipsing young Charlie Kane (Sonny Bupp) and forming a triangle of forces contending for his future

FIGURE 3.39 As Mrs. Kane and Mr. Thatcher sit down to sign over custody of Charlie, the triangle becomes pronounced as Charlie Kane is once more visible in the background

FIGURE 3.40 As the signing occurs, a new triangle forms, all eyes on the pen signing away Charlie. The diagrams give an indication of the complexity of this Oedipal ballet

Hitchcock will often use a disorienting high angle shot to show a character in physical or moral jeopardy (see Figure 3.47). In our sequence from *Kane*, the father's power is weak and diminishing further. He is about to lose his son to a man who is practically buying him from his mother. The three adults talk about their business deal while young Kane remains clearly visible through the window, on the other side, far behind them, now forming the apex of the triangle. Mr. Kane relents in his opposition to the deal the moment he understands how much money is at stake. He then goes to the back of the room and shuts the window—as if shutting his son out of his life. Mrs. Kane and Thatcher follow; she opens the window again, and, finally, after about two minutes and thirty seconds, there is a **180-degree reverse shot** of Mrs. Kane from outside the window.

This complex arrangement and rearrangement of space and figures creates a kind of Oedipal ballet in a small room, a dance of shifting parental relationships and authority that results in both gain and loss for the child. The ballet of camera and character in their dynamic spatial confines is more eloquent than the spoken dialogue and much more descriptive of narrative events.

Another less complex long take in *Citizen Kane* occurs right after Kane's electoral defeat. It is a long dialogue between Kane and his friend Jed Leland. The camera is set below the level of the floor and looks up at these two figures, one a giant just cut down to size by his election loss, the other an obsequious friend who is beginning to find his own voice. The camera moves with them, but there is no cutting. Its position is ironic; the power lies in our observation of these two figures whose place in their world is changing before our eyes.

For Welles, in *Kane* and all the other films he made in the course of an active career, the screen became a highly malleable space, a demanding space in which we, as viewers, must actively seek out the various elements in the composition. *Kane*, along with other influences, was a forerunner of **film noir**. I will speak in detail about this particular **genre** later on. But it is

FIGURE 3.41 The low angle shot of Kane (Orson Welles) and Jed Leland (Joseph Cotton) after Kane loses his election. This long shot emphasizes Kane's diminishing power. See also Figure 7.1

important to note here that its dependence on darkness, on compositions that are off center, that complicate the perspectival line, came directly from *Kane* as well as from modern art. Darkness became noir's theme as well as its visual construction. Composition is used to create anxiety rather than composure.

THE HITCHCOCK MISE-EN-SCÈNE

Psycho

The Expressionist influence spread widely throughout the history of American film, and Orson Welles was only one of its practitioners. Alfred Hitchcock was a British director who created a large body of work before immigrating to the United States. Early in his British period, he did apprenticeship work in Germany, learning much from the Expressionist style. Even in a film as late as *Psycho* (1960), we can see Expressionist composition in which emotion is expressed by the mise-en-scène. But Hitchcock's work goes even further in its compositional control and, like Welles, extends the Expressionist mise-en-scène by bringing it close to modern painting. *Psycho* is a tightly constructed film, wound like a machine, and, whenever you see it, it continues to open surprises that you would have thought were no longer surprises.

The tightness of its construction creates its dark vision of the inevitability of madness and is brought about through composition and camera movement, as well as editing in the infamous shower murder. It achieves expressiveness by constructing a closed, isolated, threatening, black and white world which is based upon an abstract compositional pattern. In other words, Hitchcock and his visual designer, Saul Bass, construct *Psycho* along controlled compositional patterns of vertical and horizontal lines, the slashing movement of a knife, and high angle shots that indicate a character in danger. As we can see in the accompanying stills, the film depends upon the control of our eye as we are allowed to approach, but never pierce, the curtain of madness.

There is a sense in which *Psycho* comes full circle to *The Cabinet of Dr. Caligari*. While not as obviously artificial as that 1920 film, it is a tale of madness told in a world that reflects the obsessive psychotic mind. Like *Caligari* it is made to scare us: horror is one of the lasting influences of the Expressionist movement.

WORKING AGAINST THE RULES

We have been looking at exceptional filmmakers, the relatively few who work against the conventions of the Hollywood style. The long take, moving camera, careful, expressive compositions in black and white or color are exceptions to the norms of loose framing, rare and unobtrusive camera movements, and flat color. But we can't understand the norm without seeing these exceptions. There is, for example, an unwritten rule that says the camera cannot be set 90 degrees to the subject being photographed. Doing so, the thinking goes, would only emphasize the two dimensions of the screen space, creating a flatness that calls attention to itself. But some filmmakers want to exploit and expose the two-dimensional compositional space of the screen by using 90-degree shots, focusing our attention on the image (see Figures 3.5–3.7). Stanley Kubrick was one who not only employed straight-on shots, but also made uncanny and unusual symmetrical compositions, just slightly off to unbalance the image and the composition. More recently, Alexander Payne's *Nebraska* (2013), the rare contemporary film made in black and white,

FIGURE 3.42 Saul Bass's credit sequence for *Psycho* (1960) sets up the pattern of horizontals and verticals, as well as the disrupting curve that will form the visual structure of the film

FIGURE 3.43 The dissolve from the credit sequence to the beginning of the narrative overlays the abstract pattern onto the image

FIGURE 3.44 The motel and the old Gothic house are the most concrete examples of the compositional structure set up by the film. This particular shot reveals Hitchcock's Expressionist roots

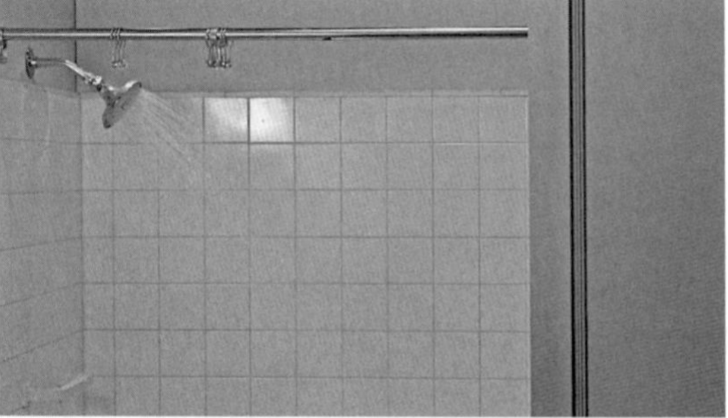

FIGURE 3.45 The structure allows Hitchcock to create an almost abstract pattern, as in this shot that occurs just after the shower murder

FIGURE 3.46 The shower scene breaks the horizontal/vertical composition with an arcing, slashing motion.

FIGURE 3.47 The high angle shot is a favorite of Hitchcock's. It shows a character in danger and creates anxiety in the viewer. Here detective Arbogast (Martin Balsam) is about to meet mother

is a road movie about an old man's search for some final validation for his life. It takes place across the flat plains of the Midwest and the wide-screen compositions are carefully made to convey a sense of emptiness mitigated by the humanity of its characters, their faces giving life to an otherwise barren wintery landscape.

Barrenness is also a quality in the images made by the Italian filmmaker Michelangelo Antonioni, whose unusual use of color we examined earlier. He revised notions of composition in radical ways. His films sometimes come close to Abstract Expressionist painting, always using composition to express his characters' states of mind, reducing them to figures in a landscape, in which the landscape, unlike what Alexander Payne does in *Nebraska*, often dominates the

FIGURE 3.48 An example of Kubrick's straight on, symmetrical compositions can be seen in this image from *The Shining* (1980)

FIGURE 3.49 Director Alexander Payne uses black and white and anamorphic wide screen to capture the figure in the Midwestern landscape in *Nebraska* (2013, cinematographer Phedon Papamichael)

characters. Abstract Expressionist painting did away with the figure entirely, something that narrative film cannot do. But in Antonioni's work, the figure and the landscape merge, often in abstract patterns that express their state of being in the modern world (see Figures 3.28, 3.48 and 3.49).

Clearly, the elements that make up composition are numerous and complex. After all, they constitute the immediate visual presence of any film. When combined with editing, a narrative—the telling of a story—is created. We therefore cut to the editing process.

FURTHER READING

John Belton, *Widescreen Cinema* (Cambridge, MA: Harvard University Press, 1992), is an excellent source for the techniques and aesthetics of wide screen.

Lotte H. Eisner, *The Haunted Screen* (Berkeley and Los Angeles: University of California Press, 1974), remains the best work on German Expressionism. The theory that horror films emerged as a response to World War I is presented in Robert Skal, *The Monster Show: A Cultural History of Horror* (New York: Faber & Faber, 2001).

An excellent study of Busby Berkeley and his treatment of the human figure is in Lucy Fischer, *Cinematernity: Film, Motherhood, Genre* (Princeton, NJ: Princeton University Press, 1996), pp. 37–55.

An extended visual analysis of *Psycho* is Robert Kolker, "The Man Who Knew More Than Enough," in Robert Kolker, ed., *Alfred Hitchcock's* Psycho: *A Casebook* (New York: Oxford University Press, 2004), pp. 205–258.

André Bazin addresses the contemplative nature of deep focus and the long shot throughout his essays in *What Is Cinema?* cited in Chapter 1.

For a discussion of the technical aspects of color, see James L. Limbacher, *Four Aspects of the Film* (New York: Arno Press, 1977). Limbacher also analyzes screen sizes.

SUGGESTIONS FOR FURTHER VIEWING

Elephant (Gus Van Sant, 2003) is a contemporary example of long-take cinematography.

Several filmmakers use wide screen as an expressive compositional element of mise-en-scène. The Japanese director Akira Kurosawa's *Red Beard* (1965) is one example. In the United States, there are John Sturges' *Bad Day at Black Rock* (1955), Nicholas Ray's *Rebel Without a Cause* (1955), *Bigger than Life* (1956) and *Bitter Victory* (1957). Ray also experimented with color schemes in *Johnny Guitar* (1954). John Ford's Westerns, which we will discuss in detail in Chapter 9, are studies in careful composition of the figure in the western landscape of Monument Valley. See, for example, *My Darling Clementine* (1946).

NOTES

1 "Cinema of Attractions" is a phrase invented by Tom Gunning, "An aesthetic of astonishment: early film and the (in)credulous spectator," in Leo Braudy and Marshall Cohen, eds., *Film Theory and Criticism* 7th ed. (New York: Oxford University Press, 2009), pp. 736–750.

2 For information on the Golden Mean, see Ocvirk, Stinson, Wigg, Bone, and Cayton, *Art Fundamentals* 9th ed. (New York: McGraw-Hill, 2002), pp. 62–65.

CHAPTER 4

The building blocks of film II

The cut

EDITING AND THE CLASSIC HOLLYWOOD STYLE

There are contemporary filmmakers, mostly from Europe or Asia, like the Hungarian **director** Bela Tarr, who depend exclusively upon the **long take**. The American director Gus Van Sant, best known for films like *Good Will Hunting* (1997) and the 1998 shot-by-shot remake of *Psycho* (1960), has made more personal works, like *Elephant* (2003), a contemplation on the Columbine shootings, that are made in very long takes with a minimum of editing. The most radical long-take directors will cut only when the scene changes. They are in the minority.

Try this experiment: choose any film and begin counting the number of seconds each **shot** lasts on the screen—in other words, start when a new image takes the place of the previous one and count the seconds until another image takes that image's place. I promise you the results will be amazing. You will discover that the average shot length of an American film is about nine seconds, usually shorter, occasionally longer, but rarely by much. This does not necessarily mean that the take made during production of the film was only nine seconds long, but it does point out the deep, abiding illusion of film called the **classical Hollywood style**: short pieces of film are spliced together to create the impression of an ongoing process of story. What we see on the screen in an average Hollywood film *appears* to be an ongoing, transparent process of narration; but it is made up of fragments carefully edited to create the illusion that they are not fragments.

We need to back up a bit to understand this fully. The shot and its **composition** are what you see on the screen. A cut or **edit** is invisible; the only thing you see is its result: another shot.

But the purpose and possibilities of what the cut produces are as complex and varied as the elements that make up the shot itself—which itself will partially determine where a cut will occur. Like the shot, editing also addresses time and space by building the temporal structure—the movement of characters and events across the **narrative** of a film—and directing our gaze as well as that of the characters to those things and events the filmmaker deems important. An edit allows our gaze to move to a new space or to a different perspective of the space within a scene. Editing creates transitions, movements from one place or time to another. A **dissolve**, for example, in which one shot fades out while another fades in, is an editing effect, as is the fade to black of a **sequence** to mark the end of a narrative moment. This was a favorite device of Alfred Hitchcock, who would, in effect, squelch a scene with a fast fade to black, leaving the viewer in a state of suspense and expectation as to what might follow. Even though such techniques are created optically, either in the camera, the **optical printer**, or digitally, they are still editing techniques. Some varieties have become cinematic conventions such as when the dissolve is created by using wavy lines, and we know a **flashback** is occurring. It became a convention by being repeated over and over again until the audience knew immediately what it signified. Today, this and other transition devices—like the dissolve or the **wipe**—have been mostly replaced by the **direct cut**. When we see a dissolve or a wipe today, we can assume that the filmmaker is consciously recalling an older cinematic technique.

FIGURE 4.1 By means of this dissolve, Rick (Humphrey Bogart) moves into a flashback of happier days in Paris. The camera has moved close to him and slowly goes out of focus as the Paris landmark is dissolved over him. (*Casablanca*, Michael Curtiz, 1941)

A shot is an actual or apparent unbroken length of film; editing is what breaks it. But editing joins together as well as cuts apart. Through editing, filmmakers build the structure of a movie by arranging its shots. Editing is what is done to a shot. Editing is cutting; but *an* edit usually refers to the joining together of two shots. There are a number of editing styles, the most dominant of which is the classic **continuity style** of American filmmaking.

A reasonable question at this point might be, why edit at all? Why not just create the sequences of film each in one shot, so the unity of time and space would be maintained without having to trick the viewer's eye into believing that parts are wholes? The answer to the question lies deep within the history and culture of Hollywood studio filmmaking and speaks to the development of the classical style. Very early in film history—at the time of Edison, the Lumière brothers, and Georges Méliès, and lasting until just after the turn of the twentieth century—films were short and usually made in one or a few shots. There was not much camera movement, and the space defined by the composition of the shot was often frontal and static. Critics have theorized that this frontal, static gaze was an attempt to represent the view of a stage from the point of view of the auditorium, a perspective most early filmgoers would have understood and found comforting. More recent theories have emphasized the aspect of spectacle in early film: a single shot that shows an amazing and attractive event—President McKinley walking across his lawn, reading a message; a fan dancer; two people kissing. Over the course of a relatively few years, as spectators and filmmakers alike became more comfortable with the spatial arrangement of the shot and the composition of the image, filmmakers began experimenting with the construction of story—the narrative—of films. The single shot seemed not to provide enough flexibility. Flexibility was a key reason for editing: filmmakers began cutting to alter points of view, keep the viewer's eyes engaged, and find ways of telling a story that could be more easily achieved by cutting scenes and sequences together.

The Great Train Robbery

This was not done easily or without concern. Nothing in filmmaking then or now is done without concern or even anxiety. Would spectators understand what was happening when two shots were cut together or a cut made from a long shot to a **close-up**? The audience did. Film is perhaps the greatest self-teacher of all the arts. New methods of building stories were taken in by audiences with apparent ease, and, as they were accepted, more editing techniques were tried out. By the early part of the twentieth century, further experiments were made. Edwin S. Porter's *The Great Train Robbery*, made in 1903, is an early example of a film that intercuts sequences—of the robbery itself, of the townspeople at a dance—and it pointed the way to great flexibility in narrative construction. For a short time in the early part of the twentieth century, control of this flexibility extended to film exhibitors—the owners of the movie houses. *The Great Train Robbery* includes a famous shot of one of the robbers pointing a gun toward the camera and firing as if at the audience. Exhibitors were at liberty to put this shot at the beginning or at the end of the film. Some eighty years later, at the end of *GoodFellas* (1990), Martin Scorsese splices in a shot of Joe Pesci's Tommy, firing his gun directly at the audience, in direct reference to Porter's early film.[1]

We shouldn't underplay the rapid development of editing in early cinema. It was largely intuited, there were no rule books (unwritten rules came later) and certainly no film school in which to study filmmaking. "School" was the process of creating, viewing, experimenting, looking

FIGURES 4.2–4.5 These images demonstrate four of the spaces that are cut together to form a narrative in *The Great Train Robbery* (Edwin S. Porter, 1903). In addition to the robbery itself (which is made up of a number of scenes)—here the robbers blow up the strongbox. A young girl in red discovers and unties the first victim of the robbery (note the rear screen projection or matted shot outside the window). She notifies the townspeople who are at a dance, and they ride in pursuit, guns blazing. These images don't directly follow each other in the film itself, but indicate the way Porter manipulates the narrative to encompass a number of actions. (The color tinting was common during the silent period)

FIGURE 4.6 Shooting directly at the audience at the end (or the beginning) of *The Great Train Robbery*

FIGURE 4.7 Martin Scorsese alludes to the shot in Porter's film by placing this shot of Tommy (Joe Pesci) shooting at the audience at the end of *Goodfellas* (1990)

for new ways to tell stories cinematically. The result was a most flexible method of storytelling that became founded in an inflexible series of assumptions.

THE DEVELOPMENT OF CONTINUITY CUTTING

Imagine this problem: A film calls for two events to happen simultaneously. A woman is held captive by a man meaning to do her harm. Her fiancé knows where she is and is coming to rescue her. As we will see in Chapter 9, this is a **dominant fiction** of film (and literature), the "**captivity narrative**." Versions of it are still with us: think of David Fincher's *Panic Room* (2002) or Pierre Morel's *Taken* (2008), or all the serial killer films and television series in which a victim is near death at the hands of a monster as the detectives race to find where the killer has hidden her. How can this information be structured for maximum effect? One method might be to show each action in a single shot, each complete in itself, one after the other. This method would extend the single-shot construction that was the mainstay of early cinema, but it would not provide temporal control. In other words, the action of the story would be at the mercy of the linearity of the shots, not the rhythm of the action: the victim is held captive, the hero rushes to her rescue, or the detectives get the information of the killer's hideout, the hero or detectives arrive and save the victim.

The successful solution of this problem creates an illusion of simultaneity by editing the sequences together so that a shot of the woman in captivity and a shot of the people coming to her rescue are intercut in an alternating sequence. Intercutting two sequences, often called **cross cutting** or **parallel editing**, provides a means to integrate story parts with finesse and flexibility. Early filmmakers—we see it in *The Great Train Robbery*—discovered that suspense could be created by changing the lengths of these alternating shots, perhaps shortening them as the hero approached the captive heroine to increase tension. Audiences accepted this structure with ease, and it became one of the foundations of the classical Hollywood style.

Other, very important, elements of cutting were developed during the period between 1905 and the early 1910s, all of them crucial to the continuity style and to cinema being created to entice and hold the viewer's gaze. One element was a solution to a seemingly simple problem. A filmmaker might need to get a character up from a chair and out of a room, catching her again from the outside of the room as she passes through the door. With a mobile camera, it would be quite possible, and very dramatic, to do a backward **track**, **dollying** the camera (moving it on tracks or another device) away from the person as she gets up and moves through the door. Contemporary television shows often use extended dolly or **tracking shots** to follow characters walking along a hallway. During the early period, however, cameras were not very mobile. Since they had no electric motor and needed to be hand-cranked, they couldn't be moved easily, unless apparatus and operator were placed in a moving vehicle, which Griffith did in *Birth of a Nation* (1915) and *Intolerance* (1916). But this would not be useful for the closed space of a room. Beyond the physical limitations, there was, as I said, a desire for a rhythmical structure in film that could only be attained by cutting, a rhythm that would keep the viewer's attention through changing shots as opposed to continuous unbroken shots. Narrative rhythm became an important driving force in the development of editing.

Cinema, early and late, is full of shots of people getting up from seated positions, leaving a room, getting into a car, going to their destinations. These are essential narrative transitions. During the pre-1910 period, however, these movements were not always cut together in consistent ways. In an early film, it is quite possible to see a person rising from a chair in the first shot and, in the second, the person rising from the same position she had already occupied before the cut. The effect is seeing the person getting up from the chair twice. This is not incompetence but rather the sign of a cinematic grammar incompletely standardized, as if one didn't know (or care) that the clause on either side of a coordinate conjunction should be different and instead saying, "She got up out of the chair and she got up out of the chair." There were no conventions of continuity cutting, no rules; they had to be invented and used over and over again before they became conventions. But as we noted earlier, "invented" is not quite accurate. The individuals who developed the grammar of continuity cutting were not theorists and were certainly not scientific.

GRIFFITH AND CUTTING

We can see the process developing across the period of early film, and especially in the short films D. W. Griffith made for Biograph, which we discussed in the previous chapter. Griffith and others learned how to match shots, so that the analysis of a single movement—the person getting out of a chair and leaving the room—would appear not to be the fragments of an action that they actually are but the illusion of one continuous action. Even the hard part, synchronizing the cut of the woman leaving the room to the shot of her exiting the door on the other side, becomes smoothed and timed to achieve the right sense of forward, purposive motion, not only of the character but of her story as well. Coordinates become, in effect, commas. Hiding the cut by editing on a continuous movement, distracting the viewer with something else going on in the **frame**, and, from 1927 on, using dialogue or sound as a cover became a major function of the continuity style.

The Lonedale Operator

Here is an example of an almost perfect continuity shot from Griffith's *The Lonedale Operator* (1911), another train robbery film. This is a brief sequence from the film that entails the telegraph operator receiving a message, getting up, and going out to greet the arriving train. The first shot frames the operator, giving a lot of space for her to actually get up and move. Griffith then offers a **point-of-view** shot of the message before cutting to her getting up and leaving the room. He then cuts to her coming out of the other side of the door. As she goes to the door that leads to the train station, she begins to wave, and Griffith cuts again, as she exits on the other side of the door, where she once again waves.

Although one can still sometimes spot a continuity error in a film, seamless continuity cutting has become the norm, and filmmakers have developed a set of conventions that allow them to cut invisibly: cuts on action, where the beginning of the action is completed on the other side of the shot; cuts on music or dialogue, so that either or both smother the obviousness of the cut; cuts to a different scene which is telegraphed by the dialogue in either the scene before or the scene following. All these techniques are formal properties of movies. They aren't natural or "given"; the cuts are made to be invisible and we learn to ignore them. The story is moved forward. There are always glorious exceptions.

FIGURE 4.8 The Lonedale operator sits at her desk in a medium shot, copying a message

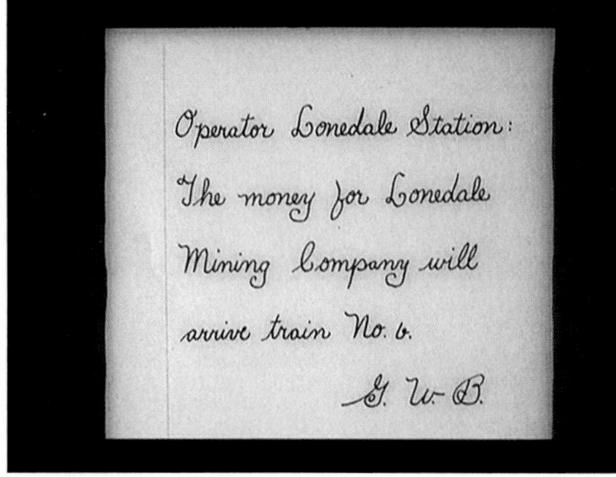

FIGURE 4.9 Griffith cuts in the message she's writing

FIGURE 4.10 The operator, in a wide shot, leaves her desk to deliver her message to the arriving train, and begins exiting through the door

FIGURE 4.11 There is a continuity cut to the other side of the door, where she continues her exit

FIGURE 4.12 She goes through the next door, waving

FIGURE 4.13 Griffith then cuts to pick her up outside where she continues to wave. The blue tint was typical at the time for outside scenes. (*The Lonedale Operator*, D. W. Griffith, 1911)

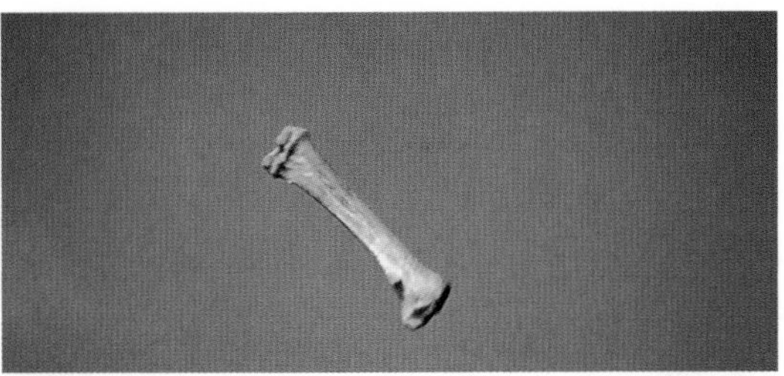

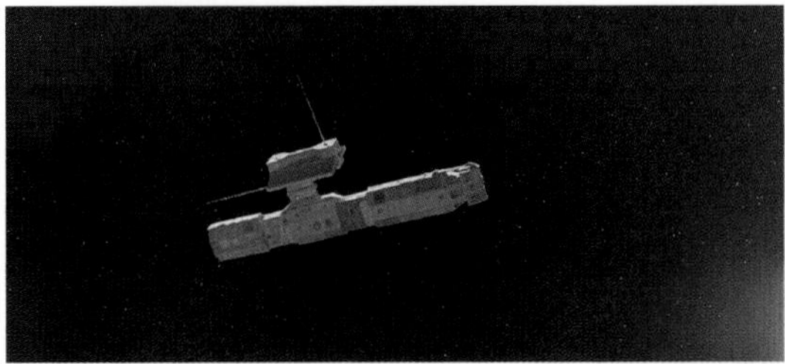

FIGURES 4.14–4.15 In Stanley Kubrick's *2001: A Space Odyssey* (1968), a cut is made from the bone hurled in the air by a prehistoric proto-human to a spaceship circling the earth, eons later

2001: A Space Odyssey

Perhaps the most audacious discontinuity cut in film history occurs in Stanley Kubrick's *2001: A Space Odyssey* (1968). The edit is made from a bone, hurled in the air by an ape who has just learned to use the tool to kill, to a space vehicle that introduces an astral ballet with a space station circling the moon. This is a discontinuity created on purpose, a temporal cut that literally cuts hundreds of thousands of years, all of which are hidden in the edit. And the discontinuity is actually ironic, since Kubrick is implying an actual continuity between the weapon as bone and the violent future of the race. Such audaciousness proves that there will always be filmmakers who go against the rules to create, even within something as complex as continuity cutting, something more complex, and more visible—something that makes us take notice that the structures of film can themselves say as much as any other narrative element.

SHOT/REVERSE SHOT

One element of continuity cutting is, in many ways, the most important, because it establishes a basic structural principle for the way narrative is created in film. We approached this in our discussion of *Jaws* in Chapter 2, and it involves the concept of the gaze, the way characters look at one another and the way we look at, and get caught up in, the looks of the characters on screen. We are connected to a filmic story largely through the orchestration of these looks, and the prime conductor of the process is the **shot/reverse shot**: one character looks (shot) and we cut to what the character is looking at (**reverse shot**), which, if it is exactly what the character is looking at, is a point-of-view shot. Making the fragments of the editing structure invisible and creating the illusion of an ongoing action depend upon building the gaze of the spectator into the storytelling or narrative space of the film. Our glance is directed, woven, sewn into the visual structure so that we forget the act of cutting and become involved in what each cut reveals. In fact, critics sometimes use a surgical metaphor, calling the process in which our gaze is stitched into the narrative the "**suture effect**." We become part of the telling of the story as well as the one to whom the story is told.[2]

Perhaps the most insistent, unvarying version of the shot/reverse pattern occurs in the presentation of a simple dialogue sequence between two characters. This structure has been so common for so many years (the pattern was developed *before* the coming of sound) that if you watch a movie or any drama or news interview program on television, you are guaranteed to see the following: two people begin a conversation with the camera framing them together in a **two-shot**. This shot will last perhaps ten or twelve seconds. The sequence will then cut to a shot over the shoulder of one of the participants looking at the other. After a very few seconds, there will be a reverse shot, over the shoulder of the second participant, looking at the first. These reverses, each one lasting perhaps three to six seconds, will continue, perhaps punctuated with **one-shots**—that is, shots of one or the other participant alone in the frame—for as long as it takes the dialogue to conclude. And it will conclude with the original two-shot of both figures. We can illustrate this pattern in almost any film. But because this cutting pattern is so universal, we can create a verbal description, a template that can be applied to any movie that you are likely to see.

Imagine the following scene: a man walks into a room, sits down at a table across from a woman, and starts a conversation. A third person in the room is standing and listening. The editing structure might be as follows. Each item indicates a shot you might see on the screen:

1 The woman looks up toward the door.
2 A point-of-view shot of the door opening as a man enters.
3 A **reaction shot** of the woman, who looks surprised.
4 The man approaches and sits down at the table.
5 Shot of the third person already in the room, who raises his eyebrows.
6 The man and the woman talk in two-shot (both are together in the frame).
7 Cut to an **over-the-shoulder** shot from the woman to the man.
8 Reverse shot over the shoulder from the man to the woman.
9 Repeat this pattern three times, perhaps inserting a one-shot of each, then return to
10 The two-shot of the two people talking.
11 A shot of the third person smiling.
12 A **wide shot** of all three participants in the sequence.

The core of this sequence might actually have been constructed out of nine separate shots. For example, the woman looking toward the door, registering surprise, might have been filmed in one shot. The man entering the room, approaching the table, and sitting down might constitute the second. The two-shot of the man and woman talking at the table would make up the third; the change in camera position from over the shoulder of one of the participants to the other would make up the fourth and fifth shots; the one-shots of each would make up two more; the shot of the man smiling the eighth, the wide shot of the whole ensemble would make up the ninth. All of the onlooker's reactions would be shot together, as would the two-shots of the couple at the table and the over-the-shoulder shots. Although nine shots are used to construct the sequence, many more would actually have been taken (they are called "**takes**" of the same shot). Each of the shots actually used would be chosen from a number of takes, in which the same setup, dialogue, and action were repeated, over and over, until the director felt she had enough good ones to choose from. Bear in mind that, traditionally, only one camera is used in filmmaking, so that each wide shot (showing the whole group), one-shot, two-shot, or close-up is done separately. Out of all these takes, the shots are chosen and cut together to create the continuity of the sequence.

Some of these shots might not require all the participants to be present. The shot of the man entering the room might include all three people, as would the initial two-shot of the conversation, and the wide shot of the whole group. But the shot of the woman looking up

FIGURES 4.16–4.21 Seduction on a train. This long conversation between Roger Thornhill (Cary Grant) and Eve Kendall (Eva Marie Saint) in Alfred Hitchcock's *North by Northwest* (1959) is made up of over-the-shoulder shots punctuated by one-shots of each. Roger does take off his dark glasses that he was wearing to evade the spies who are after him

would not necessarily require the presence of the other two actors, nor would the shot of the onlooker responding to the conversation (especially if these shots were done in medium or full close-up). In the over-the-shoulder shots that make up the dialogue at the table, it might not be necessary to have present the actor over whose shoulder the camera is gazing. If the shot shows only a little bit of one actor's face, a stand-in performer will do, and will certainly be less expensive. In television interview programs, it is common practice to shoot reaction shots of the interviewer after the person interviewed has left. These are then cut in to give the impression that the interviewer is responding to the answers given by his subject.

In the editing of a sequence, as in the composing of a single shot from different elements, the filmmakers create and we read what we need in order to understand the forward momentum of the story. In our made-up sequence, it is easy to imagine that a look of anticipation from the woman toward the door makes us anticipate something, and our anticipation is fulfilled by the cut to the man entering. The looks from the bystander serve to seal the participants and the viewer into the content of the sequence and create a dramatic context for what is going on. If the bystander smiles warmly, we believe everything is fine; if the bystander sneers or grimaces, we might suspect a bad deed is about to occur. This, however, goes beyond editing into the issue of "**coding**" in which certain looks and actions, repeated over and over again throughout the history of film, telegraph meaning to us, thereby allowing a narrative economy—a way for the visual narrative to communicate quickly and cheaply—to occur. We will examine this more closely in the chapter on acting.

POINT OF VIEW

Point of view is part of this narrative economy and in cinema means the representation of what a character sees. It is built out of the basic cinematic units of shot and cut. If a shot of a character looking at something is followed by a shot of an object or another person, we assume (because film almost never gives us reason to assume otherwise) that what we are now seeing is what the character is seeing. This is the closest film ever gets to the first-person effect in written fiction. The "I" in cinema becomes, almost literally, the "eye." We are asked to believe that we are seeing through the eyes of the gazing character. There have been very few experiments in creating film that is structured entirely in the first person. Welles wanted to make his first film, an adaptation of Joseph Conrad's novella *Heart of Darkness*, a first-person narrative, but couldn't make it work. The actor Robert Montgomery attempted to mimic the detective novelist Raymond Chandler's first-person style in his film adaptation *Lady in the Lake* (1946). The result is a wooden, silly-looking film in which the camera gets punched in the nose and coffee cups are lifted up to the lens to mimic the character drinking. The only time the main character is seen is when he looks into a mirror.

The first-person effect in film is best achieved by means of the interplay of gazes created through the intercutting of characters who look and the people or things they're looking at. Film, therefore, is mostly narrated by a mute third-person voice, the overseeing eye of the director and his camera and the controlling movements of the cutting. First-person point of view is built into this general third-person structure, articulating it with the intensity of the individual gaze. Sometimes, a film may approach first person narrative when the central character is on screen most of the time, and the world we see is the world that reflects his perceptions. Martin Scorsese's *Taxi Driver* (1976) is a case in point. The film's central character, Travis Bickle (Robert De Niro), is present in every scene but one. More importantly, we see the world as Travis sees it: an Expressionist world of shadows and violence (see Figure 5.1).

SIGHT LINES

Remember that each of the shots for a dialogue sequence, or any sequence in a film, is made independently and then cut together during the editing process to create the sequence. It is important for the purposes of constructing the sequence, and for maintaining continuity when the sequence is viewed by an audience, that the sight lines maintained by the characters remain constant. The characters must look in the same direction in each shot, for fear of breaking the rhythm of the viewer's own gaze at and within the scene. This is called an **eye line match**, and it is another constituent of the continuity style. If a character is looking to the left in one shot that eye line must be maintained in the succeeding shots of the sequence, and the other character must be continually looking to the right. What's more, as the cutting moves our gaze from one character to the other, the position of the camera must remain along the same plane in front of the characters. This is the critical and, like everything else in this process, absolutely arbitrary **180-degree rule**.

THE 180-DEGREE RULE

One of the most ironclad rules of the classical Hollywood style is the 180-degree rule. It is even stricter than the **90-degree rule** in composing the image (see Figures 3.5–3.7). Basically, the camera may not be allowed to cross a 180-degree line imagined to stretch from left to right across the scene. You can visualize this by imagining that you can look straight down at a scene of two people and see a line drawn directly behind, or even over them. The camera may be placed at any point on one side of that line, never behind it (and, as pointed out, never exactly 90 degrees in front of it because the space would appear too two-dimensional). Such rules came into being out of concern that, if the characters were looking in different directions from shot to shot, if the camera moved to the other side of the 180-degree line or was positioned at a

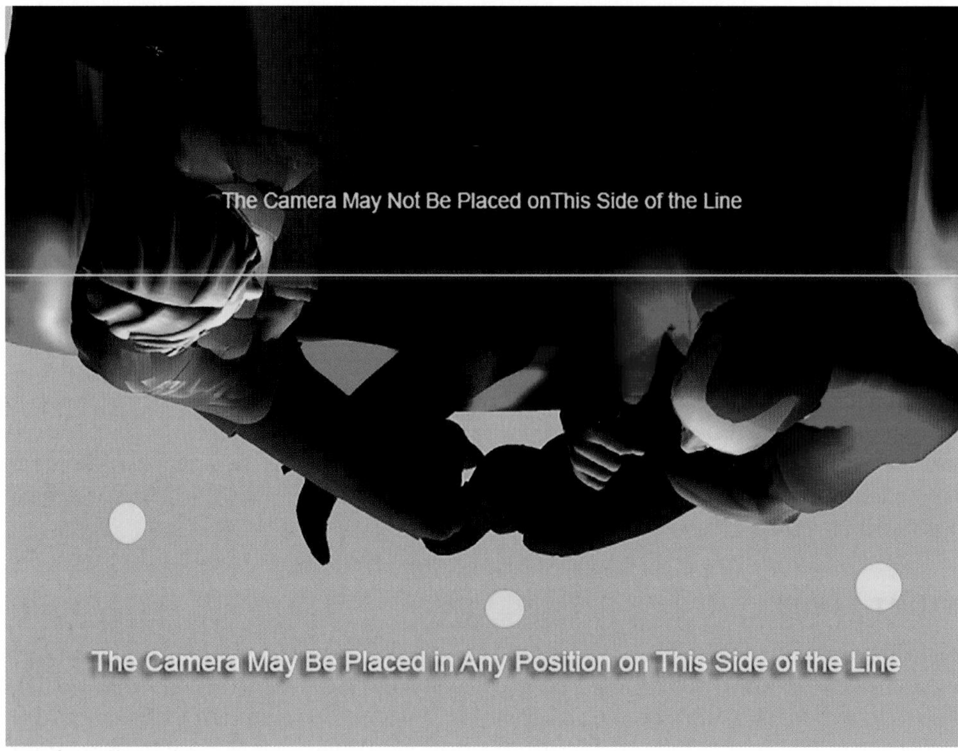

FIGURE 4.22 This diagram illustrates the 180-degree rule. The camera may move almost anywhere on one side of the imaginary line, but not on the other

FIGURES 4.23–4.24 In the bathroom scene in *The Shining* (1980), Stanley Kubrick breaks the 180-degree rule, causing surprise and a certain amount of unease, which is why the rule is rarely broken. (See Figures 3.5–3.6.)

direct 90 degrees to the figures, audiences would be confused and the artificial structure of cinematic space would be revealed.

When these and other conventions are followed with such regularity in film after film, we begin to take them for granted. Our gaze is so woven that a two- or three-way pattern is formed in which we, like the viewer of a perspective painting, are given pride of place and the illusion of ownership of the narrative space. Things happen for our eyes, and as our eyes are entangled with the gazes of the characters in the film, we feel a part of events, an element in the narrative. Like every other aspect of continuity cutting, the shot/reverse shot sequence achieves complex results from quite simple means. The shot/reverse shot is, of course, not restricted to dialogue sequences alone, and it can be fodder for unexpected results.

PSYCHO AND THE SHOT/REVERSE SHOT

Near the end of *Psycho*, Lila Crane (Vera Miles), the sister of Marion (Janet Leigh), who was brutally murdered in the shower, goes into Norman's (Anthony Perkins) mother's old, dark house to visit the old lady. From the moment she starts up the stairway leading to the house, Hitchcock constructs the sequence from a series of shot/reverse shots during which we look at Lila as she registers a response of fear or curiosity and then cut to the object of her gaze: the house, a room, a fixture, a bed. Through this construction, Hitchcock so synchronizes our expectations and fears with Lila's that he can play two jokes. The first one is on both the character and us. Lila enters Mrs. Bates's room and approaches the bureau, her eyes caught by—as the camera, in reverse shot, zooms in on—a bronze sculpture of two folded, smothering hands. As she stands by the bureau, her reflection in the mirror is bounced back from another mirror behind the one she is looking at, so that there are actually three Lilas. We look from behind and see Lila's back. In the mirror before her, we see her reflection and, in the second reflection, we see her back. These images occur very quickly, so that before we can actually make out her reflections, she is startled by them, shrieks, turns, and we shriek with her. As she turns, Hitchcock cuts to the mirror behind her, now object of her gaze and ours; she sees that the figure who startled her was her reflection, so do we, and we both relax.

The joke that's played on us alone occurs when Lila examines Norman's room. Again, Hitchcock cuts from Lila looking to what Lila sees: Norman's bed, a stuffed doll, a record of Beethoven's *Eroica* Symphony on Norman's phonograph. Lila takes a book off the shelf and

FIGURE 4.25 During her exploration of *Psycho*'s old, dark house, Hitchcock uses the shot/reverse shot to trick both Lila (Vera Miles) and the viewer, as she frightens herself with her own reflection in the mirror

FIGURE 4.26 When Lila looks through Norman's room, Hitchcock again uses the shot/reverse shot sequence to play a joke. Lila Crane examines Norman Bates's room. Her gaze is caught by something

FIGURE 4.27 She goes to the bookcase, pulls out a book, and looks at it. As she is about to turn the page . . .

FIGURE 4.28 There is a reaction shot—a shot of her reacting to what she sees

FIGURE 4.29 But, instead of cutting to the point-of-view shot that would show us what she sees, Hitchcock cuts to an action occurring elsewhere in the motel, where Sam (John Gavin) is confronting Norman (Anthony Perkins). We never get to see what's in the book (*Psycho,* 1960)

registers the fact, which we see in the reverse shot, that the book has no title on its spine. She looks at the pages and registers surprise tinged with a bit of horror in the reaction shot that follows. But Hitchcock refuses a final reverse shot. He does not show us what Lila has just seen in the book. For a moment, the suture is cut, and we are left on our own.

The shot/reverse shot convention is such a powerfully established part of the institution of making and watching cinema that a clever filmmaker can tinker with it to provoke a specific reaction. But the tinkering is rare enough, especially in Hollywood cinema. Its normalization is what allows filmmakers to work quickly and within budget and us to understand the narrative easily and quickly without our attention being diverted by the way the narrative is formed.

CONVENTION, CULTURE, RESISTANCE

It is important to note that ideology is at work in the construction of the classical style. Most film viewers have assented, across our culture and, increasingly, across the world, to what film is supposed to be and not supposed to be—what it should look like and, to a large extent, what it should say. They have agreed that film is the transparent communication of story: no work should be involved in getting access to that story, and no conscious process of reading and interpreting that story should be required. Film should give all and demand little. It should not, as we mentioned earlier, be demanding, or "deep." A film may be serious, even troubling. But in all but the rarest of instances, it should somehow relieve the trouble it has caused and redeem its characters and, if possible, its viewers. There are many levels of assumptions here, and they need to be unpacked.

As I have said, the work of imagination, no matter what its face—painting, music, novel, or film—is not a simple mirror image of reality, pure emotion, or pure story. Imagination requires mediation, of color and shape, of sound (carefully, even mathematically determined, in the case of music), of words, of moving images and the ways they are edited together. In all cases content—story, characters, emotions—is never simply there, waiting for us to see it. Content is generated by the form and structure of the imagination's work and is specific to the kind of work being done. The form and structure of painting are different from that of novel writing or filmmaking. In all cases, some kind of interpretive work is involved on the part of the viewer or listener. On some level, reading is involved, reading in its most general sense of engaging the form of a work, comprehending it, interpreting it, comparing it with other, similar examples of its kind, contextualizing it, in short, making sense of it. Sense is not a given. It must be made.

Making sense out of film is not automatic. We have to learn how to read shots and cuts and the narrative images they create. But this job is easily and quickly accomplished at an early age. Around the turn of the twentieth century, early filmmakers had to begin learning how to make images and editing legible but invisible, how to structure them so that they would be easy to read and the stories they told immediately comprehensible without us being conscious of the mechanisms that create them. "Learning," though, as I pointed out, is not quite precise, because early filmmakers did not have a body of knowledge to absorb. "Intuiting" is better, because these filmmakers were really guessing, in a haphazard manner, how image and narrative structure would work best. By the late 1910s, their guesswork was largely done. They had accomplished a task they had not even known they were beginning: the creation of a universal, legible structure of image, movement, and narrative that would dissolve into pure story in front of its viewers. The components of that structure have not changed very much. They are, with rare exceptions, routine and repeated in film after film. As with any routine, the more we do it, the less we are aware of it, and the more automatic our responses to it become.

When we watch a film, we are part of a great process of assent to its presence and wholeness, even though it is absent and made up of fragmented shots, which are themselves most often put together at different stages of production and then edited together after shooting is done. The assent is an ideological event: what we *want* to see and what we are *asked* to see are mutually agreed upon and take precedence over the "reality" of what we are actually seeing so that we usually do not question it—or even see it. Earlier, we defined ideology as the way we agree to see ourselves, to behave, and to create the values of our lives. Here we can expand that definition of ideology to include the idea of, as one writer put it, assenting to the "obviousness" of things. We take the conventions of cinematic form as "obvious" and therefore—as we are doing here—have to work through their obviousness to the structures that create the effect of that "obviousness" in order to understand how they work and how we respond to them. Shot/reverse shot structures and over-the-shoulder dialogue sequences have to be parsed like a sentence in order to see their artificiality and understand how they work their "obvious" forms on us, without our even being aware.[3]

With this in mind, we can understand that under the ideological banner of pleasure without toil, of leisure activity that demands only a positive emotional response, filmmakers and filmgoers have been joined in the process of making images and stories that are immediately understood and enjoyed, so immediately that they appear there, ready-made and unique—obvious—even though they are not there and are made with a great deal of artifice, put together in bits and pieces, and so far from unique that they have been repeating themselves, form and content, for well over a century. No other dramatic, visual, or narrative form uses these conventions (although they have been modified for use in comic strips and have been varied for television), nor does anything like them exist in ordinary experience. No one leaps from one side to the other when watching two people talking. But the conventions are so strong and ubiquitous that the first thing a filmmaker usually does when he wishes to explore alternatives to the Hollywood continuity style is refuse to do over-the-shoulder shots or obey the 180- and 90-degree rules.

Continuity cutting is an industrial standard, like driver-side and passenger-side doors on a car, like the exact tolerances that enable a nut and a bolt to fit together. Like any standard, continuity cutting creates functionality and universality and becomes the means that permit filmmaker and audience to ignore the details of structure while they go about the work of communicating emotions and advancing a story. From the principles of shot construction and continuity cutting, narrative is generated and a story is told. The key element is that the story is told with the least interference from the structure that creates it. Creative energies and viewer comprehension need not be absorbed with formal complexity because the form, as complex as it is, is so conventionalized that viewers look through it, as if observing a story unfolding on its own.

As we saw in the example from *Psycho*, an innovative director may exploit these techniques and make them yield different responses. Most filmmakers do them by rote. As viewers, we are so acculturated to these compositional and cutting techniques that we don't know they are happening—which is exactly the point. To film a dialogue sequence is to create an over-the-shoulder cutting pattern. Therefore, to watch a dialogue sequence is to watch the over-the-shoulder, shot/reverse shot cutting pattern. We take it as a given and essentially don't notice it—we see right through it. More precisely, we don't respond to the cutting except to move within its secure and comforting pattern, imagining ourselves between the glances of the participants on screen.

The classical Hollywood continuity style is incredibly economical. Since every filmmaker must know how to shoot a dialogue sequence, or a suspense sequence, or a sequence in which a woman looks at a man and knows she's in love, the setups (lighting, camera position, marks on the floor where the actors need to stand) are relatively easy to make. They are shot simply and inexpressively in a shallow space, with bright, even **high-key lighting**, the camera set quite still at eye level to the characters. Much of the narrative burden is carried by the dialogue. The rest is carried by facial gestures, body language, props, and other elements of the **mise-en-scène**, all of which are fit to make a sequence and entire film. Almost always, they are determined by a thousand such sequences made in other films.

Fragmenting a sequence into many different shots makes it possible, as we've seen, not to have all the actors present at the same time or the entire set built at once. If an intense confrontation between a good guy and a bad guy in a warehouse calls for individual shots (one-shots) of each character threatening the other, only the character in the particular shot need be present. Someone out of camera range (usually the person responsible for keeping track of the continuity from one shot to another) can read the lines of the good guy while a shot is made of the bad guy yelling threats and brandishing his gun. The two parts of the sequence can be cut together in the editing room where a better reaction from one of the actors, taken at a different time or even from a different scene, can be cut in if needed. Making a **master shot** which takes in the entire scene and then creating **coverage**, shooting the sequence from different angles and making numerous takes of those angles, ensures that the film can be put together to the **producer's** liking, in line with conventional cutting procedures in the inexpensive confines of the editing suite. As long as attention was paid to where the eyes of each of the antagonists were looking, as long as the lighting was consistent and nothing changed in the background—a clock, for example, which must not be permitted to indicate the passage of shooting time but only the passage of narrative time—the **editor** can match movement, dialogue, and sound so that the intercutting between the two characters will be subordinated to what they are saying.

As we've seen, the economy of the continuity style operates on the side of reception as well as production. As viewers, we have been so acculturated to the style's nuances that a mere exchange of glances, edited across the gaze of two characters, can tell us volumes. Suspense and horror films, for example, depend absolutely on a character's look of surprise or fright that prepares us to expect to see the object of this agitated gaze. That object can be shown in the following shot or a few shots later. But shown it must be to close the circulation of the look, the expectation, and to satisfy that expectation. Even new cinematic ideas quickly become conventionalized when they prove popular.

Contemporary thrillers and horror or science fiction films made in the classical style may use an expressive dark-blue, smoke-filled lighting for nighttime. Some horror films use exaggerated point-of-view shots to allow us to "see with" the eyes of the monster. Steven Spielberg does this in *Jaws* (1975), where we assume the point of view of the shark. But these, too, have all become conventions; we expect to see them and we know what they mean when we do. These elements of the classical style have become, like all the others, invisible and, at the same time, heavily coded. Especially in the horror film, we are wise enough about these codes to laugh at their obviousness, even while enjoying them: the recent *Scream* films (Wes Craven, 1996, 1997, 2000, 2011—see Figure 6.18) and *I Know What You Did Last Summer* (Jim Gillespie, 1997, Danny Cannon, 1998) series, as well as *The Blair Witch Project* (Daniel Myrick, Eduardo Sánchez, 1999), depend upon our understanding of the codes, the **genres** that are formed from them, and our continued willingness to be taken in by and enjoy them.

On one level, we take no notice of them, but on another level, these conventions communicate to us, succinctly, economically, what we need to know to understand the story being told and to feel the emotions that must be felt. When the camera dollies in to a close-up of a character whose eyes are slightly raised and, after the dolly-in, there is a dissolve with wavy lines from one shot to another, we know what's coming: a dream, a daydream, a memory, or a fantasy sequence (see Figure 4.1). Someone steals into an apartment or underground parking garage and hides in the shadows. A woman follows, going about her business, looking for her keys, as if nothing has happened. Our gaze is privileged by so many other sequences just like this that we see and know more than the woman does. Trained to move across the cuts, we know that women in dark spaces inhabited by a villain unseen by them are vulnerable. We experience unease and fright in anticipation of what might happen. No matter what is going on in the rest of the story, this combination of shots tells a story of its own. The characters' point of view doesn't matter, only ours. Whenever a camera moves around in an arc or rapidly dollies forward toward an object, our emotions surge (perhaps because the camera is otherwise so often still). Facial expressions or body movements, edited in counterpoint to each other, tell volumes. A nod of a head, a stiff smile, parted lips, narrowing eyes, hands held up to a wide-eyed face with mouth agape; a shot of a hand moving down toward a pocket; shoulders hunched or hands held away from the body; a head buried in open hands or a hand cupping a chin—these and dozens of other stock movements and gestures make up a rhetoric of narrative codes used by film and we will examine and illustrate them in Chapter 6.

GENDER

Gender drives many cinematic conventions. Gender-specific stereotypes of the strong man saving the weak and passive woman informed the early development of cross cutting—the editing of captivity/rescue sequences by intercutting shots of the woman in peril with shots of her approaching rescuer. In general, the structure of the gaze in film is really the structure of the male character and of the male viewer, gazing at the female character, who is built into the narrative as the object of desire. In the words of critic Laura Mulvey, she carries the quality of "to-be-looked-at-ness." The exchange of looks in film is very often erotic, and so the structure of the gaze drives the narrative, drives our emotions, and propels the characters across the cutting and into each other's arms. Even small gestures are gender marked, and much narrative material is expressed through the gender of the person who uses it. Only women put their hands up to their faces to express horror, fear, sadness. Men may jerk their shoulders back or put an arm out—often a protective arm if a woman is with him. A man will allow his head to fall on his forearm in a moment of stress or pull it down between his shoulders to express anger. Women cast eyes upward for a variety of sexually related reasons; men work their mouths, usually in a self-contained smile or smirk. Men may raise their eyes, but usually as a look of annoyance. In almost every instance, from the editing structure to the slightest movement of an actor's arm or face, form dictates content and almost always sexual desire dictates both. We will examine the codes of gesture and facial expression more fully later in our discussion of film acting.[4]

CODING

Directed by the looks of the characters and, on a higher level, by the structure of looks and cuts that are used uniformly over all of cinema, the viewer needs to be shown and told quite little.

Events, responses, emotions, narrative movements become coded. Having seen films and television, we know how to read the structure. Like a computer code, it runs our responses and, within given limits, can be assigned variables. While it would be absurd to say that *all* films are alike, that they all communicate the same meanings and garner from us exactly the same response, we can say that the ways they order our responses, code them, and communicate them are indeed quite uniform, so much so that radical variations from the established patterns become visible to us and are accepted or rejected to the extent that they disturb us with their visibility. A large part of this coding process occurs generically, that is, according to the film's genre, and this will be discussed at length as we proceed. But much of it also is the result of cutting and composing.

Viewers and reviewers remarked how director Quentin Tarantino played with narrative chronology in his 1994 film *Pulp Fiction*. Chronology is an important aspect of the classical style, and it has not advanced very far from Aristotle's classic notion that dramatic narrative construction should consist of a beginning, middle, and end. (The French filmmaker Jean-Luc Godard once commented that Aristotle was quite right: narrative should have a beginning, middle, and end, but not necessarily in that order.) A film narrative must proceed along a recognizable path of development and must come to closure. Any dissonance, any disruption to the lives of the characters generated at the beginning and worsened toward the middle, must be resolved by the film's end. *Pulp Fiction* seems to disrupt this movement. The end of the very first sequence of the film, in which the two gunmen are caught in the middle of a hold-up in a diner, takes place at the end of the film. In the middle of the film, one of the gunmen, John Travolta's Vincent, is shot to death, coming out of a toilet—meaningless, violent death being a main narrative anchor of Tarantino's movies. There he is, alive again, at the end of the film in a sequence the beginning of which we have already seen.

RESPONSES TO CONVENTIONAL CUTTING

The structure of *Pulp Fiction* is less radical than jokey and actually helps Tarantino tie up his film and leave audience members less queasy than they might have been given all the violence. It gives Vincent a reprise, while also sending him back to the toilet in an attempt at ironic counterpoint to the event that occurred earlier and to further emphasize the anal references throughout the film. It also offers a mock redemption to Samuel L. Jackson's Jules, who decides to leave his life of crime and take up religious work. The minor break in narrative continuity is amusing, only provocative enough to make an audience curious. And it has an antecedent in Stanley Kubrick's early work, *The Killing* (1956), a heist film that is constructed in a complex overlapping time scheme. Other serious efforts are found in the work of some filmmakers, most often from outside the United States, where experiments began early and still continue. There is, for example, a British film called *Betrayal* (David Jones, 1983), written by the playwright Harold Pinter, whose narrative runs backwards, starting at the end and ending at the beginning. A similar experiment occurs in Christopher Nolan's *Memento* (2000), which we will examine in more detail in Chapter 7. Mike Figgis's *Time Code* (2000) breaks its narrative into four quadrants on the screen, using sound to focus the viewer's attention on one or the other of the four interlocking events taking place. In the classic *Last Year at Marienbad* (1961), by the French director Alain Resnais, normal continuity cutting is made non-continuous, and the entire convention of linear chronology in film narrative is called into question. Any reverse shot, in this film about the uncertainty of memory, could possibly take place at another time than the shot that preceded it and therefore not be a reverse shot in the normal sense at all.

Other experiments involve the intercutting of various narrative strands in multi-character stories. D. W. Griffith pioneered this technique in *Intolerance* (1916), where four stories, taking place in four different historical periods, are interweaved. But in Griffith's film, the stories are independent of one another except for their general theme. A contemporary, more complex version of this is found in two films by Robert Altman, *Nashville* (1975) and *Short Cuts* (1993). Here, the stories of a large cast of characters are intercut so that the characters' lives intersect. The narrative time scheme is linear, but within that linearity coincidental meetings and chance encounters create complex canvases of emotional turmoil. Though the editing in Altman's films is mostly invisible, they still break with the classical Hollywood style by asking us to follow multiple narrative arcs, some of which are concluded, others left without satisfactory closure. They are all tours de force of intricate editing. Similarly, Paul Thomas Anderson's *Magnolia* (1999), Paul Haggis's *Crash* (2004), and Alejandro González Iñárritu's *Babel* (2006) weave together multiple narratives, cross-cutting between them as their stories become entangled with each other.

EISENSTEINIAN MONTAGE

Other alternatives to the classical style, classical continuity, and conventional narrative development have occurred throughout the history of film. They were occurring even as the classical style was in the process of inventing itself. One important moment occurred when continuity cutting itself was challenged as the best, the only, way to make a film. This moment occurred at a time of political turmoil. The Russian Revolution of 1917 unleashed enormous creative energies across the arts in the new U.S.S.R. Revolutionary artists were driven by a desire to make aesthetics, culture, ideology, and politics interact on a visible, formal level and make them accessible to as many people as possible.

In filmmaking, artists such as Lev Kuleshov, Alexander Dovzhenko, Vsevolod Pudovkin, Sergei Eisenstein, Dziga Vertov, and Esther Shub looked to editing—or **montage**, as it is more accurately called when applied to their work—as the means by which the raw material of film, the shot, could be turned into a statement charged with revolutionary energy. They looked closely at Hollywood films, particularly at D. W. Griffith's, to find out how they worked. What they discovered was that the continuity cutting being developed in the West was a form that led to reconciliation or redemption: men rescued endangered women, bad guys were overtaken by good. There was always climax and closure, in which "good" prevailed. In *Intolerance*, Griffith was not averse to having Jesus and the angels descend over the scene to close the narrative and unify it for eternity. The revolutionary Soviet filmmakers had something else in mind. They were looking for perception, not redemption; they wanted to pass on the charge of history to their viewers, not the calm of eternity. They found the way through montage.

Eisenstein in particular was fascinated by the ways in which montage could be used as an aesthetic and an ideological tool. In his films (*Strike*, 1925; *Battleship Potemkin*, 1925; *October*, aka *Ten Days That Shook the World*, 1928; *Old and New*, 1929; *Alexander Nevsky*, 1938; *Ivan the Terrible*, 1943, 1946) and the essays he wrote about them, he formulated a structure of filmmaking that was more than montage; it was an attempt to generate the pulse of revolutionary history in his viewers.

Eisenstein believed that the basic unit of film structure was not the shot but at the very least two shots cut together. The process of cutting shots together was not to be an operation that repressed the visibility of what was happening in the name of continuity. Rather, montage was a collision of shots hurled at the viewer. It was to be visible, legible, and powerful, a way of making the viewer sit up and take notice. Eisenstein's filmmaking colleague, Dziga Vertov—who, among many other films, made twenty-three issues of a newsreel called *Kino Pravda* between 1922 and 1925 and *Man with a Movie Camera* in 1929—referred to his own method of filming and editing as the "kino eye"—the cinematic eye. "Dziga Vertov believes in the kino eye," said Eisenstein. "I believe in the kino fist!" (see Figure 9.7).

Battleship Potemkin

For Eisenstein, the shot was raw material and montage the film artist's tool that allowed him to cut images together in ways that would cause conflict and visual dissonance. Eisenstein would play shots off one another in order to make the viewer see something greater than the individual shots alone. A montage sequence might be built from the rhythmic or dynamic elements of the individual shots: conflicting diagonal lines, the movement of figures in one shot placed against an opposite movement in another; conflicting ideas, a woman calling for peace and calm cut against the chaos of advancing soldiers and hysterical crowds. This interaction makes up part of the montage pattern of the great "Odessa Steps" sequence in *Battleship Potemkin*, in which the Czarist navy attacks civilians on shore in retaliation for a mutiny aboard one of their ships. The sequence builds from shots of the people of Odessa demonstrating support for the mutiny to the attack itself, which is rendered in rapid, often shocking cuts of gunfire, the crowd, a lone woman carrying her dead child up the steps as soldiers march with their rifles toward her in the opposite direction. Masses of people, soldiers, civilians, seen collectively, in groups, one, a few, or many, moving in opposite directions and cut together in a montage that defines the outrage of the attack and its brutality.

In the most famous montage in the film, which has been parodied by Woody Allen in *Bananas* (1971) and Brian De Palma in *The Untouchables* (1987), not to mention the crazy *Naked Gun 33⅓: The Final Insult* (1994), a woman with a baby carriage at the top of the Odessa steps is shot by the troops. As the sequence proceeds, and the montage returns to her every few seconds, she sinks lower to the ground. But these successive shots are not in continuity with one another. That is, each time we see a shot of her falling, she is not in exactly the same position as she was in the previous shot. Usually, she is in a more upright position than she was at the end of the last shot. The suspense and agony of her fall are therefore discontinuous, stretched out, repeated.

Working against the codes of continuity cutting being developed in Hollywood, Eisenstein refused to indulge in an illusion of linear time, replacing it instead with an emotional time, the time of suspense and of thought, extending the woman's fall so that the viewer understands the enormity of the crime against her (echoed elsewhere in the Odessa Steps sequence by a brief and stunning shot of an old woman in close-up, who, having exhorted the crowd to reason with their attackers, is shot in the eye). As the woman finally falls, she loses her grip on the baby carriage, which, finally, is released to roll down the steps, against the tide of the oncoming troops and the fleeing crowds, in a montage of accelerated speed toward destruction.

Eisenstein's was a cinema of ideas and huge political emotion, in which the conflicting patterns of images attempt to represent the conflict of history itself—a Marxist history of class struggle, the overturning of oppression, and the victory of the proletariat. Eisenstein wanted nothing less than to give cinema the form of dialectical materialism, that philosophy of history which sees events and ideas churning in conflict with each other, negating one another, creating new syntheses, constructing the new out of conflicting elements of the old. Nothing suited Eisenstein

FIGURES 4.30–4.33 In the Odessa Steps sequence of Sergei Eisenstein's *Battleship Potemkin* (1925), a woman with a baby carriage is shot. Each time Eisenstein returns to her, she is in a slightly higher position than she was in the previous shot, until she finally falls and the baby carriage goes down the steps. These images are selected from a larger montage

better than to create Soviet montage as the dialectic to Hollywood editing. His ambitions outstripped political reality. Eisenstein visited America in the late 1920s, shot footage in Mexico, and negotiated with Paramount Pictures to make a film of Theodore Dreiser's novel *An American Tragedy.* He lost ownership of the Mexican footage, and his ideas and politics were too radical for Paramount, which reneged on the deal. He returned to a Soviet Union in the throes of a violent retrenchment. The arts were undergoing the revisions of Socialist Realism, a state-ordered aesthetic that cut back formal experimentation and promoted a seemingly transparent representation of worker and peasant heroes. Eisenstein had already run afoul of Stalin, who was partially responsible for stopping his Mexican film. This **avant-garde** Communist filmmaker— who also happened to be gay and Jewish, working in an anti-Semitic, homophobic culture and finding himself suddenly in an anti-avant-garde political atmosphere— was permitted to make fewer and fewer films. He spent much of the rest of his life writing and teaching.

FIGURE 4.34 In *Nixon* (1995), Oliver Stone plays a variation on Eisensteinian techniques. These two images follow each other. The first is in color, the second in black and white. The juxtaposition represents Nixon (Anthony Hopkins), here delivering a self-pitying political statement—"you won't have Nixon to kick around anymore"—visualizing how his internal and external lives are fractured from each other

Eisenstein and Oliver Stone

Eisenstein's films have left only the most sporadic influence on Russian cinema or any other. His style can be recognized in some of the **documentary** films of the 1930s, including those financed by the American government, films such as Pare Lorentz's *The Plow That Broke the Plains* (1936) and *The River* (1937). In Hollywood, Eisensteinian montage was mostly turned into another variety of special effects and then largely forgotten. But his films and his theories of montage remain an important force in the history of cinema as a response to the Hollywood style. Flashes of Eisenstein briefly broke out in the cutting styles of MTV music videos (hardly a revolutionary form) and, in more interesting ways, in the work of Oliver Stone, especially in *JFK* (1991), *Natural Born Killers* (1994), and *Nixon* (1995). Here, as Eisenstein did, Stone cut against temporal expectations. He repeated a motion or a character's comment. Like Eisenstein, he turns time into an emotional and political force, a way to express an idea rather than a simple trajectory for the story to follow.

THE NARRATIVE OF THE CLASSICAL STYLE

Despite Eisenstein and so many other exceptions which demand viewer attention and response, the classical style holds sway. It speeds narrative along and places us squarely in the story. But, in an interesting way, Hollywood conventions tell another story. In many ways the classical style constitutes its own narrative. It tells its own story of stimulus and effect, action and reaction, our desire to see and respond to the continuous stream of images and movements, characters, and stories that satisfy our seemingly endless desire for cinematic stories. The formal devices of the classical style communicate meanings, transitions, elements of story that are repeated from film to film. Facial expression, hand and body movements, props, camera movement, lighting, and cutting patterns are used over and over again to ensure that we understand perfectly what is going on. The curious and fascinating thing about all of this is that these repetitions of style and gesture are not taken as a joke when they are seen in context. When have you ever said, "oh, no, not another over-the-shoulder dialogue sequence"? Unless they are self-conscious, stilted, their timing is off, or some other ineptitude is committed by the filmmaker, or they are being used to parody their own conventionality, as in those recent horror films, we simply ingest them as part of the flow of the story being told. We are not about to laugh at or question something that helps us so easily understand what's going on in the scene and in the film. We are not about to laugh when these stock gestures and movements are carrying us forward through a story that has captured our attention to itself and away from the ways it is being created.

The classical style is therefore invisible and highly visible at the same time. Its visibility and invisibility can play counterpoint. A film dependent on ordinary structures of shot/reverse shot, eye-line matches, conventionally expressive gestures may suddenly indulge in a surprising camera movement or an unusual spatial composition. A filmmaker may wrench the invisible into the foreground by exaggerating a gesture or movement, as Hitchcock does with the **cross tracking** effect in which a character in motion is intercut with a point-of-view shot of what she is looking at, also in motion, or with the leap to a high angle shot that he so often uses to express the diminished, vulnerable state of a character who has just made a terrible discovery or is in grave danger. As we've seen, some filmmakers, in and out of the Hollywood system, make up new codes, give new meanings to movement and gestures, shots and cuts, or turn the old ones on their heads. Orson Welles and Stanley Kubrick use tracking shots to turn space into expressive containers of their characters' loss of power and diminishment. Oliver Stone revived Eisensteinian montage to mold time, character, narrative, and culture into alternative views of history. Some directors are boldly breaking the 180-degree rule. As the cliché says, rules are made to be broken; in film, rules are only as strong as the filmmaker's desire to make things as ordinary as possible.

WORKING CREATIVELY WITHIN AND AGAINST CONVENTIONS

All this indicates that although the classical style remains triumphant, it is not invulnerable. Not every filmmaker depends solely upon shot length and shot content to articulate the narrative space of his films. Some directors combine the shot and the cut together to create a mise-en-scène of space and time that enables them to develop narrative subtleties. This, in turn, permits the viewer to comprehend a range of meaning and emotion in the frame and across the cut. In subsequent chapters, we will discuss a number of individual filmmakers, American and from abroad, concentrating on their styles as well as the stories they tell with those styles. This will allow us to see how filmmakers use the basic building blocks of cinema to create unique, imaginative works that prove that conventions and rules exist for two purposes: to permit the Hollywood system to work smoothly and to allow filmmakers of imagination to break the rules and explore the boundaries of cinema.

FURTHER READING

For an interesting analysis of very early film and audience response, see Jonathan Auerbach, *Body Shots* (Berkeley, Los Angeles, London: University of California Press, 2007).

In addition to Thomas Elsaesser's collection of essays, *Early Cinema,* cited in Chapter 2, two other books present a broad and stimulating examination of the early developments of the classical Hollywood style, concentrating on the development of cutting and narrative patterns: Noël Burch, *Life to Those Shadows,* trans, and ed. Ben Brewster (Berkeley and Los Angeles: University of California Press, 1990); and Tom Gunning, *D. W. Griffith and the Origins of American Narrative Film* (Urbana and Chicago: University of Illinois Press, 1991). For early editing, see Stephen Bottomore's essay "Shots in the Dark—The Real Origins of Film Editing" and André Gaudreault's "Detours in Film Narrative: The Development of Cross-Cutting," in Elsaesser's *Early Cinema.*

An excellent treatment of sound in cinema can be found in Rick Altman, ed., *Cinema/Sound* (New Haven: Yale French Studies, 1980) and *Sound Theory, Sound Practice* (New York: Routledge, 1992).

There are a number of essays and books that discuss the ideology of the classical Hollywood style. Two excellent and accessible essays are Robin Wood's "Ideology, Genre, Auteur," in *Film Theory and Criticism,* pp. 592–601. Bill Nichols, *Ideology and the Image,* cited in Chapter 1, is another good resource. For a detailed history of the classical Hollywood style, see David Bordwell, Janet Staiger, and Kristin Thompson, *The Classical Hollywood Cinema: Film Style and Mode of Production to 1960*, cited in Chapter 2.

For the male gaze, read Laura Mulvey, "Visual Pleasure and Narrative Cinema," in *Visual and Other Pleasures* (Houndmills, Basingstoke, Hampshire: Macmillan, 1989).

Eisenstein's essays are collected in two volumes, *The Film Form: Essays in Film Theory,* ed. and trans. Jay Leyda (San Diego: Harcourt Brace Jovanovich, 1977); and *The Film Sense,* ed. and trans. Jay Leyda (New York: Harcourt Brace Jovanovich, 1975).

A classic work on films made against the grain is Amos Vogel, *Film as a Subversive Art* (New York: Random House, 1974).

SUGGESTIONS FOR FURTHER VIEWING

Jean-Luc Godard, whose films will be discussed in Chapter 8, worked assiduously to counter the classical Hollywood style. See, for example, *My Life to Live* (*Vivre sa vie*, 1962).

The films of director Tony Scott offer dynamic examples of rapid editing. For example *Domino* (2005), *The Taking of Pelham 1 2 3* (2009), and *Unstoppable* (2010).

Derek Cianfrance's *The Place Beyond the Pines* (2012) does interesting things with narrative form and classical cutting.

Independent avant-garde filmmakers often use rapid cutting, sometimes a frame a second. Stan Brakhage is a major practitioner whose work is available on a Criterion DVD.

Recent turns on the horror film include films made in Japan and remade in the U.S., for example *Ringu* (Hideo Nakata, 1998) and *The Ring* (Gore Verbinski, 2002).

NOTES

1 Porter's 1903 film *The Life of an American Fireman* had been considered the "first" film to intercut sequences. In fact, a more reliable print of the film was discovered in which the scenes were linked in a linear fashion, leading to the conclusion that the intercut version was a *later* edition, made by someone after intercutting had become the norm.

2 The notion that cutting on a look to the thing looked at will create the appropriate emotional response is an old one. The story of the "Kuleshov effect" has it that, in the early 1920s, the Russian filmmaker Lev Kuleshov took a strip of film showing a neutral close-up of an actor. He then intercut that shot with one of a plate of food, a coffin, and children playing. When the film was shown, people were amazed at the versatility of the actor, who showed hunger at the food, sadness at the coffin, pleasure at the children. The standard work on the concept of the "suture," the stitching of the viewer's gaze into the narrative, is Daniel Dayan's "The Tutor Code in Classical American Cinema," in *Film Theory and Criticism* (New York: Oxford University Press, 2009), pp. 106–117.

3 The concept of "obviousness" is from Louis Althusser, "Ideology and Ideological State Apparatuses," *Lenin and Philosophy*, trans. Ben Brewster (New York and London: Monthly Review Press, 2001).

4 Laura Mulvey, "Visual Pleasure and Narrative Cinema," in *Visual and Other Pleasures* (Houndmills, Basingstoke, Hampshire: Macmillan, 1989), 14–27.

CHAPTER 5

The storytellers of film I

Who makes movies? We've looked at the structural stuff of which film is made, at the economics that are part and parcel of the structure, and at the work of a few **directors**—and will look at more, especially at those who have gone beyond the Hollywood style, in a later chapter. But, especially when dealing with Hollywood film, there is often no one creative entity, no single author that we can name, as we can with a poem, painting, or piece of music. In the world of criticism, the very concept of the individual creator has come under examination in recent years. Some theorists hold that the notion of human individuality in general is just that, a notion: individuality isn't a thing that every person automatically has, hard-wired into the brain, but an idea that a culture creates and maintains about itself and its members: a cultural construct.

One of the **dominant fictions** of movies and the culture at large is the importance of the individual and "individual freedom." Films are always telling us stories about the process of discovering and "being true" to ourselves, to the individuality we each have. But recent thinking holds that this is just part of a story we have been telling ourselves over the past six centuries. What we think of as individuality is really a complicated set of social relationships, in which "I" and "you," "we," "them," and "it" are continually shifting arrangements or positions that we all take up from moment to moment according to where we are, to whom we're speaking, or about whom we're speaking. The self, in other words, is neither innate nor permanent. The individual really is a shifting thing. The "I" writing this book is not exactly the same "I" watching *Bridesmaids* (Paul Feig, 2011), teaching a class, or complaining about life to a friend. In fact, all the "I's" I am are constructed over a long life of being in the world, a "you" to the person talking to me, "he" to someone talking about me. Individuality is a function of moment and the

FIGURE 5.1 Travis Bickle (Robert De Niro) addresses all his imaginary enemies in Martin Scorsese's *Taxi Driver* (1976)

place. Think of Travis Bickle's "You talkin' to me?" in dialogue with his reflection in *Taxi Driver* (Martin Scorsese, 1976), creating for himself the image of an angry, aggressive man.

If this is true about individuality in general, what can we then say about individual creativity? The theories that tell us that individuality and subjectivity are cultural formations rather than objective realities are powerful and persuasive precisely because they take culture and history into consideration. They counter individuality with larger forces in which the individual is one particle, always being altered. But even if all this is true and individuality in the abstract is a cultural and ideological formation, we still believe in its existence and have proof of it whenever we or others act. After all, we do feel, think, and create. Therefore, we can consider various ideas about the individual: individuality is a shared, cultural belief; acts, including creative acts, performed by an individual are always also formed by many forces, internal and external. A creative work—including and especially the creative work of filmmaking—has in fact many authors, including the audience and the culture that surrounds and infiltrates it, the moment in which it was made, the economic forces that put it into shape, the **genres** and conventions that nourish or diminish it. Individual contributions are finally determined when they are discovered *in* the work, or a collection of works by one hand, rather than beforehand. The author is, in a sense, created backward from the work to the person.

With this in mind, we can ourselves work backward to discover what some individuals do in making a film possible on the production and creative side, always keeping in mind that these people were a part of and partly created by the historical and cultural moment in which they worked. This will be useful because, if we understand the individual contributions to a film, we can continue to understand that a film does not come out of nothing but is the result of craft, calculation, and—sometimes—art, all of which are the result of human activity. We can understand as well that creative imagination need not be thought of in the romantic sense, as the unique working of an inspired individual, creating alone and calling upon the forces of solitary emotions. We can understand imagination as a collective event, the result of a collaborative project.

COLLABORATION AS CREATIVITY

Collaboration is the core of cinematic creativity. From the most independent filmmaker to the largest studio production, people work together, divide the labor, contribute their particular expertise. There may be one single, guiding intelligence that integrates or orchestrates all the collaborations, or there may be many. In the early 1930s, in the face of growing criticism about the amount of sex and violence in their films, the studios instituted an internal censoring office, called the Hays Office after its first President, Will Hays. The Hays Office vetted every script to make certain its strict moral codes (the **Production Code**, as it was known) weren't compromised. Today, the ratings office of the MPAA (the **Motion Picture Association of America**) often demands cuts in order to give a film an acceptable rating. And there are forces on the economic level: the power of the box office, which is the representative of the audience and its willingness to pay. In the studio days, the responses of preview audiences often determined how the **final cut** of the film would look: what scenes needed to be reshot; how the editing might be changed for greater effect. Today, focus groups are used to gauge audience response. We must understand, once again, that the Hollywood imagination is an economic system, an economics of the imagination. And this system now works across the world, infiltrating the filmmaking of other countries where individual creativity used to be more easily identified.

Filmmaking began in America as the work of what we like to call rugged individualists, despite the fact that Edison was a company that created many things besides film. In Chapter 2, we discussed how William K. L. Dickson, an employee of the Edison factory in the United States, and the Lumière brothers and Georges Méliès in France worked to invent the apparatus of filmmaking, film distribution and exhibition and developed some of the basic **narrative** structures that survive to this day. Early in the twentieth century, other individuals battled (sometimes physically) with the goons that Edison sent out to protect his equipment patents, and finally set up shop in Los Angeles. For a while, production in Hollywood and New York was the work of individual filmmakers working with small companies, developing and helping to invent their craft. D. W. Griffith was one of them. In collaboration with his **cinematographer**, Billy Bitzer, and working for five years for the Biograph Company, he made major contributions to the development of the **continuity style**. He then struck out on his own to create *The Birth of a Nation* (1915) and *Intolerance* (1916), two films that solidified the position of film as a social and cultural form.

But such independence was short-lived. Even Griffith understood the economic advantage of incorporation, of joining his work to that of a larger economic entity. In 1919, along with Charlie Chaplin and two other enormously popular actors, Douglas Fairbanks and Mary Pickford, he formed United Artists, a studio whose main purpose was to distribute the independent productions of various filmmakers. The arrangement never worked to Griffith's economic advantage—he was hopeless when it came to money—but it is indicative of what was happening to filmmaking at the time. The economics of production absorbed the imagination of individuals, ultimately allowing it only to push against its constraints. The **studio system** evolved as a means of industrializing the imagination—making it economically viable—and turning individual activity into the collaborative effort that enabled industrial filmmaking.

As in any manufacturing effort, speed and efficiency, established with the least cost, are essential in the mass production of film. The studios became self-contained entities, with facilities, technical staff, **producers**, actors, writers, composers, directors, all working within their sound stages, all of them under contract. Some of these workers, from electricians to writers to directors, formed unions, and as a result, clear divisions of labor were marked out. (If you are a fan of credits, you might notice the line at the end of many current films, whose story may be set in a U.S. city, indicating that the film was in fact shot in Toronto or elsewhere in Canada, in an attempt—this the credits don't say—to escape American unions and taxes. They are called "runaway productions.") In short, every filmmaking job has on-site personnel to carry it out, and every staff member knows his or her job. There is a temptation to reduce the outcome of this work to the relative anonymity of its mass production. Indeed, early criticism of popular culture did just that, implying that work of the imagination produced in a factory, for mass consumption and economic gain, could not attain the complexity and status of art. But an opposing argument would be more valid, that a new kind of art, created out of collaboration, emerged from the studio system. We can also argue that there are indeed important individuals involved in cinema's creative process, individuals who develop and use their talents in a collaborative effort in which individual skill becomes absorbed in collective effort and assumes anonymity in the resulting films.

CREATIVE CRAFTSPEOPLE

On the level of the physical apparatus itself, a number of people plied their skills and talent in the studios, and still do, though more often as independent suppliers: electricians, camera operators, sound recorders, set designers, painters, greens people, film lab technicians, and (today) **digital colorists**, assistant editors. These people rig the lights; set up the camera (as well as turn it on and off and keep it focused on the scene being shot); dress and paint the sets; put up greenery; create the special effects that synthesize actors, backdrops, painted scenery, models, and computer graphics into a single image; develop the film or "wrangle" the digital files; mix the sound; assist in the complex process of editing the **shots**; and then transfer the **edits** onto the master negative or digital file that will be used to strike exhibition prints or be placed on a hard drive.

The cadre of individuals that has been growing since the mid-1990s includes computer graphics designers, software engineers, members of a large variety of companies like George Lucas's Industrial Light and Magic and smaller digital effects houses like Rhythm and Hues. Again, a look at the credits at the end of a film will reveal just how many people are involved in the digital work that has taken over from the studios' special effects units. These artists create backgrounds and characters, starting from wireframes or the motion-captured images obtained by placing nodes on actors and capturing their movement on a computer. They add shading and shadow, color and detail, building up a digital effect or an entire digital **mise-en-scène** (see Figures 1.2, 2.13, 5.5–5.7).

The following are among the most important of the creative personnel and craftspeople who collaborate on a film's production. I've tried to group them in relationship to both their importance and whether the role they play takes place during or after a film. However, I've left screenwriters and producers near the end. They are not simply "craftspeople," and their creative talents are crucial to the entire process of a film's creation.

CINEMATOGRAPHER

The cinematographer, or **director of photography** (nicknamed the DP), is among the most important creative people involved in the production of a film. He (in a notoriously male-centric industry, there have been few women cinematographers, though recently their numbers are growing slightly) handles the lighting, chooses the appropriate lenses and film stock, decides on all the elements that determine the size of the image, its spatial qualities, density, color values or gray scale that will result in an image appearing, first on the film or digital file, and finally on the screen, when the light of the projector is focused through it. If the director wants a **wide shot** or to introduce some distortion into the image, the cinematographer may choose to put a 28-mm lens on the camera, which will produce a very wide, deep effect. The cinematographer will choose the correct combination of lights to produce the appropriate mood of the scene, and will even tinker with the color to create an overall visual effect—though today the cinematographer, director, and digital colorist will manipulate color after the film has been shot. The cinematographer and the director make the **compositions** we analyzed in a previous chapter.

At his best, the cinematographer is a close collaborator with, and an adviser and consultant to, the film's director. In the days of the studios, some major stars had their own cinematographers assigned to them in film after film. William H. Daniels, for example, worked consistently with Greta Garbo, MGM's glamorous and mysterious star of the 1930s, because Garbo and the studio felt he could light her to best advantage. This was not an act of mere vanity but of the studio's and the audience's desire to have a consistent image of its star, which the cinematographer could best provide (see Figure 3.12).

In some instances, a cinematographer exercises extraordinary creative license, expanding upon what the producer or director wants to see on film. This was the case in Gregg Toland's collaboration with Orson Welles on *Citizen Kane*. Toland signed on to the project because he felt that working with a new, young, imaginative director would give him the opportunity to experiment, which it did. He ground and coated new lenses, experimented with lighting, and figured out ways to create the deep field compositions and Expressionist style that both he and Welles envisioned. The way *Citizen Kane* looks—its dynamic articulation of space, light, and composition—had more influence on filmmaking than anything else since *The Birth of a Nation*, which like many of Griffith's films was photographed by Billy Bitzer (see Figures 3.8–3.10, 4.8–4.13). In *Citizen Kane*, that articulation is the result of the Welles and Toland collaboration, which Welles credited (see Figures 3.34–3.41). *Citizen Kane* is one of the very few American studio films in which the names of both the cinematographer and the director appear together at the end of the film. (Another is John Ford's 1940 film *The Long Voyage Home*, also photographed by Gregg Toland.) Some would argue that on many films the cinematographer should get similar or even greater credit as the originator and developer of a film's visual style.

In many instances, directors and cinematographers remain together as a team. This is more usual in Europe and in the **post-studio period** in American filmmaking, where it is less likely that individuals will be assigned to a film and more likely that writer, director, and producer will choose whom they want to work with. Among the most famous director–cinematographer teams in film history was Swedish director Ingmar Bergman and cinematographer Sven Nykvist. When Bergman quit his filmmaking career—after he had become the most widely known European director of the 1960s and 1970s—Nykvist began working in the United States. He lends his rich style, in which he sculpts fine details of interiors in carefully modulated light and shadow, to an unlikely film, the popular *Sleepless in Seattle* (Nora Ephron, 1993).

Alfred Hitchcock worked with one cinematographer, Robert Burks, on twelve films. Hitchcock, who predetermined and **storyboarded** the structure of every shot before filming ever began, needed a cinematographer he could depend upon to accurately interpret his instructions. Carlo Di Palma, who photographed two of the Italian director Michelangelo Antonioni's extraordinary color films, *Red Desert* (1964; see Figure 3.28) and *Blow-Up* (1966; see

FIGURE 5.2 Cinematographer Robert Richardson likes to reflect light from hands, as in this shot from Quentin Tarantino's *Django Unchained* (2012). See also Figures 1.1, 1.4, 1.5, 1.6, 4.34 for images shot by Richardson

Figure 2.17), had worked with Woody Allen on most of his films until the late 1990s. In Hollywood today, some directors and cinematographers remain close collaborators: Steven Spielberg and Allen Daviau and Janusz Kaminski are a primary example.

Today, when so many films are shot digitally and all go through a **digital intermediate** stage for coloring and image correction, cinematographers have had to adapt to new technologies while maintaining a consistent style. As in the studio period, a few stand out: Robert Richardson's work on *JFK*, *Natural Born Killers*, *Nixon* (Oliver Stone, 1991, 1994, 1995; see Figures 1.5, 1.6, 4.34), *Hugo* (Martin Scorsese, 2011), and Tarantino's *Inglourious Basterds* (2008; Figure 1.1) and *Django Unchained* (2012), among many others. Wally Pfister's work with Christopher Nolan on his Batman films gives them a texture in which light and dark set their brooding mood and tone (see Figures 7.19–7.24). Phedon Papamichael's black and white cinematography for Alexander Payne's *Nebraska* (2013; see Figure 3.49) demonstrates that even in a time when all films are made in color, a talented cinematographer can return to an older palette of graytones with a renewed sense of discovery. Similarly, as we see in Figure 3.23, the Polish cinematographers Ryszard Lenczewski and Lukasz Zal create an almost painterly image in black and white for the film *Ida* (Pawel Pawlikowski, 2013).

EDITOR

The cinematographer is the individual with great responsibility for the overall character of a film's visual style. He or she works closely with the **production designer**, the digital effects department, and, especially, the director. The cinematographer is present throughout preproduction and shooting. After shooting, when everyone but the director and producer have gone on to other projects, the **editor** assembles the pieces of footage into a coherent whole, in the variety of ways discussed in the previous chapter. Editing has been one of the few major roles in filmmaking open to women, a fact that is all the more significant because the editor is the person who gives a film its final shape, makes it conform to the will of the producer (during and after the studio period) or the director (who, in the post-studio period, helps oversee the editing process). But the primary talents of an editor are far more important than passivity and patience.

A film editor needs great dexterity, a sharp eye for detail and rhythm, and a prodigious visual memory.

In the studio days, the editor was the one who managed to structure pieces of exposed film into the patterns of the continuity style. Under the producer's eye, she made the film the audience would see—and often remade it if previews went badly. Few directors, then and now, shoot with the precision and economy that could dictate and control the final shape of their material. Many directors still shoot a great deal of footage, and very few "edit in the camera," thereby giving the editor little footage and therefore fewer choices. Producers are nervous when there is either too much to work with, or too little to cut, giving the editor too much material, too much to put into comprehensible shape, or too little.

Many films are saved in the editing process. Bad acting can be covered up by cutting away from a talentless actor, or even a good actor who could not deliver a particular line, to something or someone else in the scene, with newly recorded lines dubbed in to create a better performance. Many films are invented during editing. The violent stunts of action films or the fights in a martial arts film are constructed by editing. **Sequences** in which people knock each other down, fall off buildings, bash their cars into each other are constructed out of shots—themselves manufactured out of various image elements and computer graphics—carefully cut together to create the illusion of fists meeting faces and bodies falling through glass doors.

In most films, the various pieces of shots put together in the editing process do not necessarily have to have occurred at one time. If a **close-up** is needed, for example, and a good one is discovered earlier in the shooting than in the finished film, an editor will cut it in. This, by the way, should not imply that all editors and their directors succeed. There are films whose editing is completely flatfooted, containing shots that last too long after they should have been cut; editing decisions that create no sense of coherent action; no narrative rhythm. When these missteps occur and there is no attractive mise-en-scène to hold the eye, then none of the constituent parts of film hold together or hold our interest. But all this needs to be put in the larger perspective of the continuity style, in which all motion, progression, movement, and unity are illusions built out of the ways in which small fragments of exposed film are cut together—and that is the editor's task. In that sense, the editor's work is predetermined by the overriding imperatives of continuity cutting and she can only work small variations on the expected editing patterns.

In American cinema during the studio period, editors have had major responsibilities for executing the cutting style of the studio, and some important editorial names are attached to their respective companies, rather than to directors: Viola Lawrence at Columbia, George Amy at Warner Brothers. Dorothy Spencer worked at a number of studios on films as different as *Stagecoach* (1939), *The Snake Pit* (1948), *Cleopatra* (1963), and *Earthquake* (1974). Like cinematographers, some editors have worked consistently with particular directors: George Tomasini with Hitchcock, Dede Allen with Arthur Penn, Thelma Schoonmaker with Martin Scorsese, Michael Kahn with Steven Spielberg; Angus Wall with David Fincher. Some of these are creative collaborations. In others, the editor helps the director keep his film coherent, and in all cases they provide the narrative structure the audience sees.

PRODUCTION DESIGNER

The production designer (usually called "art director" during the studio period) conceives and elaborates the settings, rooms, and exteriors that together help to give a film its physical texture, its spatial and temporal orientation, and that mark its setting in the past or present as recognizable, even giving it the illusion of being "authentic." If the film takes place in a particular historical era, the work of the production designer—along with that of the costume designer—takes on a special importance. During the studio period, each company had a head production designer—Cedric Gibbons at MGM, Lyle Wheeler at 20th Century Fox, Hans Dreier (who began his career in the late 1910s at Germany's UFA studios) at Paramount, Robert Clatworthy at Universal, for example—who had great responsibility for creating the general style of a particular studio.

Since the days when studios exercised complete control, production designers have developed individual styles and can sometimes be linked with the work of certain directors. There is the careful re-creation of 1930s, 1940s and 1950s spaces and objects that Dean Tavoularis develops in Arthur Penn's *Bonnie and Clyde* (1967) and Francis Ford Coppola's *Godfather* films (1972, 1974, 1990). Cars and dusty Midwestern towns in the former film; tables, chairs, carpets, wall hangings in the latter films are chosen and placed to evoke and represent the domestic space of a certain class and time. In *Godfather I,* a newsstand on the street is arrayed with period papers and magazines, which are laid out as they might have been in the 1950s. A room in *Godfather II* is created to reflect the decorative style of the 1950s and 1960s. In *Apocalypse Now* (1979), Tavoularis creates for Coppola in the Philippines the nightmare jungle of Vietnam.

Recall the dark, fantastic urban future designed by the late Anton Furst for *Batman* (1989). Those sets, consisting mostly of hand-painted **mattes** that were processed into the shots of the film to give them a physical presence, help create the atmosphere of despair and unspoken terror that supplies much of the subtext for director Tim Burton's film. Italian production designer Dante Ferretti has worked on many of Martin Scorsese's films. In Europe, the late production designer Alexandre Trauner began work in the 1920s and helped develop the "look" of French cinema, especially the 1930s school of "poetic realism" that climaxed with Marcel Carné's *Children of Paradise* (1945). He went on to work with Orson Welles on his film of *Othello* (1952) and, in Hollywood, with the German émigré Billy Wilder. Like the work of any good production designer, his design can be detailed and crafted to catch the viewer's attention, or made invisible, not calling attention to itself, but adding incalculably to the director's mise-en-scène.

The 2014 Academy Award for production design went to an Australian, Catherine Martin, for Baz Lurman's adaptation of *The Great Gatsby* (the award was shared with the film's set decorator, Beverley Dunn). The film is a madly overproduced 3D fantasy of the 1920s, and its production design is detailed and appropriately over-the-top. It is interesting to compare the production design of this version of F. Scott Fitzgerald's novel with that of the English designer, John Box, who worked with director Jack Clayton on the 1974 version of the novel (with a screenplay by Francis Ford Coppola). Here the design is more restrained, less flamboyant. Clearly, production design is part of the larger idea the director has for a film and, if the film takes place in an earlier time, influenced by contemporary ideas of what the past might have looked like. In the course of film history, production design has become far more detailed and more or less accurate to the period the film is representing. In the case of Lurman's film, however, the production design is a reimagining of Fitzgerald's world—as, in fact, the design of any film set in the past must be.

Production designers combine the talents of graphic artist, which today includes computer-generated design, interior decorator, architect, art historian, or futurist, to create ideas that—once executed and organized by the set designer, matte painter, carpenter, greens person, and special effects people—fashion a world that the camera can photograph, or the computer generate, and the editor can assemble into a coherent representation of time and place. The production designer readies the space for the actors to inhabit and for the director of photography to film.

FIGURES 5.3–5.4 A comparison of production and costume design in two versions of the party sequence in *The Great Gatsby*. The first, relatively restrained, is from Jack Clayton's 1974 version, the production designed by John Box, costumes by Theoni V. Aldredge. The second is from Baz Lurman's over-the-top 2013, 3D adaptation, production design by Catherine Martin and Karen Murphy, costumes by Catherine Martin

SPECIAL EFFECTS AND CGI

I spoke earlier about the ways in which a shot, in almost any studio film, is built from a number of elements, including **rear-screen projection**, **matte paintings**, blue or **green screen**, and various optical devices that add images to the still undeveloped piece of film. Every studio had a special effects unit, and there have been some individuals who stood out in the field. Since the original *King Kong* (Merian C. Cooper, Ernest B. Schoedsack, 1933), **stop action** photography—photographing the minute movements of a model creature **frame** by frame—became a standard for monster movies and depicting space travel in science fiction films. Ray Harryhausen emerged as leading figure in stop action, famous for his work from the late 1940s through the 1980s, films like *Mighty Joe Young* (Ernest Schroedsack, 1949), *It Came from Beneath the Sea* (Robert Gordon, 1955), *Jason and the Argonauts* (Don Chaffey, 1963), *The Golden Voyage of Sinbad* (Gordon Hessler,

1973), and *Clash of the Titans* (Desmond Davis, 1981). He rose to the ranks of producer on the last two films.

Douglas Trumbull worked with Stanley Kubrick to create the overwhelming photographic effects of *2001: A Space Odyssey* (1968) and later with Steven Spielberg on *Close Encounters of the Third Kind* (1977). He directed *Silent Running* (1972), worked with Ridley Scott on *Blade Runner* (1982; see Figures 4.15, 9.23 and 9.24), and as visual consultant to Terrence Malick on *The Tree of Life* (2011). Like Ray Harryhausen, Trumbull's style in the creation of special effects made him close to an **auteur** of the form.

The movement from optical to digital effects was all but inexorable. The change began in the mid-1980s, when John Lasseter, who went on to direct the first two *Toy Story* films (1995, 1999) and has acted as executive producer on any number of computer-generated animations, created the digital knight in Barry Levinson's *Young Sherlock Holmes* (1985). The figure steps out of a stained-glass window and pursues a priest across a church. The digital knight is a bit awkward and two-dimensional, but nonetheless surprising and effective, and it signaled a change in the creation of special effects that would continue to grow in films like James Cameron's *The Abyss* (1989) and Spielberg's *Jurassic Park* (1993). By the mid- to late-1990s, **computer-generated imagery (CGI)** had replaced most of the older forms of optical effects. As in sound design, few major figures have emerged in this field, mostly because the companies that create the effects, companies like the aforementioned Rhythm & Hues, George Lucas's Industrial Light and Magic, Disney's Pixar, the New Zealand company WETA Digital, founded by Peter Jackson for his *Hobbit* and *Lord of the Rings* films, employ hundreds of people involved in a complex enterprise requiring a great deal of collaborative knowledge and work that combines imagination and computer science.

Computer-animated 3D films, like *Despicable Me* (Pierre Coffin, Chris Renaud, 2010) are enormous undertakings, requiring not only complex software, but the ability of the designers and animators to visualize three dimensions in a two-dimensional space. Old-fashioned animation involved drawing successive "cells" in which the action changed slightly from one cell to the other. Each cell was photographed separately on an animation stand. Computer animation requires generating a figure, either from scratch, or often, as in old-fashioned animation, by **rotoscoping**, having a live action figure filmed and then used as a reference for the computer-generated figure, building paths for it to follow, and marrying it with 3D backgrounds before the whole is transferred to film or distributed as digital files. Special effects films, anything from *Jurassic Park* to the latest *Star Wars* (George Lucas, 1999, 2005, and J. J. Abrams' version in 2015), or *Spider-Man* (Sam Raimi, 2002, Marc Webb, 2012, 2014), in fact any superhero film, mix live and computer-generated figures seamlessly. Gollum in Peter Jackson's *Lord of the Rings* films (2001, 2002, 2003), the tiger in Ang Lee's *Life of Pi* (2012), and Groot and Rocket in *Guardians of the Galaxy* (James Gunn, 2014) are digital creations.

But beyond these special effects and computer-animated films are the domestic **melodramas**, gangster films, and romantic comedies, indeed any of the traditional genres that employ CGI to one degree or another. Their virtuality is not created with models or paint, but with computer code creating pixels on the screen. On a larger scale, we have passed through one major technological change with CGI; we are now moving through a major passage from celluloid using digital imagery to the totally digital, from production design to cinematography, coloring, editing, distribution, and exhibition. Digital artists are the mostly anonymous figures creating this technological and creative shift.

FIGURE 5.5 Director James Gunn shows his CGI animators the expression he wants for the character Groot in *Guardians of the Galaxy* (2014)

FIGURES 5.6–5.7 Actors in blue act out the motions for Rocket and Groot that will later be animated by computer for the finished film *Guardians of the Galaxy*

SOUND DESIGNERS

The coming of sound to film was not an overnight event. Warner Brothers' *The Jazz Singer* (Alan Crosland) did not appear out of nowhere in 1927. The studios had been experimenting with sound for some time, but it wasn't until Warner Bros. found itself in financial difficulties and began looking for a novelty to bring large audiences back to theaters that they offered a full-length silent film accompanied with some synchronized dialogue. "Synchronized" is, of course, the operative term. As I've noted, films always had a musical accompaniment, played by piano or orchestra while the film was running; but making words that match the movement of the actors' mouths was another problem altogether. But it must be emphasized that reaching this point was an incremental process.

Roughly synchronized sound was born at the beginnings of film. Edison wanted sound to accompany his early film inventions, and his film inventor employee, William K. L. Dickson, worked on this in the late 1880s. So did others in Europe. Technical difficulties and lack of interest put sound to rest until the 1920s. There were many experiments of sound on film made during the 1920s—short films with musical interludes, for example—but it took the unexpected success of *The Jazz Singer*, which was originally recorded and distributed with sound on a disk synchronized with the projector, to assure the changeover to all sound. For a while, each studio employed a slightly different technique for sound recording until it was obvious that standardization was necessary. That standard became the **optical soundtrack**, a photographed strip of sound waves printed next to the **image track**, and it made synchronization all but foolproof.

There are few "stars" in the realm of sound recording, few who quite match the renown of some cinematographers or production designers. One reason for this is that sound people are largely engineers and technicians, working quietly to perfect their specialty. They work inventively and largely anonymously. Another reason is that sound has, until recently, never received quite as much attention as the more prominent visual aspect of film. A few gifted individuals have received recognition—Douglas Shearer at MGM, who was prominent in the early years of sound, and more recently, Walter Murch, who did extraordinary sound work for Francis Ford Coppola, especially on *The Conversation* (1974) and *Apocalypse Now* (1979).

The sound technician is responsible, obviously, for recording the dialogue. But even this is not a straightforward process. What dialogue do we hear? How do we hear it? How is dimensionality of sound achieved? In fact, just as the cinematographer must give the illusion of depth to a 2D surface, so too the sound engineer must provide a dimensionality to the soundtrack, which, without it, would be flat and lifeless. Placement of microphones and mixing sound to achieve the right balance and depth is a complex job, as is dubbing dialogue and adding and enhancing sound during editing, supplying background noise and sound effects, which is the major work of recording sound today. Dialogue can be focused by the way it is mixed so that it directs our attention, as much as composition or editing does. In all films, dialogue is mixed to complement or hide the cutting or to keep our attention focused on the shot itself. There are exceptions: filmmakers as different as Orson Welles, Howard Hawks, or Robert Altman mix sound in ways that allow many voices to be heard simultaneously, creating a complex aural canvas to complement the visual one.

These days, most sound, including dialogue, is added during editing, especially with the advent of digital techniques. **Automatic dialogue replacement (ADR)** dubs in dialogue without the dead sound and unsynchronized lip movements associated with the earlier version of dubbing. Dubbing sound after filming is called "**looping**." Digital sound and more sophisticated under-

FIGURE 5.8 This is what a film frame looked like with the image track in the center and the soundtrack running along the side. (Film unknown, possibly from the 1930s)

standing of the ways in which sound, along with music, can affect the ways an audience responds to a film have produced extraordinary sonic effects made up from a variety of found sounds as well as sounds generated by the computer. Think only of the dinosaurs' roar in *Jurassic Park* (Steven Spielberg, 1993). More important, listen beyond the dialogue in a contemporary film. In older films, dialogue was surrounded mostly with silence, unless a scene was outdoors or in a large space or had musical accompaniment. But now there is almost always something there behind the dialogue: **room tone** or **world tone**, to use older film production jargon, refers to the background sounds behind the dialogue. Filmmakers carefully complement the visual atmosphere of the shot with an aural atmosphere, sometimes in the background, heard almost subliminally, but just as often brought forward; sometimes used for shock; always to create an aural space.

Therefore, while the sound technicians and sound editors in the past received a credit at the end of a film, they are now emerging from that relative anonymity. For example, an individual whose name has become a term of art, Jack Foley, was an effects pioneer from the early days of sound film. His name has become an adjective, and you will see it in every film made during the past fifteen or more years: **foley** artist or foley design. More recently, film credits are carrying the name of the sound designer, a term indicating that, like the production designer, there is now someone who will coordinate and build the film's aural structure, from footsteps to specific effects, to the music used and the **ambient sound** that accompanies all the shots and binds them together, helping to create an aural mise-en-scène to accompany the visual.

COMPOSER

Music is the sound that has accompanied film almost since its beginnings, when a pianist played while the silent film ran. In large city theaters, a whole orchestra might provide musical accompaniment to the images. With the coming of synchronized sound, the composer attained a great deal of importance, providing not only a background to the action and dialogue, but the emotional drive of the film, evoking or even signaling the emotions appropriate to the narrative from moment to moment.

Traditionally, the composer of a film's musical track was only peripherally involved with the actual production of the film. He may not necessarily spend a great deal of time on the set. He is not directly connected with the construction of the film's visual elements, as are the production designer and cinematographer. Like the editor, he is more involved with fragments than wholes. The composer may confer with a film's producer and director, read the script, and make some melodies in advance. Even during editing, the director may use some found music to provide a temporary background, until the producer, director, and editor get a sense of the film's shape and the composer steps in to assist, through his music, organizing final narrative and emotional direction.

Only the title score and music for the final credits are written as complete, if miniature, musical compositions. (In the 1950s, a producer might commission a title song for a film to be later sold as a single recording.) The rest of the music is written as "**music cues**," brief snatches of melody, sometimes only seconds long, that are composed to fit sequences or transitions between sequences, to distract from editing effects (or even bad acting the editing can't hide), and in general to create emotional responses from the audience, sometimes greater than the narrative, the mise-en-scène, or the acting can achieve by themselves. Music can carry a film that may be otherwise weak, and in melodramas and thrillers (but not exclusively in those genres) provide cues to us, as viewers, as to when and how to react.

The history of music in film marks some of the major trends in moviemaking and the cultural forces that influence it. During the studio period, composers, like all creative people and craftspersons, were under contract to individual studios. They—like writers, cinematographers, editors, production designers, and directors—were paid labor, who worked under orders from the producer of the film, who, in turn, worked under the studio bosses. Many early composers, such as Erich Wolfgang Korngold, Max Steiner, and Miklos Rozsa, had distinguished composing and conducting careers in Europe before moving to Hollywood and becoming contract composers with various studios. Along with others, such as Franz Waxman and Dimitri Tiomkin, they made their fame and fortune writing for movies. Some worked closely with a single director. Bernard Herrmann, perhaps the greatest screen composer, started his broadcast and theatrical work in New York with Orson Welles's Mercury Players, came to Hollywood with Welles, and composed the score for *Citizen Kane* (1941). He continued working with various directors and in 1956 began an eight-year collaboration with Alfred Hitchcock. His music for Hitchcock is so intensely involved with the narrative images Hitchcock creates that you can listen to a recording of Bernard Herrmann's music and experience the emotions of the film it comes from. Think of the slashing strings that accompany the shower sequence in *Psycho* (1960) and what it might be without them.

Herrmann's work with Hitchcock coincided with the end of the first era of the symphonic score and a period of change in the constitution of the studios. As movie attendance fell during the late 1940s and throughout the following decades, and as contracts with staff and players ran out, the studios changed from complete in-house manufacturers of narratives, with a ready, salaried staff always on hand, to less centralized production facilities and distributors. These days, the studios may assist in initiating a project, provide financing, and distribute the completed product to theaters, but leave the details and the staffing to the individual production group formed for the particular film. By the 1960s, an in-house composer and a studio orchestra were among those dependable, off-the-shelf services studios could no longer afford. The same period saw a rise in popular music—rock and roll especially—and a change in film marketing procedures.

Movie audiences had always been segmented to some degree. Studios produced "women's pictures," more accurately known as domestic melodramas, to appeal to the female audience and action films and Westerns to appeal to men. But, at least until 1946, the studios had an audience they could depend upon—an audience eager for their products. By the 1960s, the studios had to seek out their audience and then discovered that the most attractive group was those between their late teens and late forties. Since this group proved to be a lucrative market, and because pop and rock music were very popular among them, the symphonic score lost favor. Many films since the 1960s use existing pop or rock music as background. Robert Altman's great Western *McCabe and Mrs. Miller* (1971) uses the music of Leonard Cohen in ways that make it so integral to the images that it might as well have been written for the film. Mike Nichol's use of Simon and Garfunkel songs in his 1967 film *The Graduate* played no small part in that film's popularity. Martin Scorsese creates such complex scores out of old rock and roll songs—especially for *Mean Streets* (1973), *Goodfellas* (1990), *Raging Bull* (1980), and *Casino* (1995)—that some have referred to the films as visual jukeboxes. Scorsese's use of pre-existing songs that are contemporary to the period of the film energizes the action and drives the images. At the same time, Scorsese is sensitive to the power of the symphonic score. He commissioned Bernard Herrmann to create the music for *Taxi Driver* (1976). It turned out to be that composer's last and, except for the music he wrote for Welles and Hitchcock, his greatest score. Unsatisfied that Herrmann was no longer available, Scorsese commissioned another older Hollywood composer, Elmer Bernstein, to redo Herrmann's score for his remake of *Cape Fear* (1991) as well as compose original music for many of his later films.

Stanley Kubrick is another filmmaker who relied on pre-existing music. For *2001: A Space Odyssey* he commissioned veteran Hollywood composer Alex North to write a score. But during production and editing, he discovered that classical and modern music by Richard and Johann Strauss, György Ligeti, and Aram Khachaturian was much more effective. The opening sequence of Richard Strauss's *Also Sprach Zarathustra*, with its colossal crescendo, and Johann Strauss's *Blue Danube Waltz* have outstripped their origins and become permanently attached to our responses and memories of that film. The use of Beethoven's Ninth Symphony in *A Clockwork Orange* (1971) plays ironic counterpoint with the film's central character, a violent predator who gets off on Beethoven's music.

Sergei Eisenstein, the Russian filmmaker whose theories and practice of **montage** we discussed in Chapter 4, worked so closely with the composer Sergei Prokofiev on his film *Alexander Nevsky* (1938) that he created a graphical representation for part of one sequence, plotting the dynamics of the music with the dynamics of the shots and the montage.

By the 1960s in the United States, the large studio symphony orchestra all but disappeared, as did the great names of film music composition. In Europe during the same period, some directors still collaborated with individual composers and carried on a sense of textual coherence between image, narrative, and score. Federico Fellini and Nino Rota, Michelangelo Antonioni and Giovanni Fusco, Sergio Leone and Ennio Morricone are some examples from Italy. Ennio Morricone, who wrote the scores for Sergio Leone's great Spaghetti Westerns, such as *The Good, The Bad, and The Ugly* (1966), also composes for American film.

In America, the cycle shifted back to the symphonic score in the late 1970s, partly because of nostalgia, partly because young filmmakers, who had been studying film history, were intrigued by the use of music during the studio period, and mainly because of the successful collaboration

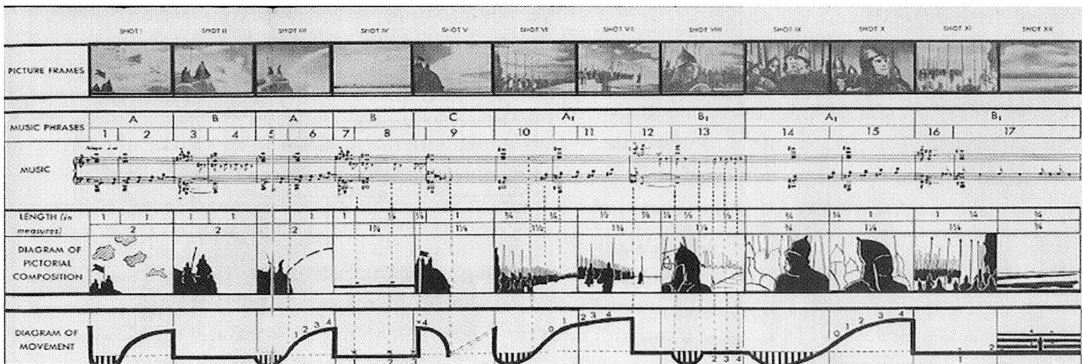

FIGURE 5.9 Sergei Eisenstein worked so closely with the music of composer Sergei Prokofiev for Eisenstein's *Alexander Nevsky* (1938) that he was able to graph how the tonalities of the score matched the composition of the images

of Steven Spielberg and John Williams in *Jaws* (1975) and, subsequently, all of Spielberg's films. Today, whether an elaborate score is prepared specifically for a film or a series of rock or rap tunes are selected for the soundtrack, music remains an important part of a film's narrative flow, part of its emotional dynamic and, in clever hands, an integral part of the film's structure. A film composer can become known for work in many fields, like Henry Mancini, and can also do wildly different kinds of scoring in different media. Danny Elfman wrote the music for the first two *Batman* films and other works by Tim Burton as well as the theme for television's *The Simpsons.* John Williams continues to compose for Spielberg and spent time as conductor of the Boston Pops, and Randy Newman, cousin of the famous Hollywood composer Alfred Newman, has largely turned from writing popular songs to creating musical scores for such films as *Seabiscuit* (Gary Ross, 2003), the *Toy Story* animations (John Lasseter, 1995, John Lasseter, Ash Brannon, 1999, Lee Unkrich, 2010), *Meet the Fockers* (Jay Roach, 2004), and various television programs. The end of the studio period seems to have released the composer into activity in many fields.

The role of the composer is oddly secure, because he can remain somewhat aloof from the production. The composer knows his role, knows that he must write to order. Little is left to speculation or temperament. There is a funny, perhaps apocryphal, story of a conference held many years ago between the famous Russian émigré composer Igor Stravinsky and the studio executive Samuel Goldwyn about the composer's working for films. There was some mutual accord until the studio executive asked Stravinsky how long it would take him to deliver a score. "A year," he responded. The meeting and the collaboration were over. For the composer, like the cinematographer, "individual genius" is subordinated to collaborative imagination. Art is put into the service of making narrative, and everything is subordinated to budget and schedule.[1]

SCREENWRITER

Every film begins with the written word. Yet, despite this truism, the screenwriter's task has not been so clear or easy. The screenwriter is the one figure in the talent pool of filmmaking who, certainly in the 1930s and 1940s, was wracked with doubts, anxieties, uncertainties, self-hatred, and mistrust. There is no great mystery as to why the screenwriter has been such a tormented figure or why we, as viewers, can have little confidence about exactly how much the persons we see listed in the credits as writer or writers were actually responsible for the film in whole or in part.

American and European culture maintain the nineteenth-century image of the writer working in splendid isolation, with complete control over his or her work. Even when subsidiary myths are bracketed off—the Hemingway myth of the brawling, hard-drinking, adventurous writer—we still think of the process of writing itself as being carried out in a hallowed space, where the creator is the controller of his or her production. Most writers believe this story too, even though, like all cultural myths, it is only somewhat true. While much writing is, indeed, done alone, not all of it is (think of coauthorship, even in fiction). And there are few writers who are free of editorial intervention—few whose work gets into the bookstores or on Amazon exactly as it was written, almost as few as there are film directors who see their own version of a film on the screen. There is, finally, nothing very romantic about writing: only people attempting to put good words on paper. If writers and their culture need to maintain their myths of isolated inviolability, film executives know better.

Writers had always worked in film—women screenwriters were particularly active during the silent period, but in the late 1920s and early 1930s, when actors began speaking dialogue, the studios wanted writers to do more than create a story and write intertitles between scenes, or written versions of what the actors were supposed to be saying, and instead write the actual dialogue the actors would speak. Studios had few places to turn to and perhaps, in their male-centered world, felt that their women writers were not up to the job or had the prestige they were looking for. Hollywood, at that moment, was not a great literary Mecca, and the studios began importing often well-known writers from New York—novelists, playwrights, essayists—at high salaries. When these writers arrived in L.A., the studio bosses put them in offices and told them to make words from nine to five. The writers found themselves used as common labor. The studio executives loved it, because, semiliterate as some of them were, they were delighted to have intellectuals under their control. Besides, they were offering a lot of money and expected their control to be heeded.

To add insult to injury, the executives rarely allowed one writer to produce all the words for a given film. The studio bosses enforced the collaborative nature of film on all levels, whether the writers were willing or not. Studio executives often put scripts through many hands, some of them specializing in very particular kinds of writing: comedy dialogue, romantic interludes, dramatic exchanges, mid-story plot and character complications ("**back stories**" in current Hollywood parlance). Some scriptwriters, then and now, are known to be good "script doctors." They don't originate material: they fix the words others have written that a producer or director thinks aren't working or won't transfer well when filmed, or they add extra dialogue where needed. The names of any of these writers may or may not appear in the credits. In fact, the writing credits are the least dependable of all, because so many hands may go into the creating of a shootable script. The screenwriting process echoes the fragmentary nature of the making of the film itself, moving through a "**logline**," or brief summary, outline, character analysis, through screenplay and shooting script, each one filling in the material with various hands playing a role at various points. The process is so rigid, in fact, that budding screenwriters can buy software that will put their ideas and words in the proper form for each stage, though perhaps not help in the imaginative expression of the words.

Some major authors in the past, like F. Scott Fitzgerald, couldn't quite manage the process. The few who could did it on a grand scale. William Faulkner contracted with Warner Brothers and worked with director Howard Hawks on such fine films as *Air Force* (1943), for which he did not receive screen credit, and *The Big Sleep* (1946), for which he did. He asked Jack Warner, head of the studio, if he could receive a special dispensation and work at home. Warner agreed, and Faulkner promptly left Hollywood for his home in Oxford, Mississippi. He wrote scripts for "them"; he wrote novels for himself and his public, and everyone, including himself, profited in many ways from both. This was a rare freedom, but it was not based on Faulkner's fame alone. Rather, it was a demonstration of a half-truth on Faulkner's and a rare amount of good faith, understanding, and self-possession on everyone's part.

Hollywood moviemaking, like any large business enterprise, is not usually based on self-possession and understanding. Power and money are the motivating forces, and power depends upon generating insecurity, resentment, and fear in order to work. That's why writers often felt miserable under the studio system. In the studio days, executives took all of this for granted, but the writers did not. An unpleasant culture was created for them, and many felt they were working in bad faith. But two good events emerged from this. One was the Screen Writers Guild (SWG), a powerful and, in its early days, left-of-center union that the writers formed in the 1930s to help protect their interests, as best they could be protected. During the 1930s, it also provided a base where writers could discuss the political and intellectual matters they couldn't deal with in their films. The second important job of the SWG was and still is to arbitrate what writer gets credit on a film. An interesting example is the list of credits on the entertaining but ill-fated *The Lone Ranger* (Gore Verbinski, 2013). Here there is a fine distinction made between "and" and "&." Screenplay by Justin Haythe *and* Ted Elliott *&* Terry Rossio. Screen story by Ted Elliott *&* Terry Rossio *and* Justin Haythe. One can only imagine the negotiations that went on to determine who got the full coordinate or the ampersand.[2]

Arbitration for screenwriting credits can be amusing for the viewer or anxiety-provoking for the people involved. But we can't lose sight of some of the sparkling writing that went on for the great studio films created between the early 1930s and the mid-1950s, films that prove the old cultural myths wrong: that it is possible to get good writing and strong narrative structure through a group effort. While few films have shining, imaginative dialogue, many of them have good dialogue. Some of it captures the rhythms of the language of the day. (Even though, because of the Production Code, which demanded a strict adherence to guidelines about what could and could not be seen and said in a film, and a general fear of offense, profanity was not heard in film until the 1960s.) Much of it delineates character and propels story and expresses powerful emotions. Abraham Polonsky's dialogue for his film *Force of Evil* (1948) sounds like blank verse. Mardik Martin creates rhythmic street dialogue for Martin Scorsese's *Mean Streets* (1973) and, with Paul Schrader, *Raging Bull* (1980). Alec Coppel, Samuel A. Taylor, and Maxwell Anderson create passionate language for Hitchcock's *Vertigo* (1958). Like the continuity style of which it is an essential part, dialogue becomes integrated within the seamless web of story and action. If a film coheres, the viewer cannot recognize the fragments of writing that come from various hands. Like the editing, like the music, it becomes unified and coherent, part of the story's presence. At its best, it drives the narrative and defines its characters.

There is somewhat less resentment and self-hatred among screenwriters these days. One reason is that there is little innocence left about the process. Most writers who go into the business know that it will be a collaborative event and that egos and romantic myths about independence and control won't work. Perhaps more important, a screenwriter stands to make a great deal of money. A quarter-million dollars is not unheard of for a first effort, millions for an established screenwriter, someone like Robert Towne (the writer of *Chinatown*, Roman Polanski, 1974) or Joe Eszterhas, who was paid three million dollars for his script for *Basic Instinct* (Paul Verhoeven,

1992). David Koepp received four million dollars for his script for David Fincher's *Panic Room* (2002).

The cynical view would be that sanctimony disappears in the face of profit; a kinder view is that more and more writers, who consciously choose screenwriting as their profession, understand what movie writing is all about and are able to join in the collaborative mix we've been discussing, doing their jobs with few fantasies about individual creativity. They *are* creative, but in ways that don't usually fit in with our preconceptions.

PRODUCER

Orson Welles once said that no one can figure out exactly what a producer does. At the Academy Awards, the "Best Film" award is given in the name of the winning film's producer. In the credits of a film, the producer's, or these days producers', title is prominent and subdivided among many individuals: executive producer, coproducer, associate producer, line producer. What do these people actually do? Depending upon a number of factors, a producer is an initiator of projects, a fund-raiser, a deal maker, an administrator. The producer is also a cajoler, a protector of egos, though often enough a tyrannical ego him- or herself. The producer and her associates get the money and represent it. He or she oversees the writing, casting, design, and direction. More often than not, the producer is on the set during shooting and in the editing room when the film is being assembled. All this control bestows a right on the producer to leave an aesthetic mark on the film itself. Even if it's just suggesting a camera angle or an actor's reading, or cutting a few frames or entire sequences during editing, or to get the appropriate rating from the MPAA, the producer likes to think that administrative creativity should also extend to the artistic.

The amount of power that a producer has cannot be underestimated and never is in Hollywood. From the time that Irving Thalberg was appointed executive producer at MGM by Louis B. Mayer in 1923 and reorganized the film production process, demoting the role of director to another contract worker, the producer has been the focal point of the American filmmaking system. Mayer and Thalberg were the ones who helped establish the film studio as an artistic version of the factory assembly line. It worked this way: the studio head, through his executive in charge of production, oversaw production in Hollywood. In New York, the studio owners (sometimes relatives of the studio head) controlled the finances. At the studio, the executive producer worked with the studio head in choosing stories and stars and assigning producers to individual films. Staffing for each production was done according to which writers, stars, director, and cinematographer best suited to the project were available, or whose contracts and schedules indicated that they were in line for some work. The executive producer assigned a producer to each film, and that producer oversaw the day-to-day operations of the film, ran interference for the cast and crew to and from the executive producer and the studio head, and supervised editing. His word was law. His creativity lay in marshaling the forces, getting them to work according to plan and schedule, and conforming the film to the studio's style and standards.

The **producer system** created a perfect hierarchy for order and control. It put someone in charge whose main obligation was to get things done the way management wanted them done. The system mediated and moderated creativity, because the studio's representative was always there to make sure the film was made the studio's way. If this system repressed great flights of imagination, it permitted small ones and, though creating something of a uniform style for each studio, allowed room for variations. From such volume came much mediocrity, but also a certain leeway for experimentation. When Orson Welles was invited to Hollywood by RKO in 1939—

because the studio needed a boost in prestige and revenue—he was offered a multipicture deal with the right to final cut. The film he made would be the film RKO released. It was the kind of contract few directors have received before or since. It was one of the things that made Welles disliked in Hollywood from the start. But, as a recent biography of Welles has pointed out, the studio never totally gave up its control. They insisted on consultation at all times and held the right to cut the films for censorship purposes. Though Welles produced and directed *Citizen Kane*, RKO never gave up anything. RKO threw Welles out when management changed, and his patron, studio executive George Schaeffer, was fired; they promoted a new slogan for the studio: "Showmanship in place of genius at RKO." This made clear, if there was ever any doubt, that experimentation was never safe in the studio system; it only had its moments. Welles was fired after beginning work on a **documentary**, *It's All True*, which he was filming in Brazil for the U.S. government. The editing of his second film for RKO, *The Magnificent Ambersons* (1942), along with the reshooting of its final sequence and throwing out of much wonderful footage, was done by the studio.[3]

In the post-studio period, the producer's role has changed only slightly. While some producers still work for studios and sometimes run them, many are freelances. There are a few women producers, like the action-film producer Gale Ann Hurd, or Emma Thomas, who runs Syncopy Films with Christopher Nolan, the director of the recent Batman films and *Interstellar* (2014). The studios themselves are no longer self-contained factories but part of large, often multinational corporations—like the electronics company Sony that owns Columbia Pictures—that have nothing to do with filmmaking, except that one of their holdings happens to be a film studio. But reduced or not, the studio still has power. Although a producer may no longer have one boss to whom she must answer, she still remains the mediator between the money and the production, which the producer often puts together (though not always: a film can now be organized by an agent, a director, or a star, who will then hire a producer, or, often enough these days in the case of a star, be listed as one of the film's producers).

Unlike the old studio days, few things are "off the shelf" and few personnel are available down the hall or across the lot. An array of service businesses has grown around the filmmaking process: equipment renters, sound recording studios, casting agencies, digital special effects companies, caterers, and powerful talent agencies who represent all those people—writers, cinematographers, composers, production designers, and the like—who used to be under contract. The business of putting together the pieces has become complex, and the producer has to work her way through the complexity and turn out a product that will turn a profit.

Have there been great producers? Certainly John Houseman, who was Orson Welles's producer before Welles came to Hollywood and really was responsible for setting up *Citizen Kane* as well as many other fine films after that, was a man sensitive to the director's work. Currently, we can look at the work of Bob and Harvey Weinstein. They formed their own company, Miramax, in 1979. They sold the company to Disney in 1993 and then formed their own company again, The Weinstein Company. They have had enormous success with semi-independent films, which they produce or distribute, like *Gangs of New York* (Martin Scorsese, 2002), and *Fahrenheit 9/11* (Michael Moore, 2004). They have produced most of Quentin Tarantino's films, from *Pulp Fiction* (1994) through *Django Unchained* (2012). They distributed the curious, fascinating science fiction film *Snowpiercer* (Joon-ho Bong, 2013) and decided to put it quickly into pay-for-view when they understood it would do better there than in theaters.

But, in the end as in the beginning, the producer's creativity is that of a manager. He has to know how to initiate, negotiate, mediate. He must believe that he possesses an excellent intuition of what constitutes popular success and impose that intuition upon the entire production, with the control of a stern administrator. He—or they—has to believe that he knows "what the public wants" and get a film made that delivers it along with what the studio or the distributor wants, in the only form his bosses understand: box office receipts, cable deals, and DVD rentals. If not, Sony, or newspaper mogul Rupert Murdoch (whose News Corporation owns 20th Century Fox), or Time Warner, or Viacom (owners of Paramount Pictures, as well as CBS), or the latest conglomerate—as of this writing—NBC Universal, owned by cable company Comcast (which includes Universal Pictures, the National Broadcasting Company and its many cable outlets) may not want him to produce any more films for them.

We have not quite yet answered the question: Who makes movies? That is, we haven't answered it if we are still looking for filmmaking to fit within the tradition of the creative individual. Even if we can comprehend the idea of collective creativity, that ideological relay switch almost always trips on, forcing us to say that anything made by a group can't be very creative. So we keep looking for answers even though the answers that come along never quite satisfy our longing for the romantic myths of creativity. Still, the cultural desire to find the creative person dwelling inside of and existing as an aura around a work of imagination is very strong, so strong that, without it, a work is in danger of getting no respect. As long as film remains a product of "them," instead of her or him, it is unmanageable by the critical mind; a handle can't be put on it. For film and the study of film to be taken seriously, a single, identifiable author (who is not a manager, a figure held in little respect in intellectual and academic circles) has to be identified. Other figures need to be looked at: actors and the director, the former, whose names are known to everyone watching movies, the second the subject of a notion about the core of creativity.

FURTHER READING

An excellent, though challenging, source of information on the individual subject and its shifting positions is Kaja Silverman's *The Subject of Semiotics* (New York: Oxford University Press, 1983).

One of the best works on cinematographers is a compilation film called *Visions of Light* (Arnold Glassman, Todd McCarty, Stuart Samuels, 1992) available on VHS and (preferably) DVD. It contains good commentary and excellent visual examples. A recent collection of essays is Patrick Keating, ed., *Cinematography* (New Brunswick, New Jersey: Rutgers University Press, 2014).

Two books on production design are Beverly Heisner, *Production Design in the Contemporary American Film: A Critical Study of 23 Movies and Their Designers* (Jefferson, NC: McFarland, 1997) and Lucy Fisher, ed., *Art Direction and Production Design* (New Brunswick, New Jersey: Rutgers University Press, 2015).

Lev Manovich covers in detail the work of computer design in film in his previously cited *The Language of New Media.* The film *Side by Side* (2012), available on DVD, contains many interviews with directors and cinematographers concerning CGI.

Douglas Gomery's *The Coming of Sound: A History* (New York: Routledge, 2005) is invaluable. A collection of essays on theories of sound can be found in Rick Altman, ed., *Sound Theory, Sound Practice* (New York and London: Routledge, 1992).

One of the best books on film editing is an old one by the director Karel Reisz, *The Technique of Film Editing* (New York: Hastings House, 1968).

There is a growing body of work on film music: David Neumeyer, ed. *The Oxford Handbook of Film Music Studies* (New York: Oxford University Press, 2014); Philip Hayward, ed., *Terror Tracks: Music, Sound and Horror Cinema* (London and Oakville Connecticut: Equinox, 2009); Kathryn

Kalinak *Settling the Score: Music and the Classical Hollywood Film* (Madison: University of Wisconsin Press, 1992); Royal S. Brown, *Overtones and Undertones: Reading Film Music* (Berkeley, Los Angeles, London: University of California Press, 1994). For the use of popular music in film, see Jonathan Romney and Adrian Wootton, eds., *Celluloid Jukebox: Popular Music and the Movies since the 50s* (London: British Film Institute, 1995). An annotated bibliography of readings about film music is James Wierzbicki, Nathan Platte, Colin Roust, eds., *The Routledge Film Music Sourcebook* (London: Routledge, 2012). Steven C. Smith's *A Heart and Fire's Center: The Life and Music of Bernard Herrmann* (Berkeley, Los Angeles, London: University of California Press, 1991) is a wonderful biography of the greatest film composer.

A good survey of Hollywood screenwriters is Richard Corliss, *Talking Pictures: Screenwriters in the American Cinema* (New York: Penguin Books, 1975). For some stories about writers in Hollywood, see Tom Dardis, *Some Time in the Sun* (New York and Harmondsworth: Penguin, 1981).

SUGGESTIONS FOR FURTHER VIEWING

Some of the footage from Welles's *It's All True* was put together in a film of the same name (1993).

Examples of the work of some major cinematographers include *The Long Voyage Home* (John Ford, Gregg Toland, cinematographer, 1940); *Body and Soul* (Robert Rossen, James Wong Howe, cinematographer, 1947); *Border Incident* (Anthony Mann, John Alton, cinematographer, 1949); *Dr. Strangelove, or How I Stopped Worrying and Love the Bomb* (Stanley Kubrick, Gilbert Taylor, cinematographer, 1964); *McCabe and Mrs. Miller* and *The Long Goodbye* (Robert Altman, Vilmos Zsigmond, cinematographer, 1971, 1973); *The Conformist* and *Last Tango in Paris* (Bernardo Bertolucci, Vittorio Storaro, cinematographer, 1970, 1972); *The Godfather* (Francis Ford Coppola, Gordon Willis, cinematographer, 1972); *Seven* (David Fincher, Darius Khondji, cinematographer, 1995); *The Matrix* (Andy Wachowski, Lana Wachowski, Bill Pope, cinematographer, 1999) *Gone Girl* (David Fincher, 2014, Jeff Gronenwith, cinematographer).

The work of composer John Williams can be heard in all of Steven Spielberg's films, as well as the *Star Wars* series and *JFK* (Oliver Stone, 1991).

Similarly, Bernard Herrmann composed the music for Alfred Hitchcock's films from *The Trouble with Harry* (1955) to *Marnie* (1964). He also scored *Citizen Kane* (Orson Welles, 1941) and *Taxi Driver* (Martin Scorsese, 1976), among many other films and television shows.

The work of the studio composer Miklos Rozsa is at its best in Billy Wilder's *Double Indemnity* (1944).

French composer Georges Delerue has written many scores, most notably for Bertolucci's *The Conformist,* and Maurice Jarre has been equally prolific, perhaps most notable for *Lawrence of Arabia* and *Dr. Zhivago* (David Lean, 1962, 1965).

Richard Sylbert was an important contemporary production designer in such films as *The Graduate* (Mike Nichols, 1967); *Rosemary's Baby* and *Chinatown* (Roman Polanski, 1968, 1974).

NOTES

1 The notion of the "visual jukebox" is from I. Penman, "Juke Box and Johnny-Boy," *Sight and Sound 3*, no. 1 (April 1993), pp. 10–11. Stories of Stravinsky in Hollywood can be found in Otto Friedrich, *City of Nets: A Portrait of Hollywood in the 1940s* (New York: Harper & Row, 1986) and John Baxter, *The Hollywood Exiles* (New York: Taplinger, 1976).

2 Here is a story that demonstrates how difficult it sometimes is to depend upon a screenwriting credit. In 1995, a film named *Bulletproof Heart* appeared. The screenwriting credit was given to one Gordon Melbourne, a Canadian. In fact, the film was written by Mark Malone, an American. The bogus name was put on the film in order to register it for a Canadian tax shelter. (See Josh Young, "The Case of the Elusive Screenplay Writer," *New York Times*, May 21, 1995, pp. H11–12.)

3 The story of Welles's *It's All True* is told by Catherine Benamou, *It's All True: Orson Welles's Pan-American Odyssey* (Berkeley and Los Angeles: University of California Press, 2007). Welles's original material for *The Magnificent Ambersons* has still not come to light. Robert L. Carringer has done a "reconstruction" in print, *The Magnificent Ambersons: A Reconstruction* (Berkeley: University of California Press, 1993). Information on Welles's contract at RKO is from Frank Brady, *Citizen Welles: A Biography of Orson Welles* (New York: Scribners, 1989).

CHAPTER 6

The storytellers of film II

Acting

Screen acting is a complex affair with an interesting history, involving not only what happens on screen—how dialogue, the gaze, body language, camera placement, and lighting inflect and communicate important **narrative** information—but also what happens off screen. Acting and celebrity go hand in hand. Stories about the lives of movie stars are sometimes as interesting as what happens on screen. Early in the history of film, both filmmakers and audiences were uninterested in the entire issue of the creative individual behind the camera and focused on the visible figures in front of them. Actors are, after all, the most recognizable, most promotable, sometimes the most memorable elements of a film. They create an illusion of embodiment, of giving story flesh and bone. They are turned into simulacra of our desire, representations of what we think we want to be and know we want to see. At their best, they become one aspect of a film's **mise-en-scène**, articulating a film's larger vision. Historically, they constitute our collective imaginary, the cultural repository of images of beauty, sexuality, romance, strength, and power. Filmmakers, who at first (long ago, at the turn of the twentieth century) tried to keep their players anonymous so they wouldn't have to pay them a lot of money, soon had to yield to public curiosity—public *desire*—and actively promote the people who turned out to be their most valuable commodity.

METHODS OF PERFORMANCE

There are a variety of film acting styles, and they have a history. But there is one consistent fact about screen acting that holds true from the early development of narrative storytelling to the present: it does not constitute a performance of the kind we know from stage acting. The creation of a performance in film does not involve a coherent, developing representation of narrative-driven emotion, at least not on the actor's part. A performance is created partly by the actor and partly by the film's editing structure and the **director** who, even more than the actors, must hold a concept of the performance in his or her mind. The actual process of film acting is part of the **continuity style**, composed out of fragments in the editing room. During filming, the actor actually "performs" in relatively short spurts and in multiple takes of relatively short pieces of business, usually shot out of sequence. (Stanley Kubrick demanded his actors deliver take after take after take until, all inhibition and resistance gone, they produced the effects the director recognized as the ones that he needed.)[1] Though an actor may deny this, it is the **producer**, the director, and the **editor** who create the final performance, if we define performance as a process in which a character and situation are developed. The director, producer, and editor emphasize what they want and hide what they don't, sometimes by no more complicated means than cutting away to something or someone else when a particular character is talking, or mixing parts of various **takes** of a **scene,** or cutting a **reaction shot** into one scene that might have been filmed for another. The director, **cinematographer** and composer can provide accents to a scene by lighting, camera angle, and movement when the scene is being filmed and by music and editing rhythm when the film is being assembled.

Delsarte

The actor must be able to call upon his or her tricks or talents for emotional delivery on demand and without a real sense of connection to what was going on before or may go on after, when the **final cut** is assembled. Like the composer, the actor creates on demand and in disconnected bits—a look, a gesture, a piece of dialogue. The continuity style creates the illusion of physical and emotional presence and continuity. The actor's body is given, if not flesh, then the immediacy of appearance, and it expresses the illusion of emotions deeply felt.

The ways in which those emotions are delivered have changed over time. Silent screen acting depended on broad, often exaggerated gestures. Before the advent of film in the nineteenth century, a systematic notation for stage actors was developed by a Frenchman, François Delsarte, as a coded description of facial expressions and bodily gestures that were carried over into the early period of silent film. A variety of emotions could be represented according to prescribed rules, down to the minute movements of the eye, as in the examples in Figures 6.1–6.2.[2]

As we will see, movements of the eye remain key to communicating emotions in contemporary film. And as these charts and directions indicate that acting, at least in the Delsarte system, was not natural, spontaneous, or realistic. The actor was expected to code her eye movements and gestures according to plan and the audience to respond in an all but Pavlovian way. One set of emotions called forth one set of gestures and gazes in what amounted to two scripts: the script for the play itself and the script for the appropriate gestures that the play script called for.

Even the earliest silent film **melodramas** toned down the exaggerated gestures of stage acting. Filmmakers and their actors understood that there was a greater intimacy between the screen and the viewer than there was with a live stage production. But still there were only the eyes, the face, and the body to communicate meaning. Some filmmakers, like Erich von Stroheim, were able to keep exaggerated movement to a minimum. D. W. Griffith modulated from film to film the way his actors would emote with face and body. The coming of sound meant that, of course, pantomime was over, but as actors began talking, another kind of exaggeration occurred,

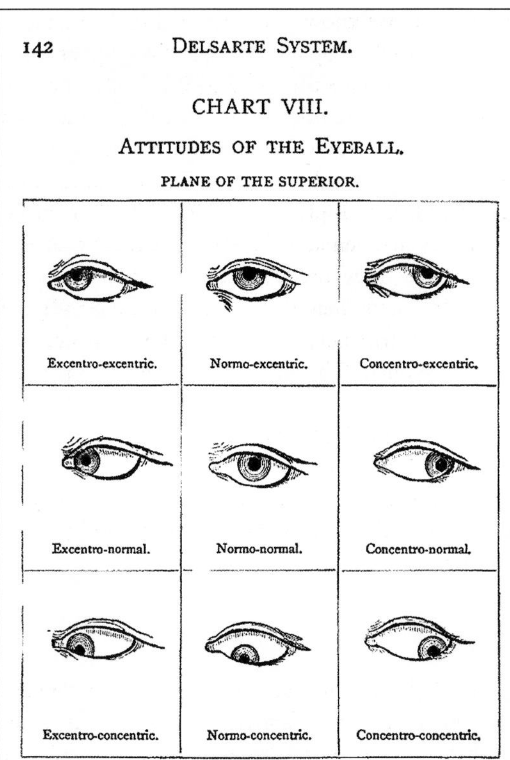

142 DELSARTE SYSTEM.

CHART VIII.

ATTITUDES OF THE EYEBALL.

PLANE OF THE SUPERIOR.

Excentro-excentric.	Normo-excentric.	Concentro-excentric.
Excentro-normal.	Normo-normal.	Concentro-normal.
Excentro-concentric.	Normo-concentric.	Concentro-concentric.

PLANE OF THE INFERIOR.

N. B.—Plane of the superior indicates the upraising of the eyeball, Plane of the Inferior the depressing of the eyeball. To object—the eyeball turned to the object. From object, vice versa.

SIGNIFICATION AND ACTION OF THE EYEBROW.

I.

Action: nor.-nor.

Signification: calm serenity of mind; vital and mental force inactive.

Description of action: brow normal.

II.

Action: con.-nor.

Signification: calm reflection; vital force concentrated; mental force full, but serene.

Description of action: ex. of brow depressed.

III.

Action: ex.-nor.

Signification: anxiety, calm suffering; vital force exalted, mental force quiet.

Description of action: ex. of brow raised.

IV.

Action: nor.-con.

Signification: timid or sterile mind; vital force in repose, mental force dormant and depressed.

Description of action: con. of brow lowered.

FIGURES 6.1–6.2 These reproductions from a book on Delsarte indicate how minutely even the movements of the eyebrows were coded in order for an actor to get the most expressive effects on stage

this time of the voice. Acting in many of the films of the 1930s is declamatory, due partly to the fact that stage actors were imported from New York (along with writers to create their dialogue) and partly to the new sound technologies that, in the late 1920s and early 1930s, caused microphones to be placed in static positions on the set—hidden in a telephone or vase of flowers—and the camera enclosed in a sound-proof baffle. Even as the technology became more limber, the camera more mobile, and sound engineering more flexible, acting in some films of the decade seems aimed at the audience rather than at the other characters within the film.

The Method

By the 1940s, the declamatory style changed to a more intimate exchange of dialogue between the characters in a film. Even gesture and the gaze of eyes are quieter and more contained. The actors seem to be talking to each other rather than the viewer. The 1950s saw another major change in acting styles that originated in Russia at the turn of the twentieth century. The Moscow

FIGURE 6.3 "You're tearing me apart!" James Dean as Jim Stark emotes in Nicholas Ray's *Rebel Without a Cause* (1955)

FIGURE 6.4 Marlon Brando as Terry Malloy in Elia Kazan's *On the Waterfront* (1954)

FIGURE 6.5 And as Don Corleone in Frances Ford Coppola's *The Godfather* (1972). See also Figures 8.5, 11.6

Art Theater was founded by Konstantin Stanislavski in 1898, and he developed an acting style directly opposite to the Delsarte system that came to be known as "The Method." Stanislavski's Method was imported to the United States by Lee Strasberg, who founded The Group Theater in the 1930s and, under director Elia Kazan, The Actors Studio in 1947. Method acting is meant to be spontaneous, interior, driven not by external coded responses, but by an actor's "emotional" or "affective memory" peculiar to the particular actor and his or her own experiences. A Method actor is asked to call upon his or her own life to inform the role and to live the character rather than merely create a notion of who the character might be.

The results of The Method are theoretically more intense and "realistic" than conventional acting, but in fact appear more mannered. Watch James Dean—a Method-trained actor who in the 1950s made only three films before his early death—in Nicholas Ray's *Rebel Without a Cause* (1955). Dean's performance is studied, halting, as if he were thinking through every sentence before uttering it. Similarly Marlon Brando, who did not study The Method, was directed in his early films (like *Streetcar Named Desire* in 1951 and *On the Waterfront* in 1954) by Elia Kazan. Brando's gestures and mannerisms, the subtle ways in which he moves a hand, tilts his head, inflects his despair, the tonalities of his vocal delivery are recognizable whether he plays a working-class union guy or, despite his dyed hair and prosthetic jowls, Don Corleone in *The Godfather* (Frances Ford Coppola, 1972).

The Method is no more or less "realistic" or authentic than any other acting style. All actors attempt to inhabit the role they play; Method actors attempt to extrude their character from within with certain mannerisms that are sometimes subtle, sometimes exaggerated. But, despite the fact that it is as artificial (in the sense of "artfully made") as any other acting style, it has had a great influence on films beginning in the 1950s. From Brando to De Niro, Scarlett Johansson and Barbra Streisand, Christopher Walken and Christoph Waltz, actors trained in The Actors Studio or, in Brando's case, directed by Elia Kazan, have brought distinctive styles to the creation of characters on the screen. The Method is by now deeply absorbed into screen acting, so much so that we are liable to find the acting in pre-1950s film artificial in the usual sense of the word.[3]

CULTURES OF ACTING

No matter what their training, actors create characters. Many of them have the talent to create not only a role within a film but a style that is carried from one film to another. These are the ones whose presence and style may either transcend the subservience to directorial and editorial manipulation or allow it to be used to everyone's best advantage. Some screen players create personae, versions of themselves that are made up of attitudes, gestures, and facial expressions so coherent and maintainable that they become instantly recognizable and sometimes more interesting than the particular film they are in. When this is combined with the elaboration of a cultural myth about the actor's persona, a story built up in the collective popular consciousness from the actor's roles and publicity, a figure is created that transcends his or her individual films. John Wayne is more than the character in this or that film; he is, even dead, an evolving idea of a hero (we will note Wayne's career in Westerns in Chapter 9). Marilyn Monroe transcends *The Seven Year Itch* (1955) or *Some Like It Hot* (1959, both directed by Billy Wilder), becoming part of the culture's collective sexual insecurity and its mythologies of the sexually active, self-destructive woman. Others take up somewhat less cultural space, but demand our attention in and out of their films nonetheless: Humphrey Bogart, Henry Fonda, Katharine Hepburn, Robert De Niro, Kevin Spacey, Julia Roberts, Bruce Willis, Samuel L. Jackson, Cameron Diaz, Ben Affleck, Meryl Streep, Russell Crowe, Leonardo DiCaprio, Christian Bale, and many others are actors with a reputation for intensity, grace, a peculiarity of gesture and gaze that draws us to them from film to film. So also the great comedians, old and recent: Charlie Chaplin, Buster Keaton, the Marx Brothers, Laurel and Hardy, Jerry Lewis, Alan Arkin, Rodney Dangerfield, Jack Lemmon, John Candy, Joan Cusack, Steve Martin, Steve Carell, Jason Segal, Seth Rogen, Jonah Hill, Adam Sandler, Maya Rudolph, Vince Vaughn, Melissa McCarthy.

Some actors can both transcend and inhabit a role. As I noted earlier, Marlon Brando had a recognizable class of attributes that he carried over from film to film. Brando was a camera-riveting presence—the way he is able to focus the viewer's gaze on the character he is making and the processes he's using to make the character foreground his presence as the central point of the film's mise-en-scène. The cliché about "taking up a lot of space" is quite appropriate to this kind of acting. He was, with the help of a good director, able to put his resources in the service of the narrative but transcend it at the same time. He could develop a role and allow the viewer to observe how he develops it. He anchors the narrative and then moves with it. But, while doing all of this, he focuses every action within the film and every perception of the viewer on his presence.

FIGURE 6.6 Marilyn Monroe in Billy Wilder's *The Seven Year Itch* (1955)

FIGURE 6.7 Meryl Streep plays a haughty fashion designer in *The Devil Wears Prada* (David Frankel, 2006)

FIGURE 6.8 Samuel L. Jackson has made his career playing tough, strong, loud characters. Quentin Tarantino changed his character into a kind of parody of his usual roles, here as a house slave in *Django Unchained* (2012)

FIGURE 6.9 Comedians from the silent period used their faces and bodies to communicate. This is Charlie Chaplin (on the right) in *The Gold Rush* (Chaplin, 1925)

FIGURE 6.10 Buster Keaton used objects of the physical world for his comedy, here in *The General* (Keaton, Clyde Bruckman, 1926). See also Figures 2.4 and 3.27

FIGURE 6.11 A clutch of contemporary comic actors: James Franco, Danny McBride, James Baruchel, Jonah Hill, Craig Robinson, and Seth Rogen in *This is the End* (Evan Goldberg, Seth Rogen, 2013)

FIGURE 6.12 Jeffrey Wright is instantly recognizable and has made a career as a low-keyed supporting actor in such films as this, *The Hunger Games: Catching Fire* (Francis Lawrence, 2013)

FIGURE 6.13 Three of the most recognizable actors, who most often play in independent films: the late Philip Seymour Hoffman with Catherine Keener and Christopher Walken in *A Late Quartet*. Actor Mark Ivanir is on the left. (Yaron Zilberman, 2012)

Some current film actors—Al Pacino, Billy Bob Thornton, Bill Patton, Glenn Close, Parker Posey, John Cusack, Edward Norton, Matt Damon, Bryan Cranston, for example—can change their styles, shifting, chameleon like, into different personae in different films. And there has always been a huge store of character and supporting actors, all but anonymous people with instantly recognizable faces who populate television and film and act as anchors: Jeffrey Wright, Richard Jenkins, Brian Cox, Catherine Keener, Allison Janney. They are more than extras, less than stars, filling out the scene, transmitting important narrative information, securing our gaze. They give us comfort, like a **genre**—always present, always changing.

HOW SCREEN ACTING WORKS: THE GAZE AND THE GESTURE

Eyes Wide Shut and *Vertigo*

Consider these two images of a couple embracing. The first is from Alfred Hitchcock's *Vertigo* (1958), the second from Stanley Kubrick's *Eyes Wide Shut* (1999).

In each, the woman is distracted, looking away from her partner, who is apparently deeply into the intimacy of the moment, face all but hidden. If you are not familiar with the films, can you "read" the distracted looks of the two women? The gaze of Madeleine (Kim Novak) in the image from *Vertigo* appears frightened and drawn to something, as if she were pulled in a direction away from the embrace. Her eyes are wide and her mouth indicates fear. Her head is tilted up and away to the right. The look on Alice's (Nicole Kidman) face is more inward, her eyes are not open wide (the film, after all, is called *Eyes Wide Shut*) and are cast very slightly downward and to the right, as is her face; there is a slight, knowing smile on her face. In both cases, the look indicates some knowledge that is diverting the women from the matter at hand, some emotion greater that the intimacy of the moment: fear in the image from *Vertigo*, perhaps a secret

FIGURE 6.14 Madeleine (Kim Novak) looks away in fear in Alfred Hitchcock's *Vertigo* (1958)

FIGURE 6.15 Alice (Nicole Kidman) looks away as if thinking of something other than the embrace of her husband in Stanley Kubrick's *Eyes Wide Shut* (1999)

in the one from *Eyes Wide Shut*. Even more intriguing is that the image from *Eyes Wide Shut* is reflected in a mirror—a reflection of a distracted gaze.

There are stories told in the eyes, the faces, the directions of the gaze of these two women. They are acting, acting out, playing roles that, at the particular point in the narrative of each of the two films, suggest to us, wordlessly, what is going on with them, with the men they are embracing, and what we as viewers might expect. They speak to us at the moment and offer questions about what may come. Such rich, silent, visual cues form the basis of film acting and grow out of film's very origins, when there were no words and much of narrative information was communicated through pantomime. Despite the changes in acting styles over the decades, some fundamentals remain the same.

The following images constitute a brief catalogue of gestures and gazes, the ways in which actors communicate non-verbally.

FIGURE 6.16 In silent cinema, looks and body language had to communicate emotions. Here is an example of the coy, averted gaze in D. W. Griffith's *The Girl and Her Trust* (1910)

FIGURE 6.17 In the same film, reacting to the threat of robbers is a universal, if exaggerated, expression of fear

FIGURE 6.18 So universal that it can be seen again in this image from the 1996 horror film, Wes Craven's *Scream*

FIGURE 6.19 Opposed to fear is this expression of rage in Sidney Lumet's *12 Angry Men* (1957). Actor Lee J. Cobb is the really angry man

FIGURE 6.20 Close to anger is malice, expressed well by Woody Harrelson in *Out of the Furnace* (Scott Cooper, 2013)

FIGURE 6.21 The wistful, far away but at the same time inward gaze expressed by Judi Dench in *Philomena* (Stephen Frears, 2013)

FIGURE 6.22 A universal expression of troubled frustration, here posed by Tom Hanks in *Saving Mr. Banks* (John Lee Hancock, 2013)

FIGURE 6.23 The faces of psychosis. Norman Bates (Anthony Perkins) in Hitchcock's *Psycho* (1960)

FIGURE 6.24 Private Pyle (Vincent D'Onofrio) in Stanley Kubrick's *Full Metal Jacket* (1987)

FIGURE 6.25 Seeing Double: in Richard Ayoade's film, *The Double* (2013), Jesse Eisenberg plays two versions of himself. The body language of each communicates their difference, one withdrawn and depressed, the other lively and energetic. In this film the doubles were created with CGI, but films have used various techniques over the course of time to create two characters out of one actor

FIGURE 6.26 When the two leads in a romantic comedy square off early in the film, you can tell by their body language and facial expressions that they will probably get together by the end. Juliette Binoche and Clive Owen, *Words and Pictures* (Fred Schepisi, 2013)

FIGURE 6.27 When the possibility of love is lost, there is a look of thoughtful regret. This is an image at the end of the Hindi film *The Lunchbox* (Ritesh Batra, 2013). The actress is Nimrat Kaur, and the look is close to the wistful gaze in 6.21

CELEBRITY

A strong argument can be made that film as we know it—with all its attendant apparatus of publicity, fandom, expectation, identification, and desire—was born when public recognition and admiration of stars forced filmmakers to acknowledge that they could extend their profits by extending the stories they told about the people in front of the camera beyond the films themselves. The film narrative became only one in a larger constellation of stories. The star system became a great attraction and convenience for everyone. Audiences could live out fantasy and desire through their favorite players both on and off the screen. Sexual fantasy, so much at the core of what movies are about, could be expanded from film narrative to publicity narrative and so journalism became one more extension of the **studio system**: they could all feed one another. A studio's filmmaking and publicity machines meshed gears with newspapers, magazines, radio, television, and now the Internet to author a super narrative of sex, wealth, marriage and divorce, good works, fantastic irresponsibility, and fall. The antics and embarrassments of celebrity can often outstrip the actor or actress; it becomes a second narrative—in some cases a primary narrative (think of the now fading celebrity of Lindsay Lohan)—of fame and misfortune that may have little to do with the primary performance talents of the actor.

A sturdy character actor, a well-known star, or a celebrity with acting ability—any talented player who can sustain an illusion of performance and build a coherent character across the film's narrative, can be thought of as a creative figure *in* a film rather than a creator *of* the film. The actor whose persona transcends a film can be considered the co-creator of another narrative: her or his mythic life, devoured by the public through other media than the films in which they appear. All this while the strong supporting or bit player works for hire, does her job, helps fill the screen and the narrative, and moves quietly on to the next role. This demands an act of recognition by another creative figure: the viewer. The viewer enjoys the actor's work in a film and observes and responds to celebrity, taking part in a story of desire, fulfillment, eventual loss, and sometimes pathetic death of the figure who is partly real human being and mostly illusory construct, the imaginary figure of the movie star.

FURTHER READING

James Naremore's *Acting in the Cinema* (Berkeley and Los Angeles: University of California Press, 1988) and Christine Gledhill's edition of essays, *Stardom: Industry of Desire* (London and New York: Routledge, 1991) are useful resources. See also Richard Dyer's *Stars* (London: British Film Institute, 1979).

The cultural historian Garry Wills has written an important book on John Wayne: *John Wayne's America: The Politics of Celebrity* (New York: Simon & Schuster, 1997).

Early film acting is discussed in Patrice Petro, ed., *Idols of Modernity: Movie Stars of the 1920s* (New Brunswick, New Jersey and London: Rutgers University Press, 2010). Contemporary acting is covered in Cynthia Baron, Diane Carson, Frank P. Tomasulo, eds., *More Than a Method: Trends and Traditions in Contemporary Film Performance* (Detroit: Wayne State University Press, 2004).

SUGGESTIONS FOR FURTHER VIEWING

The silent comedians, Charlie Chaplin and Buster Keaton, defined comic acting in silent film: Chaplin in, for example, *The Gold Rush* (1925) and Keaton in *The Play House* (1921).

From *The Petrified Forest* (Archie Mayo, 1936) through *The Caine Mutiny* (Edward Dmytryk, 1954), Humphrey Bogart played a small variation of characters that he inhabited with toughness and grace.

Marlon Brando is always interesting to watch. In addition to the films mentioned in the text, there is *The Wild One* (Laslo Benedek, 1953), *On the Waterfront* (Elia Kazan, 1954), and most especially his late work, *Last Tango in Paris* (Bernardo Bertolucci, 1972).

Robert De Niro stands out in Martin Scorsese's films, especially *Mean Streets* (1973), *Taxi Driver* (1976), and *Raging Bull* (1980).

Contemporary actors and actresses who do unusual work include Scarlett Johansson in *Under the Skin* (Jonathan Glazer, 2013); Ryan Gosling and Bradley Cooper appear together in *The Place Beyond the Pines* (Derek Cianfrance, 2013).

Meryl Streep is a chameleon actress who seems to change physically depending on her characters in, for example, *Silkwood* (Mike Nichols, 1983) and *Doubt* (John Partick Shanley, 2008), in which she co-stars with another major contemporary actor, the late Philip Seymour Hoffman. One of Hoffman's best films is *The Master* (Paul Thomas Anderson, 2012). Anderson directed the British actor, Daniel Day-Lewis—another chameleon—in *There Will be Blood* (2007). Day-Lewis morphs into another character in Martin Scorsese's *Gangs of New York* (2002).

NOTES

1 For Kubrick's work with actors, see Vincent LoBrutto, *Stanley Kubrick: A Biography* (New York: Donald I. Fine, 1997) and John Baxter, *Stanley Kubrick: A Biography* (New York: Carroll & Graf, 1997).

2 The Delsarte charts are from Genevieve Stebbins, *Delsarte System of Expression* 2nd ed. (New York: Edgar S. Werner, 1887), pp. 142–145.

3 For information on The Method, see http://www.methodactingstrasberg.com/history, http://www.methodactingstrasberg.com/alumni (accessed 16 March 2015) and *The Stanislavski System*, http://homepage.smc.edu/sawoski_perviz/Stanislavski.pdf (accessed 17 March 2015).

CHAPTER 7

The storytellers of film III

The director

I noted in the last chapter that ideally an actor should be one aspect of a film's **mise-en-scène** and tested out the notion that an actor may perform best when under the guide of a strong **director**. Unlike television, where the "show runner," the person in charge of script and production, has creative control, in theatrical film the director is the main driving force, arguably the most creative individual in the filmmaking process. At the very least, the director shares with the film's **producers** the overall control of the production. At best, the director is the imaginative engine of the film, imprinting it with a coherent look and feel; he or she transfers the inert words of the script into the (hopefully) dynamic visuals on the screen and shapes performances from the bits and pieces of acting that are often filmed out of sequence. As we will see, the director's role has been a contentious one, both in the making and in the critical analysis of film, and before we discuss the work of a few individual directors, we need to examine some of this history.

THE PRODUCER AS DIRECTOR

In all but a few instances, and throughout the history of film since the introduction of the **producer system**, a film's producer has always had the last word. He was often on set, giving directions to the director and in the editing suite, determining what the **final cut** would look like. These days, films have multiple producers, executive producers, associate producers. Just try to keep track of the number of names listed in the credits under these various headings.

Anyone who has anything to do with getting a film financed, or is owed a favor, gets their name on the screen, and they all would like some say in how the film will look.

EUROPEAN ORIGINS OF THE AUTEUR

Historically, European filmmaking was more individualized than American filmmaking. Production never occurred on the scale of the Hollywood studios, even though major outfits existed, such as Shepperton and Ealing Studios in England, Gaumont and Pathé in France, and UFA (supported in part by American studios) in pre-World War II Germany. Elsewhere in the world, for example in Japan until relatively recently, some nations had enormous production facilities. India, even now, turns out more films than Hollywood. The exotic (to Western eyes) musical–romantic–mythic–surrealistic films of "**Bollywood**" are now reaching U.S. audiences. In Europe, small crews and independent production were much more the style. A film's director often wrote or co-wrote the script and guided the editing process. The producer was basically a functionary, rarely the overriding force he is in American production. Films made abroad—especially those made for an international audience—were often more intimate and sometimes less dependent on the conventional **narratives** and stereotypes beloved of American filmmakers.

It is important not to fall into a romantic overvaluation of foreign cinema. Some of it was different, a few directors took chances, a number of films are more intense and complex than all but a few American films, and we will examine them in detail in Chapter 8. The prewar work of Jean Renoir and Marcel Carné in France, Fritz Lang and F. W. Murnau in Germany (to name only a few), and the great explosion of cinema across Europe after World War II attest to a strong, independent filmic intelligence. But two issues must be kept in mind. Films made for *internal* consumption in Europe are as grounded in clichés and narrative patterns beloved of the particular culture (as in the Indian films mentioned earlier) and some as banally executed as anything made in the United States. There is variety and a great deal of invention in international cinema, but, with the possible exception of Indian films, most people outside the United States want to see American movies more than they want to see their own.

France and the French New Wave

The myth of the individual creator—or **auteur**, the French word for "author"—in film grew, indirectly, from political and economic issues between the United States and France after World War II, and it developed directly from the attempts of a group of post-World War II French intellectuals to account for American film and react to what they did not like in the films of their own country. The political and economic issues were of the kind that develop from time to time in all countries where the popularity of American film threatens the economic viability of the country's own cinema. France tried to solve the problem by creating a policy about how many American films could be shown in relation to the number of French films. During the Nazi occupation of France, from 1940 to 1944, no American film was permitted on French screens. After the war, a flood of previously unseen movies came into the country, and filmgoers were overwhelmed and delighted. Established French filmmakers hoped to compete against this deluge of American movies and meet their quota of French films by making a "high-class" product (in contradistinction to the so-called "quota quickies"—comedies and other light entertainment—made to meet the quotas in Great Britain and other countries). They wound up producing sometimes stodgy, often stagy films, many based on popular fiction or on big literary works, like Claude Autant-Lara's film of Stendhal's French classic, *The Red and the Black* (1954).

That young group of film lovers—who were quickly becoming film critics and who, by the late 1950s, under the title of the **French New Wave**, became the most influential filmmakers of their generation—railed against their country's movies and held American films up as a model. François Truffaut, Jean-Luc Godard, Jacques Rivette, Eric Rohmer, and Claude Chabrol wrote in disgust about the filmmakers of their country, especially in the influential journal *Cahiers du cinéma*. Jean-Luc Godard said of them, "Your camera movements are ugly because your subjects are bad, your casts act badly because your dialogue is worthless; in a word, you don't know how to create cinema because you no longer even know what it is."[1]

Who did know? According to these Frenchmen, some European filmmakers, such as Jean Renoir and the Italian **neorealist** Roberto Rossellini, knew. But most important, as far as they were concerned, a handful of American filmmakers knew best: Orson Welles and Alfred Hitchcock (who started his career in England); John Ford, Howard Hawks, and Otto Preminger; Nicholas Ray, Raoul Walsh, Samuel Fuller—indeed names that many American filmgoers didn't know, then or now, were placed in the pantheon of great directors. For Godard, Truffaut, and their colleagues, these American filmmakers developed and maintained that very quality we have been searching for: individual style. These French film critics imagined something so important about American cinema that, by learning from their favorite Americans, it enabled them not only to launch their own careers in France and then internationally, but to launch film studies as a serious undertaking in the United States. What they figured out gave respectability to the movies. They decided that, despite the anonymity and mass production of the **studio system**; despite who may have produced, written, photographed, or starred in a film; despite the studio and despite the amount of money a film may or may not have made, continuity and coherence could be discovered across a group of films linked by one name: the director's.

THE AUTEUR THEORY

Andrew Sarris and the three principles: competence, style, vision

The principles of stylistic continuity were suggested by the French critics and then codified in the mid-1960s by the American film critic Andrew Sarris, who imported them to the United States under the name of the **auteur theory**.[2] The principles of the auteur theory are based on the assumption that the director is the controlling force in the structure of a film. For Sarris, that control includes three basic attributes. The first is a technical competence that marks a director's ability to understand and practice the techniques of filmmaking in an expressive way. The second is a coherent personal style, a set of visual and narrative attributes that are recognizable in film after film. Examples would be Orson Welles's use of **deep focus** and moving camera; John Ford's use of Monument Valley as the landscape for his imaginary West; Hitchcock's use of **cross tracking**, his variation of the **shot/reverse shot** in which a character, walking and looking at a threatening object, is intercut with that object, drawing closer, ominously, and his use of a high angle **shot** to show a character in a vulnerable state; Stanley Kubrick's symmetrical

compositions and careful, almost symbolic color schemes; David Fincher's dark, yellow-tinged mise-en-scène, created across the horizontal line of the Panavision screen; Oliver Stone's extraordinary **montages**; Paul Thomas Anderson's stately and eloquent compositions. The Swedish director Ingmar Bergman's intense **close-ups** of a character in a profound state of existential despair; the German director Rainer Werner Fassbinder's framing of characters in doorways or behind doors; his fellow countryman Wim Wenders' images of men driving the road from city to city in Germany or America; the Austrian Michael Haneke's pitiless gaze at violence and domestic disintegration—these are all ways of perceiving the world, of making images that mark the directors as having special ways of seeing. It is important to understand that these stylistic attributes are formal, sometimes even symbolic, expressions of ideas and perceptions. Monument Valley is for Ford a representation of the West and all the myths of the frontier that it represents from film to film. Hitchcock's camera strategies express ways of thinking about his characters and showing them in difficult, threatening, often violent situations. They are expressive of his notions of a precarious and randomly violent universe. Fincher's tight, expressive compositions and camera movements in *Seven* (1995), *The Game* (1997), *Fight Club* (1999), and *Gone Girl* (2014) are eloquent expressions of an oppressive world in which nothing is what it seems.

Style is not decoration, but the visible creation and expression of emotion and thought through the language of cinema that is varied and repeated by a director from film to film. This "language" may consist of individual inflections of the Hollywood style, or the introduction of new ways of seeing through cinema. This leads to Sarris's third and, for him, most important attribute of the auteur: a consistent view of the world, a coherent set of attitudes and ideas. Sarris calls it "interior meaning" or vision, but it might also be called a worldview, a philosophy, a kind of personal narrative that is either unique to the specific director or a major and consistent variation of larger narrative conventions, such as John Ford's turns on the Western **genre**.

The French director Jean Renoir once said that a filmmaker needs to learn everything about technique (Sarris's first attribute), and then forget it. The ability to think cinematically, to know just the right place to put the camera, to know when to create stillness or motion in the **frame**, to understand how the actors are to be composed and directed, to know exactly where an **edit** should occur—these are the initial marks of the auteur. Technique that is learned and forgotten becomes style, because style is technique put to imaginative use and becomes a reflexive part of the directorial process. Anyone with good cinematic training can create a low angle shot, in which the camera gazes up at a character looming above it. But only cinematic intelligence can turn this technique into a stylistic trait, and only true cinematic imagination can make it state a view of the world. Orson Welles loved to use the low angle shot. In his hands, and through his eyes, it became a way of tilting the horizon and distorting the world around a character. He used it to comment ironically on the strength of a character or to predict the fall of a character who might still believe in his own power. It becomes a part of Welles's vision of a labyrinthine world in which the human figure dominates only momentarily. It is matched by Hitchcock's use of the high angle shot to observe a character in a vulnerable moment or a point of moral crisis (Figures 7.1, 7.2; see also Figure 3.47).

John Ford's figures in the Western landscape transcend compositional stylistics. They articulate a changing vision of the Western myths of settlement and domesticity, of Indians as a force of the land, and of outlaws as impediments to lonely heroes in the inevitable movement from east to west. Ford's visual style fixed individuals in the landscape of a symbolic West; fixed women in the center of the domestic landscape, in the comforting interiors of homesteads, with men

FIGURE 7.1 This extreme low angle shot from Orson Welles's *Touch of Evil* (1958) foreshadows the imminent fall of the corrupt cop, Hank Quinlan (Welles). See also Figure 3.41

FIGURE 7.2 Welles will also pull up and away from his character, isolating him at his moment of vulnerability

riding out to the peripheries, making them secure. The dynamic conservatism of Ford's cinematic inquiry into our memories and mythologies of the West developed through a variety of films, written by different hands and made for different studios. He was persistent, silent about his work, recessive, a good movie worker who developed his style and his ongoing narrative without fanfare. His concept of the West kept developing and turned to critique. His later films, such as

FIGURE 7.3 The Ford landscape of Monument Valley in *The Searchers* (1956)

The Searchers (1956) and *The Man Who Shot Liberty Valance* (1962), began questioning the very notions of frontier heroism he had originally established.

Robert Altman, the director of *M.A.S.H.* (1970—the movie, not the television show); *McCabe and Mrs. Miller* (1971); *The Long Goodbye* (1973); *Nashville* (1975); *Popeye* (1980); *Come Back to the 5 & Dime Jimmy Dean, Jimmy Dean* (1982); *The Player* (1992); *Short Cuts* (1993) and *Gosford Park* (2001) to name just a few, uses a **zoom** lens almost obsessively.[3] It is a technique that became an expected part of his visual style (though it was less present in his late work). He used it as a probe, a way to move toward and beyond his characters, and a way to let us, as viewers, understand that watching a movie is, in part, a desire to come close to the image of a face, which is always slipping away from us. Altman's use of the zoom, especially when he combines it with a telephoto lens and wide-screen composition, a combination that flattens the image and makes space claustrophobic, keeps denying our desire. He plays with what we want to see, getting close, sliding away, and finally isolating our look at the characters and the connection of the characters to each other.

The zoom, along with other compositional and editing techniques, became part of Altman's style not merely because he used them all the time (in which case they would only be repetitious) but because they are essential to the way he thought about the world cinematically. They mediate, represent, and generate to the viewer his particular notions about power, the relationship of people to each other and their surroundings, the way stories get to or miss the truth, the way movies reveal and hide personal and global history.

They all prove a central point about auteurism: once you see a few films by an auteur and learn his stylistic traits, his view of people in the world, ideas about politics, history, social order, psychology, sexuality, and power, you should then be able to identify those elements as the work of that particular director in any other of his films. The British critic Peter Wollen puts it in structural terms, suggesting that, if we take the body of work by an auteur and strip away the

FIGURE 7.4 In Robert Altman's *McCabe and Mrs. Miller* (1971) the wide open spaces of the Western become the cramped, cold environs of the frontier town of Presbyterian Church. The actors are Julie Christie and Warren Beatty

narrative variations that are part of each individual film, we will discover a structure of basic thematic and stylistic traits, a kind of abstract pattern of ways of seeing and understanding the world cinematically. This pattern then becomes a template that we can see generating the form and content of each film the auteur makes. Jean Renoir put it more directly. He said that a director really makes one long film in the course of his career.

At its most fruitful, studying the work of an auteur—like studying the work of a novelist, poet, painter, or composer—becomes a way of discovering thematic and formal patterns, the way similar ideas cohere or oppose each other, how images are constructed in similar ways, how a coherent idea of history and human behavior develops across the artist's work. It is a comfortable kind of discovery, because it breeds familiarity on a personal level. We can get close to a filmmaker by recognizing his or her mark; we can find—as we do in literature, painting, or music—a creative personality. Because of this, the development of the auteur theory made film studies possible as an academic discipline. When we study the novel, we never think about anonymous creativity or a collaboration, unless the novel was coauthored. The author and the work are linked. We study Melville, Steinbeck, Hemingway, or Morrison and never refer to the author of a novel as "they." Positing, even inventing, the director as auteur put film in the same league as other humanities disciplines. We could now connect individuals with their work and analyze structures of style and meaning developed by a single imagination. Connecting a singular imagination to a group of films also allowed film scholars to recuperate film from its debased state as an anonymous commercial form of common entertainment to the imaginative expression of a serious artist who creates uncommon entertainment. Because the French discovered auteurs within Hollywood production, establishing style and vision within the studio system, American film was redeemed from anonymity.

The success of the auteur theory was enormous. Films were rediscovered, reputations of forgotten directors were made, methods of analysis were deployed, and a whole new discipline of study developed. Filmmakers themselves were now able to celebrate their medium. The originators of the theory—Godard, Truffaut, Chabrol, and the rest of the filmmakers of the French New Wave—began making films in homage to the Hollywood auteurs they had discovered or created. They alluded to American films in their own films—recalling a camera move from a Fritz Lang movie, a composition from a Douglas Sirk **melodrama**, a character gesture from Vincente Minnelli, a narrative line from Howard Hawks, a snatch of dialogue from Nicholas Ray's *Johnny Guitar* (1954). The New Wave created and honored a universe of cinema and implicitly understood what the poet T. S. Eliot said in his famous essay "Tradition and the Individual Talent." For Eliot, poems coexist and influence each other. So do films. A new filmmaker, like a new poet, responds to, is influenced by, and adds to the existing universe of films; new films absorb the old and then become part of the total film universe.[4]

Many American filmmakers who came to artistic maturity after the auteur theory were influenced by its call to individual expression. Unlike their Hollywood predecessors, who learned their trade by coming up the ranks in the studios, many of these new directors went to film school and learned filmmaking by learning film history. Like the directors of the French New Wave, they celebrated their knowledge and their medium by referring to other films within their own work and, often, by taking filmmaking as one of the subjects of their films. Unlike their predecessors, who adopted the **classical Hollywood style** and its invisible access to story, some contemporary filmmakers—and especially those who began their careers in the late 1960s and early 1970s—are less likely to hide style and make us forget we're watching a film. They are more likely to foreground the presence of cinema and its methods and invite us to see the story and understand what allows us to see it. They will often make films of complexity and ideas that run against the grain.

Robert Altman

Let's return to Robert Altman for a moment. Nowhere does Altman articulate his style and his vision better than in his film *Short Cuts* (1993). Based upon a series of stories by Raymond Carver, it is one of the most powerful statements about gender inequity and the objectifying of women ever made by a filmmaker. And it is a great narrative experiment. Through a complex intertwining of characters and their stories, taking place among mostly lower-middle-class Los Angelinos, gender difference, even gender panic, is revealed. Dozens of characters—their stories woven together through chance meetings, through amusing associations (a joke about Alex Trebeck and "Jeopardy" runs through the film)—and the restless probing of the zoom lens expose gender hostilities, both open and unconscious. The film seems to discover an almost universal thoughtlessness about feelings and inappropriate actions. A group of men go on a fishing trip and discover a woman's body floating in the water. Rather than call the police, they simply continue fishing. One of them urinates on the body. When one of the men returns home and tells his wife, she gets out of bed to take a bath, as if re-creating for herself the dead woman's experience as well as cleansing the wound of her husband's callousness. She goes to the woman's funeral and, when asked to sign the guest book, only makes a gesture of signing, preferring to retain the same anonymity that the dead woman held for the men.

The film is filled with serial cheating (by both sexes), long-held anger by one member of a couple toward what the other may have done years ago, and confrontations that lead to deep resentments and finally to violence. One of the men, a pool cleaner, bitterly resentful that his wife engages in phone sex to supplement their income, picks up a girl and kills her. As he does this, an earthquake occurs. The woman's murder is taken by the media as a casualty of an upheaval in nature, when in fact it was actually the result of an upheaval between genders.

Short Cuts is amusingly misanthropic, casting a cold and displeased eye on relationships in general, though its sympathies are clearly with the women, who are abused in so many ways.

FIGURE 7.5 Dressed as a clown, this character (Matthew Modine) from Robert Altman's *Short Cuts* (1993) expresses his rage by the squeal of air coming out of a balloon

The film is amazingly insightful into the ways gender and sexuality work to keep people cold and apart, as opposed to the melodramatic conventions of keeping them together and happy, even as they share their emotional and physical pain. It attempts to understand that life in an allegedly postfeminist world is no easier than it was when women were supposed to "know their place," and men were content being the dominant gender—as if it were all a given of nature. Women still struggle on all fronts and Altman knows that nothing in culture is a given of nature, especially in the realm of human relationships. His characters struggle against that fact, and his restless, probing camera pushes their struggles to the limits. *Short Cuts* is a summary film. In it are gathered all of Altman's concerns and techniques and views of the world garnered from almost fifty years of filmmaking, a career marked by conscious efforts to undermine the conventions and narratives of the Hollywood style.

Martin Scorsese

Martin Scorsese—at least until recently—was a shining example of the new kind of filmmaker who knows film form and history and attempts always to rework it. A graduate of and part-time instructor at New York University film school during the mid-1960s, he has since become one of the best-known and most self-conscious filmmakers in the United States. He has worked across a number of genres and for many studios, developing a consistent and recognizable style. He has spun off a number of imitators, including Quentin Tarantino and many young filmmakers who make their first and second movies in homage to Scorsese's work (think of *Pulp Fiction*, 1994; *The Usual Suspects*, Bryan Singer, 1995; indeed any first film involving gangsters). Even more mature filmmakers have done Scorsese imitations, such as the British Mike Newell's *Donnie Brasco* (1997). The popular HBO series *The Sopranos* (1999–2007) is an extended riff on *Goodfellas*.

More than his equally famous contemporaries—Steven Spielberg, Woody Allen, and Francis Ford Coppola—Scorsese has maintained an unflagging interest in exposing the grammar of film to his viewers. But, at the same time, he understands the nature of working in a popular medium. While he plays and tinkers with the classical style, often exposing its workings, he simultaneously observes the basic rules of narrative and visual construction that allow him to continue to receive financial backing for his films and acceptance from viewers. Like John Ford and Alfred Hitchcock, two of his major influences, along with Jean-Luc Godard, François Truffaut, and the British filmmaker Michael Powell, he is able to work many aspects of the system at once. He maintains commercial viability and explores and experiments. This was the kind of talent that originally defined the auteur: the director who, while working within the studio system, could also quietly subvert it, using its conventions to develop a personal style.

Scorsese began his career by making small films of consistent quality, and by varying his output. In the late 1960s he made short films and a feature, *Who's That Knocking at My Door?* (1968). His major films of the 1970s are *Mean Streets* (1973), *Taxi Driver* (1976), *New York, New York* (1977), and *The Last Waltz* (1978). The key films of the 1980s are *Raging Bull* (1980) and *The Last Temptation of Christ* (1988), which caused a big uproar from some religious groups. *Goodfellas* (1990) is the key 1990s film, along with *Cape Fear* (1991), *The Age of Innocence* (1993), and *Casino* (1995). *Gangs of New York*, a big costume drama, large on budget and small on experimentation, appeared in 2002. Of these films only *Cape Fear* and *Gangs of New York* brought in large amounts of money, and Scorsese made *Cape Fear* exactly for that purpose as an offering to Universal Pictures, which had backed his controversial *The Last Temptation of Christ*. More recently, he has moved even further from his roots with lavish productions such as *The Aviator* (2004), a biopic (as they are called in Hollywood) about the eccentric and emotionally troubled millionaire Howard Hughes. He briefly returned to his gangster film roots with *The Departed* (2006), tried his hand at a psychological thriller, *Shutter Island* (2010), and then experimented with 3D in his homage to early cinema, *Hugo* (2011). In 2013, he made a three-hour vulgar and hilarious film about the excesses of the newly rich, *The Wolf of Wall Street*. He has alternated his fiction films with various documentaries, some about rock stars, such as *George Harrison: Living in the Material World* (2011) and American and Italian cinema: *A Personal Journey with Martin Scorsese through American Movies* (1995) and *My Voyage to Italy* (2001).

I detail Scorsese's filmography to indicate the range and variety of his work. But it is the films of the 1970s and 1980s that remain his most interesting in the context of experimentation and the interrogation of consciousness. While, on the level of story, Scorsese's films often concern small-time hoods or individuals on the edge or over the edge of psychosis, they are, on a more complex level, about appearance and reputation, about how it looks and feels to *be* in the world, looking at people and being looked at, seen, recognized, and hurt by the glance of others. His films—often like Stanley Kubrick's, though executed in an entirely different manner—are existential and very physical. Bodies as well as personalities are always at stake. Characters kill and get killed, beat up others or get beaten up, thrive and do themselves in by thriving, or are nobodies trying to be somebodies by doing something to their own or someone else's body—beating, shooting, or, in the case of *The Wolf of Wall Street*, taking massive amounts of drugs.

Raging Bull is about the body. Jake La Motta tries to control his body, which is busy either damaging other people, being damaged in turn, or getting fat as he tries to control the world around him by violence and jealous rages, by aggressively imposing his body on others. The film is ultimately a violent meditation on the inability to get control, or always being controlled, just as an actor is controlled by a director and a movie viewer is controlled by a movie. *Raging Bull* focuses on a boxer whose awareness of the outside world and his place in it is dim at best. He is moved by momentary, unthinking whims and responses, and winds up becoming a parody not of himself but of movie representations of a boxer, which is, after all, what Robert De Niro's Jake *is* in *Raging Bull*—an actor, playing an "actual" boxer, in a film that grows out of a fairly

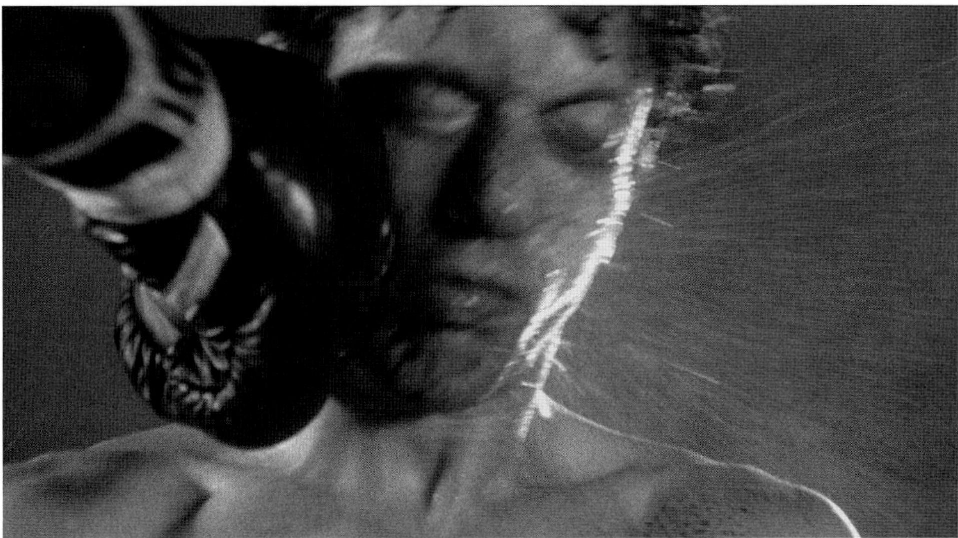

FIGURE 7.6 Jake La Motta (Robert De Niro) takes a punch in the ring in Martin Scorsese's *Raging Bull* (1980)

substantial **subgenre** of boxing films. In the last shot of *Raging Bull,* Scorsese appears partially reflected in a mirror, telling an aging, fat Jake, who has gone from champion boxer to nightclub owner to performer in strip joints, that it's time to go on stage to do his rendition of the "I could have been a contender" scene from *On the Waterfront* (1954), Elia Kazan's film of a washed-up boxer who gets into trouble with and informs on his union.

As the film ends, De Niro, as Jake La Motta, urged on by his director, playing a stage manager, does a parody of Marlon Brando playing a boxer from an older film. Jake La Motta is portrayed as a figure made up of self-contradictory parts, a reflection of a reflection. He is "real" and he is a fictional character in a film, there and not there, like film itself. Like Hitchcock, Scorsese impresses his own image on his film (like Hitchcock, he makes some kind of appearance in many of them). He focuses our attention on the artifice of celebrity, the illusory nature of film, and the fact that the film and our response to it are controlled by someone. The illusion totters, though Scorsese never permits it to collapse. The last scene of *Raging Bull* so fascinated Paul Thomas Anderson that he imitates it at the end of *Boogie Nights* (1997), just as Altman's *Short Cuts* is the driving force behind his film *Magnolia* (1999).

Illusion and celebrity fascinate Scorsese and his characters. Travis Bickle, in *Taxi Driver,* achieves fame without knowing it. Travis is crazy, an uncontrollable psychotic who can see the world only as a brutal, devastating place. His world is created out of an imaginative use of the most basic aspects of the shot/reverse shot and **point-of-view** shooting and cutting technique. Travis, like many other Scorsese characters, is menacing and sees menace around him. Paranoia rules. When Travis (or Jake La Motta in *Raging Bull*) looks at the world, the world looks back as a threatening place. One way Scorsese manages this is to generate point-of-view shots in slow motion (an effect now imitated by many filmmakers), so that the character's world appears as if it were a hallucination. Scorsese has perfected this technique so that he will change the speed of the motion in the course of a shot. The figures seen by the main character will move slowly and then subtly speed up, until they move at a normal pace. This method, which is a refinement of Hitchcock's technique of intercutting a character in motion with an object or person that character is looking at, also in motion, is disturbing because it plays against the stability of the shot/reverse shot we have come to expect. It generates an unstable space and reflects the perceptions of an unstable character. With it, point of view and the mise-en-scène are joined in an expressive definition of character and the emotional state, the emotional *space*, he inhabits and we are asked to observe (see Figure 5.1).

The result is that Travis's world is one of sharp and dark fragments, created by a mind that is both paranoid and aggressive. Travis believes that he is responsible for cleaning up the very world he imagines, first by attempting to assassinate a presidential candidate and, when that fails, by saving a young hooker who doesn't particularly want saving. In the process, he murders three people in a nightmarish episode of violence and destruction and is turned into a media hero. Some films later, Travis is reincarnated in the person of Rupert Pupkin in Scorsese's *The King of Comedy*, played by De Niro, an actor who became part of Scorsese's directorial pattern and mise-en-scène until he was replaced in the later films by a less expressive actor, Leonardo DiCaprio. Pupkin is not a crazy paranoid like Travis. He is an ordinary lunatic who can't be embarrassed. His goal in life is to deliver a monologue on a late-night talk show (hosted by Jerry Lewis), which he manages to do by kidnapping the star and threatening his way onto the stage. He gets his wish, is put in jail, and is turned by the very media he hijacked into a star.

Blundering violently, lost in the normal world, compelled by madness, high spirits, or some obsessive-compulsive drive, Scorsese's characters, from Rupert Pupkin to Jesus Christ to Howard Hughes to Jordan Belfort, try to fight the world's imposition on them and impose their own will and spirit back on the world. This question of imposition lies at the core of his characters and also at the core of the classical Hollywood style. That's where Scorsese's cinematic contention lies. Like his characters, he wants to impose his will on the structures of cinema, to undermine the impositions of the classical style by imposing his own style, his own way of seeing the world through cinema. Unlike his characters, he succeeds. He insists that we, as viewers, come to terms not only with the characters but with the way they see and are seen. He asks as well that we question our own ways of seeing movies.

One way to remind us, even on a subtle level, is to show that his films grow out of other films. In *Cape Fear*—not, by itself, a very subtle film—he constructs **sequences** that are subtly based upon Alfred Hitchcock's *Strangers on a Train* (1951). You have to be really familiar with Hitchcock to understand what's going on. Both films are concerned with apparently upright characters who become involved with, and are stalked by, figures representing their darker, corrupt natures. In each film, there are sequences in which these characters, these mirror images of dark and light, confront each other. For example, in *Strangers on a Train*, the "hero," a tennis player named Guy (Farley Granger), sees his evil other, Bruno (Robert Walker), staring at him from the stands as Guy attempts to play a match. All the other spectators except for Bruno turn their heads as the ball flies from side to side. Bruno just stares straight at Guy. In the companion scene in *Cape Fear*, the lawyer, Sam (Nick Nolte), goes with his family to watch a Fourth of July parade. The crowd watches the procession while in their midst Max Cady (Robert De Niro), the ex-con out to get Sam, stares straight across the street—the tormentor freezing his victim in his gaze.

Once you see the connections—and there are others—*Cape Fear* becomes an interesting conversation with an earlier filmmaker, as is *Taxi Driver*, which is in many ways a remake of *Psycho*, with allusions to John Ford's *The Searchers*. Sometimes, Scorsese can be downright weird about his obsession with drawing attention to the cinematic roots of his imagery. Early in *The*

Last Temptation of Christ, Jesus goes to a tent where Mary Magdalene is performing a sex act. He sits in the audience, and the camera observes him as if he were in a movie theater, looking at a screen. At the end of the film, on the cross, his fantasy of a normal life over, Jesus dies, and Scorsese cuts to a montage of abstract colors and shapes. In the midst of this montage are images of film sprocket holes. Even his meditation on the Christ story is, finally, a meditation on film and the way it represents legend and myth.

He can be very playful, too, almost teasing us about our position as viewers of a carefully made-up tale. This is what he does at the end of *Raging Bull*, and it is the main ploy of *Goodfellas*. This latter film is a more energetic and imaginative version of his earlier *Mean Streets*. It is also an examination of just what we, as audience, think we're doing when we go to see yet another film about New York gangsters. Interestingly, in *Gangs of New York*, he gives up the examination of genre to create a large, somewhat conventional costume drama with clichéd oedipal overtones about early thugs in New York. But in *Goodfellas*, Scorsese asks us to consider who tells us stories in films, to think about whom we listen to and tend to believe—an important question in the context of a film that asks us to find brutal gangsters amusing. Henry Hill (Ray Liotta), narrator and main character of the film, seems to be our guide and our eyes. His voice talks to us throughout, and we see what he sees. Or do we? One of Scorsese's favorite point-of-view techniques is to use the camera as a surrogate for one of his tough-guy characters as he moves along a bar in a club. He does this in both *Mean Streets* and *Goodfellas*.

Early in *Goodfellas*, Henry introduces us, in **voice-over narration**, to his gangster pals at a bar. The camera **tracks** along, pausing to look at each face, each character, who smiles and responds to Henry's off-screen presence. Everything here seems to guarantee that we are looking through Henry's eyes, sharing his point of view—until the very end of the **tracking shot**. The camera moves to the end of the bar, where Henry is heading to examine some stolen furs. A rack of furs appears, and so does Henry. The camera has been moving from right to left, diagonally into the frame. Henry appears on the left, opposite the direction of the camera. So, at the end of the shot, Henry himself emerges, but from the left side of the frame—not from where the camera is positioned. With this slight disruption of expectations, Scorsese brings into question who is actually seeing what, whose point of view we can really depend on.

How is this possible, if we were supposed to be seeing things through Henry's eyes? Well, of course, we are not seeing through Henry's eyes. Henry is a character in the fiction, who is constructed to appear as if he were controlling the fiction. As we've seen, Scorsese is continually questioning the reality of people's control over things. It's one of his recurring themes and a major part of the formal construction of his style. Like Hitchcock before him, Scorsese plays with his characters and his audience and their imagined relationship to the characters. In *Taxi Driver*, for example, Scorsese limits point of view, forcing his viewers to see through the eyes of a madman a dark, violent city. Playing on the conventions of **German Expressionism** and **film noir**, drawing upon Hitchcock's ability to define character by how that character looks at the world and how the world looks back, *Taxi Driver* restricts our vision to that of a single, deranged sensibility. The prizefight scenes in *Raging Bull* attempt to create a mise-en-scène of noise, distortion, exaggeration of movement and sound that represents Scorsese's idea of what it must be like to be in a boxing ring. *What it might look like to someone* is a driving force in Scorsese's films. Limiting point of view, fooling us with who is seeing what, even playing with film speed, slowing down motion when he cuts to a character's point of view or speeding up the cutting in *The Wolf of Wall Street* are some of the ways Scorsese communicates shifting feelings, uncertainties, and changing responses. For Scorsese, perception is a liquid, undependable, and tricky business. He uses a variety of cinematic properties to communicate this and to make us aware that film can teach us about perception, or keep us fooled.

Goodfellas plays counterpoint between Henry, who seems to be in control of the narrative, and another perspective—Scorsese's, perhaps, or a more abstract "voice" that speaks about film's ability to manipulate perception—with such intricacy that we are left somewhat unsettled. Henry's "story" is punctuated by freeze frames, moments in which the image is frozen while Henry meditates on what's just happened, or what will happen; by virtuoso camera movement, as in the amazing almost three minute long tracking shot that accompanies Henry and Karen as they walk from the street into the Copacabana nightclub, downstairs, through the kitchen, up to their table—all to the tune of The Crystals' "Then He Kissed Me" (see Figure 3.3).

At times, Henry's voice is taken over by Karen's, so that the woman's voice seems to run the narrative. Sometimes the editing takes over both and mimics the characters' point of view, as when, late in the film, frantic and high on cocaine, Karen and Henry believe they are being followed by a helicopter. The cutting is quick and nervous: time seems to speed up.

Finally, Scorsese takes over completely. It's his film, and one of the things he wishes to do with it is comment upon gangster films in general and our attraction and reaction to them in particular. He wants us to think about stories and their tellers. He makes Henry, the petty thug, the man who betrays his friends, a very attractive character, but he knows this is easy to do. Henry continually seems to take us into his confidence and remains aloof from the violence he and his friends commit. He is good looking, funny, and full of high spirits. But this shouldn't be enough to make us like a small-time criminal, and Scorsese needs to put more distance between us and his character. He does this by continually pointing to the tenuousness of Henry's authority, finally diminishing it entirely. Throughout the film, he plays with Henry's point of view and our sharing of it. Late in the film, after the mob has been busted, Henry goes to meet Jimmy (played by Robert De Niro in a relatively minor role for him in a Scorsese film). Henry is about to betray Jimmy and everybody else to the police. They meet in a diner and sit in front of the window, the camera placed so that it sees both men in profile against it.

Suddenly, perspective and space alter. Scorsese executes a simultaneous zoom and track, in opposing directions, so that the background—what's going on outside the diner window—seems to be moving in on the characters as they sit still. This is a technique that Alfred Hitchcock used to represent Scottie's reaction to heights in *Vertigo.* We saw how Steven Spielberg used it to communicate Sheriff Brody's response to his sighting of the shark in *Jaws*, and it has since shown up in many other films (see Figures 2.22 and 2.23). From a self-conscious device used by young filmmakers to pay homage to Hitchcock, it is rapidly becoming a cinematic cliché that can even be seen in television commercials. In *Goodfellas* it serves as a kind of outside commentary, a caution that the world created in the film is about to slip away, that the character we have been attached to has lost his moorings. Or never had any. It is an artificial gesture of camera and lens used to emphasize that everything we see through the camera's eye is artificial, in the very best sense of "artfully made."

The coup in which the director undermines the point of view of his character and our dependence on it comes in the trial sequence near the end of the film. Here, Henry simply steps out of the scene, walks through the courtroom set and addresses the camera, something forbidden by the Hollywood **continuity style**. By doing so, he acknowledges that it's all an illusion, all going on in somebody's head—Henry's, the director's, ours. As the film comes to an end and we see Henry in the witness protection program, living in some anonymous suburb, complaining in voice-over that he can't find a decent tomato sauce, he once again looks at the camera and smiles, as if to say, "We know what all this is about, don't we?" And just in case we still don't quite know, Scorsese inserts a shot of Tommy (Joe Pesci), Henry's hilariously violent friend, pointing his machine gun and firing at the camera. This shot doesn't come from anywhere else in *Goodfellas*. It alludes to another film, made in 1903, Edwin S. Porter's *The Great Train Robbery*. There, a shot of one of the cowboys firing his gun at the camera was put either at the beginning or the end of the film, at the discretion of the exhibitor, to excite the audience (see Figure 4.7).

So, with a wink at the audience and a nod to the history of film, Scorsese lets us know what we like about gangsters and violence. We like to watch. We like to be safe. We like to desire. And we like the delicate balance of control and fear. We also like a wise guy. In *Goodfellas*, Scorsese attaches us to a desirable character who seems to own the world, only to find that he is owned by the film we're watching, as are we ourselves. The director toys with his character and with us, allowing us in on the joke or allowing us to go off in a state of being deceived. It's only a movie, and the choice is ours.

Stanley Kubrick

Stanley Kubrick has made films, from *Killer's Kiss* in 1955 through *Eyes Wide Shut* in 1999, that not only are great works of cinema, but, in works like *Dr. Strangelove* (1964), *2001: A Space Odyssey* (1968), *A Clockwork Orange* (1971), and *Eyes Wide Shut*, are profound insights into and prophecies of cultural and political behavior. Kubrick himself attempted to avoid completely the public life of a film director. He began working in Hollywood, and his first studio film, *The Killing* (1956), brought him to the attention of the film community and especially the actor Kirk Douglas, who had Kubrick direct him in Kubrick's first major work, *Paths of Glory* (1957). But after finishing *Spartacus* (1960), a big Hollywood sword and sandal epic that Douglas asked him to take over after firing its original director, Anthony Mann, he began to work in and ultimately moved to England. He rarely, and later in his life, never traveled, creating his visionary worlds on sound stages, back lots, or nearby locations (like the old North London gasworks that became Vietnam in *Full Metal Jacket*, 1987) and dealt with large numbers of people only during the actual filming process. Kubrick was the one filmmaker who tried to emulate the life of a novelist, painstakingly creating his projects—cool films, filled with strong images, carefully controlled color schemes, and tracking camera shots that let the viewer know the character's state of mind and how we are to interpret it. He flaunts conventional filmmaking rules, and weaves complex themes about the cultures of violence and politics and the absolute loss of human agency. He worked long and carefully on his films that, after *A Clockwork Orange*, were made many years apart, in isolation and without any publicity. He made complex films that stay in the memory, that keep yielding information on each viewing. Films that were—most of them—commercially successful movies that managed the great, barely possible feat of combining the popular and the difficult—high art and popular art at ease with each other, capable of causing an unease in the viewer along with a sense of elation.

Kubrick was an inquisitive prophet; his films, many of them taking place at the time of their making, some set in the past, and two set in the future, think about the limits of being human. They are not optimistic, and often verge on the misanthropic—he didn't think that humans had a great future ahead of them. The figures who people his films, who bear the illusion of having an emotional life, a past and a present, are actually more ideas than conventionally formed movie characters—attitudes given a movie presence. This is a difficult concept, because we are so used to characters who are created to make us simply love or hate them, to elicit admiration—even a desire to be them—or, in the case of villains, to look forward to their undoing. Kubrick's characters do not attract us. Humbert Humbert in *Lolita* (1962) is a pedophile. Alex in *A Clockwork Orange* is a rapist and murderer. They are, very much like Hitchcock's characters, part of a larger pattern defined, most often constrained, by the environment he builds around them. And Kubrick never makes that pattern easy to see.

A Clockwork Orange, for example, stacks the deck so that we easily miss the joke—as did many critics, even this one when it first appeared. On first look (and listen—voice-over narration plays an important role in many of Kubrick's films), Alex is king. In his sordid, decaying world of the near future, he is a demonic force of violence and rape. Kubrick forces us to like a disgusting thug simply because he's the liveliest element of the mise-en-scène. When the camera tracks him through the record boutique where he meets two girls to take home for sex, he is completely in control (see Figure 3.4). When, in clockwork fashion, his control winds down in the second part of the film, after he has been conditioned to react negatively to violence, we feel sorry for him. He *tells* us to feel sorry for him. He gets his wish, and he seems to get his power returned—but as a political tool for the political party in power. He and we have both been manipulated, and when, in the midst of his last sexual fantasy, he calls out "I was cured all right," we realize that the cure may be worse than the disease.

Kubrick is that rarest thing among filmmakers, an ironist. Like Hitchcock, like many European filmmakers, he makes us look at characters and events from more than one point of view. To understand them, we have to see how they figure in the pattern of the film's mise-en-scène and how that pattern shifts and changes in subtle ways. This is why Kubrick's films don't reveal their full meaning for many viewings, and sometimes never. How many times have you watched the last sequence of *2001* and still wondered about its meaning? It is extraordinary for a film not to have one simple meaning, but rather multiple perspectives that float around possible meanings, shifting every time you see the film. But despite the shifts, the visual structure, the spectacular, head-on, 180-degree defying, symmetrical shots, the repeated vision of people losing out because they can't see beyond the internal and external repressions they've created for themselves, whether

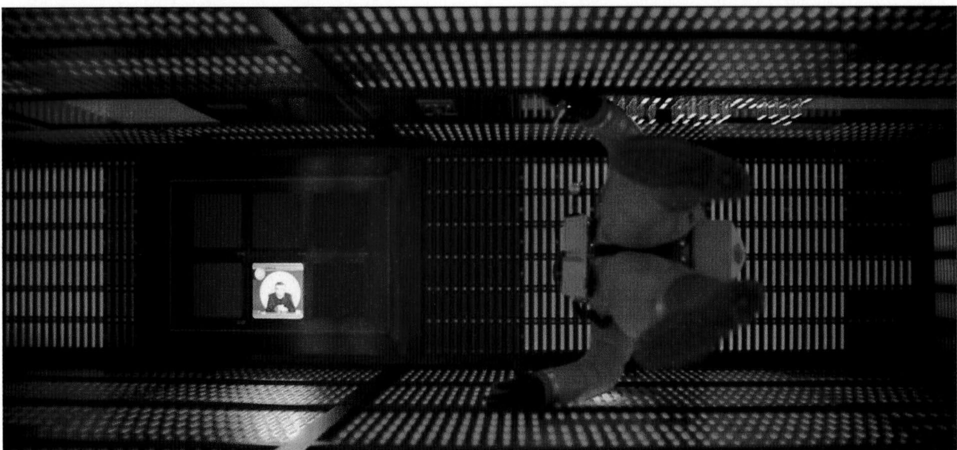

FIGURE 7.7 An ironic Kubrickian joke: as Dave (Kier Dullea) lobotomizes the HAL 2000 computer, who has attempted to take over the ship, a recorded message comes on informing him that HAL was the only one on the ship who knew about its mission to Jupiter. *2001: A Space Odyssey* (1968)

by the doomsday device of *Dr. Strangelove* that ends the world, or, after having been dehumanized by their drill instructor during training only to be undone by a female sniper in Vietnam in *Full Metal Jacket*—everyone in a Kubrick film loses (see Figures 3.26, 3.48, 4.14, 4.15, 4.23, 4.24, 6.15, 6.24, 9.25, 10.12). But the loss is the viewer's gain. As a prophetic filmmaker, Kubrick permits us to see beyond his own pessimism, to examine his images, to put the pieces of the visual and narrative puzzles together, even, if we pay attention, to find the joke that lies within every film he's made.

Alfred Hitchcock

Alfred Hitchcock carefully planned every formal move in his work well before filming actually began. Cinematic form and structure, Hitchcock understood, are the means by which narrative is made and emotion generated. Nothing would be left to chance in the creation of that structure, and no one would interfere with the finished plan when shooting began. Hitchcock was pleased to say that by the time he went to filming, he never had to look through the camera, because his plan for the film and his instructions on how to execute it were complete. As a result, Hitchcock's best films—he made some forty-eight of them between 1922 and 1976, not counting those he directed for television—are grounded on complex structures in which each composition and cut relates a great deal of information. The space of the Hitchcockian world, seen especially in films such as *Shadow of a Doubt* (1943), *Notorious* (1946), *Rear Window* (1954), *Vertigo* (1958), *North by Northwest* (1959), *Psycho* (1960), *The Birds* (1963), and *Marnie* (1964), is created by positioning characters and camera to produce a composition that often ironically comments upon the characters' situation. He will relate figures and objects through a subtle cutting between gazes, creating an interplay between a character looking at something or someone and a shot in motion of the person or object being looked at, so carefully measured that the cutting back and forth builds a sense of threat or vulnerability. This is the cross-tracking we have been discussing.

Even without cross-tracking, Hitchcock achieved extraordinary effects through the combination of composition and editing. Consider the sequence in *Psycho* when Norman invites Marion into his parlor, just before the shower murder. By cutting between the characters in their isolated

FIGURE 7.8 During the parlor sequence in Alfred Hitchcock's *Psycho* (1960), Norman (Anthony Perkins) leans forward, threatening Marion Crane and the viewer in a foreshadowing of the violence to come

worlds—their own little islands, as Marion says—and slowly increasing the visual association of Norman and his stuffed birds, including a terribly threatening, low angle shot in which a stuffed owl looms over Norman's head, the sequence reveals much of the mystery of the plot. With its emphasis on dark and threatening spaces, fear and withdrawal, its association of Norman first with passivity and anxiety and then, in a shot in which he bends forward in the frame, with a threatening look toward Marion and the viewer, the mise-en-scène of this sequence forms the nucleus of the film. Its visual structure, along with the dialogue, lets us know everything that is going on and will go on—if we care to watch and listen (Figure 7.8; see also Figures 3.44–3.47).

FIGURES 7.9–7.13 These images from the sequence in *Vertigo* (1958) in which Gavin Elster (Tom Helmore) hatches the plot to ensnare Scottie Ferguson (James Stewart) indicate how Hitchcock manipulates his mise-en-scène to communicate more information than the dialogue itself provides. The two characters start on an equal basis—even though Elster is seen comfortably seated with images of power behind him. As he begins his story about his wife being haunted by a ghost, he mounts an elevated platform in his office, dominating Scottie. As the sequence continues, Scottie continues to be dominated, even when he appears taller than Elster; the camera is in a low-angle position, emphasizing his weakness. He winds up scrunched down in a chair in the corner

Early in *Vertigo*, Scottie goes to visit Gavin Elster, the man who will set in motion an enormous ruse that will ruin Scottie's life. Scottie is already reduced and weakened. His fear of heights has resulted in the death of a fellow police officer and his own retirement from the police force. In Gavin's offices—large, ornate, overlooking the San Francisco waterfront, with a huge construction crane moving outside the window—Scottie is made to look small, sometimes almost cowering. Throughout much of the scene, Hitchcock has him sit scrunched down in a chair composed in one corner of the frame as Gavin, standing on a raised portion of the floor in his office, dominates him and the viewer. Through the spatial arrangement developed by the construction of the set and the camera, whose placement and movement keep diminishing Scottie's presence, we are allowed to comprehend undercurrents that are not articulated in the dialogue. Gavin tells Scottie a story about how Gavin's wife is possessed by a spirit from the past. In fact, Gavin is using Scottie in a plot to kill his wife, a plot that will eventually lead to Scottie's total breakdown. Scottie will become the diminished figure we see in this sequence. Like the parlor sequence in *Psycho*, this sequence in *Vertigo* gives away a lot of the film through the ways in which Hitchcock has us see his characters as part of his eloquent mise-en-scène. We will return to *Vertigo* again in Chapter 11.

WOMEN AUTEURS

An ongoing scandal in moviemaking the world over is the lack of women and minority directors. Women have always played a part in the filmmaking process. They were scriptwriters (especially during the silent period) and, most often, editors. They were "script girls," the important figure who made sure physical continuity was maintained from shot to shot. But only rarely were they in charge of putting the script on the screen, directing actors, choosing shots, working with the director of photography to light the set—all the things a director does.

Alice Guy-Blaché and Lois Weber

In the early sound period, there were two important women filmmakers. One was French, Alice Guy-Blaché, who, after making films in France, came to America and set up her own production company, Solax, in 1910. Another was Lois Weber, who, in 1916, articulated a strong statement of auteurism. "A real director should be absolute" in her control of a film, she wrote, while she was making progressive films on contemporary social issues. Both of these women made films in which women played a more active role than usual. Weber—whose career lasted into the 1920s—may have been slightly more adventurous.[5]

Her *Too Wise Wives* (1921) starts with a lovely image of a couple against a sunset and a title that says "our story should begin that way . . . but . . . ." It then presents its heroine as a completely domesticated woman—"a martyred kind of wife who lives only for her husband . . . ." Pipe-smoking, book-reading husband and his knitting wife are shown in separate shots. She cleans up his smelly pipe ashes, and he moves into a **flashback** in which he recalls an earlier flame who didn't mind his smoking. But, back in the present, he relents and offers to wear the slippers his wife knitted for him,, which he hates. The scene shifts to another wife, selfish and calculating: "A very successful wife." She performs that role. Much intrigue follows, letters, misconceptions, and at the end, the wives perform various acts of contrition. But on the way, there is an emphasis on women's power, some reference to the politics of the day, and a charming scene in which the two wives make up to each other—a rare sequence, even then, of women's friendship. The film is shot carefully and with the intent to focus on the women. While it may not be a large step from female stereotyping, it does at least bring its female characters to the foreground and honor their personalities.

Dorothy Arzner

Dorothy Arzner, like many women in Hollywood production, started as an editor and a screenwriter. She began directing in 1927 and made seventeen films through 1943. Some of her works—especially *Christopher Strong* (1933) and *Dance, Girl, Dance* (1940)—speak in complex and knowing ways about women and their reduced place in the culture. They address the ways in which genders are shifting cultural constructs (in *Christopher Strong*, the main character, played by Katharine Hepburn, spends much of her time dressed as a boy) and how women understand their status as things to be looked at by men. In one of the most celebrated feminist moments in film, one of the female performers in *Dance, Girl, Dance* talks to her audience, expressing her outrage at being the object of their gaze. It is a rare moment when a woman is permitted to speak her understanding of what film and gender performance are about from a woman's perspective.

FIGURE 7.14 "What do you suppose we think of you up here?" Dressing down her audience: Judy (Maureen O'Hara) rails at being the object of their gaze in Dorothy Arzner's *Dance, Girl, Dance* (1940)

Ida Lupino

Ida Lupino was an actress in many films from the 1930s through the 1950s (some of her best are Raoul Walsh's *High Sierra* and Michael Curtiz's *The Sea Wolf*, both 1941; and Nicholas Ray's *On Dangerous Ground*, 1952). She wanted control of her work, but instead of fleeing the country and filing a lawsuit against her studio, as the actress Bette Davis had done (and lost) in the 1930s, Lupino was able to take advantage of that moment in the history of the film in the early 1950s when contracts were running out and the monolithic control the studios had wielded for so many years was beginning to dwindle. She was able to form her own production companies so that she could direct her own films.

Lupino was a canny businesswoman as well as a good filmmaker. She also understood the cultural state of the decade in which she worked. In interviews, she always played up her role as mother and family woman, and she spoke about her directing talents as being largely passive and deferential. In the 1950s, a woman might conceivably find herself in a traditionally male role, but might also find it necessary to use the more comfortable discourse of the homemaker, who—in this case—just happens to be a filmmaker as well. Lupino's films are, at first sight, very much in the manner of 1950s noir. Their subjects are often lower-middle-class men put in bizarre situations. But there can be an interesting switch. *The Hitch-Hiker* (1953) has no female characters. It concerns two men out on a fishing trip who are kidnapped by a sadistic madman and driven through Mexico until the kidnapper is caught. In place of female characters, the two

FIGURE 7.15 Men, passive under the control of a madman in Ida Lupino's *The Hitch-Hiker* (1953)

kidnapped men, Gil Bowan (Frank Lovejoy) and Roy Collins (Edmond O'Brien), are forced into passive, childlike, or, in the terms of cultural conventions, feminine situations. They are almost in thrall to their crazy kidnapper, who taunts them for being "soft" and thinking about each other's welfare. At the end, freed of their captor (whom Roy finally beats up, after the madman has been handcuffed by the police), the two family men walk into the darkness. Gil puts his arm around Roy and tells him, "It's all right now, Roy, it's all right."

This is certainly not the only film by a man or a woman in which male characters show some affection and care for each other. However, it is not a male bonding film, because the characters do not work as a "team" or share their joy in the absence of women, despite the fact that no women are present. Both characters are oppressed by their condition: they cannot escape it, and they remain good, middle-class family men. Even though, early in the film, Roy wants to find prostitutes in Mexico, Gil refuses, in fact pretends to be asleep while Roy goes about his business. It is suggested that Roy's would-be diversion is what put them in the path of the mad hitch-hiker. Precisely these kinds of subtleties mark this as a film made by a woman: that the men get into trouble because they want to chase women; because the men are reduced to passive, even weeping childlike characters; because, despite the momentary thoughts of extramarital play, they remain attached to their unseen families through the end. Within the tough, hard lines and rigorous compositions of late noir, Lupino manages to see masculine softness and vulnerability, mock these qualities just a little, and indicate a strength that comes from places other than male braggadocio and a puffed-up sense of the heroic.

There's a similar reversal in *The Bigamist* (1953), a film that shows Lupino's talents at composing and framing sequences that achieve a proximity to her characters in ways that quietly but markedly reveal emotional states. The film is structured in flashbacks as Harry (Edmond O'Brien again, who with Frank Lovejoy was an icon of the 1950s ordinary man) takes two wives. Lupino creates a complexity here that belies the sleaziness of the story. Harry's first wife, Eve, can't conceive a child and turns to running Harry's business. This is a major and ugly 1950s stereotype: the childless woman must transfer her maternal yearnings to "man's work" in order to be fulfilled, thereby forgoing her femininity. It is even suggested by Harry that he and his wife don't have sex anymore. But Lupino refuses to take all this on face value. The Eve she depicts is a loving wife who wants to adopt a child *and* run a business. Harry, who often has to travel to Los Angeles, is shown as lonely and alienated. He falls in love with, impregnates, and marries a waitress he meets in L.A., Phyllis (played by Lupino).

The melodramatic potential of this conflict—especially when Harry's secret is discovered by the man investigating their adoption request—is underplayed. In this film, Lupino is interested in gazing closely at both male and female faces of loss and loneliness. She condemns none of the characters and gives their neediness equal attention. Even more than *The Hitch-Hiker*, the male character is endowed with what, in conventional film, are considered female traits: shifting emotions, vulnerability, failings, even weakness. Male directors also create "sensitive" men. But Ida Lupino, the only female director of the decade—of many decades—understood that gender was not something defined by the movies, only stereotyped by them. Unlike many other filmmakers, she can show sympathy to all her characters and create a film that touches upon such a taboo issue as *The Bigamist*: sympathy across the board, an understanding of what men and women might need and even get, were it not for the demands of their culture and gender.

WOMEN FILMMAKERS TODAY

With the end of the old studio system and the rise of the feminist movement, there was a hope that filmmaking would be more welcoming to films made by and about women. There seemed to be some opening in the 1970s and 1980s. Some male directors—perhaps most notably Martin Scorsese in *Alice Doesn't Live Here Anymore* (1974)—attempted to portray women freeing themselves from intolerable domestic situations. But, as in *Alice*, most of these films decided that their women characters had only to find a "better" man, thereby re-creating the traditional narrative closure of heterosexual union.

There was a brief flurry of opportunity for women directors in the 1980s and early 1990s. Diverse filmmakers undertook a variety of approaches to women's issues, such as Susan Seidelman in *Desperately Seeking Susan* (1985) and *Making Mr. Right* (1987), a film that suggested the perfect man had to be constructed like a robot. Donna Deitch's *Desert Hearts* (1985) touched on lesbian themes. Barbra Streisand, particularly in films such as *Yentl* (1983) and *The Prince of Tides* (1991), used melodrama to present images of strong women. In *Household Saints* (1993), Nancy Savoca created an extraordinary and surreal film about ethnicity and the feminine.

Some of the original contemporary women filmmakers, like Seidelman and Deitch, seem not to have been able to pursue their careers. Some have moved to television, others have flourished in different ways. Penny Marshall moved from television sitcom actress to the highly bankable director of engaging films: *Big* (1988), *Awakenings* (1990), *A League of Their Own* (1992), *The Preacher's Wife* (1996), and *Riding in Cars with Boys* (2001). She too has turned to television directing. Penelope Spheeris carved out a comfortable place, making clever comedies based upon television skits and programs, like *Wayne's World* (1992) and *The Beverly Hillbillies* (1993). Amy Heckerling was in the unusual position of making commercially popular films—*Fast Times at Ridgemont High* (1982) and *Clueless* (1995), for example. Like the others, she too is now working in television. There, woman writers and directors thrive and, especially on cable and streaming venues, explorations of politics and sexuality are more open, even daring, than is possible in theatrical films.

Kathryn Bigelow

Kathryn Bigelow, who started directing with the 1980s cohort of women directors, has managed to outlive them as an active director of theatrical films. She made her mark with her 1995 film *Strange Days* (co-written and coproduced by James Cameron), in which she tried to alter the action genre in ways that redirected male centrality and the focus of the male gaze. *Strange Days* is set in an apocalyptic L.A. at the end of the millennium. The people are up in arms, and the cops are out of control. In the midst of this chaos she creates a technological fantasy in which a recording device worn on a person's head can record and play back experiences as if they were actually occurring. One of these recordings is of a woman being raped, with the recording device placed on her head to capture her terror. The result is a gruesome sequence, and only a woman filmmaker, I think, could have created it in a manner that downplays the inherently exploitative elements and emphasizes how horrible the act is to the woman involved.

The film's "hero" is an African American woman (Angela Bassett) who is in love with a white man (Ralph Fiennes), who is definitely not a hero but a kind of human punching bag. In the climax of the uprising, and despite the fact that Bigelow seems to yield to convention by introducing the patriarchal figure of a good police commissioner to set the cops right, this couple

FIGURE 7.16 The urge to danger. Sgt. William James (Jeremy Renner) suited up to disarm an IED in Kathryn Bigelow's *The Hurt Locker* (2008)

emerges, suddenly and openly in love. They kiss—a kiss between a weak white male and a strong African American woman, a kiss that is simply given and revealed to the audience, without comment, without sensationalism, in a way that suggests that all the gun play, all the violence and mayhem, are actually a mask that allows the film to present this culturally transgressive act.

Bigelow's 2008 film about the Iraq War, *The Hurt Locker*, managed to capture the brutal anarchy of that conflict while focusing on an individual, Sgt. First Class William James (Jeremy Renner), a bomb disposal expert who is an adrenaline addict. His excitement is charged by disarming improvised explosive devices, an obsession that endangers his troops. *The Hurt Locker*, true to its subject, is a percussive film. Explosions and gunfire rattle the **soundtrack**; the enemy is uncertain, unclear, except for his signature, the bombs James rushes to disarm. Bigelow allows a small amount of sentiment as James becomes attached to an Iraqi child and is clear-eyed about the male homosocial bonding that almost gets out of hand as James pummels his colleague Sgt. J.T. Sanborn (Anthony Mackie).

Bigelow has no illusions about the war and its excesses of testosterone and adrenaline. Her attachment to her central character is tempered by an implied knowledge that his obsessive commitment to explosions is both necessary and dangerous to himself and his fellow soldiers. James is not a domesticated figure. He is at home only on the battlefield, which is no home at all. Her knowing, even cool observation is carried over to her film about the finding and killing of Osama Bin Laden, *Zero Dark Thirty* (2012). The film features a woman protagonist, a CIA agent (played by Jessica Chastain) who helps track Bin Laden down, even using torture to get the information she needs. Is this lack of sentimentality meant to indicate a measure of strength on the part of a woman director, or is it rather indicative of a director working not out of any gender motivation, but her own sensibilities about the ways to render wartime cinematically? In the end it would be foolish to say that only a woman director could do this; we can only say that a woman director did do this.

AFRICAN AMERICAN FILMMAKERS

African American directors constitute another minority in American filmmaking. There is an irony to the fact that one of the most celebrated American films of 2013, *12 Years a Slave*, was directed not by one of America's talented African American filmmakers, but by a British director, Steve McQueen. This is not to negate the power of McQueen's film, that represents the brutality of slavery with such savagery that it is difficult to watch, difficult, in fact, to learn from because the violence tends to push the viewer away.

Spike Lee

Two very different contemporary African American directors have attained a prominent position in the pantheon: Spike Lee and Tyler Perry. Lee is the director of intense films about the African American experience, who is able to move easily from relatively personal works, small films like *Crooklyn* (1994) or *Red Hook Summer* (2012), to large-scale Hollywood productions like *Inside Man* (2006) and *Oldboy* (2013), to documentaries for HBO, such as *When the Levees Broke* (2006), to the opening sequences of *The Tonight Show Starring Jimmy Fallon* (2014).

Outside of his bigger budget Hollywood films, Lee's work examines questions of race with some sensitivity and often querulous anger. *Red Hook Summer* looks at the relationship of a young boy (Jules Brown) from Atlanta, who visits his religious grandfather (Clarke Peters), the Bishop of the local church in the Brooklyn housing projects. Much of the film is an almost ethnographic study of summer life in the outer boroughs of Manhattan and the clash of cultures that results from differences in class and upbringing. The film is full of comic touches and scenes of energetic worship. Parts are reminiscent of Lee's 1989 *Do the Right Thing*, and Lee makes a brief appearance in the guise of his character Mookie from that earlier film. Unlike *Do the Right Thing* there is

FIGURE 7.17 A happy moment before the "Good Bishop" (Clarke Peters) is confronted with accusations of child abuse in Spike Lee's *Red Hook Summer* (2012)

no ongoing threat of violence until a man comes forward in the grandfather's church and accuses him of molesting him as a child. There is a premonition of this earlier in the film, when the grandfather begins to molest his nephew, to whom he has been reading the Song of Solomon. The revelation of sexual abuse causes a violent reaction. The Good Bishop is beaten and forsaken. He becomes a Christ-like figure, and the film presents us with a profound moral ambiguity: how much does a man need to suffer for his terrible misdeeds? The narrative ends with the boy taking a gift of a crucifix from his young girlfriend, Chazz (Toni Lysaith) as he rides off to return to Atlanta. Lee adds a coda with a montage of Red Hook and its people, including the players in the film, with a song, "I want you to know you make me happy. I want you to know that you make me sad" playing on the soundtrack. The film remains somewhat ambiguous about its stance towards the Good Bishop's actions, while returning its optimism to the children.

Tyler Perry

Despite the film's unsolved moral dilemma, *Red Hook Summer* insists on being a celebration rather than an outburst of anger (such as ended Lee's earlier *Do the Right Thing*) and in this, it is somewhat aligned with Tyler Perry's work. Perry is also concerned with morality and religion, but there is never any ambiguity. Rather, Perry solves conflict either with the emotional rise of melodrama or the comedic antics of his alter ego, the gun-carrying matriarch, Madea. Tyler plays her against the old stereotype of the Mammy, the happy protector of the white family—most evident in the portrayal of the slave, Mammy, played by Hattie McDaniel in David O. Selznick's *Gone with the Wind* (1939).

Full of wisdom and orneriness, Madea is not a slave to any stereotype. She promotes wisdom or, in *Madea's Witness Protection* (2012), varieties of mayhem. Perry's melodramas often concern women who make bad choices, ultimately finding the right path through religion or the help of a right-thinking man or woman. This sounds banal, but Perry has a steady and sure hand with his actors and presents what appears to be an authentic sense of African American middle-class life. The broad acceptance of his films across racial bounds indicates that Perry touches many chords—his work is viewer-friendly, he eschews the formal experiments of Spike Lee's films, and provides a degree of comfort lacking in most current cinema. His work has been accused of stereotyping his characters; but he has an attachment and kindness toward them that is quite contrary to the meanness that stereotyping most often conveys.

Julie Dash

It could certainly be argued that comfort is not what an African American filmmaker should be providing. But in fact the two poles represented by Spike Lee and Tyler Perry offer a variety of the Black experience and its interpretation by two differently talented directors. And there is one more filmmaker who needs to be accounted for, despite the fact that only one of her films, made some years ago, has achieved a measure of recognition.

Television has been one place where women can work as filmmakers. Many of the women directors mentioned earlier have gone to work in television. Julie Dash made a film for the now defunct PBS series "American Playhouse" called *Daughters of the Dust* (1991) that is extraordinary on all counts. The film was financed by PBS, the National Endowment for the Arts, and various other government, regional, and corporate grants, and it received a small theatrical distribution. The film is delicate, filled with carefully crafted imagery, in which color, the kind of lens put on the camera from shot to shot, the use of slow and fast motion emphasize and form a complex narrative of remembrance and forgetting, past and future, the physical and the spiritual. Set in 1902 in the Sea Islands off the Carolina and Georgia coasts of the United States, among the people called the Gullah, the film gathers together the members of the Peazant family, born into slavery and now, some of them, reaching middle class, a few about to head north. It is very much a family get-together film, but not in the Tyler Perry mold. This is a family from a horrific background of slavery, who have retained not only their sense of self-possession, of coherence, but a wide-ranging religious practice, African, Christian, Muslim.

Daughters of the Dust is concerned with the fuzziness of boundaries between cultures and time, about the joining of traditions and the necessity of progress. We see this in its compositional elements, which depend to a large extent on wide horizontal shots along the beach, often observing people running across the screen. But this linear visual style is undercut by the complex interweaving of the characters' memories, by flashbacks and forwards, by close-ups of objects and faces, creating a series of interlocking stories directly told or suggested. In fact, in her commentary to the film, Dash says that she based its narrative structure on the *Griot*, the traditional African storyteller and keeper of tribal tradition. Because of this, there is much magic, much imagery of dream and remembrance. An unborn child appears through the lens of a camera set up to take a family picture. A young man, attempting to sink a powerful African statue in the swamp, walks on water.

Daughters of the Dust is in many ways an ethnographic film with touches of magic realism—a style that combines a conventional realism along with the fantastic. In other words, although a narrative fiction, it also documents a way of life along with its culture and artifacts, but it envelops that documentation with a narrative of marvelous events. It looks lovingly at the women and the men of the Peazant family, at the tensions of their past and their resolution. It is never

FIGURE 7.18 The former slave and voice of history in Julie Dash's *Daughters of the Dust* (1991)

violent, even when showing the old Indigo slave plantation, where the slaves had to make toxic dyes with their hands. Indeed, the great grandmother, a survivor of the plantation, wears an indigo dress, while most of the other characters wear white. The film proves that a human horror can be effectively communicated without being represented—a far cry from *12 Years a Slave*.

Occasionally, the Hollywood production system surprises us, no more than the film *Selma* (2014), which is drawn from the history of the civil rights movement of the 1960s and directed by an African American woman, Ava DuVernay, who had previously made low-budget, independent films. The success of DuVernay's film might suggest that there is a new opening for women and African American filmmakers. History suggests otherwise; but then, history can be changed.

AUTEURISM TODAY

Christopher Nolan

I want to finish this chapter by looking at a contemporary director who is straining for auteur status. Christopher Nolan is a British director, who, after his first black and white feature, *Following* (1998), a small film shot on the streets of London about one man who follows people and another who steals from people in order to shake up their lives, came to the United States and began expanding the size and scope of his work. *Memento* (2000) is a startling film that tinkers intriguingly with time because its central character, played by Guy Pearce, has no short-term memory. The film attempts to recreate the sensation of continual memory loss by fracturing the time and space of its character's perceptions. Sequences overlap, are repeated from slightly different perspectives and perceptions. It is constructed like a layer cake whose layers don't match and keep melting into each other, the only shaky stability provided by Pearce's body, on which are tattooed names and instructions about what he thinks he needs to remember.

Nolan followed this with a film called *Insomnia* (2002), about a detective played by Al Pacino, pursuing a serial killer, played by the late comedian Robin Williams, in Alaska. In the genre of troubled cops, with the twist that this one doesn't get to sleep for a week, the film contains some brilliant set pieces, such as a pursuit in the fog over rocky terrain in the course of which the detective kills his partner, but is otherwise undistinguished. Though perhaps it is just distinguished enough that Nolan moved immediately from relatively small films to large blockbusters, namely *Batman Begins* (2005), a film that cost around $150 million to make and grossed $207 million. Batman has a long history. Starting as a comic book character in 1939, he became a mock-heroic figure in a television series in 1966, which was turned into a movie in the same year. The first contemporary Batman movie was made in 1989, directed by Tim Burton, another director who came to the big budget superhero genre without any experience of a big budget. Nolan's first and succeeding Batman films, most particularly *The Dark Knight* (2008), marked the apogee of the superhero film. What distinguishes Nolan's work in the genre are three things: a more careful and subtle (as much as the genre admits of subtlety) study of the tormented superhero figure who is drawn to violent revenge while simultaneously depressed and withdrawn; the creation of nuanced and enticing evil antagonists, most evident in Heath Ledger's attractively lurid performance as The Joker; and on the formal side, a masterful use of editing to create a propulsive rhythm from shot to shot.

Here is one example: Batman (Christian Bale) has had his first unsuccessful encounter with The Joker. (see Figures 3.13 and 3.14). There is a cut to Commissioner Gordon (Gary Oldman) climbing the steps of the bank that The Joker has just robbed, the camera tracking with him. As it swings around there is a quick cut inside the building where Gordon is receiving some papers from an aide. The camera tracks with them for a few seconds and cuts to a shot from behind them. The camera swings further to the left as they enter the bank vault and then Nolan executes a 180-degree cut to the front of them, only to cut again to a profile view of Gordon. He looks up and there is a cut on his gaze to the aide in the left foreground and Batman behind, standing at the vault door. The aide swings her head around to make sure we follow the gaze to the caped crusader. All of this occurs in a matter of a few seconds, but they are seconds that move the film forward and ensure our gaze is locked into the narrative.

FIGURE 7.19 Commissioner Gordon (Gary Oldman), in the glare of flashbulbs, mounts the steps of the bank that The Joker (Heath Ledger) has just robbed

FIGURE 7.20 There is a cut to inside the building, where Gordon talks to an aide . . .

FIGURE 7.21 and another cut behind them

FIGURE 7.22 This is followed by a 180-degree shot in front of them . . .

FIGURE 7.23 and a cut to Gordon looking around . . .

FIGURE 7.24 followed by another cut on his gaze to Batman standing by the door. *The Dark Knight* (Christopher Nolan, 2008)

It could certainly be argued that this is nothing more than efficient use of the Hollywood continuity style. But, put in the service of a large, unwieldy production, Nolan's rhythmic editing slices through the dark mise-en-scène of the Batman movies to create an intensity that belies the inherent goofiness of stories about a reluctant hero who dresses up to look like a human bat to do battle with villains more interesting than him.

Nolan is firmly in the hold of the big budget movie. Even when he returns to more personal themes, he aims for large images and spectacular special effects. *Inception* (2010) has ties back to *Memento*. In this case, instead of topsy-turvy memories, Nolan examines dreamscapes. As in the earlier film, where layers of memory intersect, here layers and levels of dreams play a similar kind of fugue but across a much larger landscape. Nolan's visualization of dreamwork is not subtle or even mysterious; rather large cityscapes rise up and enfold on themselves. People float around as the dream world moves in slow motion.

Large compositions, intricate editing, and complex **CGI** effects do not by themselves turn a director into an auteur. Sarris's formulation of auteurism culminates in "interior meaning," a coherent personal view shared across the films of a particular director. This is not to say that a relatively unknown director cannot create a strong film that meets all of Sarris's criteria, including "interior meaning." But auteurism looks at the body of a director's work. It may be too early to determine if Christopher Nolan can build out a cinematic vision of the world from the confines of the big-budget superhero genre or as he breaks out into the larger territory of science fiction in *Interstellar* (2014). But it is not too early to see that a director can emerge from the crowded field and work his way intelligently through a popular genre.

WHAT IS THE DIRECTOR?

In the United States, the auteur theory was always a theory, a way of talking and thinking about films, much more than an accurate description of how films are actually made. It was also a way to think about redistributing the hierarchies of power in the filmmaking business. Unlike the rest of the world, directorial control has been and remains very rare in the United States, at least since the early 1920s when the studio system situated the director as only one among many craftspeople working on a film. American filmmaking remains so controlled by economics and audience response that its products can't be left to one person. Besides, given the studio system and its collaborative process, and the fact that filmmaking is so much a part of the cultural churn, of the thoughts, acts, artifacts, beliefs, and politics of the society in which it is made, it is difficult to reduce American filmmaking to the imagination of a single individual. But the convenience and implied intimacy of auteurism are so seductive. So are the analytical tools it offers, permitting us to understand the structure of film as the clearly coherent stylistic and thematic operation of a singular imagination. Auteurism at least gives power to the film critic and occasionally a film viewer. "You know Spielberg," I once heard a moviegoer say after watching *Saving Private Ryan*, made in 1998 by the absolute master of the Hollywood style, "he gets me every time." But we may often need to sacrifice this clarity and control to the messier realities of film as part of a complex cultural mix. At the same time, it is perfectly possible to mix various kinds of analysis—auteur, genre, economic, and cultural—in our discussion.

The actual practice of filmmaking today—despite the existence of a few directorial stars, like Spielberg, and some who have more control over their work than others, like Martin Scorsese—has pretty much reverted back to the control of the producer and the studio chief, or simply to the current versions of the classical style. The director has become a self-censor. There is little "personal" style, and with the rare exceptions of filmmakers such as David Fincher, Paul Thomas Anderson, Todd Haynes or Todd Solondz's wonderfully, subversively perverse *Happiness* (1998), innovation is tightly controlled. But at the same time, there are opportunities for directors that never existed before. This may be the greatest legacy of auteurism: the recognition on the part of studio executives that directors, after all, can have some imaginative say in the creation of films, even if it is limited.

FURTHER READING

Peter Woolen's work on auteurism, in his book *Signs and Meanings in the Cinema* (Bloomington and London: Indiana University Press, 1972), provides some useful ideas.

Two of the clearest essays about the existence of the author are Roland Barthes's "The Death of the Author" in *Image, Music, Text*, ed. Stephen Heath (New York: Noonday Press, 1988) and Michel Foucault's "What Is an Author?" in Vassilis Lambropoulos and David Neal Miller, eds., *Twentieth-Century Literary Theory* (Albany: State University Press of New York, 1987).

The best work on Robert Altman is by Robert T. Self, *Robert Altman's Subliminal Reality* (Minneapolis: University of Minnesota Press, 2002) and *Robert Altman's McCabe & Mrs. Miller: Reframing the American West* (Lawrence, Kansas: University of Kansas Press, 2007).

Robert Kolker, *A Cinema of Loneliness* 4th ed. (New York: Oxford University Press, 2011) analyses the work of Arthur Penn, Oliver Stone, David Fincher, Martin Scorsese, Stanley Kubrick, Steven Spielberg, and Robert Altman. Jon Lewis, ed. *The New American Cinema* (Durham, North Carolina: Duke University Press, 1998) presents a number of takes on contemporary Hollywood.

For various approaches to Hitchcock and *Psycho,* see Robert Kolker, ed., *Alfred Hitchcock's Psycho: A Casebook* (New York: Oxford University Press, 2004). A collection of essays on Hitchcock's films is Marshall Deutelbaum and Leland Poague, *A Hitchcock Reader* 2nd ed. (Malden, Massachusetts: Blackwell Publishing, 2009) and in Thomas Leitch and Leland Pogue, eds., *A Companion to Alfred Hitchcock* (Malden, MA: Wiley-Blackwell, 2014). A four volume collection of essays edited by Neil Badmington is *Alfred Hitchcock* (New York and London: Routledge, 2014). The classic work on Hitchcock is the career interview conducted by French filmmaker François Truffaut, *Hitchcock* (New York, NY: Simon and Schuster, 1984).

For Dorothy Arzner, see Judith Mayne, *Directed by Dorothy Arzner* (Bloomington: Indiana University Press, 1994). A biography of Blaché has been written by Alison McMahan, *Alice Guy Blaché: Lost Visionary of the Cinema* (New York: Continuum, 2002). For the career of Ida Lupino, see Marsha Orgeron, *Hollywood Ambitions: Celebrity in the Movie Age* (Middleton, Connecticut: Wesleyan University Press, 2008).

A recent book on African American film is Monica White Ndounou, *Shaping the Future of African American Film: Color-Coded Economics and the Story Behind the Numbers* (New Brunswick, New Jersey: Rutgers University Press). The classic histories of African Americans in film are Ed Guerrero, *Framing Blackness* (Philadelphia: Temple University Press, 1993) and Donald Bogle, *Toms, Coons, Mulattoes, Mammies, and Bucks: An Interpretive History of Blacks in American Films* (London, New Delhi, New York, Sydney: Bloomsbury Academic, 2015).

SUGGESTIONS FOR FURTHER VIEWING

Of interest are the films that made up the "Hollywood Renaissance" of the 1960s and 1970s. They made the concept of the auteur briefly recognized by the studios. For example: *Bonnie and Clyde* (Arthur Penn, 1967); *The Graduate*, *Catch-22*, *Carnal Knowledge* (Mike Nichols, 1967, 1970, 1971); *Easy Rider* (Peter Fonda, Dennis Hopper, 1969); *Five Easy Pieces* and *The King of Marvin Gardens* (Bob Rafelson, 1970, 1972); *Harold and Maude*, *Shampoo*, *Coming Home*, *Being There* (Hal Ashby, 1971, 1975, 1978, 1979).

Paul Thomas Anderson's films, in addition to *Magnolia*, include *Boogie Nights* (1997); *Punch-Drunk Love* (2002); *There Will Be Blood* (2007); *The Master* (2012); *Inherent Vice* (2014).

Martin Scorsese's output is huge. In addition to the films mentioned in the text, there are: *Boxcar Bertha* (1972); *Alice Doesn't Live Here Anymore* (1974); *After Hours* (1985); *The Color of Money* (1986); *Kundun* (1997); *Bringing Out the Dead* (1999).

David Fincher's recent films include *Zodiac* (2007); *The Curious Case of Benjamin Button* (2008); *The Girl with the Dragon Tattoo* (2011); two episodes of Netflix's *House of Cards* (2013); *Gone Girl* (2014).

A recent notable auteur, whose work we will look at in Chapter 10, is Todd Haynes: *Safe* (1995); *Velvet Goldmine* (1998); *Far From Heaven* (2002); and his 2011 HBO remake of the 1940s film *Mildred Pierce*.

NOTES

1 The quotation from Godard is from *Godard on Godard*, ed. Jean Narboni and Tom Milne, trans. Tom Milne (New York: Viking, 1972), pp. 146–147; new edition (New York: Da Capo Press, 1986).

2 Sarris's essay, "Notes on the Auteur Theory in 1962," is in *Film Theory and Criticism*, pp. 551–554. His groundbreaking work, originally published in 1968, *The American Cinema: Directors and Directions, 1929–1968* (Chicago: University of Chicago Press, 1985), is the classic survey.

3 Altman's *Gosford Park* was co-written by Julian Fellowes, who expanded the idea of the film into the popular PBS series *Downton Abbey*.

4 Peter Woolen's work on auteurism is in his book *Signs and Meanings in the Cinema* (Bloomington and London: Indiana University Press, 1972). T. S. Eliot's "Tradition and the Individual Talent" is widely reprinted and can be found in the collection *The Sacred Wood* (New York: Barnes and Noble, 1960).

5 The quote from Lois Weber comes from Anthony Slide, *The Silent Feminists: America's First Women Directors* (Lanham, MD: Scarecrow, 1996).

CHAPTER 8

International cinema

We have been concentrating so far on American film, in part because—with the exception of India—it is the dominant cinema worldwide and because it is the cinema we are most familiar with. But there is a larger pattern: filmgoers around the world like American film and American filmgoers are reluctant to see films with subtitles. Despite these obstacles, a strong national cinema exists in many countries, sometimes with government or other external support, and it is important to note its presence and its history. We need also to take note of the influence of foreign film on American filmmaking. We have already seen some of this influence in our discussion of **German Expressionism** in Chapter 3. Expressionism's dark, tortured **mise-en-scène** influenced (among others) *Citizen Kane* (1941) and in turn the formal structures of **film noir** in the 1940s and after.

To cover global cinema in a single chapter would be impossible. Therefore, what follows is a survey of film as it exists outside of the United States, concentrating on the post-World War II period and focusing on its influences and its **directors**, along with, perhaps, some nostalgia for a time from the 1960s through the early 1980s when filmmakers outside of Hollywood made film history.

EARLY INFLUENCES

During the silent period, when language was no barrier, there was a vigorous exchange of films between countries. Charlie Chaplin, who came from England, became a major American and international star. Late in the silent period, European directors immigrated to Hollywood, especially from Germany, where they brought the Expressionist style to American film. Later in the 1920s, the experiments in **montage**—the rapid collision of images that creates a rhythmic visual structure quite at odds with the Hollywood **continuity style**—by the Russian filmmaker

Sergei Eisenstein caused some American filmmakers to think about alternatives to continuity editing. When the Nazis rose to power in Germany, more filmmakers came to the United States, continuing the infusion of new styles and approaches to film form and content.

The results of these early foreign transfusions were varied. Chaplin set the mark for silent slapstick comedy and his character, The Little Tramp, became recognized and revered the world over. We have already taken notice of the Expressionist influence and will have the opportunity to revisit it when we discuss film noir. Eisenstein's influence was less apparent. As we noted in Chapter 4, he believed that the **shot**, in and of itself, was less important than what happened when two shots were **edited** together. And that editing was a means to jolt the viewer into a recognition of the dialectics of history—something of a shock of recognition, of the revelation of historical forces brought home by the clash of images. This was too much for American filmmakers, too political, too against the grain of the invisible editing that by this time controlled American filmmaking (in fact, Eisenstein and his colleagues used American film, the work of D. W. Griffith in particular, as a foil, the kind of editing they would work against). An individual named Slavko Vorkapich became the montage expert in American film of the late 1920s and the 1930s, supplying, for example, the **sequence** in Frank Capra's *Mr. Smith Goes to Washington* (1939) in which Jefferson Smith (James Stewart) takes himself on a dizzying tour of the Capital's monuments. As we noted, Oliver Stone in his great films of the 1990s—*JFK* (1991), *Natural Born Killers* (1994), and *Nixon* (1995)—revived elements of Eisensteinian montage, using them to create quick changes in visual and temporal perception. **Cutting** against continuity, repeating an action from different points of view or using different film stocks, Stone revived Eisenstein's goal of startling the viewer into a recognition of film's ability to make time and space flexible, to be aware of the shock effect of cutting.

Other European filmmakers flourished before World War II and had an influence on American film. Jean Renoir, son of the famous painter, developed a leisurely, politically sophisticated style, almost poetic in its lyricism and humanity. Two of his films, *The Grand Illusion* (1937), a film about World War I, and *The Rules of the Game* (1939), a sad and ironic gaze at a society oblivious to the coming of the second of the twentieth century's conflagrations, are marked by a visual sensitivity and a regard for even the most morally corrupt of his characters. He, like many of his contemporaries, escaped the Nazis and worked in America during the mid-1940s.

NEOREALISM

On the heels of World War II came the most important movement in international film, the one that had a lasting influence on film abroad and in the United States: Italian **neorealism**. It was born of many economic, social, and political factors. Italy was badly damaged during the Allies' liberation of the country from the fascist regime, a dictatorial structure of corporate state control that managed and brutalized all facets of life, including filmmaking. (Italy's main studio, Cinecitta, was inaugurated by the fascist dictator Benito Mussolini and his son.) After the war, filmmaking as usual was neither possible nor desired, and the emergence of neorealism offered itself as a rebirth of cinema itself.

Postwar Italian filmmakers associated the commercial cinema of prewar Italy with all that was bad about the fascists. They also saw a link between Hollywood film and those fascist-era comedies and **melodramas** about romance among members of the upper middle class—called "white-telephone" movies because of their overdone decor. They knew that all of this production, with its reliance on elaborate sets, stars that were removed from the life of ordinary people, stories that addressed the lives of people who could not possibly exist in the day-to-day world, the whole artifice of middle-class fantasy, had to be overthrown. In its place would be a new kind of film that addressed poor people in their daily lives, peasants in the countryside, workers in the streets, in their apartments and meeting halls.

Stars and studios, sets, and the elaborate tricks Hollywood used to fabricate complex, unreal images would be jettisoned. Gone too were the stories about doomed love affairs among the rich and the indulged emotions of bored women and heartless men. Instead of studio melodramas, films would be made on the street, on **location**, amid the buildings, traffic, and the people of the cities or in the countryside. Instead of movie stars, ordinary people or semi-professional performers would be used. Their faces would not be familiar or associated with other films. Hollywood cinema and the cinema of fascist Italy were seen as altogether an act of evasion. People went to movies to see movie life, not the life of the world. Do away with these conventions, strip generic formulas and generic responses, get to the people, and film would in turn communicate back to the people images of life as it is.

We should understand that the neorealists were not interested in making documentaries, even though they influenced **documentary** filmmakers. They wanted to continue using fiction as a means to structure an ordered **narrative**. But for them, the narrative and the mise-en-scène would appear to grow out of the present circumstances of history and place. Many of the films they made had an immediacy and texture, a visual quality quite unlike anything ever seen before. Roberto Rossellini's great war trilogy, *Rome, Open City* (1945), *Paisan* (1946), and *Germany, Year Zero* (1947); De Sica's *Bicycle Thieves* (1948), *Miracle in Milan* (1951), and *Umberto D.* (1952); and Luchino Visconti's *La Terra Trema* (1948)—one of the few films made anywhere that addressed the poverty and hopelessness of disenfranchised rural life, in this case the life of fishermen—were raw, sometimes unpolished films of great power and clarity. All of them have a roughness and directness that move the viewer beyond the form of the film to the movement of its story and its characters. But unlike the continuity style, which also takes us beyond its form and into its content, neorealism addresses poverty and desperation, the social life of the poor, and the difficulties of forming supportive communities in a way Hollywood **genres** rarely permitted. Unlike the **classical Hollywood style**, these films demand our visual attention. By filling the screen with images of a shattered and oppressive world, they ask us to observe what we have never seen in film before.

Interestingly enough, neorealism did not experiment with form itself. The films flow with a narrative fluency that any Hollywood filmmaker would be pleased with. Rather it was the content of neorealism that in a curious turnabout, influenced form, especially the *perception* of form. Looking at working people and circumstances in the locations in which they live, with the rawness of emotions of their beaten down and courageous lives, causes the viewer to see differently. Neorealism reinvents form by forcing it to articulate a new kind of content.

Bicycle Thieves and *Rome, Open City*

In the end, Italian neorealism is, essentially, **melodrama**. But where Hollywood melodrama is about the politics of subjective suffering—individuals oppressed by gender, domesticity, and unrealizable desires to escape the conditions of their suffering—Italian neorealism is about the suffering brought on by political and economic events and the lives affected by them. The characters of neorealism are deeply oppressed, not by domesticity or gender but by war and poverty.

Bicycle Thieves, for example, has a simple premise: a very poor man gets a job putting up advertising posters. In a key sequence, he pastes up a poster of the famous late-1940s movie star Rita Hayworth. It is a kind of symbolic act that demonstrates his distance, and the film's, from the world of Hollywood glamor. In order to do his job, he needs a bicycle to get from street to street. To get the bicycle, he hocks the family's linens. At the end of this particular sequence, to indicate that his desperation is not an individual one, the camera pans away from the character to reveal huge shelves upon shelves of linens, hocked by various other people in as much economic trouble as he.

Ricci (Lamberto Maggiorani), the main character, played not by an actor but by an actual laborer, is happy at his new job. Then his bicycle is stolen by someone in even worse economic and physical shape than he is. The rest of the film follows him, accompanied by his small son, Bruno (Enzo Staiola), searching throughout Rome in a hopeless attempt to find the bike and restore his life. Ricci is seen amidst family and comrades in the houses and streets of Rome. The camera will sometimes move away from him to observe passersby and the life going on around him. At one point, when he is putting up his posters, two beggar children wander by, following a well-dressed man walking along the street. The camera casually stops looking at Ricci to follow these three peripheral characters as if De Sica were simply curious about the rich and the poor whose lives go along with or despite the doings of his main character.

FIGURE 8.1 Ricci (Lamberto Maggiorani), putting up a poster of Rita Hayworth, sees his bicycle stolen in Vittorio De Sica's *Bicycle Thieves* (1948)

FIGURE 8.2 The death of Pina (Anna Magnani) at the hands of the fascists is one of the many grim scenes of war's end in Roberto Rossellini's *Rome, Open City* (1945)

The Hollywood continuity style insists that narrative and visual focus remain at all times on the central figures of the story. The world around them is often only suggested or caught in quick cutaways. In neorealism, the world that surrounds the characters is given equal space with the characters themselves. Neorealism's mise-en-scène is created by the interplay of the characters and their world—physical and economic at the same time. Ricci's is one story among others. And his story, finally, is about anguish and hope, which are irresistible. And though De Sica focuses on Ricci with his surroundings, he cannot avoid the character's emotional state, while continuously reminding us that it is tied to the class and economy in which the character lives. He communicates these emotions and creates empathy in his audience by one of the most standard of melodramatic means, triangulating the viewer between the main character and his son. The child clings to Ricci's hand throughout his search for the stolen bicycle. His misery and tears echo his father's despair and amplify it, as when Ricci, in utter despair, attempts to steal a bike himself, only to be chased and nearly beaten by a crowd. He escapes this fate, but not the greater one of being alone and without financial means. Hand in hand, father and son disappear among the sea of humanity.

The melodrama in all this is inescapable. *Bicycle Thieves*, as well as other films in the Italian neorealist mode, plays hard on our emotions. But, it bears repeating, this is melodrama in the service of class and political awareness. The grim scenes of torture and death in Rossellini's *Rome, Open City* are shocking, and the execution of the priest that ends the film deeply moving.

But these events occur as part of the struggle of ordinary Italians to fight the Nazi occupation of the country. There is an immediacy here, all the more pressing when we know that Rossellini filmed as the Nazis were fleeing Rome at the end of the war. And like the end of *Bicycle Thieves*, *Rome, Open City* concludes with a hopeful transition to a collective future—in this case the children, who, witness to the priest's execution, go off whistling the tune used for their resistance activities. The crowd of humanity at the end of *Bicycle Thieves* and the children at the end of *Rome, Open City* point away from the sadness of the films' narratives and toward some kind of better future.

NEOREALISM'S INFLUENCE

The neorealist movement lasted in Italy for about ten years. The directors, like Roberto Rossellini and Vittorio De Sica, went on to make other kinds of films, extending the neorealist aesthetic beyond the poor and dispossessed. But the movement they started—films with social-political depth photographed on the streets—spread around the world, even to the United States, where *Rome, Open City* and *Bicycle Thieves* were popular where the burgeoning "art cinema" movement was beginning to grow. Elements of the neorealist style were absorbed into American filmmaking very quickly because of its new take on melodrama and because exterior, location shooting was so novel and suddenly economically feasible. With the **studio system** losing its hold, filmmakers were freed from the confines of the sound stage and back lot. They could move outdoors to capture the look and textures of the streets.

By the late 1940s, some films were being promoted as shot "on the streets of New York with a cast of a million New Yorkers." Neorealism's influence was immediately seen in the gangster genre. *The Naked City*, filmed in 1948 by Jules Dassin, was not a neorealist film in comparison to its Italian predecessors. Neither was it filmed entirely on location. There was still the need to manufacture images in the Hollywood style. But it used exterior sequences to a somewhat greater degree than many previous films, and it led the way for gangster films and 1950s films noir to use the streets more than the back lots, to generate images out of the material of the world rather than putting them together in an **optical printer**.

The exterior shooting influenced by neorealism reflected other economic realities. Italian neorealism emerged from the wreckage of the postwar economy and political culture. A more subtle wreckage occurred in the United States after the war. What Hollywood faced was a decline in movie attendance, a government ruling that the studios could no longer own theaters (which had guaranteed that they would have distribution of their films), and therefore a falloff in revenues. Many of the contracts that bound talent to the studios and their personnel were running out. The anticommunist witch hunts of the House Un-American Activities Committee (HUAC) helped create a blacklist of many key creative personnel for alleged subversive activities—including Jules Dassin, who directed *The Naked City*, and Albert Maltz, who wrote it. The power of the studio, manifested in its total control of the filmmaking process, and its control of distribution, was waning. Filmmakers began to form independent production companies and to shoot their films outside the studio. One of the results was the movement out onto the streets. Shooting on location in the United States was partly a matter of aesthetics and a search for novelty, but probably never, as it was in Italy, a question of ideology. Therefore, we cannot exactly say that the American version of neorealism was a social–political event, except insofar as the gangster genre concerns disenfranchised individuals attempting to make their way through violent means. The real impact of neorealism was felt in moviemaking outside of the United States.

ITALIAN CINEMA AFTER NEOREALISM

Federico Fellini and Michelangelo Antonioni

The influence of a movement often takes unexpected turns. In the United States, it was absorbed into a mainstream genre. Back in Italy, it was transformed into a novel and exciting cinema. Federico Fellini and Michelangelo Antonioni both had their start in the neorealist movement. Fellini's *La strada* (1954), a film about a brutish circus strongman (played by the Mexican-American actor Anthony Quinn, dubbed into Italian) and the simple woman who travels with him (played by Fellini's wife, Giulietta Masina), demonstrates a shift in neorealist focus. The early neorealists realized the power of composing their characters amidst the rubble and the walls of post-World War II Rome. But in *La strada*, Fellini begins something more: he begins thinking about the power of the image itself. That is, the image begins to carry visual information that outstrips the basic narrative and provides non-verbal cues or is simply startling in and of itself. Fellini and, a bit later, Michelangelo Antonioni, begin to put their cinematic talents into image formation for its own sake.

This is not unusual even in American film. Orson Welles and Alfred Hitchcock, for example, look to the power of the image to communicate on an extra-narrative level. The second-

FIGURE 8.3 Federico Fellini was one Italian filmmaker who took neorealism further by concentrating on the image, making it extraordinary—even surreal—as Gelsomina (Giulietta Masina) sits in the dark, a riderless horse walks by. *La strada* (1954)

FIGURE 8.4 Fellini in circus mode: near the end of the dreamlike *8½* (1963) in which all the film's participants, past and present, dance around the main character's half completed movie set

generation neorealists, however, developed from a different base, and when they moved beyond it, when they began focusing not on working-class people in distress but middle-class people in despair, their images grew in complexity. Fellini became enamored of the grotesque face and the large visual gesture. *La dolce vita* (1960) and *8½* (1963) celebrate the decline of the spirit and the imagination represented in great imaginative flights. *8½* concerns a filmmaker unable to complete his ninth film and, in the midst of the turmoil of his imagination, he recalls his past in dreamlike images—he sees himself and his friends, dressed in flowing capes, dance with a large woman by the sea until they are all chased off by a priest. He fantasizes himself as a child, but at the same time grown up, looked after by a gaggle of women from his past and present. He takes a whip to them as Richard Wagner's *Ride of the Valkyries* plays on the **soundtrack**.

Misogyny aside, *8½* aims for a certain delirium caused when its central character's somewhat cankered imagination is allowed to go wild. Fellini sees the world as a surreal circus while he acts as its amused ringmaster. Michelangelo Antonioni's world is hardly circus-like and his image making is not delirious but eloquently severe. His films are somewhat like abstract paintings with a quiet, restrained narrative movement amidst surroundings that made by Antonioni's eye seem strange and uncanny. These films are enigmas of perception in which the environment comments on the characters rather than the other way around. As observers, we see more than the characters do, and what we see are figures diminished by the landscape. Antonioni reaches an end point of neorealism where, instead of the streets containing the characters, they define them and become at times mysterious. At the end of *L'eclisse* (*Eclipse*, 1962), the third of Antonioni's early 1960s trilogy—including *L'avventura* (1960) and *La notte* (1961)—two lovers plan to meet on a particular street corner. They don't show up and in their place Antonioni creates a seven-minute montage of almost deserted streets; a water sprinkler; a building wrapped in scaffolding; a geometrically arranged wood pile; water dripping into and pouring out of a barrel; there are faces, blank and staring. Night falls. People emerge from a bus. Human habitations have become at once dehumanized and expressive of human isolation. The world that people have built becomes a strange, even terrifying place.

Antonioni's work became popular enough that he was able to work in English and thereby reach a larger audience. *Blow-Up* (1966), *Zabriskie Point* (1970, filmed in the United States), and *The Passenger* (1975) with Jack Nicholson in the lead further investigate plays on perception and loss, seeing and uncertainty, diminished figures in a landscape that mark one of the major formalists in contemporary European cinema. (See Figures 2.17 and 3.28 for images from Antonioni's films.)

Bernardo Bertolucci

A figure who might be considered part of the third wave of neorealism is Bernardo Bertolucci. In his early films, he was a master stylist, a creator of powerful images, carefully color coded, marked by eloquent camera movements. He is famous for his film *The Last Emperor* (1988), which won nine Oscars. But his best work came earlier. *The Conformist* (1977) is an almost surreal film about an individual (played by Jean Louis Trintignant) who becomes a fascist because of his internal struggle with his sexuality. He extrapolates fear into authoritarianism, becoming a willing tool in the full flower of his cowardice. Bertolucci treats this character with a kind of delirium, as if countering the collapse of his moral energy with a counterweight of cinematic energy.

Bertolucci's best known film is the controversial *Last Tango in Paris* (1972), a film that distracted viewers by its open representation of sexuality—distracted because the film is more profoundly interested in questions of power and control. The film is focused on Paul, an individual oppressed by the suicide of his wife, who acts out his overwhelming grief through anonymous sex with a young woman (Maria Schneider) while slowly succumbing to his need to master his loss and

FIGURE 8.5 Marlon Brando as Paul in Bernardo Bertolucci's *Last Tango in Paris* (1972). Compare this with the heavily made up Brando in *The Godfather* (Figure 6.5), made around the same time, and a much younger Brando in Figures 6.4 and 11.6

rediscover a stable sense of self. What makes *Last Tango* such an important work is the way in which Bertolucci and Marlon Brando, who plays Paul, manage to express a powerful emotionality in an intensity rare in film of any language. That intensity is also reflected in Bertolucci's mise-en-scène, so powerfully seen that each image becomes an eloquent expression of his characters' anxieties. *Last Tango in Paris* may be the epitome in Method filmmaking and acting in which director and actor called so deeply on their emotional resources that they tapped themselves out. Bertolucci went on to make other films, none as powerful as this. Brando never again acted with the force and presence that he achieved here.

THE NEW WAVE

The influence of neorealism on French film took about ten years to appear. In Chapter 7 we discussed the accords that were reached with France after World War II that created a quota for how many American films could appear on French screens as a means to generate production and interest in films made at home. The result was a very literary, somewhat static cinema that was called, derogatorily, "The Tradition of Quality." The reaction to these films came from a young cadre of film enthusiasts who watched all the American films that became available after the war and were shown at the Paris Cinémathèque under the direction of an important film archivist, Henri Langlois.

Langlois was indiscriminate in the best way. He showed films, film after film, and the young viewers watched and watched. They learned about the power of the director while watching all these American films, discovering coherent stylistic and thematic continuity that could only be connected to the name of the director. They began to write about films, working under the tutelage of the great French film critic André Bazin—whose theories of the **long take** were of enormous influence—and their criticism was often celebratory of American film and condemnatory of the current French cinema. When François Truffaut's *The 400 Blows* was chosen to represent France at the 1959 Cannes Film Festival, Jean-Luc Godard wrote the words we quoted in part in the previous chapter. He went on to say:

> We won the day in having it acknowledged in principle that a film by Hitchcock, for example, is as important as a book by Aragon. Film auteurs, thanks to us, have finally entered the history of art. But you whom we attack have automatically benefited from this success. And we attack you for your betrayal, because we have opened your eyes and you continue to keep them closed. Each time we see your films we find them so bad, so far aesthetically and morally from what we had hoped, that we are almost ashamed of our love for the cinema.
>
> We cannot forgive you for never having filmed girls as we love them, boys as we see them every day, parents as we despise or admire them, children as they astonish us or leave us indifferent; in other words, things as they are. Today victory is ours. It is our films which will go to Cannes to show that France is looking good, cinematographically speaking. Next year it will be the same again, you may be sure of that. Fifteen new, courageous, sincere, lucid, beautiful films will once again bar the way to conventional productions. For although we have won a battle, the war is not yet over.[1]

François Truffaut and Jean-Luc Godard

The film enthusiasts turned critics had now become directors. François Truffaut, the best known of this group of innovators, made tender, lyrical films about "boys as we see them every day, parents as we despise or admire them, children as they astonish us or leave us indifferent; in other words, things as they are." Especially in his early work, he drew from the neorealist tradition, which had now been transformed into the **French New Wave**. *The 400 Blows* follows the journey of a boy at odds with his parents, walking the streets of Paris, getting into trouble, free and trapped at the same time. It ends with what is probably the most famous and imitated **freeze frame** in contemporary film as Antoine Doinel (Jean-Pierre Léaud) comes to the sea, stares out, free and trapped at the same time.

Truffaut's second film was an homage to film noir called *Shoot the Piano Player* (1960). American gangster films were an enormous influence on the early New Wave films. Jean-Luc Godard, who went on to become the most influential filmmaker since Orson Welles, made his first full-length film a celebration of the gangster genre called *Breathless* (1960). But this was no ordinary gangster film. Its main character, played by Jean-Paul Belmondo, is a smart, alienated admirer of Humphrey Bogart. He is a creature of the movies as much as his creator was. He is reckless and, when necessary, violent. In appropriate film noir fashion, he is betrayed by a woman.

But more important than plot—and for Godard, as for any great filmmaker, plot was the least important item—is the visual form of the film. *Breathless* was shot outdoors, on location, in the streets and rooms of Paris, in long takes (Godard put his **cinematographer**, Raoul Coutard, in a wheelchair with a handheld camera and had him pushed or pulled, following the characters), or cut with a nervous, elliptical style that gained the name "**jump cut**," removing excess movement not unlike placing three dots into a quotation to leave out the parts we don't need. The jump cut fractured space and moved the narrative through the point of view of its character, whose attention is never focused for long on any one thing. Godard would go even further—Godard was always going further—and in 1965 made *Alphaville*, a film that places the noir detective inside the science fiction genre and has its tough-guy hero travel the universe in his

FIGURE 8.6 The freeze frame that ends François Truffaut's *The 400 Blows* (1959) has the young Antoine Doinel (Jean-Pierre Léaud) staring out to sea, trapped, his future uncertain. The freeze frame rapidly became something of a cliché

FIGURE 8.7 Figures 4.8–4.13 demonstrated how early filmmakers learned continuity cutting, including the apparently simple process of getting a character out of the door. In his first film, *Breathless* (1960), Jean-Luc Godard decided to go back to zero and break with the tradition of continuity cutting, creating what has been called the "jump cut." Here, Godard's existential thief and cop killer (Jean-Paul Belmondo) leaves his girlfriend and betrayer (Jean Seberg). He heads for the door, but Godard removes all the intermediary steps, cutting directly to the character out in the street, flagging down a car. This kind of elliptical cutting has since become commonplace

Ford Galaxy. Lemmy Caution (Eddie Constantine) confronts all the standard science fiction conventions: a mad scientist, a city of the future—actually Paris in 1965—run by a computer. The detective destroys the computer and the City through a series of dialogues with the machine. "What separates light from darkness?" the computer asks him, and he answers: "Poetry." The computer is made aware of its own self-consciousness and finally destroys itself, as the detective and his girlfriend drive back across the galaxy in his Ford Galaxy.

Godard was not idle between *Breathless* and *Alphaville*. He made seven feature films and a number of short ones before his brief venture into science fiction. Every film, and all that followed, experimented with genre, narrative form, and the basic conceptions and preconceptions of cinema. For Godard, and the movement he was part of, these films were neither imitations nor parodies. They were homages, energetic celebrations of the American films that nourished their directors' imaginations, and they were vehicles for rethinking how genres work and how audiences respond to them. Their films interrogated the ways genres operate and, further, the ways in which films told their stories and developed mise-en-scène. For Godard, the gangster of *Breathless* or the private eye of *Alphaville* become figures of existential anxiety, not that far from Chandler's Philip Marlowe, who interrogates his identity and speaks philosophically about who he is and how he is to be known.

The latter becomes the key question for Godard and his viewers: How do we *know* what we see in a film and learn about characters? What is the nature of the cinematic image and the genre-driven cinematic narrative? When we see the same characters in roughly the same story, with basically the same outcome in film after film, are we lulled into a sense of acceptance, of ideological complicity with the filmmakers and their work, both of which request our uniform response? Can genres be altered in a way to make us ask questions rather than respond with the same feelings?

Godard's answer to these questions, like Robert Altman's in the United States, was to take genres, the cinematic image, and the narrative apart, in order to make us look and understand that what we were seeing was just an image. "This is not a just image," Godard would say, "this is just an image." And these images are freighted with ideological and cultural baggage, which he tried to unpack. His films break all the rules: they give up straightforward continuity editing, avoid **over-the-shoulder** shots; they gaze at length from a position directly in front of or at the back of the characters, who talk not only to one another but to the audience. His narratives shift mood and direction, interrupted by titles, cartoon images, or other graphics. His characters stop to tell stories or make speeches; literary and cinematic allusions abound. Closure is not promised, and loose ends, popping out all over the narrative, even in the music that accompanies the images, need not be tied up at the end. In all of this, Godard followed the precepts of the German playwright Bertolt Brecht, who held that by means of various techniques that would break the illusion of identification with the work and its characters, the viewer could be kept at a distance from the work. This would permit the viewer to understand the *work* of art, how it is made, and what ideological baggage the work is carrying. As a result, Godard's films grow in complexity and in political energy, questioning why we look, what we look at, how representation itself is an act of power that we, as viewers, can counter by examination, by keeping our distance, by learning and interpreting.

Weekend, made in 1967, is the climax of the first major and most influential period of Godard's filmmaking career. A surreal road movie, a condemnation of middle-class complacency, a prophecy of the uprising that nearly toppled the French government in 1968, *Weekend* is a mad burst of cinematic energy, bizarre and violent, its characters devolving into cannibalism; it ends with a fervent wish for a new kind of moviemaking. The film's closing titles read: "End of Story. End of Cinema." Godard moved into an intensely political phase after this, making films in support of a Marxist revolution. Today, in his eighties, he continues making movies. They are less revolutionary, less exciting than his earlier work. But then, having changed the face of cinema, how could he return to the very cinema he changed?

FIGURE 8.8 Godard's post-apocalyptic world, preparing a feast of some tourists. *Weekend* (1967). Godard was once asked why there was so much blood in his films: "Not blood," he answered, "red"

THE NEW GERMAN CINEMA

The baggage of World War II and Nazism weighed on the German film industry, which, after the war, tended to recycle American films and pornography. It took some time for the neorealist and French New Wave revolution to excite German directors. In 1962, a group of filmmakers at the Oberhausen festival of short films issued a manifesto. It ended with a call for a new cinema:

> We have concrete intellectual, formal, and economic ideas regarding the production of the new German film. Together, we are prepared to take economic risks.
>
> The old film is dead. (*Papas Kino ist tot.*) We believe in the new one.[2]

What followed was a reorganization of film financing mainly through television stations in the various German states and the formation of a production and distribution group known as the Verlag der Autoren—the auteurs' publishers. The influx of finance and the pent-up urge for imaginative cinematic expression created throughout the 1970s some of the most important films of the decade. Freed up financially, German filmmakers began actively to confront the tortured past and present of their country and experiment with the formal construction of their films. A number of important directors emerged, but three figures dominated the New German Cinema, at least in the sense of being well known outside of Germany, and they could not be more different in approach and world view.

Wim Wenders

Like the directors of the French New Wave, the filmmakers of the New German Cinema were heavily influenced by American movies, none more than Wim Wenders, who was deeply, emotionally involved with American rock and roll and the American road movie. His best films trace the melancholy movement of characters across the landscape of Germany and, later, when he began filming in the United States, the Southwest. Wenders' early films, particularly those made in black and white by cinematographer Robby Müller, are richly toned in grayscale, embracing characters and landscape in a quest for calm and enlightenment, an escape from past and present, Germany's history and their own personal anxieties. *Kings of the Road* (originally titled in German *Im Lauf der Zeit—In the Course of Time*, 1976) plays out its three hour course of time by following a movie projector repair man, Bruno Winter (Rüdiger Vogler), and Robert (Hanns Zischler), who he has picked up on the road as they travel along the border of what was then East Germany, in search of people, friends, lovers, Germany's history and their own. It is a languid, melancholy journey, leavened by a gentleness that marks most of Wenders' work and the abiding love of film that informs it.

Wenders' quest is at one with his characters. His films probe the byways of contemporary Germany and America. He became friends with Nicholas Ray, the director of *In a Lonely Place* (1950) and *Rebel Without a Cause* (1955), who was dying of brain cancer. The two cooperated on a film of Ray's last days called *Lightning Over Water* (1980). Inevitably, Wenders tried his hand at making a Hollywood film; two, in fact. *Hammett* (1982) was made for Frances Ford Coppola's company, American Zoetrope. Wenders' first version was so disliked by its **producers** that Wenders filmed it over again. The result was less than interesting, except for one thing: his experience led him to make a film called *The State of Things* (1982), a black and white film about a film crew stranded in Lisbon while its director seeks funding. The first part quietly

FIGURE 8.9 Bruno (Rüdiger Vogler) and Robert (Hanns Zischler) take time off from the road to perform shadow cinema for a group of children in Wim Wenders' *Kings of the Road* (1976)

follows the dead time of actors and crew waiting. In its second half, the director, Friedrich Munro (played by Patrick Bauchau and named after the German expatriate director of *Sunrise*, F. W. Murnau) drives around Los Angeles in the back of a recreational vehicle with his producer, Gordon (Allen Garfield). Friedrich has lost his funding, and eventually his life, killed because he made a film in black and white. The potential grimness of all this is leavened by the absurdity of a mob-backed production shot down, its director assassinated, because it was not shot in color. *The State of Things* is a dark and funny satire of the vagaries and vulgarities of Hollywood filmmaking, a cautionary tale for filmmakers and audiences alike.

Wenders learned his lesson and stayed alive to shoot (in color) what is probably his best known film, a U.S.–German coproduction: *Paris, Texas* (1984). The film is a Southwestern road movie and confessional. Travis (Harry Dean Stanton) searches for his estranged wife and a way to settle his deep bereavement with himself, looking for roots, seeking, perhaps, for a cure for what Wenders called a "world-wide homesickness." After *Paris, Texas* the director himself eventually lost his place. Imagination dwindled, and Wenders' subsequent films became less connected with the road and the cultures it traverses. But in his prime, he created visually and narratively powerful studies of men in the throes of existential *angst*, alive, despite their pain, travelling roads that might lead to redemption or that might lead to more roads.

Werner Herzog

The same is not true for Werner Herzog, a filmmaker whose imagination has sustained him across both fiction film and documentary, interrogating characters either completely mad or so far on the periphery of sanity that they sometimes seem to inhabit a parallel universe. Among the many films he made in Germany during the 1970s, *Aguirre: The Wrath of God* (1972) stands

FIGURE 8.10 Killed for shooting in black and white. Friedrich Munro shoots his own shooting in Wim Wenders' *The State of Things* (1982)

as an example of Herzog's obsession with the obsessed. Ostensibly about a sixteenth-century conquistador searching for the City of Gold in South America, the film becomes an allegory of fascism as Aguirre (played by the mad German actor Klaus Kinski) plows deeper into the jungle and deeper into madness and megalomania. Herzog's camera here as in his other films assumes an ironic distance, allowing his characters to be seen near and far, surrounded always by an uncanny landscape of mountains and falls, in a persistence of vision that, along with a score by the German band Popul Vuh, produces an almost hypnotic effect.

Aguirre is a figure of attraction and repulsion. At the end of the film, as Aguirre is alone on a raft filled with monkeys, Herzog's camera circles around and around the isolated madman, lording it over the monkeys and his own oblivion. There is a persistence in the madness, a need for violent exertion of will, occasionally leading to oblivion and death. In his documentary *Grizzly Man* (2005), Herzog takes found footage of one Timothy Treadwell, who liked to live among and photograph the deadly bears in Alaska. "I found that beyond the wildlife film," Herzog narrates in his soft voice, inflected by his German accent, "in his material lay dormant a story of astonishing beauty and depth. I discovered a film of human ecstasies and darkest inner turmoil. As if there was a desire in him to leave the confinements of his humanness and bond with the bears. Treadwell reached out, seeking a primordial encounter. But in doing so, he crossed an invisible borderline." Indeed, in the course of loving his bears, he and his companion were eaten by them.

Herzog spares the viewer the sight and sounds of the slaughter, but leaves her with the question about whether Treadwell was an intrepid enthusiast or a simpleton who had no idea what he was getting into. The wise fool is one of Herzog's favorite subjects, along with the darkness that inhabits the actions of obsessive loners. *The Enigma of Kasper Hauser* (1974), taking place in the eighteenth century, concerns a strange man who has been kept in a cave and suddenly released into the world. For *Heart of Glass* (1976), he hypnotized the actors, eliciting performances in which the characters seem always to drift away into another realm. There are the scientists in

FIGURE 8.11 Alone with the monkeys, Herzog's camera circles Aguirre (Klaus Kinski) in the solitude of his madness. *Aguirre: The Wrath of God* (1972)

the Antarctic in the documentary *Encounters at the End of the World* (2007), who purposely seek out their isolation. And the loneliness of an unknowable past is elicited in his documentary on prehistoric cave paintings in France, *Cave of Forgotten Dreams* (2010). He brings to all his films, fiction and documentary, a sense of wonder tinged with irony, a commitment to the strange, the outsider, the tainted innocent.

Rainer Werner Fassbinder

Innocence is never the subject of Fassbinder's films. In his short career, from 1969 to 1982, he made over forty films, some of them multi-episode series for German television. His subject was always the intersection of the private and the political, the ways in which individual exercises of power, often on the level of intimate, sexual relationships (Fassbinder was himself openly bisexual and observed the range of sexuality in his characters), mirrored the larger structures of power in German culture, past and present. His style broke into two periods. In his early films, he adhered to the Brechtian formula of the "alienation effect," which, as we pointed out in discussing the films of Godard, means that the work of art should distance the viewer. As a result, rather than being absorbed in the work and identifying with its characters, the viewer should be kept at a distance in order to understand how the work of art works and in so doing, understand the workings of larger structures of power in the culture. Unlike Godard, Fassbinder's early films are rather rigid and rigorous. He views his characters with a mostly static camera, as they stand talking, aimless and broken.

In the early 1970s, Fassbinder discovered the work of Douglas Sirk, a German director who came to the United States in the early 1940s and in the 1950s made a series of melodramas for Universal Studios. These films were themselves inflected with a certain Brechtian influence, their huge emotions tempered by Sirk's mise-en-scène, his use of mirrors and screens, a schematic

FIGURE 8.12 Rainer Werner Fassbinder combined melodrama with a carefully contained, often fanciful mise-en-scène, evident in this image from *The Bitter Tears of Petra von Kant* (1972)

color scheme, and a somewhat ironic stance toward the emotional excess the melodramatic form demands. The Fassbinder–Sirk connection is so important that we will return to it in Chapter 10 when we compare the two remakes of Sirk's 1955 film, *All That Heaven Allows*, Fassbinder's *Ali: Fear Eats the Soul* (1974), and Todd Haynes's *Far From Heaven* (2002). The influence of Sirk brought a small degree of softness to Fassbinder's work, a compassion that was still inflected by observations of power and exploitation among working-class Germans, often revealing the sometimes invisible residue of fascism. His mise-en-scène remained distant and he stressed the artificiality of the image. He would double frame his **compositions** by gazing at his characters through doorways. He would sometimes have his characters stop acting and look at the camera. He reached, on occasion, for the bizarre, and almost always for the disaffected and lonely.

There is a great deal of pain expressed in Fassbinder's films. Humiliation, embarrassment, harassment, and love that almost always ends badly. Throughout the many genres he worked in, including a Western, *Whity* (1971), and a science fiction series for German television, *World on a Wire* (1973), there is both tenderness and mercilessness. His was a cold and compassionate eye, and his films marked one climax of the wave of cinematic invention that swept postwar Europe. Other movements have since emerged, particularly the stringent Dogme 95, originating in Denmark. It took some of its rules from neorealism but demanded such a strict formula of film-making purity that it has been honored more as an idea than a practical filmmaking guide.[3]

CHANTAL AKERMAN

Jeanne Dielman

In the previous chapter, we discussed American women filmmakers. Women filmmakers abroad face similar difficulties to those in the United States. As in the United States, there are important exceptions, like the French directors Agnes Varda and Claire Denis, who have gained international reputations, as has the Polish filmmaker, Agnieszka Holland, who, like many of her American colleagues, has been directing for American television, including episodes of *The Killing* (2013) and *Treme* (2010–2013). I want here to look at a film by the Belgian filmmaker, Chantal Akerman. One of the most successful attempts to question the male gaze and the entire genre of female melodrama occurs in her film *Jeanne Dielman, 23 Quai du Commerce, 1080 Bruxelles*, made in 1975. Akerman transforms the conventional male gaze at the female character. She makes us look, but removes the pleasure, that is, the heterosexual male pleasure of gazing at a woman. The woman who is the subject of Akerman's gaze is not desirable and certainly not erotic.

For over three hours, her camera spends much of its time simply watching the central character, a lower-middle-class Belgian housewife (played by Delphine Seyrig), who lives in a tiny apartment with her teenage son and practices prostitution in the afternoons to supplement her widow's pension. The camera looks, unmoving, slightly below eye level, at a distance that prevents intimacy, as this woman goes about her obsessive tasks, cooking, shining her son's shoes, making up the rooms, going to the store, looking after a neighbor's child, talking to her son, joylessly entertaining her clients. The camera looks and looks. There is rarely a cut unless there is a change of place, and the change of place is usually to another space in the apartment. Everything is slow, deliberate. The camera looks, relentlessly, but coolly.

The act of looking demystifies everything. The woman and her work, the woman and her sexuality are reduced to the routine of her doing them and our own gazing at them. She and her life become objects, just as so many women characters in film have often been. In the excesses of traditional melodrama, the assumed intimacy of our gaze and the forward propulsion of the continuity style allow us to identify with the character. We look at her, we look with her. We want her, we want her to succeed, to be punished. Melodrama transfers desire back and forth. But in *Jeanne Dielman* there are no distractions, no excess—except the excess created by the camera's unrelenting gaze. Desire is diverted from the character back to our own looking. We either want to keep looking to see if anything will happen or want not to look. In fact, nothing happens to the woman until late in the film, when her obsessive actions begin to unravel. She forgets part of her routine, does some things over again. Then she sits in a chair for a very long time, the camera gazing at her without a cut. Later, a client arrives. The woman experiences an orgasm with him—perhaps her first—takes a pair of scissors and stabs him. Her order disrupted, her emotions brought to the surface, she seems to have no recourse but to destroy in an attempt to get the order restored.

Jeanne Dielman is the opposite of those later post-feminist films about a sexually liberated woman who is really crazy and murderous, films like *Fatal Attraction* (Adrian Lynne, 1987) or *Single White Female* (Barbet Schroeder, 1992) or *Basic Instinct* (Paul Verhoeven, 1992), or *Gone Girl* (David Fincher, 2014). Rather it is a commentary on melodrama and its attempts to sexualize and then redeem from sexuality the central female character. *Jeanne Dielman* thinks about what melodrama might look like if we were allowed to look at it without embellishment, given the distance that the classical Hollywood style forbids. *Jeanne Dielman* explores how women are

FIGURE 8.13 Jeanne Dielman (Delphine Seyrig) goes about her chores as Chantal Akerman's camera passively records her relentless order. *Jeanne Dielman, 23 Quai du Commerce, 1080 Bruxelles* (1975)

represented in film and how that representation turns them into automatons. It also explores the conditions of our own watching of melodrama and—by draining that watching of all spectacle, of all excess, music, elaborate mise-en-scène, camera movement, and cutting—takes us to the bare level of the gaze and makes us very, very uncomfortable. Discomfort, other than the scare produced by a horror film, is not usually the place we want to go when we watch a film.

FILM IN ASIA

Japan and Yasujiro Ozu

Film in Asia is thriving. At one time, Japan had studio production as great as the United States. India still does. We owe *Godzilla* (Ishirô Honda, 1954) to the post-nuclear fears of the Japanese, and today the country is best known in the West for horror films that are remade for the European and American market, like *Ringu* (Hideo Nakata, 1998) remade as *The Ring* (Gore Verbinski, 2002). Korea, whose popular culture is enormously influential, has made films that have influenced American production. Wai-keung Lau's and Alan Mak's 2002 *Infernal Affairs* was remade by Martin Scorsese as *The Departed* in 2006. Chan-wook Park's *Oldboy* (2003), a strange film about a man kept in a room, was remade by Spike Lee in 2013.

In Japan's filmmaking past, Akira Kurosawa made (among other genres) Samurai films that gained the director international recognition. But here I want to examine another Japanese director, one whose subtlety and responsiveness to contemporary Japanese culture make him among the most unusual of filmmakers.

Though he began his career in the 1920s, Yasujiro Ozu made his most important domestic melodramas that addressed the quiet change of culture in that country after World War II. Films as moving and beautiful as their titles—*Late Spring* (1949), *The Flavor of Green Tea Over Rice* (1952), *Tokyo Story* (1953), *Early Spring* (1956), *Late Autumn* (1960)—examine the Japanese middle-class family from an ironic, quiet distance. Ozu places his camera in the "tatami" position, low on the floor, emulating the traditional seating of the Japanese at home on a tatami mat. But this emulation does not define the point of view of a particular individual in the frame. It is, rather, a cultural gesture, looking at the world from a domestic, Japanese perspective. That perspective includes a respect for space, an interest in rooms and surroundings that is not confined to the narrative of a particular film but speaks the narrative of the culture as a whole. There is a stillness in Ozu's mise-en-scène that bespeaks patience and understanding, a desire to stay and observe.

American films rarely maintain interest in or focus on spaces that have no human figures in them. Ozu loves these spaces, because, though no human figures may be present, they are still humanized, made by people to live in; and therefore they retain and define human presence, even in their absence. His camera gazes at a room before someone enters it and after she leaves. He cuts away from the main narrative progression to create a montage of the city, a train passing, a rock garden, clothes hanging on a line. Ozu's world is defined by its particular cultural articulations: the things made by and representing both permanence and transience.

But there is no mistaking the melodramatic base of Ozu's films. They are about families in turmoil. Parents die, daughters marry, fathers get drunk, sisters are mean, the domestic center does not hold. None of these situations is addressed with the hysteria and overstatement beloved

FIGURE 8.14 The middle-class Japanese family, viewed from the "tatami" position—that is from a mat placed on the floor—in Yasujiro Ozu's *Tokyo Story* (1953)

of American melodrama, nor is the viewer asked to deliver emotion on the basis of a character's death or the redemption of a misguided soul. The viewer is asked only to observe and put things together and to recognize within Ozu's mise-en-scène a harmony that transcends the particular upheavals of the domestic.

Hong Kong and Wong Kar-wai

Hong Kong has long been a center of filmmaking activity, especially in the production of martial arts films that feature amazing fight scenes, characters flying through the air, editing that creates the effect of rapid, violent movement in which a single master dispatches an overwhelming number of assailants. One Hong Kong filmmaker, Wong Kar-wai, stands out as an unusual stylist, a filmmaker of unusual visual elegance who creates films in which mood outstrips content, or perhaps more accurately mood *is* content.

In the Mood for Love (2000) is nominally about two people whose respective spouses have left them and who nurse an unrequited desire for each other. But the film is really a kind of lyrical elegy about lonely people in small rooms. Wong's camera moves gently and tends to peer at its subjects, framing them through doorways, sometimes obscuring them completely, looking at the objects that surround them—a clock, cigarette smoke, rain falling on the pavement. This concern with the objects of life is somewhat like Ozu in its focus on the quotidian and the slow passage of time. There is a poetry of time and space in this film, of muted, shifting colors, and people constricted in their movements. There is politics as well, though unstated. The film takes place in Hong Kong during the 1960s, when the city-state was still a British colony, some thirty years before it would be returned to China. Hong Kong was a liminal place, Chinese and British, fluid, like Wong's camera, unsettled like his main character, Chow Mo-wan (Tony Leung), who ultimately comes to another politically sensitive place, Cambodia's Angkor Wat, to the ruined temples of a country destroyed by war.

Politics also quietly inform Wong Kar-wai's martial arts film *The Grandmaster* (2013), a film about rival fighting clans during the Japanese invasion of China, focusing on the historical figure of Ip Man (Tony Leung), who trained Bruce Lee. Ip Man refuses to collaborate—unlike his

FIGURE 8.15 The minute gestures of martial arts in the rain. Wong Kar-wai's *The Grandmaster* (2013)

rival—after the Japanese takeover in 1938 and loses two of his daughters. But the atrocity of Japanese rule serves less as a background than as a lingering reminder that the interfamily struggles portrayed in the film are small in comparison to the larger suffering China was undergoing at the time. The film is focused on Ip Man's triumph as a fighter, his overcoming his isolation when he moves to Hong Kong.

The fighting in *The Grandmaster* is even more stylized than usual in the genre. The opening of the film is a fight in the rain, water splashing as hands and arms move in slow motion through the downpour. Ip Man manages to keep his straw hat on as he battles an entire gang. The mise-en-scène of the film is made up of shadow and gold or blue light. Tight **close-ups** of faces and fists and breaking objects prevail during the fight sequences. Even more balletic than usual in films of the martial arts genre, Wong's camera is as graceful as his fighters. A foot hitting a floorboard, sending up a puff of dust, captures his attention as much as Ip Man and the woman opponent practicing their art. Like all of Wong Kar-wai's films, *The Grandmaster* is a work of cinematic impressionism, a kind of visual rapture with a world created and observed.

BOLLYWOOD

India's film production is booming, with a vibrant star system and an adoring audience that has spread so far across the world that American and multinational studios and distributors are beginning to distribute and even finance some films. India's film production is widespread across the subcontinent and made in many languages, though Hindi films are the most popular.[4] International recognition first came to the early films of Satyajit Ray, whose Apu trilogy (mentioned in Chapter 2 and Figure 2.14) was rooted in the neorealist tradition, focusing on the rural poor with a lyricism unmatched by the Italian originators of the form. Part of that lyricism was created by the music of Ravi Shankar, playing on the Indian instrument, the sitar. Shankar went on to be an internationally recognized artist and an enormous influence on popular music.

Music and dance is a key element in Indian film, more so than in many other national cinemas. There is a tendency, no matter what the genre—costume drama, romantic melodrama (especially romantic melodrama), or political thriller—for a musical interlude to erupt. In this way, much Indian cinema is structured in something akin to operatic or musical comedy style, where music is integral to the narrative. At least these are the forms Western viewers are familiar with. The conventions of Indian film don't quite conform to those expectations. There is a heightened sense of artificiality and a melodramatic surge that is unique to this cinema and that takes some getting used to.

Satyagraha

For example, *Satyagraha* is a 2013 film, directed by Prakash Jha, and coproduced by UTV–Disney, a major player in Indian film production. This is a serious film focused on political corruption in a small town and, by extension, the country as a whole. Its title means roughly "zeal for truth," and originates in the movement of the great Indian figure of liberation, Mahatma Gandhi. Images of Gandhi appear throughout the film, and one of its main characters, the school teacher Dwarka Anand (Amitabh Bachchan), like Gandhi, goes on a hunger strike to bring justice to his hot, dusty town. While the overall tone of the film is deeply serious—at one point one of the

FIGURE 8.16 A political demonstration, complete with song, in Prakash Jha's *Satyagraha* (2013)

demonstrators against corruption sets himself on fire and Dwarka himself is shot and martyred under orders of the official he is demonstrating against—there is a romantic interlude between two of the main characters and the demonstrators themselves tend to break into song from time to time. But the impression of all this is not of an **avant-garde** piece, stretching the conventions of genre like the work of Jean-Luc Godard, for example. Rather, director Prakash Jha is pulling together the conventions of Indian cinema to satisfy expectations while directing them toward a serious end.

Satyagraha does not have the neorealist gravitas of Ray's Apu trilogy with its lyrical gaze on the lives of poor rural inhabitants. It is a long (2½ hour), color, wide-screen extravaganza that to Western eyes and ears contains an odd mixture of seriousness and playfulness, political passion and melodrama. And characters breaking into song. This is a *different* popular cinema with different conventions that indicate the vitality of a national cinema serving a huge population around the world. Indian cinema is deeply embedded in the country's culture and part of a complex growth of media that marks India's emergence as an economic power. Its *difference* from Western melodramatic conventions is rapidly becoming accepted and enjoyed by audiences worldwide.

The Lunchbox

At the same time, there is the urge to make films somewhat closer to Western melodramatic conventions. The Mumbai film *The Lunchbox* (Ritesh Batra, 2013) is without song and with a great deal of restraint. Essentially a loss-of-love story, it tells of a neglected wife (Nimrat Kaur) who finds long-distance intimacy with a quiet bureaucrat (Irrfan Khan) by means of notes passed by a lunchbox delivery service, who confuses him with her husband. The two never meet and their epistolary romance is not consummated. That is essentially all there is to the film, which works through a tender regard for its characters and a trust that its audience will respond without the usual melodramatic resources to force emotional reaction. It is another indication that "Bollywood" cinema is evolving and changing in a search for new formats and new audiences (see Figure 6.27).

EUROPEAN CINEMA TODAY

Much of the experimentation that marked the Italian film of the early 1960s, the playful, political films of the French New Wave, and the New German Cinema of the 1980s is now over. Some European films are made in English for United States and international distribution. These can occasionally be somewhat odd hybrids. Take, for example, a moderately interesting science fiction film, *The Last Days on Mars* (2013). It stars two American actors, Liev Schreiber and Elias Koteas, along with an international roster of lesser-known players. It was funded by the British Film Institute, the Irish Film Board, and a Scottish company, Qwerty Films. The director, Ruairi Robinson, is Irish. The film picks up on the craze for zombies, this time putting them on the red planet. Similarly, *Frank* (2014), about a horrifyingly dysfunctional rock band, also has an Irish director, Lenny Abrahamson, and, like *The Last Days on Mars*, is coproduced by the British Film Institute and the Irish Film Board (among other companies). Its star, the German born Michael Fassbender, spends most of the film covered up with a fake head.

Jean-Pierre and Luc Dardenne

This by no means is meant to imply that contemporary European production is all genre films aimed for a quick return on investment. There are talented directors at work, exploring their medium. The Belgian brother team of Jean-Pierre and Luc Dardenne makes small films—most recently *Two Days, One Night* (2014)—about children and parents, unsentimental, closely observed —they will sometimes **track** a character's movement from behind his ear, hewing close to his emotional turmoil, while keeping a distance that allows us to see but never quite empathize. Their plotlines are slight, their characters quiet in their innocence or vulnerability. In *L'enfant* (*The Child*, 2005), a hapless young father sells his baby to get some extra money. The little boy in *The Kid with a Bike* (2011) is abandoned by his father (the father in both films is played by the same actor, Jérémie Renier) and becomes quite lost and vicious and is treated viciously in return. These events are depicted as quite human if somewhat desperate acts; the emotional temperature is kept relatively low; the focus on small actions and reactions is sharp. The viewer looks at sometimes uncanny images—the boy with a bike silently, violently, falls from a tree— and is left alone with her thoughts.

Michael Haneke

Austrian by birth, making many of his films in French, Michael Haneke has emerged as perhaps the most interesting, inquisitive, even daring of contemporary European directors. Violence and class, and the tricks of perception are his central concerns. Like many Europeans, he has a sharp and satirical eye trained on the middle class—the moderately well-to-do, wracked with doubts, pressed by forces over which they have no control, ultimately turning on themselves in the face of personal doubts, pathological behavior, or the forces of history that are internalized as vulnerability or amorphous guilt. His visual style is built on the hard, steady gaze of the long take and a playful recognition about the artificiality of his medium.

He made the film *Funny Games* in German in 1997, and then, as a kind of dare to himself, remade it almost shot by shot in English in 2007.[5] Two young men, wearing white gloves, invade the vacation home of a middle-class family and proceed to brutalize them for the duration of the film. There is, throughout, an expectation that something or someone will intervene to relieve the violence and the tension. At one point, the wife, Anna (Susan Lothar in the German version, Naomi Watts in the American), grabs a shotgun and shoots one of the intruders. This doesn't suit either the filmmaker or his characters; the surviving intruder complains that the film is not long enough yet, so he picks up the TV remote, rewinds, and the dead intruder is back to life and ready for the final mayhem.

Which is the funny game? The sadism committed on an innocent family by two psychopaths who torture and kill? The game played with the viewer, repelled and attracted to representations of horror? "Do you think it's enough?" asks Paul (Michael Pitt in the American version, Arno Frisch in the German), looking at the camera. "You want a real ending, right? With plausible plot development, don't you?" But there is no "plausible plot development" in *Funny Games*. At the end, the duo, now in a sailboat, throw Anna over the side, continuing their brutality, discussing reality and fiction and what you, the viewer, think you see in the movies.

Funny Games is a small machine for testing the limits of audience tolerance for violence as well as the discomfort at being reminded that the horror we are exposed to is fake; that the "realism" we feel so acutely is an artifice made by film that only calls on our fears and feelings of revulsion while at the same time tweaking us for falling for it. As gruesome as it is, *Funny Games* is really a joke about our tolerance for mediated violence. When Haneke gets serious, especially when he brings into play psychology, politics, and history, extraordinary things occur.

Caché (2005) is a film that draws upon many threads. In its formal structure, it practices and interrogates the theories of André Bazin (which we discussed in Chapter 1) and his notion that the long, unedited take is the most profound method of capturing the reality of duration and space on film. As its immediate antecedent, *Caché* draws upon Michelangelo Antonioni's *Blow-Up*, a film about a fashion photographer who thinks he has photographed a murder. *Blow-Up* is a perceptual detective story, about what the photographer thinks he sees when all he sees is the grainy patterns of a blown up image. The paranoia of the barely visible extrudes itself from its color-coded surfaces (see Figure 2.17). The paranoia of images both visible and hidden weave throughout Haneke's *Caché*.

The film opens with a very long static shot taken from an alley, looking across the street at a well-to-do Parisian house. The credits spread across the screen. A man walks by. A woman walks by. A man on a bike. A car. A woman leaves the house. We hear voices asking where it was found. At the point of uncertainty as to what we might be looking at, we cut to night as Georges crosses the street to the alley, looking for the camera that has taken this image. When the image returns, it begins to show tearing scan lines like an old VHS tape, speeding up and moving backward and forward. The characters talk further, saying that the tape of their house goes on for two hours. Someone apparently has Georges (Daniel Auteuil) and Anne (Juliette Binoche)—Haneke's couples are always named Georges and Anne—under surveillance.

The film's strategy is to confuse our perception and the characters' so that within the film and from our view of the film, we can never tell the source of the tapes or various other images, such as a drawing showing a child with blood dripping from its mouth that they receive along with the tapes. However, if we think through the details of the film, these images begin to make some sense. They are an enigma that is up to us to decode. When we think it through, we come to realize that the tapes are deeply entwined with personal and political history. Georges's past, which he recalls as the film progresses, is also the past of France itself. As a child, living on a farm, Georges's parents had taken in an Algerian child, Majid. Algeria was a French colony, which revolted against its rulers. In 1961, there was a demonstration in Paris of pro-revolutionary Algerians, and the police responded by attacking the demonstrators, throwing them into the river Seine, killing perhaps as many as 200 people.

Georges recalls that Majid is the son of two of the victims of the massacre that his parents took in and sheltered. As a child, Georges turned against Majid and his parents sent the boy away to an orphanage. Now, believing Majid to be the source of the tapes, Georges tracks him down. What he finds is a sorry little man living in a sorry little apartment, observed from the point of view of the all-seeing surveillance camera. In a horrendous act of violence, Majid (Maurice Bénichou) attempts to end his misery and seal Georges's guilt—and by extension that of the French and all colonialists—by blood. The film ends with two long shots, held at a distance from the action and suggesting the presence of the mysterious camera. The first might be a dream, because a distraught Georges takes some pills and goes to bed. The scene is a replay of the moment when Majid is taken away from the farm, his despair and agony viewed coolly, unblinkingly. This is immediately followed by a view of a school letting out for the day. The camera looks and looks, and if we look, we can see, almost hidden in the background, Pierrot (Lester Makedonsky), Georges's and Anne's son, talking to Majid's son (Walid Akfir). They talk (we can't hear them) and go their separate ways.

Are they responsible for the tapes? Earlier, Majid's son had denied any responsibility for them. Are they somehow in league against their respective fathers? Or are they a hope for the future untethered to their respective country's violence? Are the tapes themselves "real," or metaphors of guilt and bad faith? The answers are hidden, *caché*. It is Haneke's way of allowing the film's long takes to expose not their intrinsic meaning but our reading of their meaning. André Bazin insisted that the long take would allow the viewer to pierce the veil of reality and grasp meaning by means of a dedicated gaze. Haneke, as is his wont, turns things around, and the more we see, the more remains hidden—unless we expand our notion of reality, of taking what we see literally. Seeing does not necessarily lead to believing.

FIGURE 8.17 A sudden outburst of violence in Michael Haneke's *Caché* (2005) as the mysterious camera records the dreadful moment in which Majid (Maurice Bénichou) takes his life as Georges (Daniel Auteuil) looks helplessly on

FILM CULTURE

The post-neorealist Italian filmmakers, the New Wave, the New German Cinema, the Swedish filmmaker Ingmar Bergman, the "kitchen sink" films from England that, like *Saturday Night and Sunday Morning* (Karol Reisz, 1960), drew on neorealism, were relatively popular in the art cinema movement that flourished in American cities and university towns from the 1950s until the 1980s (relative, that is, to the overwhelming popularity of American films). They were part of the flourishing film culture in which filmmakers at home and abroad were celebrated, written about, their films eagerly anticipated. Complexity in films was expected and embraced. Critics like Pauline Kael in *The New Yorker* and Andrew Sarris in *The Village Voice* analyzed and debated the auteur theory and the work of European directors. The New Wave in France influenced the brief "Hollywood Renaissance" during which new, young directors like Francis Ford Coppola, Martin Scorsese, Steven Spielberg, and Arthur Penn got their start. Before Penn took over direction of the groundbreaking *Bonnie and Clyde* (1967), the film's screenwriters, David Newman and Robert Benton, and its producer and star, Warren Beatty, approached both François Truffaut and Jean-Luc Godard to make the film.

There was such a vital and dynamic interplay between American and European cinema during the 1960s and 1970s that, for young, creative people, making a film took the place of writing a novel as their artistic goal. Film courses were added to the curriculum of a broad range of colleges and universities, and new programs and departments in film and media studies were instituted. It is only a small exaggeration to say that out of the passion of the young filmmakers of the French New Wave the course for which you are reading this book was made possible.

As we have seen, that excitement of discovery and creativity has leveled off to a great degree. There are still important films made abroad as they are in the United States. But the urge toward international productions, films that will make money by appealing to a broad audience worldwide, is tending to diminish the role of the star director whose personal, atypical style might not have mass appeal.

As in the United States, the star director is becoming harder to find in other countries. There are, of course, exceptions, as we have seen in the case of Michael Haneke. Another example is Abbas Kariostami, an Iranian filmmaker, whose early film *Taste of Cherry* (1997) followed a lost character travelling the mountain roads of Iran, looking for someone to help him commit suicide. Recently, he has become a worldwide filmmaker, working in Italy and in Japan. Other filmmakers may not want to travel that far, but rather make films in their country that will be popular in the United States. British filmmakers have a particular advantage in this, but occasionally a foreign language film, the French *Intouchables* (Olivier Nakache, Eric Toledano, 2011), for example, makes a small commercial dent in the U.S. market. Sometimes a foreign language film will be remade in English. Such was the case with *Le diner de cons* (Francis Veber, 1998), which was made into the Steve Carell vehicle, *Dinner for Schmucks* (Jay Roach, 2010). This translation process is more common on television. Another Steve Carell vehicle, *The Office*, was based on a British series, as is the Netflix *House of Cards*, one of whose producers is David Fincher, who directed the first two episodes. The cable series *The Killing* is based on a Danish television production.

The last two pose interesting challenges to the auteur theory, given the fact that they maintain a consistent visual style—especially the dark, rainy mise-en-scène of *The Killing*—despite the fact that there are multiple directors. The auteur on a television show may be the "show runner," the person supervising scripts and production. The **director of photography** and **production designer**, who tend to remain constant from show to show, may have more to do with the unified mise-en-scène of a television, cable, or streaming series than does the director.

This is an important digression, indicating that the director may be receding from the scene and perhaps, on the small screen at least, be reduced to the role played during the studio system, when he was merely one craftsperson on the production line, albeit the person responsible for turning a script into images. Until relatively recently, the director was the major figure in filmmaking outside the United States. Now, as we've seen, there are relatively few who have gained international prominence. That decline marks the vanishing of the film culture that was so vibrant in the 1960s and 1970s both in the United States and abroad. Is interesting filmmaking giving way to television and streaming sources? Is film in a recessive mode ready to reemerge as the dominant art form it was just a few decades ago, perhaps on television as opposed to the movie screen? Pessimism may be premature.

FURTHER READING

An excellent overview of global cinema is Roy Stafford, *The Global Film Book* (London and New York: Routledge, 2014).

An analysis of postwar European and international cinema is in Robert Phillip Kolker, *The Altering Eye*, originally published in 1983, available online from Open Book Publishers, http://www.openbookpublishers.com/reader/8.

A large survey is Geoffrey Nowell-Smith, ed., *The Oxford History of World Cinema* (Oxford, New York: Oxford University Press, 1996).

For Italian film, see Peter Bonanella, *A History of Italian Cinema* (New York: Continuum, 2009).

Current theories of transnational and global cinema are found in Nataša Ďurovičová and Kathleen Newman, eds., *World Cinemas, Transnational Perspectives* (New York and London: Routledge, 2010).

The best discussion of the French New Wave remains James Monaco's *The New Wave: Truffaut, Godard, Chabrol, Rohmer, Rivette* (New York: Oxford University Press, 1976). Richard Brody's *Everything is Cinema: The Working Life of Jean-Luc Godard* (New York: Metropolitan Books, Henry Holt and Co., 2009) is a clear, intense reading of Godard's films in the context of the New Wave.

Thomas Elsaesser has written *New German Cinema: A History* (New Brunswick, New Jersey: Rutgers University Press, 1989). The influence of Brecht's theoretical writing is collected in *Brecht on Theatre*, trans. John Willett (New York: Hill and Wang, 1979).

Recent work on Bollywood includes Raminder Kaur, Ajay J. Sinha, eds., *Bollyworld: Popular Indian Cinema Through a Transnational Lens* (New Delhi, Thousand Oaks, California: Sage Publications, 2005).

SUGGESTIONS FOR FURTHER VIEWING

Neorealists

Luchino Visconti: *Ossessione* (1943).

Roberto Rosselini: *Paisan* (1946); *Germany Year Zero* (1948); *Stromboli* (1950); *Europa 51* (1952); *Voyage to Italy* (1954).

Vittorio De Sica: *Miracle in Milan* (1951); *Umberto D.* (1952).

Ingmar Bergman was a popular Swedish director whose films include *The Seventh Seal* (1957), *Wild Strawberries* (1957); *Through a Glass Darkly* (1961); and *Persona* (1966).

Some additional films of the French New Wave

François Truffaut: *Jules and Jim* (1962); *Fahrenheit 451* (1966); *The Wild Child* (1970); *Day for Night* (1973).

Jean-Luc Godard: *Contempt* (1963); *Pierrot le Fou* (1965); *Masculin Féminin* (1966); *Two or Three Things I Know About Her* (1967); *La Chinoise* (1967).

Eric Rohmer: *My Night with Maud* (1969); *Claire's Knee* (1970); *Chloe in the Afternoon* (1972).

New German Cinema

Wim Wenders: *Alice in the Cities* (1974); *The American Friend* (1977); *Wings of Desire* (1987).

Werner Herzog: *Even Dwarfs Started Small* (1970); *The Great Ecstasy of Woodcarver Steiner* (1974); *Nosferatu the Vampyre* (1979); *The Bad Lieutenant: Port of Call—New Orleans* (2009).

Rainer Werner Fassbinder (this is a small sample of a huge output):

Why Does Herr R. Run Amok? (1970); *Beware of a Holy Whore* (1971); *The Merchant of the Four Seasons* (1971); *Effi Briest* (1974); *Fox and His Friends* (1975); *In a Year of 13 Moons* (1978); *The Marriage of Maria Braun* (1979); *Berlin Alexanderplatz* (1980; a 14-episode German television series); *Veronika Voss* (1982).

Bollywood

Representative titles suggested by India media scholar Manjunath Pendakur. They are subtitled and readily available.

Sholay (Ramesh Sippy, 1975); *Coolie* (Manmohan Desai, 1983); *Roja* (Mani Rathnam, 1992); *Dilwale Dulhaniya Lejayenge* (Aditya Chopra, 1995); *Lagaan* (Ashutosh Gowarikar, 2001); *Rang De Basanti* (Rakyesh Omprakash Mehra, 2006); *Omkara* (Vishal Bharadwaj, 2006).

Wong Kar-wai

Chunking Express (1994); *Happy Together* (1997); *2046* (2004); *My Blueberry Nights* (2007).

Jean-Pierre and Luc Dardenne

La promesse (1996); *The Son* (2002); *The Silence of Lorna* (2008); *Two Days, One Night* (2014).

Michael Haneke

Benny's Video (1992); *71 Fragments of a Chronology of Chance* (1994); *Code Unknown: Incomplete Tales of Several Journeys* (2000); *The Piano Teacher* (2001); *Amour* (2012).

NOTES

1 The quotation from Jean-Luc Godard comes from *Godard on Godard*, ed. Jean Narboni and Tom Milne, trans. Tom Milne (New York: Viking Press, 1972), pp. 146–147.

2 The quotation from the Oberhausen Manifesto is from the website http://www.moma.org/visit/calendar/films/1311 (accessed 16 March 2015).

3 A list of Dogme 95's rules can be found at http://cinetext.philo.at/reports/dogme_ct.html (accessed 16 March 2015). Some of Rainer Werner Fassbinder's crew are now active in America. His cinematographer, Michael Ballhaus, has worked for Martin Scorsese, filming such diverse projects as *Goodfellas* (1990), *The Age of Innocence* (1993), and *Gangs of New York* (2002).

4 Manjunath Pendakur writes in a note to the author: "Produced in multiple languages in nearly a dozen cities, Indian cinema has an extraordinary variety and range. Hindi language cinema, although it totals 16% of the more than 1200 films produced annually, has a global reach. It is the dominant force culturally and commercially." His article "Twisting and turning: India's Telecommunications and Media Industries under the Neo-liberal Regime" in *International Journal of Media & Cultural Politics*, Volume 9, Number 2, 2013, 107–131 is an excellent survey of the current media landscape in India.

5 Haneke's reasons for remaking *Funny Games*—"it became almost a gamble with myself, whether I was able to do the exact same film under very different circumstances"—can be found at *Cinema Blend*, http://www.cinemablend.com/new/Interview-Funny-Games-Director-Michael-Haneke-8141.html (accessed 16 March 2015).

CHAPTER 9

The stories told by film I

THE STORIES WE WANT TO SEE

It's a Wonderful Life

Frank Capra's *It's a Wonderful Life* (1946), a film that grew in popularity years after its initial release, pulls its hero and its audience in many directions as it tries to reconcile post-World War II anxieties with a story that wants to be upbeat and morally responsible in a conventional way. In the process, the film tries to make up its mind whether it is a comedy, a fantasy, a nightmare, or a **melodrama**. It is full of high emotion but also has plenty of jokes and silly characters; an angel guides the main character through a dark alternative world; and the film ends, as comedies do, with a reconciliation, a reaffirmation of harmony and happiness. Everyone forgives; everyone appears ready for long-term happiness. But the film's central character, George Bailey (James Stewart), is not a comic figure. He is wracked with doubts; he fights against the calls of his community, he wants to break with his father and leave the constraints of the small town of Bedford Falls. During much of the film, he is represented as a man on the verge of a nervous breakdown. He attempts suicide and is saved only because he has a guardian angel (Henry Travers), who brings him to his senses by presenting him with a vision of the town as it would be without him: dark, corrupt, violent—almost like the inside of George's mind.

The film, like George, is a bit schizophrenic, split between various fantasies and nightmares of its own making. Coming at the end of World War II, it tried to create a story that would bring the culture together, remind it of its responsibilities, reinstate the nuclear family headed by the working man, nurtured by the stay-at-home mother. It wanted to be a good populist warning

FIGURES 9.1–9.2 The dark side of the post-World War II period: anger and violence, and the happy, redeemed man and his family. Two images of James Stewart in Frank Capra's *It's a Wonderful Life* (1946)

about the need to shift large capital out of the hands of single owners into the community. But it too fully absorbed the uncertainties of its moment, and all it can do in the end is breathlessly proclaim a happy ending. Its vision of George's conversion, and the town's sudden unity; its images of the smiling family and presumption that everyone will live happily ever after are as great a fantasy as Clarence the angel's vision of the bleak Bedford Falls that would have been without George.

CLOSURE

Despite the tensions within the film that threaten to break it down, it manages to reach closure, that conventional **narrative** event in every kind of fiction that stitches together the loose ends, the broken lives, the ruined love affairs, the villains still at large, the people physically and emotionally lost, all that has come unwound as a narrative moves along. More than simply ending a story, the act of closure brings back into harmony and balance lives and events that have been disrupted. That harmony and balance is always contrived to fit with what filmmakers believe to be dominant cultural values: victory over evil, as defined by the film, comfort to the previously afflicted, the affirmation of true love, redemption of the lost and abused, reassertion of the family as the most valued cultural unit.

DOMINANT FICTIONS

Despite the tensions, *It's a Wonderful Life* manages to position itself within the framework of what might be called the **dominant fictions** of the Hollywood style. Harmonious closure is a major part of the stories we like to see and, by reaching closure, Capra's film positions us within it as amused, intrigued, and delighted spectators. (It is interesting to note that the word "closure," formerly a critical term, is now part of everyday cultural discourse, referring to the desire to end the sense of loss following a disaster.) Like *Casablanca* (Michael Curtiz, 1942) before it, *It's a Wonderful Life* has become even more popular than when it was first released, not only because it tells a "universal" story, a grand narrative applicable to all people throughout time (keep in mind that "universal" is a culturally generated idea) but because it generates a large and inviting fantasy out of a style that carefully and invisibly propels us through a narrative of desire, sadness, fear, reconciliation, to a final proclamation of self-worth and fulfilled communal need. Such dominant fictions contain the elements that please us with their ease of access, with the way they raise our expectations and satisfy them, generate fears and then quiet them, and conclude by assuring us that all is right with the world. A dominant fiction is like a template or a blueprint of stories the culture wants to hear and it partakes of the ideological structure of the culture.

The concept of a dominant fiction is of large culturally, historically, and economically determined constructions, many of them formed long before film. They are part of a culture's collective ideology, its generative concepts of family, order, self-possession, righting of wrongs, individuality over community, property ownership, religion, and so forth. Dominant fictions can be thought of as a top level of abstraction, the reigning stories of the culture. **Genres** give words and flesh to those most comforting abstractions of love, family, sin and redemption, life and death, and our deepest fears of disruption of order, of violence and despair. Dominant fictions and the genres that give them immediacy own our imagination. *It's a Wonderful Life*'s story of a man who overcomes his fantasies of independence to settle down and be the center of his family and community derives from a dominant fiction of individual and domestic responsibility that overcomes disruption to reach harmonious closure. In this case, the generic form of the dominant fiction is a mixture of comedy and melodrama.

I suggested that the dominant fictions were important constituents of the Hollywood style. But, we could stretch a point and consider the **classical Hollywood style** is itself a dominant fiction. It is not only the form that the majority of films use to tell their stories but a narrative in itself. It offers an invitation to pleasure without work, invites us to see without really having to understand what we see, and gives us an illusion of continuity and process without asking us to understand the way the links work. Through the genres that are generated by the dominant fictions, we are asked to allow ourselves to be enfolded within a comforting space between the gazes of the characters, and it constitutes tales of excitement, danger, transgression, terror, romance that are satisfied by the film's end. The genres of the classical Hollywood form embrace and drive individual films, narratives of love and hate, fear and desire, male heroism, female dependence, the liberal virtues of racial equality, self-respect, the conservative notions of demonizing and destroying selected enemies and the imperatives of "normal" domesticity, and all the other good and bad stereotypes of human behavior that films talk to us about.[1]

NARRATIVE CONSTRAINTS

Dominant fictions and the genres they generate do not exist "out there," though many exist outside of film and have been constructed out of the long lineage of beliefs held by our culture and others. They have a history, and most important they can be varied, told and retold, reworked at different times and for different needs. Dominant fictions in particular shift with the culture's ideology. Film can trace the lineage of its dominant fictions back to Renaissance comedy and nineteenth-century melodrama, stories of love lost and reclaimed, virtuous women attacked by corrupt men, families and other beloved institutions imperiled by greedy and immoral individuals, the sanctity of home and the order of the nuclear family, the innocence of children, the patience of women, the resolvable confusions and violence of men.

The structure of the dominant fictions and the genres that they drive are based on constraints. Cultural contexts, social norms, and dominant beliefs dictate their form and evolution. In a capitalist society, cultural constraints encourage narratives that promote close families and dependent women because this is a manageable structure that urges the woman to stay at home and care for children—the future homemakers, workers, or managers, depending on their gender—while the male is freed to be in the workplace. In the past, Socialist countries attempted to generate narratives of communal activity rather than families and celebrate the laborer's and the farmer's work. Socialist narratives were constrained by state ideological necessity—celebration of the revolution or of workers, for example. In a capitalist system, constraints are created by the need for a film to make a profit. Story and structure that push too hard against what has already been proved to work are discouraged. An audience's displeasure threatens the studio's bottom line. There are other constraints as well.

CENSORSHIP

In the history of Hollywood film, events occurred in the early 1930s that further restricted the contours of its dominant fictions and genres. Responding to pressures raised by the Catholic Church over what it perceived as licentiousness in film—especially the films of the sexy actress Mae West and the violence of gangster films like *Little Caesar* (Mervyn LeRoy, 1931), *The Public Enemy* (William Wellman, 1931; see Figures 3.18 and 3.19), and the original *Scarface* (Howard Hawks, 1932), along with an open approach to sexuality in general—and faced with falling revenues caused by the Great Depression, the film business decided to censor itself before local authorities or the government stepped in. As noted in Chapter 5, the studios adopted a "**Production Code**" written and administered by a Catholic layman, a Jesuit priest, and a Catholic publisher. The Code essentially forbade films from showing anything sexual—married couples had to sleep in separate beds—or allowing any crime to go unpunished. Films could not show the details of a crime or any explicit violence. There was to be no profanity or any other activity suggestive of the ordinary or the extraordinary behavior of flesh-and-blood individuals. No one in a film narrative could be allowed to get away with anything that transgressed the culture's most conservative notions of legality and morality. A woman having an extramarital affair or, worse, bearing a child while single, had to be punished in some fashion. Nothing might be shown that wasn't within the formal strictures of the Code, because every script had to be vetted by the censors. Films had to restrict themselves to the stereotypes of heroism, virtue, reward and punishment that they themselves had imported from the Victorian stage and reworked into their native language.

If the Code had been followed religiously, movies of the 1930s, 1940s, and 1950s would have been banal to the point of being unwatchable. But screenwriters and **directors** created their own codes through images and editing that suggested things rather than stated them. Rain and cigarettes, for example, were often coded to signify sexuality. A discreet fadeout or a **dissolve** to a fireplace or a storm might indicate lovemaking. A look or gesture was loaded with meanings that might otherwise have to be spelled out in dialogue. Often, screenwriters put in outrageous **sequences** in early versions of their scripts—a visit to a brothel, perhaps—guaranteed to throw the censors off so that they would not notice more subtle elements elsewhere.

A good argument can be made that the Production Code forced film to be more indirect, more implicit and subtle than it is now in the post-Code period. Today, even with the Code long gone—and with violence, profanity, and sexuality rampant across cinema—the stories films are telling remain largely the same. In the great majority of films, evil is still punished, the complexities of individual, communal, political, economic, and cultural behavior are often ignored or reduced to bite-sized chunks. Redemption stands as the promise offered by almost every film and demanded by every audience: the promise that lost men will find their way, that a confused and threatened people will find clarity in the action of a male hero, that women desiring more than the culture allows will finally understand that the love of a man and the raising of a family will bring their lives to fruition, that domestic harmonies will be restored, that the right way—as defined by the dominant culture and the stories it loves—will be found.

GENRE

All of this constraint and repetition must be understood within the cultural contexts of film. The ability to interpret the dominant fictions means that they must respond to important individual, social, and cultural needs. We respond to films because we want to; we want to because films show and tell us the things we want them to. Subtleties and variations are continually added to the genres driven by the dominant fictions. They have to be rearticulated at different times for different audiences. Genres always have to be given concrete details to create a story because dominant fictions are abstractions, strings or algorithms of culturally accepted actions and reactions that become concrete in the individual films that give them immediacy. "Genre" literally means the *type* of film narratives that relate the stories we want to see and are structured against regular patterns, recurring themes, locations, and characters.

Genre is, finally, the major formal constraint within or out of which a particular film is generated.

We invoke genre whenever we classify a film narrative. A cable or online streaming service will do it when arranging titles by categories such as "Action," "Comedy," "Drama." Like any generic classification, these categories help prepare viewers for what they will see, though they are often broad and imprecise. To better understand genre, we need to create categories that are not only inclusive but also more definitive. When we do this, we find there is a moderately stable group of major genres—comedy, melodrama, action-thriller, crime, **film noir**, war, musical, Western, science fiction, horror—that flesh out and individualize the dominant fictions and tell us the stories we like, with the variations and invention that keep them interesting.

SUBGENRES

From within these large groupings, **subgenres** emerge. The action-thriller genre, for example, spawns such subgenres as spy films, terrorist and evil corporation films. Under and around crime film are its satellites, the gangster movie, the detective film, the heist movie, the serial killer film, and film noir, which began as a subgenre and quickly emerged into a full-fledged genre of its own. Road movies like *The Hitch-Hiker* (Ida Lupino, 1953; see Figure 7.15), *Bonnie and Clyde* (Arthur Penn, 1967), *Easy Rider* (Dennis Hopper, 1969), *Thelma and Louise* (Ridley Scott, 1991), *Natural Born Killers* (Oliver Stone, 1994), *Identity Thief* (Seth Gordon, 2013), *Nebraska* (Alexander Payne, 2013, see Figure 3.49)—to name a tiny fraction of this popular subgenre—emerge from the crime genre. Comedy and the road movie often cross. So do comedy and melodrama. *Forrest Gump* (Robert Zemeckis, 1994) is a melodrama with comedy; *Sideways* (Alexander Payne, 2004) is a comedy with melodrama. *Mars Attacks!* (Tim Burton, 1996), the *Men in Black* films (Barry Sonnenfeld, 1997, 2002, 2012), and the *X-Men* movies (Bryan Singer, 2000, 2003, Matthew Vaughn, 2011, Bryan Singer, 2014), the *Spider-Man* series (Sam Rami, 2002, 2004, 2007, Mark

FIGURE 9.3 The face of the female hero: Katniss Everdeen (Jennifer Lawrence) in *The Hunger Games: Catching Fire* (Francis Lawrence, 2013)

Webb, 2014), Ang Lee's *The Hulk* (2003), and so on through the list of superhero films mix the genre of comic books and trading cards with the action/science fiction genre.

Genres are sometimes inflected and changed by gender. The ongoing *Hunger Games* series (*The Hunger Games*, Gary Ross, 2012, *The Hunger Games: Catching Fire*, Francis Lawrence, 2013, and *The Hunger Games: Mockingjay—Part 1*, Francis Lawrence, 2014) are dystopian fantasies, taking place in a future world where the elites control the population by sending adolescents out to confront each other on survival missions. Men are usually the lead figures in such films, but Katniss Everdeen (Jennifer Lawrence) takes on the qualities of courage and cunning that allow her to barely survive the cruel machinations of the effeminate rulers. The woman hero takes on conventionally masculine qualities while maintaining an essential gentleness that informs her strength.

Genres, though born of constraint, can be quite supple, stretching and moving with the cultural demands of the moment. They help the viewer negotiate with the film, promising to provide certain narrative structures and character types that the viewer finds satisfying. But they have definite limits. For example, the Western—a genre we will examine in detail later in this chapter—has had a well-defined set of conventions. When those conventions were stretched too far, and the cultural climate that supported the Western collapsed, the genre went into recession. Attempts to revive it have met with mixed success, and sometimes downright failure. *The Lone Ranger* (Gore Verbinski, 2013), a film we have referred to earlier, is by turns serious and funny, often parodying itself as it conducts its revenge narrative. Audiences hated it. If a film is too self-conscious, the narrative bonds are in danger of being broken. If the audience feels it is not being taken seriously enough, people may not show up.

GENERIC ORIGINS

Genres, as we noted, preexist film by a considerable stretch of time. Tragedy, epic, comedy, and satire emerge in ancient Greek and Roman literature. Melodrama is of more recent origin, beginning in the eighteenth century, when the English novel gave a voice to middle-class romantic fantasies aimed at a female audience. In the drama of pre- and post-revolutionary France and

America, melodrama at first personalized the great political aspirations of a middle class yearning to be free of aristocratic baggage. After the revolutions in both countries, melodrama expressed middle-class moral principles of virtue rewarded and vice punished. In nineteenth-century French and English novels—Dickens and Balzac, for example—melodrama still combined the personal and the political, addressing issues of gender and class, discovery of lost identity, strenuous pursuit of freedom from oppression, and self-sacrifice for the cause of others. These dominant fictions would continue to generate the genres of cinema.

The transformation was made through the Victorian stage, where the passions of melodrama were played out with exaggerated abandon and the clichéd gestures that are now referred to whenever the genre is parodied. As we discussed in Chapter 6, in the nineteenth century, these gestures were, in fact, codified, illustrated, and written down so that actors would know how and when to use them. Exaggeration was required in the pantomime of silent film. Intertitles, which interrupted the action with printed words, might represent the intended dialogue or summarize narrative events, but emotional continuity needed to be maintained by physical movements and facial expressions. In many countries during the silent period a live speaker might be present to narrate the events on the screen. "Melodrama" means drama with music. Silent films were rarely shown silent. By the 1910s, orchestral scores were distributed with major film productions and were played by orchestras in urban movie theaters. In smaller theaters, a pianist might play from a score or improvise music to the film. Music provoked the emotions and made connections between what the characters on the screen and the viewers in the audience were supposed to be feeling. Music persists, now on the **soundtrack**, and it remains a major element of film in general and melodrama in particular.

The great dynamics of emotion generated by melodrama were supported by the economic dynamics of an audience willing to pay to see virtue rewarded and vice punished, to be assured that heroic men would save women from disaster and that the moral balance of the world would be restored. These dynamics were set into motion by writers and **producers** who worked in concert with what they intuited or analyzed as audience desire. Audience desire and creative supposition were more often in sync than not.

In literature, genres were born out of the complex interactions of form, structure, individual imagination, and social need. Forms of storytelling developed and were repeated, rules were constructed, obeyed, and repeated, in acts of collusion. An artist's imaginative needs, the audience's desire, and larger class and cultural events conspired to establish specific forms and formulas that generated specific meanings and maintained them in the social conscience. Tragedy, originally stories of kings and rulers, evoked the social profundity of the cyclical movements of power and pride, authority, self-deceit, and fall from power. The pastoral became the form for discriminating between the simplicities and complexities of a culture by contrasting an innocent, rustic world against the corruptions of the city. The epic told the large, complex story of the origination and formation of a society and its politics from the perspective of a great hero.

In film, genres are also born out of social need and continue as long as the need is there. But while they have literary and theatrical origins, film genres rarely emerge out of the work of individual artists. In fact, some have argued that, in film, individual imagination is the enemy of generic purity. The genre transcends the artist and is therefore the perfect example of the mass production of narratives that constitutes studio filmmaking. A genre film is the result of many imaginations, including the collective imagination of the audience, the dominant fictions it cherishes and that nourish it. And, as in all imaginative issues relating to film production, it is economically determined.

GENERIC PATTERNS: THE GANGSTER FILM

Establishing a genre means establishing a pattern out of a blueprint, constructed as a dominant fiction. As in the making of a car, once the pattern is established, it is easier and cheaper to turn out many versions of the same pattern than to reinvent a new one for each unit. Here is a brief example: during the 1930s, when Warner Brothers decided to make a gangster film—a genre that the studio came to specialize in and, with *Little Caesar* and *The Public Enemy*, practically invented (though it had its origins in silent film)—a number of events would occur almost automatically. A basic story line would be at the ready: a young man from the slums would wander into a life of crime. Since these early films were set during a period of prohibition against alcohol, the life of crime would usually be illegal trafficking in booze. In contemporary gangster films, it is usually drugs or human trafficking.[2] The young man would collect around him a close male friend and a girlfriend. They would be seduced by fame and fortune, build a gang, gain riches through violence, reach for more than they could grab. The young man would become entranced by his fame and wealth, fall out with the friend, the girlfriend, or his mob, be betrayed, and finally get gunned down by the cops or a rival gang.

This narrative appealed to the Depression audience's desire to break out of the difficult, poor life many of them suffered during the decade and helped them fantasize a life of power, riches, and comfort that ran parallel to the "legal" system. At the same time, it appealed to the dominant fiction that spoke to the moral prohibition against easy wealth and provided a cautionary restriction on the too easy satisfaction of desire. If wealth came too easily and illegally to someone, he needed to be punished. The gangster film offered the fantasy of wish fulfillment and the reality of cultural restraints all at the same time. The audience was tempted and was redeemed from temptation, though apparently not redeemed enough to keep censors from getting nervous.

Along with the gangster narrative, the apparatus for the gangster film could be easily constructed. The studio would have everything at hand: the city street already built on the back lot, a cutout of a car placed against a **rear-screen projection** of a city street in motion, guns of all kinds, fedora hats, sharp suits for the men, low-cut gowns for the women. The actors were under contract: Edward G. Robinson, Humphrey Bogart, James Cagney. Writers and directors, also under contract, would be assigned to the latest gangster production. In short, all the elements were there and ready to make a genre film. As long as the audience and the censors remained receptive, the economies for this kind of production were sound and returns on investment were guaranteed. Unfortunately, the censors soon cracked down on the studios and so they modified the genre, sometimes turning the actors who played gangsters into FBI agents, repeating the patterns but with the "good guys" in the foreground.

But the gangster genre has prevailed. It was reborn in the 1940s and became a major element in film noir. We love the outlaw; we wish to see him prevail; we know he must fail. But the genre—as all genres must—changed with the times. After World War II, with the growth of corporate power and the advent of the American mafia, the gangster moved from lone hero to member of a "syndicate," and a number of films, like Raoul Walsh's *White Heat* (1949), began to show the gangster as a fading figure, destroyed by modern technology, or, in the case of one of the most extraordinary films of the genre, Abraham Polansky's *Force of Evil* (1948), becoming part of organized crime. The gangster as heroic figure and—of all things—strong family man emerged again in the first of Francis Ford Coppola's *Godfather* films. In the second, the gangster as a man diminished by the burden of his success reemerged.

The *Godfather* films, along with Italian director Sergio Leone's *Once Upon a Time in America* (1984), brought the gangster genre into the ranks of big-budget, sweeping narratives of male bonding, the inevitability of corruption in a corrupt world, along with a certain amount of sentimentality for strong men in a world of power. And the gangster genre lives on most brilliantly in Martin Scorsese's films *Goodfellas* (1990), *Casino* (1995), and *The Departed* (2006), and in action-adventure films, like the *Ocean's Eleven* series (Steven Soderbergh, 2001, 2004, 2007; the first a

FIGURE 9.4 The face of the early movie gangster. Rico (Edward G. Robinson) pulls off a big job in *Little Caesar* (Mervyn LeRoy, 1931)

FIGURE 9.5 "Made it Ma. Top of the world!" Raoul Walsh's *White Heat* (1949) marks the end of the gangster as lone gunman. James Cagney's Cody Jarrett is a psychotic thief and killer, too much in love with his mother. At the end of the film, he goes up in an apocalyptic explosion

FIGURE 9.6 Gangsterism as a business. Mobsters and corporate executives meet in pre-revolutionary Cuba. *The Godfather: Part II* (Francis Ford Coppola, 1974)

remake of a 1960 film). Following Scorsese, the ethnic gangster surfaces in HBO's *The Sopranos* (1999–2007). But ethnic stereotypes undergo change and these days, now that organized ethnic crime has gone through a change in the culture itself, various films feature the Russian Mafia in place of Italian bad guys.

GENRE AND NARRATIVE ECONOMY

By the 1930s, as the studios geared up production, many of them releasing a film a week (six major studios and a number of smaller ones averaged over 300 narratives a year for about twenty years), originality in story line was not a practical or affordable quality. Genres—fed by adaptations from existing novels, stories, plays, or other films—allowed this vast production of narratives to go on with ease. The question of originality was rarely raised, perhaps even frowned upon. Audiences became habituated to seeing variations on a theme with apparent ease. The studios continued the variations on a theme with obvious ease. Each part of the process—production and reception, filmmaker and audience—remained in contact through genres. The studios negotiated generic form and content with an audience that signified its acceptance of the contract by buying tickets.

In the days of the studios, executives would hold previews in the Los Angeles suburbs. The film's director and producer, perhaps even the studio head himself, would travel to a theater and, from the back of the house, watch the audience watching the film. Afterward, they would collect note cards from the audience. Depending on the audience's reaction during the film and on their written comments after the screening, the executives might order retakes, demand an alternative ending be filmed, ask to have more funny lines added, or have the entire film recut to increase or slow down its rhythm. Based on audience response, the film would be reshaped, the variations on a theme reworked.

Previewing still goes on. Some moviemakers hold focus groups, in which a representative collection of people are invited to discuss their attitudes about a particular film or about film in general. But currently the main negotiating power of the audience is mediated through the money they pay in film admissions, DVD rentals, and, though difficult to calculate accurately, streaming. The most important "preview" is a film that makes a great deal of money during its first weekend. If a film is successful, it becomes a model for films to follow. The audience resides mostly inside the gross receipts a film earns. On the basis of those receipts, writers, agents, producers, and directors attempt to guess what variations on the successful genre or story might make them more money still. They guess wrong more often than right. But every right guess usually pays for the wrong ones. Think of how that single variation of the old 1930s action-adventure film, *Raiders of the Lost Ark* (Stephen Spielberg, 1981), led to a string of imitations. When *Batman* (Tim Burton, 1989) came along and was a major success, filmmakers seized the opportunity to combine comic book action, heroism, fantasy, and elements of the science fiction film in a variety of ways. There were the sequels of the films themselves (three for *Raiders: Indiana Jones and the Temple of Doom,* 1984; *Indiana Jones and the Last Crusade,* 1989; *Indiana Jones and the Kingdom of the Crystal Skull,* 2008; all directed by Steven Spielberg, with another to come; and a seemingly endless number for *Batman*). As we noted in Chapter 7, once Christopher Nolan took over the franchise, the Batman movies became **auteur**-driven productions.

But we cannot simply blame the studios for churning out generic clones. In fact, no one entity is to blame. The key to genre is the circulation of stories, and as long as audiences enjoy the product and pay for it, the circulation continues. As long as the stories keep shifting and changing shape, but not too much, the studios keep making them applicable and acceptable to a large enough audience, and audiences keep seeing them and making them applicable to themselves, a large enough generic community will be achieved. The films will be successful and the genre will thrive.

DOCUMENTARY

At first thought, **documentary**—sometimes called nonfiction—film seems to stand outside the usual categories of film genres: Westerns, science fiction, action-adventure, comedy, romantic comedy, melodrama, thriller, gangster film, and so on. It stands outside because it is not fiction, not "made up," and therefore not driven by the large narratives of make believe. The dominant fiction of documentary is supposed to be its truthfulness, a faithful gaze at the world and the lives of the characters it observes. Observation is the guiding force of documentary, and the illusion of neutrality of the documentary filmmaker makes up its central generic element.

In fact, the history of documentary, which is as long as the history of fiction film, proves otherwise, and the documentary turns out to be not only a genre but, like narrative film, host to a number of subgenres. Earlier we spoke about the old notion that fiction film derived from the work of the Lumière brothers, who often set up their camera and simply recorded the events in front of it, while Georges Méliès crafted fictions inside his studio. In fact, Méliès also filmed historical events and the Lumières set up little fictions to film. Between them, they set in motion complexities of documentary filmmaking that move all the way through the horror film, like *The Blair Witch Project* (Daniel Myrick, Eduardo Sanchez, 1999), the *Paranormal Activity* series (2007–2015), and *Willow Creek* (Bobcat Goldthwait, 2013), to the Iraq War film *Redacted* (Brian De Palma, 2007), fiction films made to look like documentaries or contain documentary-like material. Recent television shows like *The Office* are made to appear as if they were documentaries, with characters addressing the camera. These complexities have made it a difficult genre to define with any certainty.

Newsreels and television

Documentaries break down into a number of subgenres. Originally, documentaries were made to observe and record events that might have gone on without the camera's presence. Newsreels were one manifestation of this kind of documentation. They were a part of almost every filmgoer's experience from the 1930s throughout the 1950s. In cities, there were theaters devoted to showing only newsreels. One major hybrid of newsreel documentary was *The March of Time*, a weekly newsreel produced in the 1930s through the early 1950s by Louis de Rochemont and *Time Magazine*. (*The March of Time* is parodied in the "News on the March" sequence in *Citizen Kane* (Orson Welles, 1941).) *The March of Time* rarely depended on newsreel footage alone and, like many turn-of-the-twentieth-century silent newsreels, would boldly create sequences in order to achieve maximum dramatic effect.

Today, networks and cable television and the Internet have taken over the work of the newsreels that were common in theaters, and while the re-creations of events are less radical than the theatrical versions, TV and online news skew and shape the events they observe in other ways. Television news loves to show blood and tears, and it is the major outlet for prepackaged political messages. While much of the footage is of events that have actually taken place, the footage is edited for maximum emotional effect, like a movie. And because everyone from politicians to special interest groups is now quite savvy about the power of television, events, especially political ones, are more often than not staged by their participants to be filmed in a certain way. If *The March of Time* pointed the way to the mixture of fact and fiction to produce what appeared to be fact, television news turns fact into fiction and attempts to control viewer attention to maximize viewership itself.

TV news is also the great fear-monger to the culture. Unlike film, in which the convention is to avoid a direct gaze at the camera, the TV newsman makes direct eye contact with us, telling us of disaster, murder, and disease. Invading our private, domestic space, the face on the screen can pretend intimacy and evoke a narrative of participation and proximity, an invitation into a fantasy world of threat and violence (the news) or desire and pleasure (the commercial), which flow together seamlessly. And with the advent of politically centric cable outlets—MSNBC on the left; Fox News on the right—the news is documented within large ideological narratives that play, for the most part, to audiences in agreement with the political slant of either one of the two cable networks.

The advent of "reality TV" has blurred the lines even more. Pretending to observe the ongoing lives of often brash, sometimes vulgar individuals in ordinary or extraordinary situations, reality television shows are, in fact, heavily edited. Like a fiction film, they arrange the best scenes, the best takes, the best **reaction shots**, supply an overlay of music, and produce, in effect, a fiction in which everyone involved is aware of being observed and acts accordingly.

EARLY MASTERS OF THE DOCUMENTARY

Newsreels, news footage, television news and "reality" programming are in fact a special and one might say especially corrupt aspect of documentary filmmaking. Much more prominent and lasting are films made by a variety of independent filmmakers whose purpose is to show an aspect of human activity, promote social programs, record societal problems, or comment on war. Some of these filmmakers work entirely on their own. Others—especially in the 1930s and 1940s, in Russia, the United States, and Great Britain—worked for government agencies and created some of the most important and exploratory films that we have.

Dziga Vertov and Esther Shub

We have examined, through the work of Sergei Eisenstein, the powerful, structurally complex political films that were made after the Russian Revolution. Other filmmakers of the period made films that were documents of events before, during, and after the revolution (see Figures 4.30–4.33). Dziga Vertov, best known for his inventive celebration of filmmaking, *Man with a Movie Camera* (1929), also made a long series of films about daily life in the postrevolutionary U.S.S.R. The *Kino Pravda* films were instructive, observant, and playful. They would, for example, demonstrate the making of a loaf of bread by running the process in reverse, from the loaf to the bakery, the flourmill, the field of wheat. Vertov's "kino eye" made the camera a kind of reality probe to show people how the world worked. Esfir (Esther) Shub, on the other hand, rarely filmed out in the world and instead made her films out of found footage. Called **compilation films**, nothing is shot specifically for the new work, which is created in the editing room. Like so much of post-revolutionary Russian film, Shub's compilations are about **editing**, about choosing available images and so ordering them that they are given new meaning. Unlike Eisenstein's muscular, dynamic **montages**, Shub's *The Fall of the Romanov Dynasty* (1927) is amazingly linear, a history lesson moving across revolutionary time.

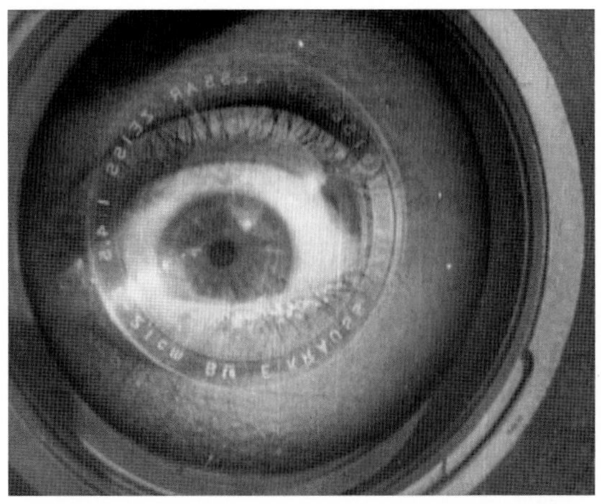

FIGURE 9.7 Dziga Vertov looked at the world with a "kino eye." The camera became his tool for exploring post-revolutionary Russia. *Man with a Movie Camera* (1929)

FIGURE 9.8 Esfir (Esther) Shub used found footage of the Russian Revolution—here Lenin greets a crowd in *The Fall of the Romanov Dynasty* (1927)

Robert Flaherty

The American Robert Flaherty still holds a place as a founding figure of the documentary. In fact The Flaherty Film Seminar is held regularly as a forum for discussion and exhibition of documentary and experimental work. Flaherty was a perfectionist and a creative force, pulling together his material and the people whose lives he was documenting, and when necessary arranging their environment to create the perfect scene and effect that, though often staged, would bring home the points he was making about his subjects even better than unmanipulated observation might show. His most famous film, the silent *Nanook of the North* (1922), despite its mildly patronizing attitude and stereotyping of the "simple savage," creates a kindly, engaged, and often lyrical observation of daily Inuit life in the 1920s. Flaherty loves to look into the faces and actions of his characters with both an anthropologist's curiosity and a desire to find the homely and comprehensible attributes of what, to an outsider, is an exotic culture: Nanook listens to (and tries to eat) a phonograph record, the family gives medicine to a child, the group builds an igloo, or they simply engage in play. In some of the film's most famous sequences, we observe Nanook fishing (he kills the fish with his teeth) and his capture of a walrus and a seal.

The latter event is a fake. Flaherty had a dead seal placed beneath the ice. But this production history does not take away from the power of the sequence and representation of authenticity of the film as a whole. Flaherty's talent at placing his camera at exactly the right place to compose the person in the landscape, and the time he allows for events to take their course, mark the film as a kind of touchstone for documentary filmmaking to come. Unfortunately, Flaherty's own career did not fare well. Film was a perfect vehicle for the culture's desire for the exotic: foreign people in strange lands who fit stereotypes of the primitive and childlike. *Nanook* fit that desire well enough that the studios attempted to cash in on it. Flaherty went to work for Paramount on a variety of projects, often with a codirector whom the studios either trusted or—in the case of the German filmmaker F. W. Murnau, who collaborated with Flaherty on

FIGURE 9.9 Digging a seal out of the ice. A reenacted sequence in Robert Flaherty's *Nanook of the North* (1922)

Tabu (1931) until the latter abandoned the project—apparently thought would add to the exoticism and make it more sentimentally attractive.

These films barely adhere to anything but the vaguest requirements of documentary and it wasn't until Flaherty turned to government and corporate sponsorship that his talents shone again. He made *Man of Aran* (1934) for the British, and it is one of his best and least compromised works. The rawness of the life of a fisherman in an inhospitable environment is presented with little flinching; the brutal landscape and hopeless labors of its inhabitants are represented without sentimentality. Flaherty ended his career with *The Land* (1942), made for the U.S. Information Service, and *Louisiana Story* (1948), sponsored by Standard Oil. Somewhat compromised because of its sponsor, which wanted a film to show what a good environmental neighbor it was, this film is a lyrical glorification of both place and alleged corporate goodwill.

Pare Lorentz

Documentaries are never big moneymakers, and documentarists have often turned to government and corporate support in order to make their films. This does not, of course, mean that the films are automatically more ideologically charged than films financed by the studios, or that they have to toe a particular line. *Louisiana Story* survives as a well-made documentary apart from its

FIGURE 9.10 Pare Lorentz creates visual poetry out of the dustbowl Midwest in the government-sponsored *The Plow That Broke the Plains* (1936)

corporate sponsorship. There have been periods in the history of film when many governmental bodies understood the importance of film in representing the culture, creating images for it, and, yes, propagating some important ideas that the sponsoring bodies wished to have known.

The U.S. government under Franklin Roosevelt in the 1930s became, briefly and through various agencies, the funder and producer of some of the best documentaries we have. Pare Lorentz, for example, made two films about the work of the government in land reclamation: *The Plow That Broke the Plains* (1936) and *The River* (1938). The films are composed with a precise photographer's eye (indeed Lorentz used prominent still photographers to film his work), and an editor's rhythm, heavily influenced by the montage practice of Sergei Eisenstein, drives the films forward with grace and purpose. Indeed, it is the visual rhythm of *The Plow That Broke the Plains* that turns a powerful statement about the reclamation of the 1930s dustbowl into a splendid piece of filmmaking with political urgency. Its precise montages of land and people, of the deadness of the first threatening the lives of its inhabitants, make it a strong prelude to the saving of the land by government intervention.

Leni Riefenstahl

Lorentz was one of many American documentary filmmakers in the 1930s who used government sponsorship to provoke their political and aesthetic imaginations into visually stimulating cinema. There were also many European documentarists, perhaps most famously Joris Ivens, who worked through a variety of subjects, including *The Spanish Earth* (1937), a film about the struggle of the Spaniards against the right-wing insurgency of Francisco Franco, with a commentary by Ernest Hemingway.

One filmmaker, however, did not use her government sponsorship well. Or perhaps she did—too well. Leni Riefenstahl remains, even after her death in 2003 at 102, one of the few prominent women filmmakers across the history of world cinema and one of the most controversial. She was the filmmaker of the German Nazi Party. Her two best-known films, *Triumph of the Will* (1935) and *Olympia* (1938), were financed for and made in the service of Adolf Hitler.

Triumph of the Will is a film about a gigantic Nazi rally that was staged precisely so that Riefenstahl could film it. The purpose of the film is to provide visual and ideological stimulation to the viewer of people in large, geometric masses, marching, saluting, looking at and listening to Hitler, the object of their adoration. A part of the hypnotic effect lies in Riefenstahl's editing, which proved so tight that filmmakers were unable to extract footage from *Triumph* to compile an anti-Nazi film. Stimulation is not the same as stimulating, however. The incessant parading and the huge massing of people, along with Hitler's harangues, may have had a hypnotic effect

FIGURE 9.11 Leni Riefenstahl's staged documentary of a Nazi rally, *Triumph of the Will* (1935)

FIGURE 9.12 . . . is echoed by George Lucas in the first *Star Wars* film (1977). The question is why Lucas would imitate a film that documents absolute evil in his film about the triumph of good

on a willing and ideologically committed fascist audience. Today the film is long, noisome, and tiring.

Curiously, the film maintains some kind of perverse influence. For reasons best known to himself, George Lucas imitated not the cutting but the compositions of *Triumph of the Will* to celebrate the victory of the heroes at the end of the first *Star Wars* (*Star Wars: Episode IV—A New Hope*, 1977). Perhaps there is something in the **composition** of geometrically massed people that attracts an innocent (or not so innocent) cinematic eye.

Triumph of the Will, obviously, has remained in the global cultural consciousness and has sparked many arguments about aesthetics versus politics. This controversy reaches as far back as the non-documentary film *The Birth of a Nation* (1915; see Figure 3.10), D. W. Griffith's groundbreaking work that celebrates and led to the renewed popularity of the Ku Klux Klan. It leads us to ask if film—or any work of the imagination—can be separated from the social and political contexts in which it was made, even if those contexts are less virulent than fascism or racism. I think the answer is no, and this book is an ongoing attempt to integrate film not only with other films, but with the cultures from which it comes.

JOHN GRIERSON AND THE BRITISH DOCUMENTARY MOVEMENT

Leni Riefenstahl proclaimed her innocence to her dying day, insisting that her interest lay in art, not politics. She has even become the subject of someone else's documentary, Ray Müller's *The Wonderful, Horrible Life of Leni Riefenstahl* (1993). She remains, perhaps with D. W. Griffith, among the most interesting, unredeemable figures in film history. Happily, while she was making Nazi films in Germany, John Grierson, a Scotsman with large humanist-socialist leanings, began overseeing a complex filmmaking process in England through funding first by the Empire Marketing Board and then—more in keeping with his notion of film as a means to disseminate information—through the General Post Office. Though Grierson directed only two films himself, he produced or oversaw many, many others. The films were as varied as they were brilliantly made. Harry Watt and Basil Wright's *Night Mail* (1936), with its narrative written by the poet

W. H. Auden and music by Benjamin Britten, showed how the British mail system worked. Basil Wright's *Song of Ceylon* (1934) demonstrated the growing and production of tea, though perhaps not the status of Sri Lanka (the name of Ceylon after it became independent) as a British colony. All of the films represented information through a synthesis of word, sound, and imagery photographed in bold, large compositions, edited with an Eisensteinian imagination, a rhythm that drives the viewer through and with the film's information.

If this weren't enough, Grierson went to Canada in the late 1930s and founded the Film Board of Canada, which was in its time a major and influential government filmmaking agency. Grierson also wrote about film. He invented the very word "documentary" in a review of Robert Flaherty's *Moana* (1926) and propagandized the social power of the documentary film with grace and persistence:

> The "art" of documentary is, as always with art, only the by-product of an interpretation well and deeply done. Behind the documentary film from the first was a purpose, and it was the educational purpose. . . to "bring alive" to the citizen the world in which his citizenship lay, to "bridge the gap" between the citizen and his community.[3]

WORLD WAR II

During World War II, the U.S. government, through the Office of War Information, continued the production of documentary films, all of which were "propaganda" films in the sense that they propagated the rightness of the American cause and pushed, sometimes to extreme racist proportions, the horror of Nazism and, most especially, the Japanese. Many of these films were produced or directed by major Hollywood figures: Frank Capra, for example, oversaw production of a large number of films grouped into two categories, *Why We Fight* and *Know Your Enemy.* These films combined narration, war footage, reenactment, and animation (supplied by Walt Disney) in films that compelled the viewer into an assent to the just war.

Other directors of great stature also made wartime documentaries. John Huston, for example—the director of films such as *The Maltese Falcon* (1941), *Treasure of the Sierra Madre*, *Key Largo* (both 1948), and *The African Queen* (1951)—made two dark, troubling nonfiction films about the war and its aftermath. *The Battle of San Pietro* (1945) is something like an engaged though reenacted newsreel with a probing, troubled intelligence behind it, so troubled that the army itself was uncomfortable with its unrelenting images of destruction and wanted it cut for public release. Similar trouble confronted Huston's *Let There Be Light* (1946), a documentary of emotionally disturbed soldiers in an American rehabilitation facility. In this case, it was (presumably) fear of revealing the identities of these soldiers suffering from what we know as post-traumatic stress that kept the film out of circulation until relatively recently.

The trauma of World War II does not diminish with time. It has long been known that in 1945, Alfred Hitchcock attempted to assemble footage of the liberation of prisoners from Nazi concentration camps at the end of the war. The film was never completed, partly because Hitchcock was so deeply affected by what he saw that he could not finish the work, but also because the British did not want to upset German postwar denazification by reminding them of the horrors they had unleashed. Years later, the footage was assembled for the Berlin Film Festival and an American Public Broadcasting program broadcast in 1985, called *Memory of the Camps*. In 2014, the material Hitchcock worked on was discovered again at the Imperial War Museum in London, edited and released under the title *Night Will Fall* (André Singer).[4]

CINÉMA VÉRITÉ

Much of early documentary was carefully planned and structured. Flaherty's films, as we pointed out, contained staged sequences, and the best of the 1930s and 1940s documentaries were composed and edited more artfully than many fiction films. There was a tendency in most studio-made documentaries to use **voice-over narration**, providing a shell of words to envelop the images. The term "voice of God" was coined to describe the stentorian tones of the narrator of *The March of Time* series, imitated in the newsreel sequence of *Citizen Kane*. But the influence of **neorealism**—discussed in the previous chapter—led to a change in these documentary structures. Beginning with the work of Jean Rouch in France in the 1950s—and moving to the United States in the films of Richard Leacock, D. A. Pennebaker, Frederick Wiseman, and David and Albert Maysles—a surge in new documentary, often referred to as **cinéma vérité**, occurred in the 1960s. Cinéma vérité is marked by the absence of voice-over narration and strives to achieve a perfect illusion of ongoing life, casually observed by the camera. Vérité is meant to appear seamless: in other words, it attempts to imitate some aspects of the Hollywood **continuity style**. But this continuity is meant to communicate the ongoing process of everyday life, of people doing their work, conducting their personal affairs.

David and Albert Maysles

For example, David and Albert Maysles' *Salesman* (1969) follows Bible salesmen on their door-to-door rounds, and watches and listens to them give their pitch to prospective customers, talk to colleagues, and ruminate about their profession. The film attempts to represent a neutrality, which, given the very nature of its subject and their work, it cannot quite manage. While not melo-dramatic, and never reaching for the large emotions of that other great work about salesmen, Arthur Miller's 1949 play *Death of a Salesman*, the film cannot avoid pulling our emotions toward the comprehension of a rather small, sad life devoted to the selling of religion. It also cannot avoid a very careful editorial structuring of events. The film's sequences may actually have been recorded as they occurred, but they are arranged to create a particular and affecting narrative flow.

It was another Maysles Brothers film, *Gimme Shelter* (1970), that brought the vérité movement to its climax. One of a number of rock music documentaries following in the wake of Michael Wadleigh's *Woodstock* (1970, one of whose editors was Martin Scorsese), *Gimme Shelter* contained a major difference: it showed a murder. The film documents the infamous Rolling Stones' Altamont concert, for which the band hired Hell's Angels as security guards. The Angels fought with the crowd, and one of them stabbed to death a man brandishing a gun. In the film, the Stones are very aware that trouble is afoot; they ask the audience to "chill out." But in a sequence staged for the observing camera, the Maysles sit the members of the rock group in front of an editing machine and show them the footage of the fight. Mick Jagger asks, "Can you roll back on that, David?" And in slow motion the stabbing is clearly seen.

From one point of view, *Gimme Shelter* is a perfect documentary in that it shows us events happening that even the crew shooting them were unaware of at the time. At the same time, it is so edited that the discovery of the murder becomes the film's climax, and the filmmakers' presence is clearly announced. The Maysles argued that it couldn't have been done otherwise, given the notoriety of the event. However, it does demonstrate how carefully a good documentary is structured and crafted, given form not by the passing of the daily world in front of a neutral lens but by the creative intelligence of the filmmaker.

FIGURE 9.13 Mick Jagger looks at the image of a murder committed at the Altamont concert captured by documentarists David and Albert Maysles in *Gimme Shelter* (1970)

In their subsequent work, the Maysles intruded further into the documentary process. *Grey Gardens* (1975) is a film about a mother and daughter—relatives of Jacqueline Kennedy—living in squalor in a decaying house in the upscale town of East Hampton. The Maysles talk to the Beales, mother and daughter, on camera, and even allow themselves to be seen directly or reflected in a mirror, filming. The lack of pretense of objectivity marks an important change in the documentary urge and becomes most evident in the work of Michael Moore and those documentary filmmakers who followed in the wake of his success.

MICHAEL MOORE

Fahrenheit 9/11 (2004) was the most critically and commercially successful documentary ever made. Moore adopted the persona of an engaged, angry, bemused, pushy reporter and explainer of the most culturally and politically charged issues of the moment. In *Roger and Me* (1989) and *Bowling for Columbine* (2002)—the first about the decay of his hometown of Flint, Michigan, when General Motors downsized their operations; the second about the mass shooting in Columbine High School—he pursued his subjects with humor, irony, and outrage. *Fahrenheit 9/11* is a frontal assault on the administration of George W. Bush and the Iraq and Afghanistan wars. Combining television footage and original material, including Moore himself cornering members of Congress on the Washington streets, asking why their sons aren't serving in Iraq,

Moore's film is a politically potent indictment of American foreign policy driven by the director's sense of humor and anger. It touched a nerve and set the stage for the documentaries about the Iraq conflict that followed.

ERROL MORRIS

Errol Morris is no less angry than Moore, but considerably more restrained. His format seems at first glance quite conventional. He interviews his subjects. More accurately, he allows his subjects to talk, while he, off camera, poses questions which allow his subjects to talk more, expose themselves, revealing truths and lies that have often global ramifications. He intersperses his interviews with footage consisting of newsreel or television images, reenactments, and digitally created effects.

Mr. Death: The Rise and Fall of Fred A. Leuchter, Jr. (1999) consists mainly of interviews with its subject, a former inventor of and consultant for human execution devices, who becomes, through his own obsessive behavior, a Holocaust denier—that is, someone who claims that the Nazis did not kill six million Jews. The latter part of the film intercuts the interviews with images of Leuchter endlessly chipping away at the walls of a Polish concentration camp, gathering samples to prove that gas was never used. Another interview, with someone who actually knows what he's talking about, completely demolishes Leuchter's theory, and the rest of the film allows Leuchter to reveal himself as a kind of innocent, amoral idiot, who seems simply to have followed ideas without actually having any. The film joins with the great documentaries of Marcel Ophuls—*The Sorrow and the Pity* (1971) and *Hotel Terminus* (1988)—which allow past and present participants in human atrocity to expose themselves before the gentle, ironic, and completely knowing eye of the filmmaker.

FIGURE 9.14 Canted off center, former Secretary of Defense Robert S. McNamara tries to defend himself about his role in the Vietnam War in Errol Morris's *The Fog of War: Eleven Lessons from the Life of Robert S. McNamara* (2003)

Morris's more recent work is even more powerful in its indictment of power misused. *Standard Operation Procedure* (2008) unpacks the confusion surrounding the grotesque images of torture at the Abu Ghraib military prison in Iraq. *The Fog of War: Eleven Lessons from the Life of Robert S. McNamara* (2003) allows the former Secretary of Defense under the John F. Kennedy and Lyndon B. Johnson administrations to quietly, amazingly, infuriatingly admit his complicity in the lie of the Vietnam War. Morris has less success in his interviews with Donald Rumsfeld, George W. Bush's Secretary of Defense and prime mover of the Iraq War, in *The Unknown Known* (2013). Rumsfeld is a recalcitrant, unredeemable, unembarrassed figure. And it is just these qualities that Morris elicits in his documentary, as Rumsfeld talks and talks and reveals nothing except his own lack of self-knowledge—or his unwillingness to admit that he lacks the same.

Morris's films about the Iraq and Afghanistan conflicts are part of a larger documentation of those awful wars in films unflinching in their observation of combat and pain. Alex Gibney's *Taxi to the Dark Side* (2007), like Morris's *Standard Operation Procedure*, studies the use of torture by the United States, while Tim Hetherington's and Sebastian Junger's *Restrepo* (2010) documents the day-to-day lives of a platoon in Afghanistan.

These films don't quite carry through the Griersonian ideal of documentary film as a government funded, civilizing force, though they do continue one aspect of his desire to have film as an educational medium. "Educational" is a word poisonous to both filmmakers and film viewers, but the work of Michael Moore, Errol Morris, and the documentarians of Middle Eastern conflicts *are* teaching by means of drama, irony, and unflinching observation. Their films are not only of the moment, but of the histories that have led up to the moment; they observe, attack, denounce, and expose. They are works about the political culture in which cinema is made and which it can reveal.

THE GENRES OF FICTION FILMS

The malleability of the documentary appears, potentially at least, to be greater than that of the fiction film genres we are familiar with. Fiction films seem more bound by the rules and conventions imposed—self-imposed—very early in the history of film than the more independent (and, until *Fahrenheit 9/11*, much less seen) work of documentary filmmakers. Even most so-called independent filmmakers adhere to generic rules if they want their films to be well distributed but these restrictions can sometimes be superficial. Many filmmakers expand, manipulate, or otherwise subvert generic expectations in ways that refresh the genres or, sometimes, destroy them. However, before change or destruction can occur, we, as well as the filmmakers themselves, need to understand the structures that might be changed. To do that, we need to move backward in film history to the time when genres were a bit more straightforward.

Genres are such complex things that I want—for the sake of clarity and in order to see in strong detail how their structures, themes, and variations work—to focus on just a few of them: the Western, science fiction, film noir, and melodrama, while also referring to others in the course of our discussion. The Western is an interesting case of a genre that has all but died. Science fiction literature and film are almost contemporaneous. Film noir is relatively new and particular to film. And melodrama is, as we have seen, very old and predates cinema. These case studies will allow us to examine a range of structures and meanings across the history of film and understand further the relationship between culture and film form.

THE WESTERN

Documentary films, for the most part, are driven by political and ideological belief; they read the world through a lens of personally held conviction about the powerful, the corrupt, or the victims. Melodrama, as we will see in the next chapter, concerns itself with personal politics, the politics of power and desire, of suffering and sacrifice. Film noir is born of wartime and postwar politics and the cultural anxieties created by them. The fact is that all film genres are based in certain ideological and cultural imperatives—those dominant fictions we spoke about earlier. Film grows out of ideology, out of cultural beliefs and desires which in turn feed back and nourish the films themselves. Sometimes, when the ideology shifts radically or the desire is redirected by historical reality, a genre can either vanish or go into a recessive state. The Western film is an interesting example of a genre that bent and then snapped under shifting ideological pressures, perhaps because it was the genre most tightly connected to our country's historical legends.

The Western began practically at the same time as narrative film and went on to become one of its most popular genres. It was invented out of our myths of the American frontier and the white man's destiny, an embodiment of the 1840s doctrine of "Manifest Destiny"—the inexorable movement of European civilization westward across the country to the Pacific, destroying everyone in its path. Western films drew on the nineteenth-century literature of the West, but quickly established their own generic patterns. The Western's settings of chaparral or desert, of small, dusty frontier towns bordering on vast, open land, created a representation of the culture's wilderness fantasies that may once have existed for some people, but were set in memory through movies, and became part of its visual conventions. Narratives of white settlers fighting savages, of heroic gunmen protecting small communities from outlaws, were rapidly set and confirmed our belief in the rightness of expansion and in the structuring authority of law and order. They confirmed for us as well that there were always enemies that threatened "our way of life." Gender was another structuring principle. The creation of the civilized community in the heart of the wilderness, so essential to the dominant Western narrative, involved the melodrama of women creating the cultural hearth in a barren land where men broke horses and shot Indians and outlaws and then returned to the domesticity they helped secure. All of this seemed to reassure the audience that our movement west was close to a divine imperative. After all, we believe, settling the West made our current life possible.

Many pre-1950s Westerns were anonymous studio products, some with unusual casting, like Warner Brothers' *The Oklahoma Kid* (Lloyd Bacon, 1939) with Warner Brothers' stock gangsters of the time, Humphrey Bogart and James Cagney, playing cowboys. There were Gene Autry and Roy Rogers movies—the singing cowboys who were fixtures of the genre. There were serials, ongoing Western narratives presented in one episode a week. There were studios, especially Republic Pictures, that specialized in the Western, repeating its stereotypes and clichés on a regular basis and all but inventing one of the classic Western codes, the hero in the white hat and the outlaw in black.

The Western landscape

Among the most important generic codes of the Western is its visual location, representing history and nation by means of visual space. The desert was at its center: open spaces, a big sky with large clouds—those "wide open spaces" that beckoned the cowboy hero, who wanted his freedom and in which he could act out his obligation to help create a safe domestic space.

These are the same spaces that still lure our imagination, even as they quickly shrink. The counter to the open Western landscape is the enclosed town, and within it the closed domestic space—which finally closes the cowboy out as it becomes impossible for him to be part of the very domestic sphere he fights to create and preserve. In some Westerns, the free spirit of the open range cannot be held within domestic bonds (unless the cowboy marries the schoolmarm) and so the genre winds up creating a space that makes him even more of a loner, as he rides off back into the wilderness (see Figure 7.3).

Therefore, two basic kinds of composition create Western spaces: the cowboy on the desert or plain, often fighting off Indians and outlaws, and the frontier community, often concentrating on its representative space, the saloon in the town that needs cleaning up and to be made safe. The saloon is the intrusion of the untamed wilderness within the community, a place of misrule and violent action. More accurately, the saloon is the place in transition, and making it safe, killing the outlaws, is the significant narrative of the genre. To consummate the dominant fiction of Manifest Destiny, the enemies of order (and therefore of expansion) must be destroyed.

The obstacle to westward expansion

The Western posited a gender and racial basis of continental expansion. The women of the West were largely the passive representatives of the *need* to pacify the western territories. Therefore two varieties of passivity are engendered in the woman of the West. She was stereotyped as the "schoolmarm," the one who maintained knowledge and domesticity. The "schoolmarm" herself contains stereotypical remnants of the quiet, retiring woman who could thrive and teach only when lone, heroic males cleared the wilderness. Therefore, passive by nature, she had to have her very environment pacified—perhaps feminized—in order for her and domesticity to thrive. At the other pole is the saloon girl, often figured as the prostitute with a heart of gold, who assists the Western hero despite her shady profession. Mrs. Miller in Robert Altman's *McCabe and Mrs. Miller*, discussed below, is a parody of this figure.

The racial basis of the Western is superficially simpler: Indians. The Western wilderness took many forms: the desert itself, whose inhospitable barrenness needed to be made green and secure; outlaws—white men who took the wilderness as land open for their violence—and the Indians. There is a large literature on who Native Americans actually were and what white people did to them. But until the late 1960s, movie-made Native Americans mostly conformed to old, cultural stereotypes of the vicious savage, a flesh and blood representation of the wilderness itself, acting in opposition to the dreams of expansion. They were the "Other," barely human, existing mainly to be destroyed. And therefore, from the beginning, the Western represented Native Americans as a violent obstacle that had to be obliterated. "Circling the wagons" has become a cultural cliché, and it is repeated visually in almost every Western film as a generic convention in which the travelers or settlers must protect themselves from savage onslaughts.

The Western star and the Western director

Robert Warshow, one of the rare early critics of popular culture to take film seriously, said that for a genre—the Western especially—to remain pure, it could not be altered by an individual's style that tinkered with its conventions. Warshow's argument is particularly cogent. Because a genre is made up of conventions negotiated between filmmakers and audience, tinkering with them, adding personal touches, stretching their generic bounds, only complicates the negotiating process that is essential for a genre to work. Too much tinkering and the audience may simply refuse to negotiate.

Warshow imagined an ideal genre represented by what he considered classics of the form. He singled out William Wellman's *The Ox-Bow Incident* (1943) and Stuart Gilmore's *The Virginian* (1946), and out of them built his ideal of the West. But the fact is that, although many directorial hands and many actors attempted Westerns, with varying degrees of success, the genre was dominated by two men, the actor John Wayne and the director John Ford. They shaped it, and Ford eventually pointed the way to its change and its ultimate move to a recessive place. But that is getting ahead of ourselves. The point is that the Western is a genre that owes much not only to the build-up of conventions, but to the ways in which those conventions were inflected, shifted, and changed by two individuals. At the same time, it confirms the fact that film is a complex mix of collaboration and individual imagination.[5]

Let's first consider the actor. John Wayne has been among the most admired actors during and after his life. His self-assuredness, swagger, and on-screen heroism and bravura made him the perfect film action hero. He was not the first such—during the silent and early sound periods, Douglas Fairbanks emerged as perhaps the first universally admired action hero, and there have been many since in a variety of films. Wayne himself starred in other genres, mainly war films, but he is best known as the moral and powerful figure in the Western landscape. His figure is part of the genre's landscape. His best director was John Ford.

Stagecoach

Ford, too, directed other film genres, most famously such melodramas as *The Informer* (1935), *The Grapes of Wrath* (1940), and *How Green Was My Valley* (1941). He began his work in the Western as far back as *Cheyenne's Pal* (1917), gained renown with *The Iron Horse* in 1924, and solidified his connection with the Western with *Stagecoach* in 1939. *Stagecoach* launched John Wayne into stardom. He had a minor career before meeting up with Ford, but with this film, the two of them together began defining the West and the Western hero, and quite consciously and conspicuously. Wayne's first appearance in the film is by means of a fast **dolly**-in, so fast that the camera goes briefly out of focus. Wayne's character, the Ringo Kid, is an "outlaw," but in a film that attempts to work out the right balance of morality in the West, he is an outlaw who protects the outcast and fights the Indians. His importance is marked by the way Ford introduces him.

Stagecoach is a Western road movie in which a collection of people—a gambler, a crooked banker (who is given a long, suspicious **close-up** when he mouths the cliché "what's good for the banks is good for the country," a comment bound to get a rise from a depression-era audience and perhaps today's audience as well), a drunken, kindhearted doctor, who redeems himself by delivering a baby, a whiskey salesman, a "proper" lady, a prostitute with a heart of gold, who is being driven out of town, and Ringo—are all traveling together on the coach, fighting Apaches, working out their moral differences, creating a small universe of character types that have to be reconciled with the new world of the West and have to reconcile that world to their own differences.

What were quickly becoming the genre's conventions are solidified, although the play on the outlaw as ultimately a moral hero already marks Ford as a director thinking about other directions in which he could drive those conventions. Ford's film not only presents stereotyped Indian savages, but fights sanctimony and fake moral virtue, taking another "outlaw" (the prostitute) to its heart, and then goes on to articulate that major generic element of settling down and creating domesticity in the wilderness.

Beyond the plot, other elements mark this as an important example of Ford's command of the genre. Much of the action is set in Monument Valley, which constitutes Ford's West throughout his filmmaking career. Here, as in all of his Westerns, he composes it from varying angles and with all the variations of lighting that were possible. He also treated interiors differently, putting ceilings on his sets, allowing the light to show the dust in the air. His compositions led Orson Welles to say that *Stagecoach* was his textbook before filming *Citizen Kane*. "I ran it over forty times."

Fort Apache and *The Man Who Shot Liberty Valence*

Among the most important aspects of Ford's Westerns is the ways he kept pushing the genre. This is precisely what Warshow was worrying about—adulterating the genre by the intervention of individual imagination—and precisely why Ford defined the genre and kept it exciting and meaningful as long as he could. He took the conventions, questioned and refreshed them. He rarely undid them, but he did make them respond to changes in the culture, particularly after World War II. He was able to take, if not an ironic, at least an ambiguous view—as in *Fort Apache* (1948), which pits a soldier (Wayne) against his superior, a rule-bound and ultimately dangerous man (Henry Fonda, playing against his usual nice guy type). The Indians are here depicted as more knowing than the military leader, part of their land and wise to its ways. The inability of the officer to understand Indians except as hateful brutes results in a rout of his troops. The military is brought into question—but only to a point. Wayne gives a rousing defense of the military at the film's end. *Fort Apache* is an ambiguous piece. It celebrates the military and its ability to survive in a desert outpost, mainly because of the work of the soldiers' wives, who domesticate this unpleasant place. It celebrates community, mainly through the dances that the inhabitants hold—dances that are interrupted by the unfriendly martinet, Col. Thursday (Fonda). Thursday leads his men to destruction. But, the film—through Wayne's Capt. York—insists, he is only an anomaly. The military is greater than its occasional bad actors.

In a late film, a kind of indoor Western, *The Man Who Shot Liberty Valence* (1962), the John Wayne character, Tom Doniphan, has settled the town and lives in the desert outside of it. One vicious outlaw, Liberty Valence (Lee Marvin) and his gang still reign, however. A politician from the East, Ransom Stoddard (played by Jimmy Stewart and called "Pilgrim" by Doniphan) comes to town and shoots him, or so he thinks. Ford shows this event at two points in the film, but from two points of view. In one, it appears that Ransom has shot Liberty. In the second Doniphan makes it clear that he, in fact, shot the outlaw. The story is being narrated by Stoddard to a newspaper man, and as he finally understands that it was not he but Doniphan who did the shooting, he questions the newsman about whether he should correct the record. The man refuses: "This is the West, sir. When the legend becomes fact, print the legend," he says. And this was the motto of all Westerns, until the legends no longer worked.

FIGURE 9.15 John Wayne's spectacular entrance in John Ford's *Stagecoach* (1939).This film strip attempts to capture the tracking shot

The Searchers

A few years earlier, Ford had made a film with Wayne called *The Searchers* (1956), which has become the most influential movie made in the United States, second only to *Citizen Kane*. The film is mirrored in Scorsese's *Taxi Driver*, in Lucas's first *Star Wars*, in Tarantino's *Kill Bill* 2 (2004), and in almost every film by Steven Spielberg. The reason lies in its complexity and simplicity; its ability to question generic assumptions and confirm them simultaneously; its affirmation of the struggle to maintain the domestic enclosure against the encroachment of wilderness; and, most important, the power of its images. The cyclical nature of the film, the door opening on the desert at the beginning and closing on it at the end, stays in memory like few others.

Some background is needed. Ford had already begun rethinking the genre in his late 1940s films. While still presenting the cavalry as heroic, he questioned some assumptions of the Western, even as he had done as far back as *Stagecoach*. By the 1950s, the Western film had reached the zenith of its popularity. The Western almost seemed necessary in order to confirm the culture's always tenuous faith in its rightness and strength. The genre sometimes became overtly political, as in the anti-McCarthy Westerns *Johnny Guitar* (Nicholas Ray, 1954) and *High Noon* (Fred Zinnemann, 1952). In *High Noon*, the townspeople are cowards who refuse to help the sheriff face down the outlaws; they reflect the passivity of the country in the face of McCarthy's bullying. Ray's film is more complex. It too presents a community easily swayed by a leader with a grudge and turns lynching into a metaphor for the ease with which McCarthy could accuse and condemn his imagined enemies. Both these films also had women who were stronger and more active than their male counterparts. In *High Noon*, the sheriff's wife (the sheriff is played by another icon of Western films, Cary Cooper; his wife by Grace Kelly) helps him gun down the outlaws as the town cowers. Johnny Guitar (Sterling Hayden) is a passive man, and the town's feud is between the two women characters, played by Joan Crawford and Mercedes McCambridge. In fact, many 1950s Westerns began to change the contours of the Western hero, though none as radically as *The Searchers*.

John Wayne's Ethan Edwards rides from out of the desert with a shady past and an obsessive, racist hatred of Indians. When his family is wiped out and his niece taken captive, he swears revenge. Worse, he considers his niece no longer human because she has become a "squaw." His racism (he was a member of the Confederate army) is overwhelming and he spends five years hunting down her and her captor. The film is driven by one of the oldest master narratives, the

FIGURE 9.16 The doorway opening on the Fordian wilderness at the beginning of *The Searchers* (1956)

FIGURE 9.17 The gaze of hatred and fear as Ethan Edwards (John Wayne) looks at the white women captured back from the Indians in *The Searchers*

captivity narrative, which we discussed in detail in Chapter 4. Its dominant fiction is the individual or even nation held captive by a stronger power, figured in early literature as a woman (occasionally a man) held captive by a vicious, murderous "other." Played out in literature and film, it occurs in the narratives of history itself, and has never lost its power. We have seen it at work in D. W. Griffith's films. In postwar political and cultural fantasy is was played out in the fears that the U.S.S.R. would imprison "the free world." In *The Searchers*, it is turned into a fiction of obsession in which the hero is close to psychotic and even closer to the "savage" he claims so much to hate. Ethan's hatred of Indians seems to echo the obsessive anti-communism the culture was going through at the time: mindless and bordering on the criminal and insane.

Ethan finds Debbie's captor, Chief Scar (played by a white actor, Henry Brandon), who is almost his double in hatred. But it is his nephew Marty (Jeffrey Hunter), who has Indian blood and is therefore despised by Ethan, who kills Scar. After five years of his quest, his anger and recklessness, Ethan seems spent and rather than kill Debbie, he takes her in his arms in a rhyme with the beginning of the film, when he scoops the young Debbie in his arms, and he takes her back to the domestic refuge that he himself cannot enter, condemned to wander the desert.

THE WESTERN AFTER THE 1950s

The power of Ford's revision of the genre, along with the power of the images he uses to create it, marks *The Searchers* as the apex and perhaps the climax of the Western as it was to that point. By the end of the 1950s the Western had perhaps been tinkered with too much; by the 1960s, fact began to interfere with legend. A number of things happened to the Western that finally destroyed it. One was the series of extraordinary films made by the Italian Sergio Leone: *The Good, The Bad, and The Ugly* (1966) and its sequels, and his huge homage to every Western ever made, *Once Upon a Time in the West* (1968). These films exploded generic conventions to the proportions of grand opera, with huge, long held **wide shots** and close-ups, with actions drawn out past any normal stress point, forcing the viewer to think about how we look at Westerns, not to mention how we think about cinematic time.

The Western, so sensitive to history, was under attack from the outside by a growing awareness of the realities of America's expansion and by contemporary events that challenged Western myths. By the 1960s, we could no longer, in good faith, hold on to old narratives of the savage Indians raping and pillaging. Native Americans were not "savages," but rather deeply spiritual builders of complex nations and laws. The truth of Manifest Destiny was that it was merely raw imperialism and destroyed the original inhabitants of the country. The Indians were not the bad guys. We were. The Vietnam War also put a temporary hold on those captivity narratives that drive us as a country to want to free the "oppressed," even when the oppressed are the liberators and we are not. The war against insurgents abroad reflected back badly on our stories of war against the original inhabitants of our own country.

The Wild Bunch, Little Big Man, McCabe and Mrs. Miller

Three films of the late 1960s and early 1970s—Sam Peckinpah's *The Wild Bunch* (1969), Arthur Penn's *Little Big Man* (1970), and Robert Altman's *McCabe and Mrs. Miller* (1971)—took these new realities, shifted the genre's conventional myths of male heroism even more than *The Searchers*, questioned the stereotypes of Native Americans, and even the place of women, on the frontier. They turned tables on the genre.

The Wild Bunch declared the end of the all-male community of gunfighters propounded by the Western and showed the violence of gunfighting as a terrible tearing up of the body. It also did what few earlier Westerns attempted: it examined the politics of violence, the male bond, and the taking of sides. *The Wild Bunch* was the most violent film since *Bonnie and Clyde*, two years earlier. Blood spurts in slow motion and its climactic sequence is a grand ballet of slaughter. But this is violence for a purpose. The film's heroes are old men at the end of the West. The best they can do is rob an army train to supply guns for the Mexican government fighting a peasant uprising. The parallels with Vietnam are clear. And, when the Bunch realize their mistake, all they can do is wipe out the Mexican fort and be destroyed themselves. *Little Big Man* turned the relationship of Indian and white man on its head, declaring that the "savages" were really the "human beings" and the white men crazy. General Custer is depicted as a raving lunatic, and the Battle of Little Big Horn a righteous cause for the Indians. *McCabe and Mrs. Miller* showed the Western community as a cold place of mutual betrayal, the hero as the joke of his own legend, and women as the marginalized, self-protective maintainers of rationality and sexuality. McCabe is a bumbler in a town that is not enclosed in the open spaces, but in the constrained, freezing rain of the Northwest (see Figure 7.4). The film has an Indian and two outlaws, but they are the "hit squad" of the mining company that wants to take over the town. McCabe—who everyone in the town decides is a gunman—does, in fact, kill the three and is himself shot. However, the town church, which everyone had ignored, catches fire. In a sequence whose editing is worthy of D. W. Griffith stood on his head, Altman cuts between the townspeople fighting the fire to save the town and McCabe dying alone in the snow, having saved the town. But unlike Griffith's work, the two parts of the editing structure do not come together. McCabe is buried in the snow; Mrs. Miller, the madam who literally has a heart of gold, the box in which she collects her money, withdraws to an opium den. As we noted in Chapter 7, Altman pulls and twists genres, taking them far past their borders, and creates worlds in which his often desperate and more than sometimes stupid heroes can't exist.

FIGURE 9.18 The end of the West and the Western. The old men of Sam Peckinpah's *The Wild Bunch* (1969), heading off for their last violent confrontation

Both *The Wild Bunch* and *McCabe and Mrs. Miller* are elegiac films. They mourn the very genre they are taking apart. And it would be too strong to say that these and other films of the period destroyed the genre by themselves, but only that they were reflecting cultural changes that no longer allowed the Western to exist in its old forms. Certainly it has popped up again from time to time, most notably in the hands of Clint Eastwood, in films like *The Unforgiven* (Clint Eastwood, 1992). But Eastwood came to fame as an actor in Sergio Leone's operatic Westerns, and the influence is from them more than from the classic genre. We also noted the attempt to resurrect an old Western hero, *The Lone Ranger* (Gore Verbinski, 2013), and its failure to convince audiences that even a dead genre could be mocked. A genre exists only as long as history, culture, and the viewers who are the products of both can maintain belief in their conventions. Warshow was right, a genre cannot take too much self-examination.

SCIENCE FICTION AND HORROR

At first glance, it might seem that these two genres, both of which began at the very beginning of film itself, should not be conjoined. They seem to have separate conventions, are aimed at different audiences, and have completely different goals. Science fiction creates awe and wonder at the imaginings of alternative worlds and beings, of space flight and alien creatures; horror aims to scare us with monsters and mutilation, with things hidden in the dark that jump out and go "boo!". Science fiction, as the name implies, imagines what happens when the creativity of science is extrapolated into the world of make believe, replete with spectacular special effects; horror films speak of unnatural beings, of hauntings and violence. But consider this: Dr. Frankenstein and his monster, originating in an early nineteenth-century novel by Mary Wollstonecraft Shelley—wife of the poet—addressed contemporary notions of creation, science, consciousness, and imagination. Frankenstein entered movies as early as 1910, when the Edison studios did a fourteen-minute adaptation. Of course, it is the 1931 Universal Pictures version, directed by James Whale and starring Boris Karloff, that has become part of film history. And here again a scientist uses an array of fanciful electronic equipment to create his monster. Jump ahead to 1979 and Ridley Scott's *Alien*. Here a spaceship takes the place of the old dark house, variations of which make up the scary space in which almost every horror film is located. Into the spaceship is brought a horrific monster that, one by one, decimates the crew until only Ripley (Sigourney Weaver) is left to tell the tale. Horror and science fiction mix nicely together.

Science fiction is another example of a genre that came from literature and appeared early in film, but, unlike the Western, it has been able to remake itself from decade to decade. One reason is obvious. Science fiction is about speculation—about the future, about alternatives to the present, about technology and its use and misuse. Science fiction is also, like the Western, open to allegory. It can tell one narrative that is wrapped around or infiltrated by another, which may be of cultural concern or political import. But, unlike the Western, its allegories are changeable from moment to moment. Like any other film, no matter when its narrative is supposed to take place, science fiction is about the present, it cloaks contemporary concerns in visions of a usually dystopian future.

The generic conventions of science fiction are not as simple as those of the Western, partly because the genre pulls in so many elements. Some are from the outside: science fiction depends upon technological imagery, speculation on the use and misuse of science, images of outer space, and, of course, robots, computers, and aliens. Today, the generic expectations of science fiction involve complex **CGI** effects, which have taken the place of the **matte paintings** and models of older science fiction.

Fritz Lang's *Metropolis*

In 1927, in Germany, Fritz Lang made one of the first full-fledged science fiction films, *Metropolis.* (The Russians had made *Aelita: Queen of Mars*, directed by Yakov Protazanov, three years earlier.) Expressionist in set design and acting style, *Metropolis* is a politically complex film that seems at first glance to take the side of the oppressed workers, forced to live like automatons in a grotesque underground city, but concludes with a reactionary notion of joining the "head" of the owners with the "heart" of the workers. The film was written by Lang's wife at the time, who went on to write films for the Nazis.

Metropolis introduces important elements that, with its intersections of gigantic machinery, a mad scientist, and a robot, would become inseparable from the science fiction and the horror film. The term "robot" had only recently been introduced in 1920 by the Czech playwright Karel Čapek, in his play *R.U.R.* (*Rossum's Universal Robots*), and was quickly adopted after that. *Metropolis* is science fiction because it speculates on the future, creates what has been called a "visionary architecture" in its city of the imagination, and imagines the capabilities of science to create a robot and then make that robot humanlike.[6] It is a horror film because the mad scientist, Dr. Rotwang (Rudolf Klein-Rogge), like Dr. Frankenstein, plays with nature and creates an inhuman form that then takes the life of a human being and creates tremendous discord. The sequence in which this occurs is a marvel of special effects, created by means of animation and multiple exposure.

SCIENCE FICTION IN THE 1950s AND BEYOND

Like the Western, science fiction bloomed like a flower in the desert during the 1950s, and it did so for very specific cultural/political reasons. My metaphor is not so fanciful, given the fact that the desert was the location of so many of these films, and the culture itself was living in a dry, scary place of political fear and accusations, of blacklistings and firings because of political views. This was the fertilizer for the genre's popularity.

The 1950s Western responded to the culture's need for reaffirmation of its greatness and rightness. It took over from the war film as an examination of the hero and his role in nation building and in the process began to question it. Science fiction, conversely, responded to the culture's terrors. The 1950s were burdened by a fantasy of Communist infiltration. Between the hearings of the House Un-American Activities Committee and the hateful, destructive games played by Joe McCarthy, the culture was scared. The fear was literally of *alien* invasion—that is an alien ideology that would destroy our souls—so it was relatively easy to represent this fear by making the aliens come from outer space rather than the Soviet Union.

Historically, the fear of space-borne alien invasion started at least as far back as Orson Welles's infamous 1938 radio dramatization of H. G. Wells's novel *War of the Worlds* (1898), concerning a Martian invasion. The radio play, presented in the style of a newscast of "breaking events," broadcast on Halloween, at a time of great anxiety over the growing unrest and hostilities in Europe, caused people to panic and take to the roads to escape the Martians. This was certainly one of the most visible early examples of the effect mass media could have on its public, and it made Welles's career. Within a few years he was in Hollywood, making *Citizen Kane* (1941).

The Day the Earth Stood Still

The real deluge of alien sightings began in 1946, shortly after World War II, and was spurred on by the presumed crash of a UFO in Roswell, New Mexico, which many people believed contained an alien hidden away by the government. Without arguing the validity of any of this (I don't believe it), the point needs repeating that World War II left a culture full of anxiety, that the atomic bombs that ended the war provoked a fear of science's unknown dangers, and that the birth of anticommunism added the final fear to the mix. The new round of science fiction film was spawned out of this volatile mix.

Three films started it: Irving Pichel's *Destination Moon* (1950) was a non-alien, pro-interplanetary discovery film, using clay animation to represent astronauts performing extravehicular activity. Robert Wise, the man who edited Welles's *Citizen Kane* and *The Magnificent Ambersons*, and who became a prolific director, whose films include *The Sound of Music* (1965), made *The Day the Earth Stood Still* in 1951, a brilliant piece of work, and perhaps the only "liberal" science fiction film of the decade. A Christ-like alien, named Klaatu (Michael Rennie) visits Washington, DC, to warn earth about its "petty squabbles" and its danger to a peaceful universe. He is accompanied by his own anti-Christ, a spectacular robot named Gort, whose laserlike eye incinerates whatever it touches.

FIGURE 9.19 Klaatu (Michael Rennie) and Gort, promising peace or destruction in Robert Wise's *The Day the Earth Stood Still* (1951)

The film is especially media savvy, understanding even this early in the 1950s how television—it uses actual broadcasters of the time—influences public perceptions. It is "liberal" in the sense that Klaatu wishes to bring the warring parties of the postwar world together and is shot (twice) for his pains and resurrected by Gort. But, as an indication of things to come, the film pulls its punches and introduces fear. In his parting speech, Klaatu warns the scientists, gathered by a figure representing Albert Einstein, that the world, if it doesn't solve its "petty squabbles," will be destroyed by the race of omnipotent robots, of which Gort is but one. "The test of any such higher authority is, of course, the police force that supports it," Klaatu tells the assembled group. Not exactly a progressive sentiment after the United States had fought a war against a nation that believed the same thing. But despite this curious ending, its noirish mood and style and its polished effects point the way for much science fiction to come.

The Thing from Another World

The third film in the opening trilogy is *The Thing*, also known as *The Thing from Another World* (1951), "produced" by Howard Hawks and "directed" by Christian Nyby. The film essentially belongs to Hawks, who was a veteran Hollywood director and whose style and narrative of men in groups, bonding in stressful situations and permitting a strong-willed woman to enter their enclave, is very much evident in this film. But it is indicative of the rather low esteem in which science fiction would be held in 1950s Hollywood—despite its popularity with filmgoers—that Hawks gives directorial credit to his editor. *The Thing* is a prime example of the intersection of horror and science fiction. The alien beast, who arrives in a giant flying saucer, is a vegetable—a blood-sucking vegetable which invades an arctic military outpost. The film is roughly but craftily made, noirish in its use of shadow, with the dark corridors of the arctic military base becoming the threatening spaces of horror film's old dark house.

Three figures stand out in the film (other than the monster, who is played by James Arness, who would go on to star in one of television's longest running Westerns, *Gunsmoke*). One is Capt. Hendry (Kenneth Tobey), whose calm and humor under pressure keeps his men in line. Another is the woman, Nikki (Margaret Sheridan), whose 1950s common sense, her understanding of how to cook a vegetable—boil it, steam it, fry it—leads to the monster's destruction. The third is the mad, slightly effeminate scientist, who wears a Russian style hat, Dr. Carrington (Robert Cornthwaite), who wants to study the Thing, make friends with it, make it feel welcome. He is the film's representation of 1950s anti-intellectualism, precisely because he is an intellectual whose curiosity leads to more deaths, retards the work of the "real men"—the military—and who represents the 1950s fear of doubters and conciliators, of those who did not believe the Red tide of Russian aliens was about to flow over the country—"eggheads." Carrington is a curious version of a great man, Adlai Stevenson, a smart, witty, and knowledgeable politician, who twice ran for and lost the American presidency because he too was an "egghead." He is at the same time a surrogate for the "Communist threat," another version of the alien, a danger to the clear-thinking community of soldiers protecting the American way of life.

Forbidden Planet

The Thing sets the tone for the genre in the 1950s: low budget, dark, desolate, fearful, and fear-provoking. It is a film of people huddled together against a monstrous unknown until they find

FIGURE 9.20 The electrocution of the vegetable from another planet. James Arness as *The Thing from Another World*. (Christian Nyby, Howard Hawks, 1951)

a way to defeat it. The variations in the many films that followed were few, because almost all involved some kind of alien threat, even, as in the case of Don Siegel's *Invasion of the Body Snatchers* (1956), where the aliens are invisible, coming to earth as seed pods to take over our bodies, turning us into emotionless zombies—as the Communists might do. Almost all of them involved this danger of losing our souls to an alien force; almost all of these films depended on the military to save us. There were a few exceptions. MGM made a big-budget science fiction film, Fred Wilcox's *Forbidden Planet* (1956), which was based on, of all things, William Shakespeare's play *The Tempest*, with a good measure of one early-twentieth-century intellectual who was especially popular in the 1950s, Sigmund Freud.

The film is in color, as opposed to the dull gray of most low-budget science fiction, and the visuals, especially the matte paintings of the planet Altair, are beautiful. Many moments in the film had a direct influence on both *2001: A Space Odyssey* (Stanley Kubrick, 1968) and *Star Wars* (*Episode IV—A New Hope*, George Lucas, 1977). An old scientist, Morbius (Shakespeare's Prospero, played by Walter Pidgeon), who traveled to this distant brave new world, has lived with his daughter, Altaira (Shakespeare's Miranda, played by Anne Francis), alone, since the rest of the colonizers were killed. They are served by one of the greatest (and friendliest) of screen robots, Robby (Shakespeare's Ariel), built like a 1950s juke box, productive of all needs, and protective of his owners. *Forbidden Planet* eschews the anticommunist politics of its generic relatives and instead addresses issues common to science fiction literature and usually diluted in films: alien worlds with enormously intelligent beings.

But the beings of Altair, the Krell, are dead. They weren't merely intelligent, but too intelligent. Their huge machines and fantastic energy sources overpowered their unconscious, which, repressed, forced itself back as "creatures from the Id," the film's version of *The Tempest*'s Caliban. Once again, 1950s anti-intellectualism raises its anti-egg head. By the time the planet is visited

FIGURE 9.21 Morbius (Walter Pidgeon) shows how Robby the Robot will short out before firing on a human in *Forbidden Planet* (Fred Wilcox, 1956)

by a military rescue crew, Morbius has himself fallen victim to these monsters—which are wonderfully drawn by Disney animators—and eventually dies. The level of inquiry in *Forbidden Planet* is not terribly deep, but deeper than in most other representatives of the genre.

Alien, Blade Runner, and *Dark City*

If we move forward many years and consider Ridley Scott's two extraordinary science fiction films, *Alien* (1979) and *Blade Runner* (1982), we see how the genres become inextricably mixed. *Alien* is a science fiction monster film in which, as we noted, the spaceship becomes a version of one of the major conventions of horror films, the Old Dark House, that place of mystery, threat, and fear that we find in a variety of places from Dracula's castle to Norman Bates's house in *Psycho* (1960). In the unknown spaces of the spaceship the monster roams, having been born bursting out of the body of an unsuspecting host, devouring everyone except Commander Ripley (believe it or not), one of the few women heroes of the genre. *Blade Runner* develops in a direct line from *Metropolis.* It depicts a city, specifically Los Angeles, of the future—but, as is always the case in science fiction, a future based on the present. A reigning cultural myth of the 1980s was that the Japanese were taking over the United States. Scott takes this contemporary myth and creates a Los Angeles that is all but a huge Asian slum, so overpopulated that "off world" colonies are created for those who can afford to escape.

In this fetid world, in a huge building like a modern version of an Aztec pyramid, a scientist has created robots—Replicants—to guard the colonies. Like Frankenstein's monster, the Replicants gain self-consciousness. They are also given memories and a limited life span, which stirs their rebellion as their consciousness develops. One, replicant Roy Batty (Rutger Hauer), kills his maker by taking out his eyes. Seeing is an important metaphor in this film, seeing memories that may or may not be real or implanted; seeing more completely and passionately when one is conscious of the brevity of one's life. But also, the scientist is the "father" of the Replicants and Roy Batty, the longest lived and most self-conscious of them, takes his revenge in a reverse of the Oedipal story. Rather than taking out his own eyes, he destroys the sight of his maker. Roy finally does epic battle with Deckard (Harrison Ford), a policeman, a blade

FIGURES 9.22–9.23 "Visionary architecture." The city of the future as imagined by Fritz Lang in *Metropolis* (1927) and Ridley Scott in *Blade Runner* (1982)

runner, whose job is to round up the errant robots, and Batty proves to have not only self-consciousness, but a soul and poetry.

To complicate things further, *Blade Runner* pulls in elements of film noir, with its dark city and quest for the sources of the darkness. But the irony of *Blade Runner* is that in searching for rebel replicants Deckard discovers—perhaps, though it's barely hinted at—that he's a replicant himself. Like Alex Proyas in *Dark City* (1998), a science fiction film whose very title comes from a 1950 film noir, and also has its roots in *Metropolis*, Scott pulls genres into a mix that remains science fiction but revitalizes it with other conventions that merge together nicely.

Proyas's film turns the noir city of dreadful night into a dream of alien mind control, which turns out to be the unrealized desires of the city's inhabitants, themselves quite possibly the dreams of the aliens. All of noir's attributes, from the encompassing darkness to a nightclub scene that is almost a prerequisite in any 1940s noir, as well as specific borrowings from Fritz Lang's

FIGURE 9.24 The replicant Roy Batty (Rutger Hauer) holds the dove of peace at the end of Ridley Scott's *Blade Runner*

early Expressionist films, are at work in *Dark City.* It is one of the many "virtual world" films of the 1990s and 2000s—think of Cameron's *Avatar* (2009) which, picking up on the virtual and immersive reality games of the digital world, and the parallel universes posited by science fiction literature (and quantum physics), as well as old narratives of illusion versus reality, questions the very trustworthiness of perception. Of course *The Matrix* films (Andy and Lana Wachowski, 1999, 2003) are the primary examples of this thread, but all the threads lead to the uncertainties of knowing and seeing, which constitute the very questions of cinema itself and which are taken up by many filmmakers, like Scott, and Kubrick in *2001: A Space Odyssey*, who concentrate their images on the fragile veil between what the astounded eye may or may not be seeing.

2001: A Space Odyssey

2001 is the climax and the rebirth of the science fiction genre. It appeared after the boom of the 1950s had died down and in its turn influenced the revival of the genre some ten years after its own appearance—revived it with such intense visual power that there is hardly a science fiction film made since *2001* that does not carry some of its traces. *2001* itself carries all the traces of science fiction film that came before it and gives them depth and resonance. The film deals with three basic generic issues: the loss of human emotion, "aliens," and the robot/computer. Kubrick's characters have already been taken over by the boredom of modernity. They are without affect, emotionless, but not because of an alien takeover. The spectacle of the film that awes us, as viewers, has no effect on the characters in the narrative itself. They are oblivious. Space and the possible existence of alien life is, for them, as ordinary as the everyday is for us. They are as empty as space itself.

The emotion that does occur in the film lies within and is caused by HAL, the computer who runs all operations on the spaceship bound for Jupiter, and who has consciousness. He is Kubrick's Frankenstein monster, and the only one on the voyage who has been told the source of the "aliens," whose monoliths push the narrative forward. Only he has full knowledge of the mission, which he deems too important for humans. He tries to kill all of them off, and almost succeeds. One survives and dismantles the computer's higher functions. HAL's expression of fear is the closest thing to a human response we get in the film, and it is unnerving.

I've been putting the word "aliens" in quotation marks because they constitute the film's biggest question. Like all of Kubrick's films, everything has multiple layers, ambiguous meaning. They force us to see things from multiple points of view. The film's famous monoliths seem to have been placed at strategic times and places first to push proto-humans in the "Dawn of Man" sequence to discover that bones can be used to kill, and later, on the moon, to push men to further exploration of space, where HAL kills most of the crew members. A monolith appears at the foot of the bed of the strange hotel room of the mind inhabited by the surviving astronaut. He ages before our eyes in a series of **over-the-shoulder** shots in which he sees himself at different stages of his decrepitude and then, through a **point-of-view** shot, seems to pass through the monolith to emerge as a fetus circling the Earth.

Does Kubrick believe that aliens have guided our destiny? I don't think so. The monoliths are visual metaphors of obstacles in the development of human intelligence that must be overcome. But the obstacles are not, and this is typical of Kubrick, overcome for the better. The apes at the beginning of the film experience the monolith and learn to kill and, as mentioned earlier, the spectacular cut from bone-weapon to spaceship indicates a perpetuation of violence

FIGURE 9.25 The end of time. Astronaut Dave Bowman (Kier Dullea) in the mysterious room "beyond the infinite" at the end of Kubrick's *2001: A Space Odyssey* (1968). See also Figures 4.14, 4.15, and 7.7

throughout human history (see Chapter 4 and Figures 4.14, 4.15 and 7.7). The movement to "Jupiter and Beyond the Infinite" results in HAL killing the hibernating astronauts. This journey is also a fantasy of a human going beyond the known and returning in an uncanny, strange rebirth, as a fetus entrapped in the universe's womb.

No science fiction film before or after *2001: A Space Odyssey*, with the possible exception of *Blade Runner*, has realized the genre with the complexity that usually belongs to science fiction literature. But the genre survives—think of Steven Spielberg's great science fiction films *Close Encounters of the Third Kind* (1977) and *E. T. the Extra Terrestrial* (1982)—because our imagination for the monstrous (or in Spielberg's case the friendly) alien, our need to develop fictions to explain science, to tell stories of the threats of computation and cloning, which make up such a large part of the genre today, and our fantasy, our dominant fiction of creating life outside of normal biological methods, remain undiminished and therefore perpetually filmable.

THE POST-APOCALYPTIC WORLD AND ZOMBIES

Another dominant fiction has infused the science fiction genre and tilts it further into the mode of horror, that of the apocalypse and the ruined world that follows upon it. During the 1950s, there were a fair number of movies about atomic-bred monsters who arose, usually from the sea, to ravage the world. Japan's *Godzilla* (*Gorija*, Ishirô Honda, 1954) is the most famous, and has spawned a number of remakes, most recently by Gareth Edwards in 2014. But home grown films, *The Beast from 20,000 Fathoms* (Eugène Lourié, 1953) and *It Came From Beneath the Sea* (Robert Gordon, 1955) create prehistoric beasts or a giant octopus that lay waste New York and San Francisco respectively. Digital monsters, in films like *Cloverfield* (2008)—one of those quasi-documentary horror films we spoke about earlier—have taken the place of creatures spawned by atomic energy and continue to ravage our cinematic cities.

These films might more accurately be assigned to the subgenre of monster movies, with the variation that the beasts are awakened by nuclear activity and before their inevitable destruction they destroy with abandon, leaving death and desolation in their wake. The films do not permit a prolonged view of the aftermath of this destruction. After all, a 1950s audience still would want a notion of optimism amidst the chaos. Even the original *War of the Worlds* (Byron Haskin, 1953), while leaving the world pretty well battered, allows for a hopeful rebirth when the Martians die off at the end. The more recent post-apocalyptic films, going as far back as *On the Beach* (Stanley Kramer, 1959), but really starting with *Mad Max* (George Miller, 1979, 2015) and continuing with such films as *I am Legend* (Francis Lawrence, 2007) and *The Road* (John Hillcoat, 2009) are grim studies of a ruined world with their respective protagonists fighting off the remnants of civilization, mostly rapacious and vicious, sometimes mutants or even zombies.

The popularity of movies and television shows featuring zombies is extraordinary. The walking dead, who go as far back as Val Lewton's and Jacque Tourneur's *I Walked with a Zombie* made in 1943, but who got their recent incarnation in George Romero's low-budget *Night of the Living Dead* (1968), are monsters and therefore their films belong to the monster subgenre of horror films. This would seem a self-evident answer to the question of their popularity: we love movie monsters, the more horrifying the more we feel secure in our seats while enjoying the fear that is contained by that security. But the lurching, chomping living dead are a different order of monster. No matter their origin—a mutant virus is the favorite cause—they are a kind of alter ego. They are ugly versions of ourselves, mean minded, singular of purpose, and at the same time perfectly vulnerable. A shot to the head and their ravenous behavior is finished. Yet they keep on coming, hordes of them in *World War Z* (Marc Foster, 2013). Unbeatable and beatable at the same time, populating a despoiled landscape, they are somehow representations of the fears of what we might become, or might face in our fellow humans when they are rendered semi-human, as we suspect many of them may be already.

We love our monsters and love our ability to be horrified by them, and filmmakers are pleased to return the favor. Variations on the horror film are so well inscribed in our own generic imagination that filmmakers are ready to stretch them to their limits, as Stanley Kubrick does in *The Shining* (1980) or parody them, as in *I Know What You Did Last Summer* (Jim Gillespie, 1977) or *Scream* (1996), by one of the major directors of contemporary horror, Wes Craven (see Figures 4.23, 4.24, 6.18). In *The Shining*, the horror film's old dark house becomes the brightly lit labyrinthine corridors of the Overlook hotel, complete with a secret room containing a

FIGURE 9.26 Computer generated zombies by the thousands in *World War Z* (Marc Foster, 2013)

"monster," an attractive naked lady who, in a perverse use of **shot/reverse shot**, turns into a diseased old crone in the arms of Jack Torrance (Jack Nicholson). There are intimations of past murders, and in the end the monster turns out to be Jack himself, a drunk who slowly degenerates under the pressures of forced isolation with his family and believes that the spirits of the place are forcing him to kill them. In Alfred Hitchcock's *Psycho*—the model for all the slasher *Halloween* and *Friday the 13th* movies to follow—the old dark house is exactly that, complete with a dank cellar in which the monster turns out to be a charming young man who has become his own psychopathic mother (see Figures 3.48, 4.23, 4.24 and 10.12).

We love horror films for their darkness, their reminders that chaos and violence are unpredictable, even as we can predict their occurrence in the film we are watching. But there is a dark side to the darkness, a group of films that have been appropriately called "torture porn." These are horror films without a modicum of self-censorship, that depict brutal, disgusting acts of mutilation and murder, films like *Hostel* (Eli Roth, 2005, 2007, Scott Spiegel, 2011), or the appallingly ridiculous *Human Centipede* (Tom Six, 2009, 2011). There is in these films a kind of dare to the viewer: Will you actually watch this? There is also a bizarre sense of play with the genre: just how far can we go before we move so completely out of bounds that we are beyond genre itself?

FURTHER READING

An ideological reading of genre can be found in Robin Wood, "Ideology, Genre, Auteur," in *Film Theory and Criticism,* pp. 717–726. See also Terry Lovell, *Pictures of Reality: Aesthetics, Politics, and Pleasure* (London: BFI, 1980).

Studies of genre can be found in Nick Browne, ed., *Refiguring American Film Genre: History and Theory* (Berkeley: University of California Press, 1998), Steven Neale, *Genre* (London: British Film Institute, 1983), and Rick Altman, *Film/Genre* (London: British Film Institute, 1999). There is interesting discussion about the tension between genre and individual expression in Leo Braudy's *The World in a Frame* (Chicago: University of Chicago Press, 2002), and by Robert Warshow in his essay "Movie Chronicle: The Western" in *The Immediate Experience: Movies, Comics, Theatre, and Other Aspects of Popular Culture* (Cambridge, MA: Harvard University Press, 2002). See also "The Gangster as Tragic Hero" in the same collection.

David Cook presents an excellent history of Hollywood censorship in *A History of Narrative Film* 4th ed. (New York: W. W. Norton, 2004).

A study of the Production Code can be found in Thomas Doherty, *Hollywood's Censor: Joseph I. Breen and the Production Code Administration* (New York, Chichester, West Sussex: Columbia University Press, 2007).

A lively history of the Warner Brothers gangster film and biography of its stars is in Robert Sklar, *City Boys* (Princeton, NJ: Princeton University Press, 1992). A classic study of the genre is Jack Shadoian, *Dreams and Dead Ends: The American Gangster Film*, 2nd ed. (New York: Oxford University Press, 2003).

Useful histories of documentary are Richard Meran Barsam, *Nonaction Film: A Critical History* (Bloomington: Indiana University Press, 1992), Erik Barnouw, *Documentary: A History of the Non-Fiction Film* (Oxford and New York: Oxford University Press, 1993), and Jack C. Ellis and Betsy A. McLane, eds., *A New History of the Documentary Film* (New York and London: Continuum International Publishing Group, 2005).

A strong analysis of Leni Riefenstahl's work is in Susan Sontag's essay "Fascinating Fascism," in *A Susan Sontag Reader* (New York: Vintage, 1982). For current theory on nonfiction film, see Bill Nichols, *Representing Reality: Issues and Concepts in Documentary* (Bloomington: Indiana University Press, 1991).

A fine study of World War II documentaries and their directors is Mark Harris, *Five Came Back: A Story of Hollywood and the Second World War* (New York: The Penguin Press, 2014).

The best book on John Wayne is by the historian Garry Wills, *John Wayne: The Politics of Celebrity* (London: Faber and Faber, 1999). There are literally dozens of books and articles on John Ford. An old but sturdy survey of the Western is Philip French, *Westerns: Aspect of a Movie Genre* (N.Y.: Viking Press, 1974). Also, see Edward Buscombe and Roberta E. Pearson, eds., *Back in the Saddle Again: New Essays on the Western* (BFI Publishing, 1998).

A collection of essays on *The Searchers* is Arthur M. Eckstein, Peter Lehman, eds., *The Searchers: Essays and Reflections on John Ford's Classic Western* (Detroit: Wayne State University Press, 2004). For the idea of the cowboy hero creating a domestic space he can't inhabit, see J. A. Place, *The Western Films of John Ford* (Secaucus, NJ: Citadel Press, 1974).

For the science fiction genre, see J. P. Telotte, *Science Fiction Film* (New York: Cambridge University Press, 2001) and Vivian Sobchack, *Screening Space: The American Science Fiction Film* 2nd ed. (New Brunswick: Rutgers University Press), 1997.

SUGGESTIONS FOR FURTHER VIEWING

Gangster films

Scarface (Howard Hawks, 1932; Brian De Palma, 1983)
The Roaring Twenties (Raoul Walsh, 1939)
Force of Evil (Abraham Polonsky, 1948)
White Heat (Raoul Walsh, 1949)
Casino (Martin Scorsese, 1995)
Heat (Michael Mann, 1995)
The Godfather (Francis Ford Coppola, 1972)
American Gangster (Ridley Scott, 2007)

Documentaries

Michael Moore
Sicko (2007)
Capitalism: A Love Story (2009)

Errol Morris
The Thin Blue Line (1988)
A Brief History of Time (1991)

The Western

John Ford

My Darling Clementine (1946)
She Wore a Yellow Ribbon (1949)
Rio Grande (1950)
Sergeant Rutledge (1960)

Other Westerns

Pursued (Raoul Walsh, 1947)
Winchester '73 (Anthony Mann, 1950)
High Noon (Fred Zinnemann, 1952)
The Far Country (Anthony Mann, 1954)
Shane (George Stevens, 1953)
Rio Bravo (Howard Hawks, 1959)
High Plains Drifter (Clint Eastwood, 1973)
Deadwood (HBO Series, various directors, 2004–2006)
The Assassination of Jesse James by the Coward Robert Ford (Andrew Dominik, 2007)

Science fiction and contemporary horror

Things to Come (William Cameron Menzies, 1936)
The War of the Worlds (Byron Haskin, 1953)
It Came from Outer Space (Jack Arnold, 1953)
Creature from the Black Lagoon (Jack Arnold, 1954)
The Incredible Shrinking Man (Jack Arnold, 1957)
Night of the Living Dead (George Romero, 1968)
The Exorcist (William Friedkin, 1973)
Invasion of the Body Snatchers (Phil Kaufman, 1978)
The Thing (John Carpenter, 1982)
The Fly (David Cronenberg, 1986)
War of the Worlds (Steven Spielberg, 2005)
I, Robot (Alex Proyas, 2004)
Super 8 (J. J. Abrams, 2008)
District 9 (Neill Blomkamp, 2009)
Halloween (various directors, 1978–2009)
A Nightmare on Elm Street (various directors, 1984–2010)
Star Trek (various directors, 1993, 1995, 2009, 2013)

NOTES

1 The term "dominant fiction" is suggested by Kaja Silverman in *Male Subjectivity at the Margins* (New York and London: Routledge, 1992).
2 "Prohibition" was a United States Constitutional amendment that outlawed the use of alcohol. It lasted from 1923 to 1930.
3 The quote from Grierson comes from *Grierson on Documentary*, ed. Forsyth Hardy (New York: Praeger, 1971), p. 289.
4 Information on WWII documentaries can be found in Mark Harris, *Five Came Back: A Story of Hollywood and the Second World War* (New York: The Penguin Press, 2014). Information about Hitchcock and the concentration camp footage comes from the following websites:

   "Alfred Hitchcock's Unseen Holocaust Documentary To Be Screened," the *Guardian* (8 January 2014). http://www.independent.co.uk/arts-entertainment/films/features/alfred-hitchcocks-unseen-holocaust-documentary-to-be-screened-9044945.html (accessed 16 March 2015).
   "Memory of the Camps (1985): The Holocaust Documentary that Traumatized Alfred Hitchcock, and Remained Unseen for 40 Years," http://www.openculture.com/2014/01/memory-of-the-camps-hitchcock.html (accessed 16 March 2015).
   "Frontline: Memory of the Camps," http://www.pbs.org/wgbh/pages/frontline/camp/ (accessed 16 March 2015).

5 Robert Warshow's "Movie Chronicle: The Westerner" can be found in *The Immediate Experience*, cited in the Further Reading section. His essay, "The Gangster as Tragic Hero," also in *The Immediate Experience*, is an important source for our discussion of the gangster film.
6 *Visionary Architecture* is the title of a book by Ernest E. Burden (New York: McGraw-Hill, 1999) and is used by Annette Michelson to refer to the future visions of science fiction film.

CHAPTER 10

The stories told by film II

FILM NOIR

In the mid-1940s a new **genre** developed, though it might be more correct to say that it invented itself. The genre, which was named **film noir** some years after it appeared, changed some elements of **melodrama** and disrupted some Hollywood stereotypes about gender and the inevitability of sacrifice and suffering. Hollywood didn't know it was making a new genre as the elements of noir were put into place. Few filmmakers or film viewers were aware, at least on a conscious, articulate level, that a new story was being told to them in a new visual style. It was the French in the 1950s who finally recognized that something was happening and gave it a name. But this does not mean that film noir was born out of nothing. Like any other genre, it came forth as a response to cultural need and developed out of cinematic elements already in existence.

During the Nazi occupation of France (1940–1944) there was an embargo on American films. *Citizen Kane* wasn't seen in Paris until early in 1946, five years after it was made. At the end of the war, American films flooded into France, a country that has had a deep and serious love of cinema since its invention. An eager group of young intellectuals—including François Truffaut and Jean-Luc Godard, who would go on to be immensely influential filmmakers, the **French New Wave** discussed in Chapter 8—began watching these films with an intense interest. They had a good location in which to do this, the Paris Cinémathèque, run by Henri Langlois, who showed whatever films he could get his hands on, twelve hours a day. They watched everything they could and especially loved American films, the spoken language of which they couldn't understand. They learned what they needed to know from the visual **narrative**, the images and their construction. They noted across the films of the mid-1940s a darkening of visual style and a darkening of thematic content. After a series of French detective stories called *Série noire*, one of these critics gave the name "film noir" to this new kind of film. But noir went far beyond the detective genre.

Expressionist roots of noir

Three main currents fed into the development of noir: **German Expressionism**, the hard-boiled detective fiction of the 1930s, and the cultural turmoil of World War II. Noir's visual style harks back to the Expressionist movement in German film, literature, theater, and painting that flourished after World War I and had a major influence on the Universal Pictures horror films of the early 1930s and on Welles's *Citizen Kane* (1941). I described this influence in Chapter 3, but it is important to repeat that Welles's dark and deep **mise-en-scène**, its combination of **chiaroscuro** lighting and **deep focus** cinematography that creates a mysterious world in which space is both inviting and threatening, had a major influence on noir.

Because its story was too closely modeled on the life of the newspaper magnate and millionaire William Randolph Hearst, who tried to have the film destroyed, and who refused to advertise it in his papers, *Citizen Kane* was not a commercially successful film. But even though its popular appeal took many years to form, its appeal to movie professionals was immediate. **Directors**, **cinematographers**, and **production designers** were taken by its radical style. The influence of Welles and his cinematographer, Gregg Toland, on the style of 1940s cinema was enormous. Darkness descended on Hollywood filmmaking.

Hard-boiled fiction

Citizen Kane was the main conduit into film noir, fed by the tributary of German Expressionism as well as some late 1930s French film, the "poetic realism" that figured in such dark and moody films as Marcel Carné's *Le jour se lève* (1939). Another source of influence came from literature. In the 1930s, a popular school of detective-fiction writers emerged, the most famous of whom were Raymond Chandler and Dashiell Hammett. Their work became known as the hard-boiled school of detective fiction, and they were masterful at creating visions of a dark, corrupt underworld of dopers and robbers, of sexual exploiters and an omnipresent immorality infiltrated by their cynical but morally secure detective characters—Hammett's Sam Spade and Chandler's Philip Marlowe. Their detectives were unheroic, ironic, self-aware, and also persevering and cunning but flawed and vulnerable, barely surviving their exploits with their moral centers intact.

A third figure connected with this school did not write detective fiction. James M. Cain told stories of sleazy, lower-middle-class families falling apart under the pressures of infidelity, murder, and general moral corruption. Almost all his novels—*Double Indemnity*, *Mildred Pierce*, *The Postman Always Rings Twice*—were made into films in the 1940s (*The Postman* had actually been made twice before in Europe). Cain's work and that of the hard-boiled school did not fit well with the Hollywood of the 1930s, however, burdened as it was with its self-imposed censorship code and need to provide ideological uplift for a Depression-ridden culture. But this wasn't for lack of trying. Warner Brothers had acquired rights to Hammett's *The Maltese Falcon* very early on and filmed it twice during the 1930s, once as a Bette Davis vehicle. They didn't actually get it right, though, until 1941, when John Huston directed the film with Humphrey Bogart as Sam Spade. During the 1930s, MGM was more successful with Hammett's *The Thin Man*, which the studio made as a series of **screwball comedies**—bright, fast-paced narratives about an upper-class married couple who drink a lot and verbally spar with each other while they do a bit of detective work on the side.

The Maltese Falcon

The 1941 version of *The Maltese Falcon* was not a comedy, though it did have a more ironic and wry tone than its predecessors. It is also somewhat slower paced and more intensely composed and **cut** than most films of the 1930s. It maintains much of Hammett's tough-guy dialogue, as Spade finds his way through a morass of blind alleys and murderous types as he searches for the mysterious figure of a gold-encrusted bird, and it catches the sense of an infinitely corrupted world that, because of censorship, was difficult to do in 1930s studio film. Visually, while the film was darker in tone than was usual during the preceding decade, it did not employ the deep chiaroscuro that would occur in films after the appearance of *Citizen Kane*. That darkness began to take over about 1944.

Murder, My Sweet, Double Indemnity, Scarlet Street

The third current that made film noir possible occurred outside of film and literature. The darkness of noir owes much to the darkening mood of the culture during and right after World War II. Noir's themes of male isolation and weakness, of female treachery and murderousness, grow out of a multitude of insecurities occurring in the American psyche. These themes infiltrated film noir through both form and content. The genre's visual darkness and its obsessive, damaged men reflected the culture's anxious postwar state.

Three landmark films solidified the look and the thematics of the new genre in 1944 and 1945. RKO, the studio that made *Citizen Kane*, produced an adaptation of Raymond Chandler's novel *Farewell, My Lovely*, directed by Edward Dmytryk, that they called *Murder, My Sweet*. Presumably the name was changed because the film was a vehicle for Dick Powell, a lead player in musicals, who was attempting to broaden his serious acting capacity; the studio feared that audiences would think the original title would be interpreted as another Dick Powell musical. *Murder, My Sweet* is, along with Howard Hawk's *The Big Sleep* (1946), the best of the Chandler adaptations. Powell delivers Philip Marlowe's **voice-over narration** with a grim irony, while the world the characters inhabit is bathed not in 1930s light but in darkness only occasionally relieved by light. "A dirty stupid little man in a dirty stupid world," a character says of Marlowe at one point, a comment that exemplifies the reduced existential circumstances of the noir male in a world he cannot quite see through, cannot accurately detect.

In the same year, 1944, the German director Billy Wilder made *Double Indemnity* for Paramount. Based on a James M. Cain novel with a screenplay by Raymond Chandler, it synthesized noir's essential generic elements—bitterly ironic dialogue, a weak male character who falls prey to a female predator, and a mise-en-scène not quite as dark as *Murder, My Sweet* but unrelentingly gray and claustrophobic. The film contains some rare (for its time) exterior footage: a nighttime city street is pierced by the headlights of a careening car and the spark of a workman's blowtorch; a gray suburban Los Angeles street, its cracks filled with veins of black asphalt, adds to the pervading atmosphere of diminished, sleazy lives. Interiors are dusty and gray. The living room of Phyllis Dietrichson (Barbara Stanwyck)—the woman who lures the poor insurance salesman, Walter Neff (Fred MacMurray), to murder her husband and finally shoots him and is shot by him in turn—is cut through with light coming from behind Venetian blinds. The light makes palpable the swirling dust in the air. The image of the shadowy slits of light from Venetian blinds occurs in almost every 1940s film from this point on.

Double Indemnity can be read in two ways. It is either a misogynist film about a terrifying, destroying woman—the classic "femme fatale"—or it is a film that liberates the female character from the restrictive and oppressed melodramatic situations that render her helpless. Feminist critics are divided in their views of the film and the noir genre as a whole. If it is in fact a film that gives its female character more strength and control, no longer situating her as the secure center of the family but as its destroyer, it marks a shift in the **dominant fiction** that speaks of women's passivity. However, the fact that both she and her doomed male prey die at the end diminishes its radical potential. What is unambiguous is the film's attitude toward such sacred cultural institutions and generic mainstays as the protective family and the brave, heroic, self-possessed male.

Walter Neff is dying from the very beginning of the film, which is narrated in **flashback** as, slowly bleeding to death from Phyllis's gunshot, he dictates his sorry tale onto a recording machine in his office. And while Neff is never self-pitying and remains verbally dexterous and self-deprecating in his narration, he is also clearly a loser, whose lust for Phyllis undoes his reason and self-control. Phyllis, we learn, creates families in order to destroy them. The family into which Walter comes, as an insurance man trying to make a sale, are a bunch of snarling whiners. Phyllis's husband is fully worthy of the death she plans for him. She manipulates first him and then Walter through a morally (and visually) degraded world of cheap houses, crowded office buildings, supermarkets, and dark railroad tracks where Walter dumps the husband's body. There is as little sentimentality in this narrative as Hollywood could allow.

The following year, Fritz Lang, a director from Germany who was an important figure in the Expressionist movement (in Germany, he made the classic science fiction film *Metropolis* in 1927 and the early sound film *M* in 1931), made a film called *Scarlet Street*. Here, a meek, henpecked husband, Christopher Cross (played by Edward G. Robinson, an actor from the early gangster film days, who plays Walter Neff's boss and would-be friend, Keyes, in *Double Indemnity*), becomes

FIGURE 10.1 "A dirty stupid little man in a dirty stupid world." Drugged and hallucinating, Philip Marlowe (Dick Powell) falls into the depths of corruption in the Expressionist mise-en-scène of Edward Dmytryk's *Murder, My Sweet* (1944)

FIGURE 10.2 Walter Neff (Fred MacMurray) and Phyllis Dietrichson (Barbara Stanwyck) succeed in killing each other in the shadows of Billy Wilder's film noir *Double Indemnity* (1944)

sexually in thrall to a young woman named Kitty (Joan Bennett). His enthrallment is climaxed by the kind of image Hollywood loves to use to indicate male debasement: he paints her toenails. Painting is a major issue in this classic noir film. Chris Cross is a would-be painter, and Kitty has her boyfriend, Johnny (Dan Durea), pass off Chris's work as hers. Chris kills Kitty in a rage, and Johnny is sentenced for the crime. The meek man is given power only through his reaction to being played a chump, and though Johnny deserves punishment for many reasons, his execution is the cause of overwhelming guilt, borne by the ironically named Chris Cross.

This grim little narrative is given considerable substance by Lang's ability to reproduce the desire and paranoia, the failure and miserable triumph of his meek and hopeless main character. The narrative is given existential portent in its climax, as Chris becomes a kind of eternally guilty everyman. He becomes a street person, wandering a city that is empty of other people. He is the only man alive, carrying his guilt and despair alone.

Scarlet Street announces a universal anxiety and a reduction of individual agency that are usually associated with great modernist literary fiction. The point is made over and over again by film noir. The world is dark and corrupt. Women are predators. Men are either violent and brutal or the passive, unwary prey of the violent or the sexually manipulative woman. Any way out is hard to see. As one film noir character says, "I feel all dead inside. I'm backed up in a dark corner and I don't know who's hitting me."[1] All of this was remarkable in a cinema usually devoted to the bright and harmonious or to the safe excesses and reassuring closures of melodrama. While none of the filmmakers had a term for the genre that rapidly took over production across the studios, the darkness reigned, and by the mid-1940s most films from Hollywood that were not comedies shared some noir characteristics, even if only the core image of a room banded by shadows of light coming through Venetian blinds.

Anthony Mann

One figure stands out in film noir's mature period in the late 1940s. Anthony Mann, collaborating with his cinematographer John Alton, created among the darkest, most misanthropic films of the

FIGURE 10.3 Anthony Mann created some of the most astonishing noir images, as in this image in a steam bath from *T-Men* (1947)

genre. His characters are cold and merciless; extraordinary acts of violence explode unexpectedly; and his mise-en-scène is the darkest, his **compositions** the most disorienting until Welles's *Touch of Evil* in 1958. Mann took noir seemingly as far as it could go, turning the screen in films like *T-Men* (1947), *Raw Deal* (1948), and *Side Street* (1950) into a tunnel of despair and anxiety. He even made a film noir Western, *The Furies* (1950), before he turned to color cinematography and a string of Westerns. He ended his career making sword and sandal epics, the overripe Roman and biblical films made in the late 1950s and early 1960s, and was briefly Kirk Douglas's director on *Spartacus*, before being replaced by Stanley Kubrick.

NOIR'S CLIMAX

In a Lonely Place

Noir lasted through the early 1950s, climaxed by four films that were self-conscious about what they were doing. Nicholas Ray's *In a Lonely Place* (1950) combines elements of noir with the male melodrama we will discuss. Humphrey Bogart, who had helped form the male noir character in *The Maltese Falcon* and *The Big Sleep*, constructs a figure of repressed rage, a screenwriter who lives in the shadows of his own uncontainable violence. He is recessive and aggressive at the same time, and when he emerges into the light and falls in love, he is undone by his rage. Along with Alfred Hitchcock's very different *Vertigo* (1958), *In a Lonely Place* is as complex and moving an analysis of male angst and the turmoils of gender as exists in the canon of American cinema. This is the rare American film that allows the fact—indeed, the "reality"—that love may not, actually, conquer all; that differences in gender response may be insuperable; and that the central characters and their narrative may not be resolved.

FIGURE 10.4 Humphrey Bogart's Dixon Steele can barely restrain his excitement as he "directs" a scene of violence for the benefit of his friends. *In a Lonely Place* (Nicholas Ray, 1950)

The Wrong Man

Alfred Hitchcock's *The Wrong Man* (1956) took a "true story" and created a quasi-**documentary** style to narrate the events of an ordinary family man accused, arrested, and tried for robbery. His wife sinks into madness as a result of the events. Much of the film—visually as dark and claustrophobic as Hitchcock ever made—doggedly follows the process of its central character's incarceration and trial. It has a slow, almost trancelike pace, emphasized by Bernard Herrmann's thrumming score, and refuses to mitigate its characters' unrelenting misery. For much of the film, Hitchcock restrains his camera, but at key moments, he allows it to reflect its character's battered state of mind. When Manny Balestrero (Henry Fonda) is thrown into a prison cell, the camera assumes his point of view, inscribing vertiginous circles around the enclosure to indicate his stomach-churning anxiety. Even more than *Scarlet Street*, made over a decade earlier, it uses the structures of noir to address the loss of individual power and identity in the post-World War II world. *The Wrong Man* constitutes a kind of allegory of the anticommunist witch hunts being carried out by the House Un-American Activities Committee in Hollywood and by Joseph McCarthy nationwide. Manny is hounded and humiliated like the witnesses hauled before the various committees investigating a non-existent "Communist threat."

Loss, powerlessness, the inability to pull out of oncoming chaos—the elements of a bad dream drifting from the individual unconscious into the culture at large—had marked noir from its beginning. Now near the end of its first cycle, these noir elements spoke to the 1950s with even more immediacy. In a decade characterized by extreme governmental interference into the intellectual freedom of the country, by big corporate growth, by the construction of the myth of Communism, the super-enemy ready to infiltrate the very fabric of the culture, the decade's paranoia was addressed quite profoundly by film noir as it was addressed somewhat less profoundly by the alien invasion science fiction film, a major 1950s genre that we examined in the previous chapter.

Kiss Me Deadly

Robert Aldrich's *Kiss Me Deadly* (1955) used the private detective version of film noir to address Cold War issues directly. The film is based on a novel by Mickey Spillane, who wrote vulgar,

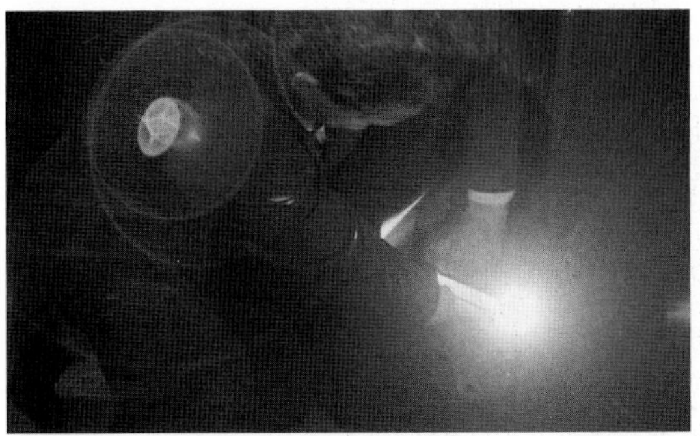

FIGURE 10.5 An example of intertextual allusion: The blinding light of an atomic device hidden in a box in Robert Aldrich's *Kiss Me Deadly* (1955)

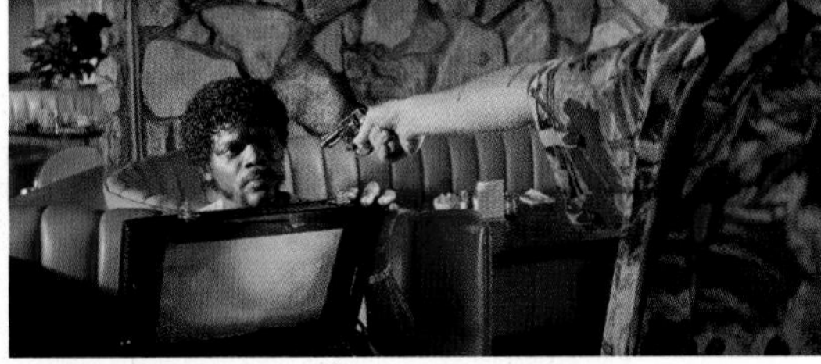

FIGURE 10.6 Quentin Tarantino is thinking about Aldrich's bomb when Jules opens the mysterious suitcase in *Pulp Fiction* (1994)

violent, woman-hating detective fiction that was enormously popular during the decade. Aldrich's screen version of Spillane's detective, Mike Hammer (Ralph Meeker), removes some of the vulgarity, turns the sexual violence into a peculiar kind of sexual reticence, but leaves the physical violence much intact. *Kiss Me Deadly* is about the search for a mysterious box that contains nuclear material. When opened, the box roars, screams, and glows with a deadly light: Quentin Tarantino got the idea for the mysterious suitcase with the golden light in *Pulp Fiction* from the mysterious box in *Kiss Me Deadly.* The box is discovered and opened by a curious woman—the film plays on the Pandora myth with a special 1950s misogyny—and it blows up the world.

Noir is usually about implosion rather than explosion. But as the poet T. S. Eliot pointed out in the 1920s, the end of the world does not have to come with a bang. A whimper is more likely, and a whimper is what's heard in *Scarlet Street* or *The Wrong Man* or *In a Lonely Place. Kiss Me Deadly* turns the whimper back into the more conventional bang. When light pierces through the noir darkness, the world comes apart. When the detective finds out the secret he's been looking for, he gets fried. This is the peculiar double-edged paranoia of the 1950s. Men will collapse into lonely isolation, or, if they really find out the world's secret, they and everything else will be destroyed.[2]

Touch of Evil

Between implosion and external destruction, there is another possibility. Create a world that appears as an ongoing nightmare of dizzying perspectives, long, dark streets, bizarre individuals careening around an unstable landscape of strip joints, hideous motels, oil fields, barren gray intersections, and open sewers. In other words, update the Expressionist vision to address the modern age. This is what Orson Welles does in *Touch of Evil* (1958), the last film noir of the genre's first cycle. It is fitting that this climactic film should be made by the director who

FIGURE 10.7 The dark, off kilter mise-en-scène of Orson Welles's *Touch of Evil* (1958). (See also Figures 3.2, 7.1 and 7.2.)

originated the genre seventeen years earlier. Welles had been away from the United States, making films in Europe for almost eight years and returned to find a project based on a second-rate novel about corrupt police, starring Charlton Heston as a Mexican cop. He took the challenge and created the most intriguing and inventive film noir to date. Filming mostly in the streets of Venice in Los Angeles, and inside actual buildings, Welles turned the "real world" into a bad dream of a border town trafficking in corruption, a local cop who plants evidence to catch his man (the cop is played by Welles himself, puffed up, limping, and growling), and a sappy, moral Mexican official out to save his country's name and protect his American bride (Janet Leigh).

Touch of Evil is, in part, an outsider's view of mid-1950s America just coming out of the grip of Joseph McCarthy and the anticommunist, evidence-fabricating witch hunts—a morass of moral and political corruption. It is also an ironist's attempt to play sympathy for the devil. Welles's Hank Quinlan, the corrupt cop—a Joseph McCarthy surrogate—is, in fact, weak and spiteful, out for revenge against "my dirty job." The world Welles creates for these characters, on the other hand, is of his imagination only, insinuated by his camera, which **tracks**, **cranes**, cants, sinks far below eye level and then rapidly cranes high above the characters. The long opening **shot** of *Touch of Evil* tracks a car moving through the dark labyrinth of a Mexican–American border crossing. The shot lasts for almost three minutes and is one of the most famous **long takes** in contemporary cinema. The camera articulates the characters and the audience's perceptions of them by means of dizzying, off-center compositions and enfolds them in its dark, nightmare world. It is the definition of how mise-en-scène can be created.[3]

NOIR'S REBIRTH

There was not very much further one could go past *Touch of Evil* in creating a dark, decaying, Expressionist mise-en-scène. The genre was spent, and films were beginning to respond to television in ways that made noir obsolete. The deeply shadowed black and white of the 1940s was giving way to a more evenly graded spectrum of graytones in the 1950s. Then in the 1960s, black and white gave way to color. Since film noir was so essentially dependent on the dark end of the black and white spectrum, a move to color would seem to mark the end of its visual life, despite at least one notable noir color experiment, Henry Hathaway's *Niagara* (1953). But in the hands and eyes of a talented director and **director of photography**, color turned out to be a very flexible medium. To understand why, a review of the short history of color film is necessary.

As we discussed in Chapter 3, film had always been tinted and toned in the silent period, with a red tint signifying passion, blue standing for night, gold for day. We see this in the various images from silent film throughout this book (see, for example, Figures 3.10, 3.22, 4.2–4.6). Experiments with a more "realistic" color stock began in the early 1920s, and the three-color **Technicolor** process was introduced in the early 1930s. Here, the color spectrum was filtered into its primary components and photographed on three strips of black and white negative. The making of a positive print involved marrying the three strips and using dyes to create the final color product. Color remained a specialty process until the early 1960s, used mainly for musicals and fantasy films, which is why the Oz **sequences** of *The Wizard of Oz* (Victor Fleming, 1939) are in Technicolor.

"Realism" required black and white. We have been discussing all along how conventionalized film is, how it is based on repeated patterns and recognizable structures. This is nowhere more apparent than in the fact that "reality" for film before the 1960s meant black and white cinematography. Of course there is nothing inherently "realistic" in either color or black and white. The latter was considered "real" only because it was the dominant mode and color wasn't. But that changed in the 1960s. By the early 1960s, television began to broadcast in color, and, because the final distribution point for any film is the television screen, by the end of the decade all films had to be made in color.

The influence of film noir was powerful, and young filmmakers, many coming out of film school in the late 1960s and early 1970s, felt a response similar to that felt by those French intellectuals in the early 1950s: the discovery of something extraordinary in the style and content of American film from the 1940s and early 1950s. They began to revive noir, rethink it in color, and use noir as a way to make color cinematography responsive to their imaginative needs. Arthur Penn made a key film in the noir revival in *Night Moves* (1975), and Martin Scorsese was at the center of the revival. *Taxi Driver* (1976) captures the dark Expressionism of original film noir, with its creation of an urban landscape that reflects the paranoia of its main character more thoroughly than any film since *Touch of Evil*. Such films are now referred to as noir or neonoir, like Christopher Nolan's *Batman* series, because the call of darkness and helplessness seems to come from deep within the culture as an antidote to the redemptive urge of our dominant fictions and continue to be given form—and now even parody—in film. The genre named by the French became, by the 1970s, a genre recognized by many filmgoers. By now, "film noir" has entered the language. It is one of the few terms from French film criticism that everyone knows, and it has become the most written about American film genre. The spell of film noir has infiltrated our culture and our consciousness.

MELODRAMA

As we noted earlier, melodrama is not original to film. As an old and popular form, it is even represented by a popular stereotype. Because it is the dominant serious dramatic and narrative form of so many cultures, it contains within it the seeds of its own parody. In popular usage, "melodrama" is often used to describe an exaggerated, emotionally overblown situation, even in our daily lives. But in this case, parody turns out to be a form of flattery (or self-protection) because melodrama has never lost its power to make grown people cry. It is the central cinematic form that creates empathy and identification. A while ago, when radio and then television soap opera were in their prime, it demanded the attention of millions of listeners and viewers around the world. Soap opera remains enormously popular in Latin American countries.

Melodrama is about feeling or, more accurately, about provoking emotions, perhaps more intense than what are called for by the story being told. The desire to provoke emotions, and, for the audience, to have them provoked, was a driving force in the development of American cinema's classical style. Its formation and the development of film melodrama went hand in hand. Knitting the viewers' gaze within the narrative space of a film; emphasizing glances, faces, hands (D. W. Griffith especially liked **close-ups** of women's hands, wringing, twisting); and finding ways to mold the viewers' response into a narrative flow of despair, loss, anxiety, hope, and eventual triumph, suffered or instigated mainly by women, helped filmmakers establish a style of visual, narrative, and emotional continuity.

As we have seen in Chapter 6, exaggerated as they might seem to us now, the gestures of silent film melodrama were in fact a refinement, even a rethinking, of their stage originals, providing an emotive language of look and gesture that created and maintained a connection with viewers. An intimacy between the audience and the representations of actors on the screen was greater than that achieved when live figures gesticulated on a distant stage. These looks and gestures and the way they were edited together became conventionalized codes that triggered conventionalized responses, predictably, time and time again. In their predictability lay their security. It lies there still. The gestures and looks are less broad now, but still codified. It must be so, because melodrama is about security, about the safe expression of overwhelming passion, safe because confined within the known bounds of cinematic codes. Circumscribed, predictable, closed, the codes of melodrama can permit extravagant stories to be told, stories that articulate deep, subjective passion and terrors, which are always contained within the bounds of the dominant fictions.

Broken Blossoms

D. W. Griffith was as central a figure in the development of the contours and contents of film melodrama as he was in the development of the classic style itself. He was a man of a conservative, populist, Southern character, and his background and ideology colored his films. His racist film *The Birth of a Nation* (1915) not only expanded the narrative scope and running time of theatrical film but celebrated and managed to revitalize the then dormant Ku Klux Klan. Griffith spent much of the rest of his career attempting to atone for the appalling social–political results of his "masterpiece." His racial attitudes were matched only by his attitudes toward gender (though it should be emphasized that these attitudes were shared with large parts of the contemporary culture, as were his appalling views of race). Women, in most of Griffith's films, fulfilled conventional roles of wives and mothers. They were weak and got into trouble, often at the hands of desperate, angry men. They needed saving by the opposite: good, virile men. One of the essential, primary structures of narrative film, the **cross-cutting** editing pattern that links a sequence of captivity and a sequence of rescue, is based on this response to gender difference. The pattern was not invented by Griffith, and it was used in comedies as well, but he fully exploited it, made it essential to melodramatic construction, and climaxed it, in fact, in the great rescue scene of *Way Down East* (1920), where the woman—passive, trapped, stranded on rapidly dispersing ice floes—awaits rescue by her man, who is desperate to arrive before she goes over the edge.

Griffith helped institutionalize this formula and made it a permanent part of the language of melodramatic cinema. He could also reverse it. In *The Mother and the Law*, a film made right after *The Birth of a Nation* and included as one of the stories in *Intolerance* (made in 1916, the first of the films he made to atone for the racism of *The Birth of a Nation*), it is the woman who leads the rescue of her son, imprisoned because he is wrongly accused of labor violence (Griffith's populism occurs in other films, like the 1909 short film *A Corner in Wheat*, where he takes the side of labor against business). Such a reversal in gender expectations is nowhere as startling as in *Broken Blossoms* (1919), a melodrama in which gender positions are set askew, and both the male and female characters suffer an enormous amount of repression. *Broken Blossoms* sets some basic patterns for the family melodrama that have persisted, with much variation but little fundamental change, to the present.

Griffith's overt theme for the film is a rather weak-willed wish for "universal brotherhood." What the film crucially investigates is miscegenation (interracial sexual relations) and brutality to women. The central male character is a Chinese man, played by a white actor (Richard Barthelmess), who is referred to in the intertitles as "The Yellow Man." He comes to London—

a mythical movie-set London, a place removed from any reality, a perfect mise-en-scène for this fantasy of domestic terror—on a religious mission to calm the savage white man. He lives an isolated life in the East End ghetto. He takes no part in the pursuits of opium smoking, which Griffith portrays in an extraordinary tableau, showing men and women lounging sensually in a smoked-filled opium den, and maintains a spiritual aloofness as a small shop owner. His revulsion to violence, his features and gestures, the very way he holds his body are strongly marked as female. That is, they are marked by what the culture recognizes as feminine—small, mincing gestures; hands and arms drawn close to the body; a non-aggressive personality.

"The Yellow Man" is doubled by the film's female character, Lucy (Lillian Gish). In gesture and demeanor she is his mirror image, and they are even composed by the camera in similar ways. Lucy is also an outcast, a poor, withdrawn, helpless creature of a monstrous father, the prizefighter "Battling Burrows" (Donald Crisp), who looms forward in enormous close-up, almost threatening the viewer as he does his daughter, whom he beats with ferocious violence. The melodramatic triangle set up by these figures is fascinating in its complexity and in the ways it reveals basic principles of the genre. Lucy is oppressed by a paternal figure of such violence that she attempts to escape him by turning to the gentle, feminized male—a vulnerable, regressive figure like herself—for comfort. But the comfort she receives is also threatening in its otherness.

Melodrama must create a world of threat, not only to its characters but to its audience, before it resolves itself. Filled with desire of his own, "The Yellow Man" turns Lucy into a fetish object, making her up to look like an Asian doll and placing her on his raised bed. This really frightens her—and us. In one close-up from her point of view, "The Yellow Man's" face moves toward her filled with lust—a shot that will be echoed later when Battling Burrows' face moves toward Lucy, filled with violent hatred. But "The Yellow Man" has sublimated his lust and is no threat to her; he worships her. The look on his face actually reflects her own fears. Everything, the erotic in particular, remains repressed. In melodrama, sexuality and desire must be sublimated into something else. In *Broken Blossoms*, their sublimation results from the cultural prohibition against miscegenation and the notion that protection is stronger than the need for sexual satisfaction.

The sublimation turns "The Yellow Man" into a maternal figure, a strangely desexualized but somehow still erotic figure who both worships and cares for the battered Lucy. But this adoration and care is no match for Battling Burrows. The tension of the narrative is built when he finds his daughter. The brutality of the crazed patriarch will destroy the apparently innocent pleasures of this odd couple. He drags Lucy back to their hovel and beats her to death after she flees to the confines of a closet. "Battling" breaks down with an ax the walls she hoped would protect her, the camera capturing Lucy's entrapment and exposure through a sequence of **point-of-view** shots that is chilling and unrelenting. It is a scene so grueling and so expertly done that Hitchcock does homage to it in the shower scene in *Psycho* (1960), as does Kubrick in *The Shining* (1980) when Jack breaks down Wendy's door with an ax.

It is typical of melodrama to create an experience of such extremity, a cruelty so enormous that it seems impossible to correct it. But it must be corrected, because without closure, without recuperating the situation, the internal melodramatic world would be in perpetual disruption. It might be useful to think of melodrama spatially, as a kind of bell-shaped curve. The narrative starts out with a forced and weakened harmony between the characters. Events become complicated as when, for example, an abused white woman and an Asian man seek affection for each other. These complications raise the emotional graph to sometimes unbearable peaks. But these excesses must be themselves reclaimed—melodrama is always about subduing the excess it

FIGURES 10.8–10.9 Mirror images in D. W. Griffith's *Broken Blossoms* (1919). Lucy (Lilian Gish), the abused woman and "The Yellow Man" (Richard Barthelmess)—both characters marked by vulnerability and sensitivity, separated by gender and race

FIGURE 10.10 Battling Burrows (Donald Crisp), Lucy's brutish father, looms out of the frame

FIGURE 10.11 He takes an axe to the closet where Lucy tries to hide from his rage

FIGURE 10.12
Stanley Kubrick has this scene in mind in *The Shining* (1980)

creates—and a kind of harmony is reestablished by the film's end. Often, when the narrative situation appears to have no probability of closure, the film will simply kill off its participants, which is what happens at the end of *Broken Blossoms.* Griffith tries to create a standard intercut sequence of rescue. But "The Yellow Man" doesn't arrive in time to save Lucy. She is murdered, and he shoots "Battling Burrows" and then himself.

Melodrama is structured on the containment and release of desire. It calls for the end of repression and then reimposes it at the end. That is because melodrama is essentially a cautionary form. Yes, it says, people live constricted and hurt lives. They want more, should have more. But too much more will damage the fragile emotional equilibrium, the sets of oppositions, the dominant and regressive states of freedom and containment that the culture needs to survive. So melodrama always enacts, at its end, a process of recuperation, bringing its characters back to a kind of cultural health or, more accurately, a "health" prescribed by the dominant values, and the dominant fictions, of the culture. Melodrama is an expression of the dominant fiction of closure and equilibrium, of bringing characters and culture into a manageable steady state; and if it cannot recuperate its characters into a steadier state than the one in which they began, or if they cannot be recuperated because they have transgressed too far, or if they have a disease (think of *The Fault in Our Stars*, Josh Boone, 2014), it will enforce an equilibrium through their absence and kill them off, usually in the name of their being too good or too bad or too damaged to survive.

As a dynamic genre, depending upon a close interaction with the audience who view it, we can almost say that melodrama has a life of its own. "It" can do things to characters and to viewers. All genres can do things, because they are prescriptive mechanisms. Within a genre, certain actions can and *must* be taken by or occur to certain characters, and the narrative that directs their lives must follow a prescribed and proscribed path.

Broken Blossoms deals with one of the ultimate cultural transgressions, miscegenation. And while the film pretends a tender understanding of how "The Yellow Man" and Lucy find comfort in their bizarre, asexual union, it cannot possibly allow that union to prevail or endure. Melodrama is self-censuring. It always assumes to know how much passion and transgression the audience, within its cultural constraints, will or should manage. In the process of built-in censure, it will also gauge the maximum emotional capital it can cause the audience to expend in exchange for the images they are watching. So, while Griffith has his three characters killed off because the triangle was simply more than cultural reality in the late 1910s could bear, he manages to wring from his viewers as much sympathy, or even empathy, as they can muster or commit.

Caution and exploitation are two of melodrama's main attributes. If tragedy, the dramatic form that preceded melodrama, asked of its audience a profound recognition of great human achievement undone by greater human limitation, melodrama asks for a less lofty but more emotional recognition of the necessity to contain all aspirations within comfortable and known boundaries. "Asks" is wrong, though. Melodrama demands. For melodrama to work, an audience must be told what to feel and when to feel it; viewers must be hooked and reeled in. Narrative movement must be unstoppable and not allow any questions to be asked. If, at any point, melodrama permitted an opening through which the viewer could look and say, "This is ridiculous, such events, such suffering could or should never occur," the structure would fall to pieces. Melodrama demands continuous assent and uses all the force of the **continuity style** to get that assent. It **sutures** the viewer into its fabric and makes the viewer's emotional response part of that fabric's pattern.

The pattern is often enough based on very primal stuff. Simple human need for emotional comfort in the face of outrageous brutality is the baseline of *Broken Blossoms.* But elaborated into a narrative of interracial romance, gender diffusion, and a grotesque representation of an abusive father, the baseline is built up just to the point of collapse. Griffith's delicacy and restraint (not qualities he shows in many of his other films) and the constant fascination of his mise-en-scène—the mythic constructions of East End London streets; the conversion of "The Yellow Man's" room into an exotic, erotic temple; the oppressive grunge of "Battling Burrows's" room—keep the viewer contained within the narrative. The simple cutting, the connections of gaze and response, ease the viewer into this mise-en-scène of gender hysteria. The sexual ambiguities, the continual threats to Lucy of violence and rape, even her ghastly attempts to smile at her beastly father by pushing up the corners of her mouth with her fingers, fascinate because of their very outrageousness. Melodrama turns the outrageous into the plausible and asks us to believe that plausibility is close to reality.

Now, Voyager

Melodrama throws pain and dissatisfaction in our faces, insists we can do better, and then, in the end, takes it all back, assuring us that we'll be fine if we only modify desire and deflect pain somewhere else—or end it with death. In 1942, Warner Brothers made a rich and complex melodrama called *Now, Voyager,* directed by Irving Rapper. With Bette Davis, one of Warner's major contract players, as its star, it combines an Oedipal narrative with the story of Cinderella to create the classic structure of melodramatic proposal and denial. A superb example of the classic Hollywood continuity style, *Now, Voyager* knits its pieces together within a narrative of such perfect continuity that the viewer is compelled across its parts into an illusion of a seamless flow of events. *Now, Voyager* substitutes an oppressive, upper-class mother for *Broken Blossoms'* brutal working-class father. Mother (Gladys Cooper) is always shown rigid and dominating the frame, even if it is only her fingers, ominously taking up the foreground of a composition, impatiently tapping on a bedpost. The subject of her oppression is her daughter, Charlotte Vale, seen early in the film as a mousy, gray, emotionally arrested, neurotic middle-aged woman.

The film plays out the introduction of Charlotte as long as it can, in an interesting display of the intimacy filmmakers knew existed between viewer and film. Audiences already knew very well what Bette Davis looked like from her many other films: she was a major star who had gained even wider recognition by unsuccessfully attempting to break her contract with the studio because she did not like the roles she was being given. Viewers could be depended upon to have read stories of her lawsuit and also to have read publicity that stressed how homely she was made to look early in the film. Therefore, *Now, Voyager* takes its time introducing her and, when it finally does, shows her legs first, descending the stairs, to further heighten expectation. In a similar way, as described in Chapter 2, Warner Brothers' *Casablanca* (Michael Curtiz), made at about the same time as *Now, Voyager,* and retaining some of the political structure of melodrama's origins, also withholds the appearance of its star, Humphrey Bogart, building audience expectation and defining the character through his surroundings.

Now, Voyager posits two men who come to Charlotte's rescue, each one a "foreigner," each one offering a different kind of assistance and release. One is a psychiatrist, a figure with a mixed history in American film. The cinematic role of psychiatry and psychiatrist reflects the profession's mixed reputation in the culture at large. Feared and admired, looked to as someone to deliver us from emotional pain, or as a personification of individual defeat and helplessness, or as the embodiment of evil influence, the psychiatrist can help or destroy. In *Now, Voyager* psychiatry is salvation, and its incarnation in Dr. Jaquith—a wise, ironic, and self-contained Britisher (Claude Rains)—enters Charlotte's mother's house at the very beginning of the film and rescues Charlotte. He is an asexual individual, emotionally potent but no romantic threat. Because the sexual is so foregrounded in melodrama and placed as a primary cause of most of the characters' activities, the genre often needs clean divisions between those for whom sex is a central issue and those for whom it plays no role. These non-threatening figures (very often represented as the friend of the central character, like Sam in *Casablanca*) are mediating forces. They act a bit as our presence in the film, guiding, threatening nothing, seeing everything, assuring the success of the main character. In *Now, Voyager*, Dr. Jaquith figures as a pleasant, though aloof, patriarchal counter to Charlotte's mother—understanding, supportive, curative where she is negative, mean, and destructive. Though the film does not show the details of her cure, Charlotte is indeed transformed by her stay at Dr. Jaquith's sanitarium and emerges, as if from a cocoon, to appear as the glamorous Bette Davis everyone in the theater would have been familiar with—as familiar as now we would be with Scarlett Johansson.

Dr. Jaquith helps execute the Cinderella myth embedded in this particular melodrama. The genre demands, however, more than physical and emotional transformation. Sexual transformation must occur as well. Jaquith provides the paternal guidance. Jerry, an architect with a European accent (he is played by Paul Henreid, Victor Lazlo in *Casablanca*), provides the sexual awakening. Charlotte meets Jerry on a cruise. This is an important moment in her life. In a flashback to an embarrassing moment in her past, on another cruise, we learn the reason for her repression: her mother caught her making love to one of the ship's crew. The incident is coded to indicate that the mother's oppression of Charlotte's sexual awakening had lasting effects on her sexuality, constricting her, bringing her to that condition so abhorred by melodrama, as well as the culture at large that melodrama addresses, of being an "old maid."

In melodrama, repressed sexuality is a standard starting point, liberated sexuality its apparent goal, moderated sexuality its favored closure. *Now, Voyager* pursues this path with relentless determination. In Brazil (Latin America being a stereotyped place of the erotic in classic American cinema), Charlotte and Jerry fall in love and make love, in the spaces of a fade-out between a glowing fireplace and its afterglow embers—a lovely substitution for the physical contact the censors forbade showing on the screen. Their affection is signaled by one of those great Hollywood inventions that hooks a film into our imagination. Jerry begins a habit of lighting two cigarettes in his mouth. One is for himself, the other he hands to Charlotte. The gesture is repeated many times in the film, and, with the recurring theme music on the soundtrack, it becomes a correlative of the couple's passion. The critics Thomas Elsaesser and Geoffrey Nowell-Smith point out that in film melodrama, music and mise-en-scène often express the excess of emotion experienced by the characters. The lighting of the two cigarettes in *Now, Voyager* and the swelling soundtrack that accompanies it are excellent examples of gesture, movement, and sound that express to us a world of emotion.[4]

As if in response to her daughter's romance, Charlotte's mother feigns illness and a crippling fall in an attempt to reclaim her daughter, who wavers momentarily and, out of touch with Jerry, thinks she will marry a local Bostonian of good family. She also discovers that Jerry is married. This decline and dangerous reversal are an important part of melodramatic structure, which depends upon graphing our emotions in predictable patterns. Having shown Charlotte a way out of her misery, melodrama insists on letting her—and the viewer— know that a return to the darkness is not far out of sight. Suspense and fear for the central character are constructed by means of comparing where she was, how far she has come, and how tentative her liberation remains. The female character of melodrama is always on a precipice, with the narrative line acting as a kind of tightrope, and we are depended upon to agonize over the chances of her falling back to where she was.

So tentative is Charlotte's situation that she winds up back in Dr. Jaquith's sanitarium, where a series of events occurs that is less important as a matter of story than indicative of what melodrama must do to recuperate its characters, even at the expense of strained credulity. The intolerable paradox of melodrama is that the liberation of its characters is also their transgression. To make themselves free they break culture's rules and have to pay. Through Jaquith's intervention and Jerry's intimacy, Charlotte achieves a degree of sexual freedom and emotional maturity. But a narrative and cultural tension is thereby created. As far as our identification with the character in her narrative is concerned, her freedom is a relief and our emotions soar with her. Charlotte has become an independent agent. But in terms of what is culturally allowable and the **Production Code** forbade, what she has done is impossible.

In the early 1940s, when restrictions on the representations of sexuality in film were stronger than they are now, Charlotte could not be permitted to go much further in her explorations of

FIGURE 10.13 "Don't let's not ask for the moon . . . we have the stars." The melodramatic gaze: Charlotte (Bette Davis) and the man she loves but cannot have, Jerry (Paul Henreid) in *Now, Voyager* (Irving Rapper, 1942)

independence. But even in the wake of the feminist movement, even though women characters in film and television are permitted an exploration of sexuality unheard of during the years of the Production Code, many films still compromise their female characters in one way or another. If such a film is a romantic comedy, the strong-willed woman will be convinced that marriage is the only final outlet for her energies. This is not surprising, given the fact that, as a genre going back to Shakespeare and earlier, comedy ends in marriage. Marriage remains the ritual representation of harmony and rebirth in most cultures, the joyous reproduction of the family, and the unstated representation of sexual containment. If the film is a melodrama, the unrepressed woman is as often as not depicted as crazy or evil, threatening the man and his family. Think about *Fatal Attraction* (Adrian Lyne, 1987), *Single White Female* (Barbet Schroeder, 1992), and *Basic Instinct* (Paul Verhoeven, 1992), films made as part of the backlash against feminism. David Fincher's *Gone Girl* (2014) heightens the convention of the violent mad woman who lies, murders, and creates mayhem out of an unarticulated urge that may be psychosis or high spirits that get melodramatically out of hand.

Crazy if repressed, crazy if unrepressed, melodrama catches women in a double bind and allows few escapes other than death or a falling back into some barely tolerable compromise. The latter is what happens to Charlotte in *Now, Voyager.* In Dr. Jaquith's sanitarium, she meets a depressed little girl, the double of Charlotte in her former state. She nurses the child back to mental stability and discovers she is Jerry's daughter, product of an unhappy marriage in which Jerry nobly remains because his wife is an invalid. The metaphor of sickness and health overwhelms the film. Disease is melodrama-friendly, because it represents people in extreme states. Curing disease, or succumbing to it, parallels melodrama's accordion-like structure of repression or restriction, expanding outward to emotional or physical health and then collapsing again into a more culturally acceptable situation of moderated health and constrained emotional activity, or death. James L. Brooks's *Terms of Endearment* (1983), which seems to begin as a romantic comedy, ends with the onslaught of fatal disease that reawakens a mother's love for her daughter. *The Notebook* (Nick Cassavetes, 2004) ends its tale of a complex love affair with death by Alzheimer's. Larry Kramer's play *The Normal Heart*, made into an HBO movie by Ryan Murphy (2014), uses the illness and deaths of HIV to engender compassion and understanding from heterosexual viewers. The aforementioned *The Fault in Our Stars* depends upon disease as the motivating force of emotion throughout. The local fiction of any given melodrama is less important than the dominant fiction of sickness in body or mind that produces sacrificial acts on the part of an individual, a family, or group member, not to mention extraordinary empathy from the viewer.

As the reigning metaphor of *Now, Voyager*, the cycle of sickness and health is passed from one character to another—to Charlotte, her mother, Jerry's wife, and his daughter. Charlotte gets well. But her cure is entirely local. She's happy, but her happiness does not satisfy the film's or the culture's melodramatic requirements. Individual happiness is never sufficient for melodrama. Perhaps because it has never completely shaken off its class origins, perhaps because audiences find insufficient gratification in a character whose happiness is complete, melodrama must do something to temper events. A selfish indulgence in sexuality might do well for Charlotte the fictional character, but it does not satisfy cultural demands for self-sacrifice and moderate behavior, qualities found if not always in life then in the ideal representation of life in melodrama. Melodrama mediates between desire and social probity, what we want and what the culture thinks it should allow. Its characters must conform to the impossible demands to be free *and* restricted, liberated *and* domesticated, sexual *and* chaste. For Charlotte, and all her predecessors and heirs throughout the history of film worldwide, a series of internal mediations is the only means to salvation. She must bring her desires down to a manageable level and once again contain her passions in a semblance of respectability.

She will not marry Jerry. She will not return to her mother's domination. She chooses to become a surrogate mother. She will care for Jerry's daughter, sublimating her passion for him through the child. Sex is out. Marriage is out. Sacrifice is the key. Liberation from emotional repression is gained by means of another kind of repression. "Don't let's ask for the moon," Charlotte tells Jerry, after he lights two cigarettes and asks if she will be happy, "we have the stars." Why ask for passion, when our ideal love is mediated through the innocence of a child and the perfection of being close and separate at the same time? This is not happiness, only its perpetual promise. The music swells.

Melodrama's insistence on self-sacrifice or self-denial is a trait even more remarkable than its excessive emotions or piling up of incredible coincidence. It is more remarkable because self-sacrifice is largely an invisible trait. Hysteria and passion can be made visible in the mise-en-scène, on the character's face, and audible on the soundtrack. Self-sacrifice is an internal condition, the external manifestation of which is usually *not* doing something rather than taking a visible action. Therefore, unless the act of sacrifice is the ultimate one of dying, melodrama asks us to build our own response to the negative gesture of the character, to Charlotte's withdrawal from adult contact in order to love Jerry through his daughter. Sometimes, if a film is part of a larger social movement, the negative sacrifice can be given positive, even political overtones.

Casablanca

I mentioned that *Casablanca* has parallels to *Now, Voyager.* Rick gives up his beloved Ilsa (Ingrid Bergman) to Victor Laszlo (played by Paul Henreid, who is Jerry in *Now, Voyager)* and turns to Captain Renault (Claude Rains, who plays Dr. Jaquith) for the greater good of the war effort in *Casablanca.* As in its companion film, sexuality is again repressed, but here in the name of political allegiance. Rick is very much the melodramatic figure in this film. He suffers for his love, overcomes—or represses—it in the name of getting involved in the French Resistance against the Nazis with his old enemy and friend, Captain Renault. "Our problems don't amount to a hill of beans in this crazy world," he tells Ilsa, as he allows her to fly to safety with Victor and he goes off with Renault to fight the good fight. Like Charlotte, Rick represses his love for a cause, though in this case a global, political one.

Charlotte, after freeing herself from her mother's domination, willingly falls under Jerry's by becoming his daughter's surrogate mother. In classic melodramas, women sacrifice their desires for freedom and self-expression by reclaiming a cultural respectability that affirms the gross imbalance of conventional gender behavior. Ilsa, in *Casablanca,* gives up her love for Rick to support her husband, even as Rick gives up Ilsa because he knows Victor's cause is bigger than his own emotions. Even in contemporary melodrama, where the conventional ideologies of family and self-sacrifice have become ever more strongly posited, we see women gaining freedom and then returning to the family fold or often suffering alone. Women are still seen as instigators and victims of distraught and failing femininity or, in some instances, as strong survivors.

CONTEMPORARY MELODRAMA

The Fault in Our Stars

I mentioned earlier *The Fault in Our Stars*, a touching film about teenagers suffering from cancer. Illness, in this case, is spread among three of the main characters, whose pluck and high spirits are the melodramatic foil against their inevitable death. Like the classic melodramas of the 1930s and 1940s, the film insists that we understand and respond to the tension between the inevitable end of the characters and their insistence that they live fully despite that knowledge. Unlike earlier melodramas, the emotional response is all the more acute because the characters are young, vulnerable, with their lives cut short. In fact, more than the classic studio melodramas, a film like *The Fault in Our Stars* makes us as viewers more vulnerable. There is little distance between the viewer and the dying teens represented in *The Fault in Our Stars*. Little to do but grieve with Hazel Grace (Shailene Woodley) over Gus's (Ansel Elgort) death. Unless we gather around us a protective cloak of cynicism we are not permitted *not* to respond. This becomes our melodrama, plying our pity for the characters and our fear for our own wellbeing.

Flight

In addition to suffering adolescents, some contemporary melodramas—like *Casablanca* earlier on—focus on the emotional turmoil of a male character. The Denzel Washington vehicle *Flight* (Robert Zemeckis, 2012) offers an interesting example. Washington often plays strong but flawed characters, and in this film he is deeply flawed, a pilot suffering from alcoholism, who is responsible for the crash of a plane. Drawn to this nerve-wracking center of an admired actor playing a badly damaged character, the viewer is asked to search for a redemptive moment that only comes when Washington's Whip Whitaker finally admits his problems. He sits in front of a prison talk therapy group as the camera circles and then slowly tracks into him. His sacrifice is having his privilege of flying revoked and being imprisoned. But his redemption lies in the fact that he now, paradoxically, feels liberated, because he has gained self-knowledge, is free of booze, and regains the respect of his son. He also, in the course of the film, breaks yet another cultural taboo, in effect piercing the melodrama of the audience itself, their own barely repressed racial fears. This occurs in a sequence, played simply and without fanfare, in which Whip makes love to a white woman.

All of which is to say that the power of melodrama remains undiminished and, as in its beginnings, can have ramifications beyond the films themselves. We want to watch suffering at a distance and, at the same time, we love to feel it, close to home, close to our own emotional turmoil; we love to pierce that inevitable screen of mediation between us and the characters in order to have something like direct experience.

Brokeback Mountain

An interesting challenge to melodrama's draw on audience desire is Ang Lee's *Brokeback Mountain* (2005). Here is a melodrama that is both cautionary and transgressive. The cowboy lovers Ennis (Heath Ledger) and Jack (Jake Gyllenhaal) cannot help their love, cannot quite deal with the effects it has on the women in their lives, cannot avoid the inevitable melodramatic loss of a passion that they try to hide or even deny. Ennis and Jack express the inexpressible. They are in love within a culture that in the past regarded homosexuality as something needing to be destroyed. What makes this film unusual—beyond its sexual subject—is that the central characters are helpless in the face of their attraction to each other while maintaining a patina of normal life. In classical melodrama, the repressed subject looks for a way out of her repressed state. Ennis and Jack express their desire, their sexuality, and at the same time fall into a struggle to repress that expression, to live "normal" lives, only to have repression take its inevitable toll. Like any good melodrama, the film ends with a death, Jack's, most likely at the hands of a homophobic mob, a frightful, violent event that Ennis and, given the way it is represented on screen, we too can only imagine. And in the end, Ennis is left alone with a remnant of cloth, the shirts he and Jack wore on the mountain, one wrapped in the other. The film quietly posits the question of what causes suffering. Is it the oppression of a callous culture; the fears and denial on the part of Jack and Ennis; or simply the turmoil of desire that, gay or straight, overwhelms us and turns things upside down?

Brokeback Mountain is not only a moving contemporary melodrama, it also, I think, played a role in the gradual softening of homophobic prejudice that worked its way through American culture in the 2000s, leading to many states legalizing same-sex marriage. *Casablanca* helped, in its way, to promote American involvement in World War II—a melodrama with political weight. *Brokeback Mountain* had a certain cultural weight, showing the pain of repressed love between two men, who, as cowboys (one a rodeo performer), carry the cultural weight of strong masculinity. Their forthrightness, pain, and loss are as irresistible as the pain and loss of the teenagers in *The Fault in Our Stars*. We can, finally, carry the emotions wrought by melodrama with us—they can be that strong. They can enter the cultural consciousness.

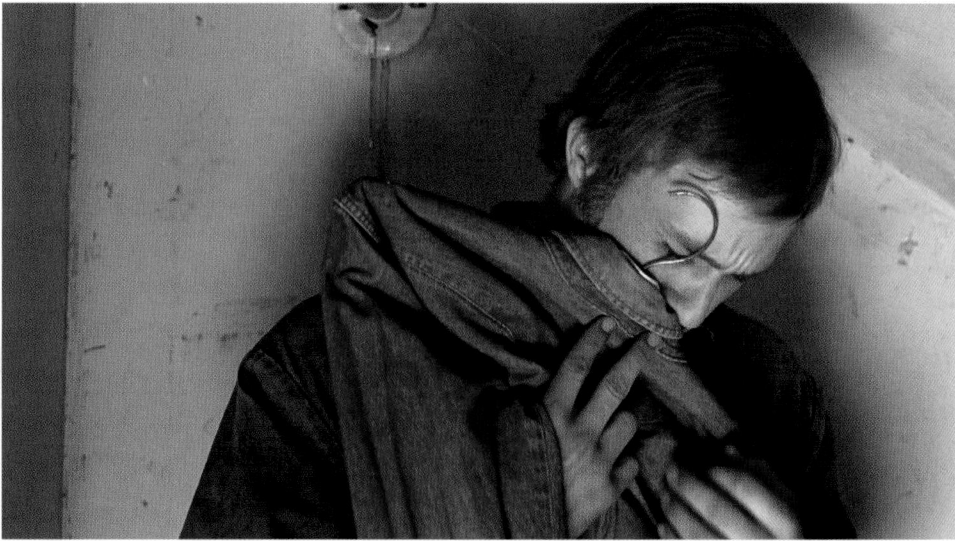

FIGURE 10.14 This tough, intense image of emotional pain occurs near the end of *Brokeback Mountain* (Ang Lee, 2005). Ennis (Heath Ledger) cradles his dead lover's shirt that is draped around his own shirt. The prominence of the coat hanger's hook against his face suggests the hardness of his loss and the "hook" that an uncomprehending world holds on his passion

ONE GENRE, TWO COUNTRIES, THREE DIRECTORS

All That Heaven Allows, Ali: Fear Eats the Soul, Far From Heaven

We have discussed what happens when directorial intelligence intrudes upon a genre and changes it. To conclude our discussion, we will turn to a melodramatic narrative that has been molded by three very different directors: Douglas Sirk, Rainer Werner Fassbinder, and Todd Haynes. The first is a German immigrant working in Hollywood, the second a German in Germany, the third a contemporary American director.

Always, in the end, as in the beginning, there is melodrama. This is the most flexible genre and the most international. Even though it is very hard to break its conventions, they prove resilient and able to be molded by individual filmmakers, forcing them into new configurations without actually changing them. Two of our films—Fassbinder's *Ali: Fear Eats the Soul* (1974) and Haynes's *Far From Heaven* (2002)—are remakes of the original, Sirk's *All That Heaven Allows* (1955). Remakes are a standard method of wringing the most out of a successful film. If a film is well received, why not do it again? Even a great director may do this. Alfred Hitchcock filmed *The Man Who Knew Too Much* in 1934 and 1956. In the studio days, it was not unusual for the production of a remake to put a **moviola**—the old standard film-editing machine—on the studio floor and copy the older version of the film **frame** by frame. Less usual are multiple versions of a single film, from different hands, indeed, in our case, from different countries, each approaching the film's subject from different personal and cultural points of view. When this happens, we have the unusual opportunity not only to see three ways of creating a similar narrative, but to understand how creation is inflected by period, country, culture, and the temperament of the filmmakers involved.

THE FILMMAKERS

Rainer Werner Fassbinder

As we saw in Chapter 8, the German filmmaker Rainer Werner Fassbinder looked for melodrama to deliver insight into history and politics and to discover in the family a microcosm of large power structures in the culture. He brought together a remarkably talented stock company of cast and crew, who set out to rethink American film melodrama as a means of addressing the politics of the family and the state.

Douglas Sirk

After a period of imitating Jean-Luc Godard and other European filmmakers, Fassbinder discovered Douglas Sirk. A German émigré to America, Sirk, in the 1950s, working for Universal Pictures and **producer** Ross Hunter, directed over-the-top, bigger-than-life melodramas that pushed the genre to its limits, making the viewer aware of how the excesses of emotion, and the spilling over of those excesses into the mise-en-scène, were the marks of the genre's artifice rather than illusory imitations of life. Sirk knew that melodrama was not a reflection of life, but a concentrated, stylized representation of it. He was a commercial director who was smart enough to give an audience the tears they wanted while at the same time stretching melodramatic boundaries, but only so far. Fassbinder took the genre's conventions and reflected them back in on themselves, exploiting them not as reflections of personal anguish, but as larger statements about a culture and its politics (which, in fact, is where melodrama started). Sirk showed him the way, his films giving Fassbinder a visual and thematic methodology he could both imitate and turn upside down. Many of Sirk's films, like *Imitation of Life* (1959), were comments on 1950s social failings and selfish excesses. Fassbinder pushed this commentary by making the social and the political state of postwar Germany unmistakably intertwined.

Todd Haynes

Todd Haynes's work veers less to the overtly political than to the gently satirical. More than Sirk or Fassbinder, he seems genuinely to like his characters, even when they are Barbie dolls, as they were in his first major film, *Superstar: The Karen Carpenter Story* (1987). This has become one of the few films that can seriously be called "cult," because it was, literally, occulted, removed from view by the Mattel Corporation, Barbie's owners, who, disliking the way their major profit item was used, enjoined the film from ever being shown. It now exists on YouTube. Haynes's subsequent films are varied in subject and style. *Safe* (1995) is almost Kubrickian in its starkness and pitiless gaze, concentrating on a woman who, believing she is sensitive to allergens, winds up allergic to the very material and emotional stuff of the contemporary world and withdraws into isolation. *Velvet Goldmine* (1998) is an energetic film about the London Glam Rock movement, full of music and general high spirits. His biography of Bob Dylan, *I'm Not There* (2007) uses multiple actors, including Cate Blanchett, to embody his subject. His HBO series, *Mildred Pierce* (2011), a remake of the 1945 film, but closer to its source novel by James M. Cain, is a remarkable piece of concentrated acting and visuals that both understand and press against the constraints of the television screen.

FIGURE 10.15 Todd Haynes and production designer Mark Friedberg capture an idea of the 1950s during a painful domestic moment between Cathy (Julianne Moore) and her husband (Dennis Quaid) in *Far From Heaven* (2002).

Far From Heaven was Haynes' most commercially and critically successful theatrical film. This is curious. *Far From Heaven* is a moving, understated, quietly filmed melodrama, set in the 1950s. It has none of the elements that usually make up a contemporary popular film, except for good acting and a quietly effective mise-en-scène that captures the colors and décor of the decade. Perhaps because it touches upon some vital social issues by filtering them through the past, allowing us a certain superiority to the very problems that still plague us precisely because they are made to appear old problems, viewers were made to feel comfortable, believing, perhaps, that they no longer exist. Maybe its popularity was based on the fact that it is a well-made, emotionally complex film.

THE COMMON THREAD

A driving force of our discussion throughout this book is that plot is a product of the film narrative, and is not the film itself. A film cannot be reduced to plot, because plot is only one thing that the narrative—the construction of story by the formal structure of the film—produces. However, when dealing with three films, two of which work and rework the first, we do have to find the common thematic threads before we see how they are woven and rewoven, how their patterns and meanings change each time, and this involves abstracting plot from the narrative. *All That Heaven Allows*, *Ali: Fear Eats the Soul*, and *Far From Heaven* are each about a woman who makes a romantic choice that is outside the realm of the social and cultural norms of her time. In Sirk's film, an upper-middle-class suburbanite and widow, Cary Scott (Jane Wyman), falls for her nurseryman, Ron Kirby (Rock Hudson). He is a free spirit, with friends who read Thoreau and talk of no longer living lives of quiet desperation. In Fassbinder's film, Emmi (Brigitte Mira), an elderly Polish housekeeper, widow of a German, both of whom were members of the Nazi party, falls in love with and marries Ali (El Hedi ben Salem), a Moroccan *Gastarbeiter*—literally "guest worker," an immigrant brought in to do the low-paid work the country's citizens won't and who are reviled for it. Todd Haynes's Cathy Whitaker (Julianne Moore), of the same suburban class as her Sirkian forbear, is attracted to her nurseryman, Raymond Deagan (Dennis Haysbert), who is African American. To complicate matters, her husband, Frank (Dennis Quaid), realizes he is gay and eventually leaves her.

All of this is the stuff of romantic melodrama, particularly the fact that each film presents a woman acting on desires forbidden for various social reasons. In each film, the characters undergo extreme emotional turmoil, and in each film, their environment, the people around them, indeed the films' entire mise-en-scène serve as containers for the excess of the turmoil. Yet each film is remarkably different, while together they act as resonant echo chambers, each one playing against the other, opening up their ideas and their styles when seen side by side.

All That Heaven Allows and *Far From Heaven*

The two American films are closest, by virtue of the similarity of their characters and the familiarity of their surroundings and social concerns. *All That Heaven Allows* is, on one level, quite straightforward in its melodramatic import: Cary suffers terribly for her romantic and sexual desires. She is spurned by neighbors and children, and closure is reached with the appropriate sacrifice on her part. The mise-en-scène, however, is extraordinary. Like most of Sirk's films of the period, the colors are rich, saturated, and often completely unnatural in ways that emphasize

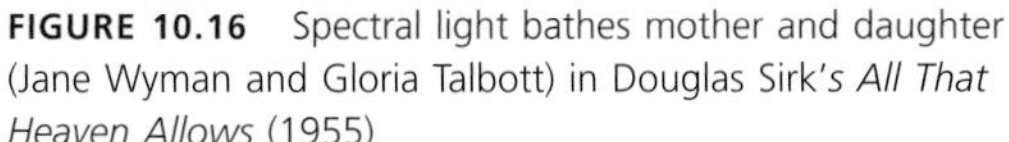

FIGURE 10.16 Spectral light bathes mother and daughter (Jane Wyman and Gloria Talbott) in Douglas Sirk's *All That Heaven Allows* (1955)

FIGURE 10.17 Shadows and screens separate mother and son (William Reynolds) in *All That Heaven Allows*

mood and the characters' situations. In one scene, where Cary is talking to her daughter, the light comes in as if through a spectrum, bathing them in red, green, and blue lights as her daughter whines about her mother ruining their lives by marrying the gardener. Not completely averse to 1950s stereotyping, the daughter is portrayed as a glasses-wearing intellectual, spouting Freud, and sounding ridiculous. Of course, she finds a husband and comes to her senses, and she wears scarlet clothes when her sexuality is realized. When Cary's son berates his mother, he steps behind an elaborate screen, creating a composition that broadly represents how purposefully he cuts himself off from her feelings and needs.

Mirrors and screens figure prominently in Sirk's compositions, either visually representing a blocking off of feelings, as when Cary's son steps behind a screen when expressing his disapproval of his mother, or reflecting the characters back to themselves, making us see them twice, doubling their passion. The most telling use of a mirror image occurs when Cary's children forget their passionate anger at her choice of a lover. As the film progresses, the grown children get involved in their own affairs, but not before they've forced her to give up her plans to marry Ron. The son is off for a new job overseas. The daughter, dressed in scarlet, has discovered her own sexuality, which she denied to her mother, and found a husband. They leave Cary alone with the Christmas present they've gotten for her: a television set. We have to remember that even in the mid-1950s, television was, like so many things, both embraced and distrusted. It was sold as the lonely housewife's companion. In fact, the salesman who delivers the children's present promises Cary she will now have "life's parade at your fingertips." The irony is bitter—Cary is given a replacement for passion by the children who were so violently against her passion to begin with. The TV is rolled in and Cary's own reflection is given back to her. The TV screen receives nothing but the image of her own loneliness.

Such exaggerated images, reflections, and colors serve not only to heighten the emotion but to allow us to step back from them. There is enough artificiality in Sirk's films for us to understand that what we see is an artful representation of life and its turmoil; through the images, there is enough commentary on the wretched behavior of people toward events and feelings to allow a 1950s—and a twenty-first century—viewer to understand that film was not life but an image representing it. Sirk wants it all ways. He absorbs a 1950s audience into his characters' melodrama and simultaneously creates distance from it, by means of emotional and visual exaggeration, in order to allow them to understand that what's happening on screen is not life, only a Technicolor representation.

FIGURE 10.18 The lonely image: Cary reflected in the TV screen in *All That Heaven Allows*

Far From Heaven, on the other hand, is visually more subdued than *All That Heaven Allows.* Haynes captures a great deal of the Sirkian style, but in a lower key, with only occasional flashes of fall color to brighten an autumnal and winter light, metaphorical of the fall and decline of the main character. There are the mirror images and even the exaggerated 1950s décor, but less flamboyantly displayed. There is a reason for this. *Far From Heaven* is *All That Heaven Allows* seen through a glass darkly. Seen through a number of glasses, in fact. Made in the early twenty-first century, it is set in the same period as Sirk's film and has Fassbinder's film on its mind as well. The issues faced in the film are articulated by the way we know them now and the way they may have been experienced then, more accurately, the way Haynes, Fassbinder, and their audiences experienced them *through* Sirk's film. By setting the film in Sirk's period, Haynes can't openly bring the 1950s up to date to the early 2000s, the way Fassbinder does by setting *Ali* in 1970s Germany. Haynes can use the 1950s as a mirror for the early 2000s and create a kind of ping-pong effect directly with Sirk's film and indirectly with Fassbinder's. *Far From Heaven*, therefore, changes its characters and its narrative in quiet and often highly ironic ways.

RACE

For example, Cathy's attraction to her gardener remains a focal point and that gardener is African American. Two things are happening. There are no African Americans in Sirk's film. They do not fit into the lily-white Connecticut suburb in which his film is set. This is not to say that either Sirk or the 1950s ignored racial issues. Amidst the crushing repression of that decade, the one thing that Hollywood can be proud of was its progressive treatment of race—and not only progressive: one film, Joseph Mankiewicz's *No Way Out* (1950), borders on the revolutionary. Sirk himself attempted a liberal reading of racial issues in *Imitation of Life* (1959, itself a remake of a 1930s film), in which a white woman and her maid become close and confront the maid's daughter's attempt to pass as white. But in *All That Heaven Allows*, it was enough for Sirk merely to have Cary have sexual feelings for a white man below her age and class in order to start tongues wagging, people staring, and misery to ensue. For Haynes, Cathy and Raymond are attracted out of mutual gentleness and loneliness, amidst a sea of racist hatred, which is alluded to in various ways. At a party, a guest jokes that there is no racial problem in their town because there are no Negroes. Haynes cuts to the African American wait staff quietly looking on. In one gruesome scene, where the family vacation in Miami, an African American child innocently steps into the hotel pool. He is pulled out as the guests look on with horror and disgust.

The interracial relationship between Cathy and Raymond is played out quietly, between them, at least; but when it surfaces, they are so reviled and even physically threatened that Raymond chooses to protect his daughter and himself, leave town, and leave Cathy miserably alone. The scenes between Raymond and Cathy are among the most moving in the film, even though some interesting touches are given to her character that modify her gentleness. She's startled whenever she comes across an African American, even after she gets to know Raymond. She's strict and unpleasant with her children. But when she becomes comfortable with Raymond, their relationship is created in a straightforward way, usually in two shots, to indicate their closeness. Unfortunately, whenever they are together with other people, the potentials for a deeper intimacy are always suppressed. Whenever people are around, they are the subject of merciless stares and outright hostility; they seem filled with a predetermined sense of loss and are always the objects of hatred. It is typical of Haynes's women that they are perpetually vulnerable and isolated. In *Safe*, suburban wife Cathy White, also played by Julianne Moore, is globally vulnerable, so alone, so inward, that the outside world becomes an overall threat, rendering her helpless. *Safe* is an allegory of a woman's difficulty in asserting herself and inserting herself into the world. The world, in its turn, attacks her and renders her painfully alone. *Far From Heaven*, like Haynes's version of *Mildred Pierce*, is a melodrama of a wife who cannot hold her center—which, in the 1950s, as today, means her family—together. One reason is her transgressive attraction to a man of another race. Another is a subject that Sirk could not possibly touch.

GENDER

Far From Heaven enters the subject of homosexuality into the narrative variations of the two previous films. Until fairly recently, there were few gender issues that created more cultural dissonance and downright violence than this one, and Haynes treats it not only with great delicacy, but also by placing it in the past. In the 1950s, in fact throughout the history of film, gays could not be portrayed on screen except under the subterfuge of a usually fussy, comic character, or a wink and nod joke. Outside of film, the 1950s were particularly hard on gays in the culture, often harassing them as subversives. But the fact is that, despite the negative majority attitude toward homosexuality, it has, of course, always existed. Perhaps because gay women and men have, until quite recently, had to live an underground existence, it has indeed been subversive. This is true in the arts, where many creative people are gay and, happily, if not so secretively, making their presence felt.

This sets up an intriguing set of reasons for the entry of a gay character in *Far From Heaven*. Todd Haynes is openly gay. Douglas Sirk's producer, Ross Hunter, was gay; Rainer Werner Fassbinder was bisexual; and perhaps the most subversive element coursing through the three films, if only by inference, Rock Hudson, who plays the nurseryman in *All That Heaven Allows*, was gay. Rock Hudson was a major Hollywood star in the 1950s and early 1960s and in television during the 1970s. His homosexuality was known throughout the film business, and his studio, Universal, tried with the greatest success to keep knowledge of his sexuality from his adoring public. He almost always played macho characters—he even played an Indian in, of all things, a Douglas Sirk Western, *Taza, Son of Cochise* (1954). We must not forget that Sirk was a studio director and took the projects that came his way, forging them with his personality only when he was able. And, of course, Hudson's role in *All That Heaven Allows* is as a strong, self-sufficient, totally independent, yet gentle, man, gentle enough to tend to plants; strong enough to build a dwelling for Cary and himself. Under Sirk's hands, if I may play on a cliché, Hudson's "feminine" side was often allowed to appear—and he appeared in five Sirk films.

Hudson's gayness was not known to the public, at least until the early 1980s when he had HIV/AIDS and, in the television series *Dynasty*, was visibly wasting away. It is this very secrecy that allows Haynes to make homosexuality a point of focus in *Far From Heaven*. He had a delicate job. By the 2000s, though still reviled from many quarters, homosexuality was, after much struggle, pretty much open. Television shows and some movies dealt with it if not matter-of-factly, at least as a societal and cultural given. But Haynes's film is set in the 1950s, when the question was not openness but furtiveness. He does two things to take care of the problem without making it less problematic.

He casts Dennis Quaid, an actor best known for smirky, macho roles, as Cathy's husband. He is made up to look quite unattractive, given an ugly nose and directed to act with a kind of sorrowful, depressed air of hopelessness. If Rock Hudson was the 1950s gay man pretending to be straight in romantic melodramas and comedies, Quaid, the laid-back tough guy, becomes a 1950s gay man in a 2002 film, trying hard, but failing, to be a good father and provider. Before yielding totally to his sexuality, he goes to a psychiatrist to get "cured" of his homosexuality—which was, until relatively recently, considered a disease—and has clandestine affairs with pick-ups in his office late at night, until he is caught by his wife.

The result of all of this is continuing and growing despair on Cathy's part, caught between two—both for the 1950s and for the early 2000s—impossible loves. She discovers her husband's "secret" and is as helpless before it as he is. When, finally, both he and Raymond leave (Raymond is threatened by other African Americans because of his friendship with Cathy and his daughter is attacked by white children), she is left utterly alone. At the train station, waving goodbye to Raymond, she walks into the stark late winter street. The camera, reversing its opening movement, where it imitated the beginning of *All That Heaven Allows*, cranes up to a branch in early blossom. But everything else on the street is so gray, Cathy is in such a hopeless situation, that this sprig of hope can't even close the melodrama with more than a suggestion of nature's ongoingness as opposed to people's meanness and sorrow.

Cary, in *All That Heaven Allows*, suffers a different kind of repression. The only question reigning over this melodrama is exactly how much will heaven allow? We know already from our previous discussions of the genre that it allows only so much, which Haynes acknowledges by showing just how far his characters' lives are from heaven. In Sirk's film, Cary's friends and relatives forget their cold rebuff of her romance, which she has already broken off. She is forced to a doctor to see about her headaches—a nice 1950s displacement for sexual repression. She decides to return to Ron, only to see him fall from a snowdrift and become seriously injured. As a result, she must become his caretaker, his nurse. A doe appears outside the window where Ron lies ill and Cary sits by him, and the conclusion promises a return to gentleness and perhaps even a recuperation of their love. But on what terms? 1950s terms. Cary assumes a maternal role; Ron the passive "son." No notion if they will become lovers again. Melodrama thrives on sacrifice. "Don't let's ask for the moon . . . we have the stars."

Ali: Fear Eats the Soul

When Fassbinder made *Ali: Fear Eats the Soul* in 1974, he was working not only at the peak of his own imaginative energy, but at a peak of creativity in cinema worldwide for an audience looking forward to films that experimented, that took genres and stood them on their heads. This is exactly what Fassbinder did with Sirk's films. He took the essential banality of Sirk's premise—the romance of an older woman with a younger man beneath her class—and turned it into political and social allegory. I've noted that the social and political is already present in Sirk's film, that *All That Heaven Allows* is a kind of mirror of 1950s repression and prejudice. But Fassbinder goes further. He takes an overt, contemporary political problem in Germany at the time, the country's importing of foreign workers, whom native Germans both needed and hated, and makes it the driving engine of his work. He's not merely working through social and political issues, but talking, and not very indirectly at that, about social policy.

But there is much more happening here. Fassbinder opens up the latent social commentary of Sirk, and also takes the melodrama of *All That Heaven Allows* and subverts it, down to its very mise-en-scène. In place of Sirk's opulence, his gorgeous and carefully integrated color scheme, Fassbinder moves between the plain and the garish. Since his subjects are poor Germans and Moroccans, there are no fancy houses, but cramped apartments, dull streets, and a seedy bar (Haynes imitates a scene from *Fear Eats the Soul* when he has Cathy and Raymond dance in a bar beneath a Champagne ball). Fassbinder indeed uses lighting for effect. Like Sirk, he will play with red to indicate passion or, ironically, its impossibility. But mostly he uses fairly stark, **high-key lighting** in this film. Everything is brought to light. He also plays upon a Sirkian camera strategy for particular effect. I noted how Sirk loves to photograph his characters through things, framing them behind screens or observing their reflections in mirrors, for example. Fassbinder

FIGURE 10.19 Trapped in small rooms: the use of frames in Rainer Werner Fassbinder's *Ali: Fear Eats the Soul* (1974). Ali (El Hedi ben Salem) and Emmi (Brigitte Mira)

FIGURE 10.20 From time to time, the actors in *Ali: Fear Eats the Soul* will stop acting and engage the viewer in a distant stare

almost always double frames his characters, in the screen frame and then in doorways or the room dividers of apartments. He will put his camera at a distance, staring at his characters, isolating them in our gaze and the gaze of others, and sometimes allowing the characters to stare directly back at us.

The influence of Bertolt Brecht

In Chapter 8, we touched briefly on the influence of German playwright Bertolt Brecht on the films of Jean-Luc Godard and Fassbinder. We need now to consider this influence more fully. Fassbinder does not only invert melodramatic principles and turn them inside out; he does this to show how they can be made to work, to expose their mechanisms by showing their artificiality. Instead of absorbing the political into the personal—or absorb the viewer into the melodrama—Fassbinder shows how personal suffering and emotional repression can be understood as political events on both the micro and macro levels. He frames his characters, for example, to show that these are characters framed in a film, and also are subject to the constraints, the pressures of the world that diminishes them.

He also shows how melodrama can be made to work on an intellectual level, usually fatal to the genre, by inviting the viewer to step back a bit and look with some detachment—as when he frames characters at a distance through doorways, inscribing frames within the movie screen frame. These various formal methods show the influence of Bertolt Brecht, who said that the work of art should not mystify or make itself invisible but rather open itself up to interrogation. For Brecht, the more invisible the form and structure of a work, the more the viewer is fooled into believing an illusion. The more fooled, the more she is taken advantage of. The more visible the form and structure, the more the viewer understands how form and ideology operate, and how they are in fact inseparable. Made visible, the work of art becomes a tool for understanding larger structures of power in the culture. Brecht would have the playwright and, by extension, the filmmaker build into his work effects that create distance between it and the viewer and thereby make its workings and its reception visible.

Fassbinder frames his characters in doorways and within rooms so that we become conscious of the framing of the camera and how that framing comments upon the characters and their situation. He creates outrageous narratives with characters who are physically unattractive by Hollywood standards. This is a major break with Sirk—and even Haynes can't quite carry this one through: his actors are mostly attractive people. Instead of an attractive upper-middle-class matron as the central female character, Fassbinder presents us with an old German washerwoman, Emmi, a widow who was a member of the Nazi party ("everybody was, back then," she says without thinking about her words). Instead of a handsome young nurseryman, there is Ali, a homely, bumbling Moroccan, an immigrant worker, who suffers the indignities, scorn, oppression, and diseases faced by people of color who are brought in by a rich culture to do their dirty work. Here, of course, is an elision made by Todd Haynes in his version: the nurseryman is an African American who suffers scorn in a similar way to Ali—his daughter is stoned by her classmates—and like him, is the object of everyone's cruel gaze.

The old German woman and the young, black immigrant fall in love and marry. Fassbinder makes this all so touching that we have to shake ourselves to realize how perfectly absurd it is. It simply couldn't happen. And this is part of the Brechtian moment. In "real life," the conventional absurdities of ordinary melodrama could never happen. The narrative structure and events of

Ali: Fear Eats the Soul only point up these absurdities and make us examine our assumptions about them. The film invites us to come to understand how much we take for granted in melodrama, and how much goes unexamined. And this is itself a distancing device. At the same time, Emmi and Ali's love is as emotionally touching an event as any melodrama can present, and as impossible.

There are other Brechtian effects. Fassbinder will literally stop dramatic action and have his characters look up and stare at the camera, forcing us to recognize the artificiality of the scene. After their marriage, Emmi and Ali go to a fancy Munich restaurant—she does not fail to mention to Ali that it was Hitler's favorite. They are condescended to by the maitre d' and confused by the menu. It is an appallingly embarrassing sequence, ended with a cut to outside the doorway of the dining room, the camera framing and staring at the poor couple, who simply stop acting and stare back, for a long time, at the camera . . . at us. A bit later, in the film's most emotional scene, Emmi and Ali sit in an open-air restaurant, she weeping over the hatred they receive, both of them isolated by the gazes of the people around them. Fassbinder tracks far from them as, again, they stop acting and simply stare at one another.

The gaze

The gaze itself becomes a distancing device. Everyone stares at Ali and Emmi, and Haynes picks up on this device in *Far From Heaven*. These benighted characters become objects, the Other to other people's eyes. Of course, film is all about the gaze. When we discussed the Hollywood continuity style, we spoke about how shots are built by characters looking and the audience being shown what they are looking at. We examined the gendering of the gaze, the look by male characters at women. In Fassbinder's and later in Haynes's eyes, the gaze is turned into both a narrative device—a way to tell us about hatred and fear—and a reflection of the cinematic act itself. They make it an attention-drawing effect that forces us to think not only about the cinematic gaze in general, but about the larger cultural conditions that make people outwardly or implicitly stare at those who are different, and the effect on people who are turned into objects by the stare.

FIGURE 10.21 The withering, humiliating gaze in *All That Heaven Allows*

FIGURE 10.22 Emmi's family glowers at the announcement of her marriage to Ali. Director Fassbinder is the second from the left

FIGURES 10.23–10.24 The racist glare in *Far From Heaven*. Cathy and Raymond (Dennis Haysbert) are forced to leave the diner because of the open hostility of those around them

Fassbinder's narrative

Like Cary and Ron and Cathy and Raymond, Emmi and Ali, the unlikely couple, are visited by a string of humiliations, even more exaggerated than their cinematic predecessors and heirs. Emmi's neighbors scorn her; her family reviles her. They take out their anger on her and her possessions. Recall how in *All That Heaven Allows*, Cary's children buy her a television set to keep her mind off the loneliness for which they are largely responsible. Emmi's son—after a slow panning shot of her children staring at her and Ali in disgust—kicks in her television set to show his anger at her impending marriage. It is part of the climax of rejection: her neighbors shun her and call the police when she has Ali's friends over to the apartment. The local grocer won't sell his food to Ali. And everyone stares. The destruction of the television is just one displaced act of anger, violence to a possession instead of against the transgressing parent. (In *Far From Heaven*, television functions quietly but persistently: Cathy's husband works for a manufacturer of television sets.)

Then Fassbinder reverses the situation. After all, a major component of melodrama is a sudden, often coincidental turn in events. Suddenly, Emmi's children realize that mother is a good resource for babysitting; the neighbors want Ali to help them move furniture; the grocer, realizing that

FIGURES 10.25–10.26 In *Ali: Fear Eats the Soul*, repression returns like a rhyme as the foreign worker is imprisoned in the same composition as Emmi was, locked in the stares of her coworkers. In the second shot, Emmi becomes one of the starers

his business is being hurt by supermarkets, welcomes Emmi back to his shop. But as outsiders change their tune to fit their needs, Ali and Emmi go through a reverse change and become their own exploiters. Emmi humiliates Ali by showing off his muscles to her neighbors and refuses to allow his friends to visit the apartment. He, in turn, flees to the arms of the woman who runs the local Moroccan bar. Earlier, Emmi was cast out by her coworkers. Now she joins them in taunting and isolating a foreigner who has joined her cleaning crew at the office. Fassbinder makes a special point of this by literally rhyming a shot. Earlier in the film, his camera looks at Emmi sitting alone on the stairs, eating her lunch, as her co-workers group together making fun of her. She is composed between the spokes of the banister, as if imprisoned. Later, when Emmi joins her coworkers taunting the newcomer, this poor soul is framed by the camera in exactly the same way that Emmi was. Oppression returns like rhyme.

Happiness is not always fun

For Fassbinder, oppression is not merely internalized. Repression is not only sexual. Unhappiness is not always the result of a bad romance or a failing marriage. Repression and unhappiness are social and political phenomena; they are about power and one-upmanship (an exercise of power)—about how someone with a little power exercises it by oppressing someone with even less. This cycle of oppression and hurt is itself contained within a larger cycle of power and repression exercised by the state, in which the powerful continually manipulate those with no power. With the promise of a melodramatic renewal of romance, Emmi and Ali have a reconciliation. They meet at the bar for Middle-Eastern immigrant workers where they first found each other, and they dance. A happy ending threatens—but Fassbinder has warned us by means of the epigraph to the film, itself taken from Godard's 1962 film *My Life to Live*: "Happiness is not always fun." In the middle of the dance, Ali collapses.

All That Heaven Allows ends with Cary assuming a maternal position at Ron's bedside, while a doe plays in the snow outside. He may get better if she gives him her all-devoting care. Ali's collapse has nothing to do with Ali and Emmi's reconciliation. He is suffering from an ulcer. The doctor at the end of *Fear Eats the Soul* offers no hope and tells Emmi that Ali will never get well. His condition is a common physical response of immigrants to the terrible conditions and humiliations they face in their host country. He is a victim, finally, of state power and cultural prejudice. The humiliations and the ulcers will keep occurring until he dies. The film ends with the image of Ali in his hospital bed. There is no deer at the window, only the cold light of a Munich afternoon. As in *All That Heaven Allows* and *Far From Heaven*, the woman is left alone, turned into nurse and nurturer in Sirk's film, into a completely isolated figure in Fassbinder's and Haynes's.

GENRE RESILIENCE

The amazing thing is how flexible generic boundaries are. With the exception of the Western, which starved because of changes in the historical and cultural events that once fed it, most of film's established genres thrive. For example, with the likes of producer/director Judd Apatow, comedy keeps changing with the cultural climate of the times—and we will look at Apatow's films in the next chapter. Gangsters always attract our fearful and envious gaze. With **CGI**, science fiction has gotten, if not better, certainly more visually spectacular. The key to genre is its ability to be reworked, to renew itself. For some filmmakers, testing the boundaries and even pushing them beyond the breaking point are ways to define a subjective approach to filmmaking, to move beyond the **classical Hollywood style**. By working from a generic base, filmmakers can find their voice, change viewer perceptions, change the genre, and, perhaps, change cinema.

The variations on *All That Heaven Allows* show us how cultural history itself is refracted through cinema. We have, throughout this book, considered the ways in which films and the culture that they are part of interact. At this point, we turn our attention more fully to the concepts of culture and cinema, concluding our study by attempting to understand how the movies are part of our greater cultural lives.

FURTHER READING

So much has been written on noir, but the best remains an essay by the screenwriter (of *Taxi Driver,* among others) and director Paul Schrader, "Notes on Film Noir," in *Schrader on Schrader*, ed. Kevin Jackson (London: Faber & Faber, 2004). A good visual analysis is offered by J. A. Place and L. S. Peterson, "Some Visual Notes on Film Noir," in Bill Nichols, ed., *Movies and Methods,* vol. 1 (Berkeley and Los Angeles: University of California Press, 1976), pp. 325–38. See also Frank Krutnik, *In a Lonely Street: Film Noir, Genre, Masculinity* (London and New York: Routledge, 1991), James Naremore, *More Than Night: Film Noir in Its Contexts* (Berkeley: University of California Press, 1998), and Jonathan Auerbach, *Dark Borders: Film Noir and American Citizenship* (Durham, N.C. and London: Duke University Press, 2011). For a feminist reading, see E. Ann Kaplan, ed., *Women in Film Noir* (London: BFI, 1980).

For discussion of whether noir elaborates a destruction of the women-based family or merely recuperates it, see Claire Johnston, "Double Indemnity," in the previously cited *Women in Film Noir,* pp. 100–111; and Joyce Nelson, "Mildred Pierce Reconsidered," in Bill Nichols, ed., *Movies and Methods,* vol. 2 (Berkeley and Los Angeles: University of California Press, 1985), 450–457.

There are two excellent anthologies of essays on melodrama and film: Marcia Landy, ed., *Imitations of Life: A Reader of Film and Television Melodrama* (Detroit: Wayne State University Press, 1991); and Christine Gledhill, ed., *Home Is Where the Heart Is* (London: BFI, 1987). The standard essay is Thomas Elsaesser's "Tales of Sound and Fury: Observations on the Family Melodrama," reprinted in *Home Is Where the Heart Is*. See also Geoffrey Nowell-Smith, "Minnelli and Melodrama," in *Imitations of Life*. For melodrama and early film, the standard book is Ben Singer, *Melodrama and Modernity: Early Sensational Cinema and Its Contexts* (New York, Chichester, West Sussex: Columbia University Press, 2001). A study of melodrama in literature (quite applicable to film) is Peter Brooks, *The Melodramatic Imagination: Balzac, Henry James, Melodrama, and the Mode of Excess* (New Haven: Yale University Press, 1995).

SUGGESTIONS FOR FURTHER VIEWING

Film noir

Confessions of a Nazi Spy (Anatole Litvak, 1939)
Woman in the Window (Fritz Lang, 1944)
The Postman Always Rings Twice (Tay Garnett, 1946)
The Blue Dahlia (George Marshall, 1946)

Kiss of Death (Henry Hathaway, 1947)
Brute Force (Jules Dassin, 1947)
The Lady from Shanghai (Orson Welles, 1947)

Melodrama

Dodsworth (William Wyler, 1936)
Stella Dallas (King Vidor, 1937)
Mildred Pierce (Michael Curtiz, 1945; Todd Haynes, 2011)
Magnificent Obsession (Douglas Sirk, 1954)
Bigger Than Life (Nicholas Ray, 1956)
Imitation of Life (Douglas Sirk, 1959)
Come Back to the 5 & Dime, Jimmy Dean, Jimmy Dean (Robert Altman, 1982)
Steel Magnolias (Herbert Ross, 1989)

NOTES

1 The quotation "I feel all dead inside . . ." is from Henry Hathaway's *Dark Corner* (1946) and is quoted in Frank Krutnik's *In a Lonely Street: Film Noir, Genre, Masculinity* (London and New York: Routledge, 1991) p. 101 (see Further Reading above).
2 The implied destruction of the world at the end of *Kiss Me Deadly* is apparently a studio addition. In a recent "director's cut," the detective and his girlfriend escape.
3 There is a wonderful sequence in Tim Burton's film *Ed Wood* (1994) in which the momentarily dispirited director of very bad films goes into a dark bar in the middle of a bright Hollywood day. He finds Orson Welles sitting in a corner working on a script. "Tell me about it," Orson tells Ed Wood. "I'm supposed to do a thriller at Universal, but they want Charlton Heston to play a Mexican!" The long take at the beginning of *Touch of Evil* is lovingly parodied in the opening of Robert Altman's film *The Player* (1992). Altman makes his shot even longer, and the characters who move around in it keep referring to Welles's film.
4 Thomas Elsaesser's essay is "Tales of Sound and Fury," Nowell-Smith's is "Minnelli and Melodrama"—full citations in the Further Reading section.

CHAPTER 11

Film as cultural practice

Our concluding chapter is something of an experiment. I want first to step back from the analysis of film that has occupied us for most of this book and see cinema as part of broader concepts of cultural theory and practice. Second, I want to take two very different films—Alfred Hitchcock's *Vertigo* (1958) and Judd Apatow's *This is 40* (2012)—to see how we might read them both as cinematic works, unique or conventional, and as part of the **culture** that they belong to.

FILM IN THE REALM OF CULTURE

We have been examining film from the minute particulars of the **shot** and the **cut** to the economics of production, to the people responsible for the various parts of moviemaking. We have seen that film is a part of industrial production—the making of films follows principles of mass production and, in purely economic terms, is now one of the largest commercial endeavors in Los Angeles, beating out the military as the city's industrial base. We have looked at films from other countries. We have begun to examine how film creates and satisfies its consumers' desires. But unlike other industrial goods, and conforming more closely to what we usually think of as art, movies have emotional and moral designs on us. They ask us to respond with our feelings and to think of the world in moral certainties, to assume there are clearly defined good and bad people, ethical acts and unethical ones, all clearly discernible. They even suggest ethical solutions to the problems of how we should act in the world. Their characters seek redemption. Yet when compared to a novel or a painting or a symphony, the emotional demands made by many films seem shallow and unambiguous. Unlike the traditional high arts, film—with the exception of the international films referred to earlier, films by such as Fassbinder, Godard, Bertolucci, Antonioni, Fellini, and others, made during the 1960s through the 1980s, as well as the work of some American filmmakers like Kubrick, Welles, and Hitchcock—does not demand great intellectual powers to understand it. Film is too often condemned, like popular music and fiction, as being exploitative, commercial, and stupid.

While many movie studios, small and large, do have units that produce "independent" films for an adult audience, who want, the **producers** hope, to see films that aren't made up of explosions or the epic battles of superheroes, and while there exist **directors** in the United States, like David Fincher and Paul Thomas Anderson, seeking alternative ways of telling stories through explorations of cinematic style, many producers believe that they must pay prime attention to the prime male audience between the ages of fifteen and forty-nine.[1] The films so made feed into the notion that the people, young and old, who admire and enjoy popular culture are being pandered to and willingly enjoy the bad effects of the pandering. That willingness somehow reflects a debasement of the culture. Politicians continue to rail against the moral danger posed by Hollywood—especially "Hollywood liberals." Fear that cultural standards are being lowered by popular culture and mass media causes distrust, which is followed by condemnation. But condemnation seems to have no effect. We still love movies; we still watch television and listen to rock and roll and hip-hop. Distrust then turns to cynicism, sometimes on the part of filmmakers and professional film reviewers as well.

CULTURE AS TEXT

There is an element of truth in everything negative that is said about popular culture, although blanket condemnations are not useful in helping us understand its richness. What is useful is to attempt a broader definition that takes into consideration the negative things about pop culture, but also sees it in all its seriousness and playfulness. In this larger view, we need to start with a definition of culture and then an examination of popular culture (or, more accurately, cultures) to discover ways to fight cynicism with the understanding of unexpected complexity.

Culture can be understood as the text of our lives, the ultimately coherent pattern of beliefs, acts, responses, and artifacts that we produce and comprehend every day. Coherence, system, and order are the highlights of what constitutes a text. We usually think of a book as a text, but anything with known boundaries that produces meaning, even self-contradictory meaning, even meaning that keeps shifting, can be a text. The idea of culture as text means first that culture is not nature; it is made by people in history for conscious or even unconscious reasons, the product of all they think and do. Even the unconscious or semiconscious acts of our daily lives can, when observed and analyzed, be understood as sets of coherent acts and be seen to interact with each other. These acts, beliefs, and practices, along with the artifacts they produce—the music we listen to, the clothes we wear, the television we love, the websites that fascinate us, the social media that consumes our time, the films we watch—have meaning. They can be read and understood.

By "read," I mean that we can understand the musical and lyrical complexities of popular music just as we can analyze a Beethoven symphony or a Philip Roth novel. Reading as a critical act is applicable to all meaning-making entities or texts. People drive cars and select certain makes; they go to school, open a bank account, make paintings, post on Facebook, watch television, accept racial and sexual differences (or don't), hate Democrats or Republicans (or don't), believe in free will and a free economy (or don't), behave well or badly, love classical music or rock or hip-hop, and somehow make perfect sense of most of this behavior. With a little study and an open mind, we can understand the sense we make of it and the needs that are fulfilled by the choices we make and the things that entertain us. We can understand why and how our entertainments affirm or deny our beliefs. We can see that none of this is natural; it is all born of class, gender, race, education, acculturation, and the ideologies that drive us all.

SUBCULTURES

Our culture—or that part of our culture that makes divisions between high and low, serious and popular art—defines culture much more narrowly than we just have. It defines as culture those serious works made by independent imaginations that are complex and acceptable only to the few who have, want, or like "culture." In other words, culture segments and segregates itself. The culture's culture is what we normally think of as the difficult, personal art we have to engage deeply in order to understand: paintings in museums, symphonies played in concert halls, poems and novels analyzed in the classroom, foreign films that used to be shown in "art houses." If other kinds of imaginative products are allowed in, they become part of a hierarchy and are referred to as "low" or "popular" culture and relegated to the margins.

Popular culture is often scorned by admirers of "high" culture, and the high is often scorned by the popular. This mutual antagonism is sometimes expressed through allusions to stereotypes. Classical music, art, and poetry lovers are the effete, the intellectual elite, with all the implications of class and sexual otherness this implies. People who enjoy the popular arts are sometimes represented as working or lower-middle-class, poorly educated, people without a life, or people of color, or teenagers, all of whom threaten dominant values. The negative view of the popular is further nourished by the fact that mass culture is commercial culture ("commercialized" would be the popular, pejorative term). Movies, television, rock music, social media, romantic novels, and newspapers are commodities, objects of commercial desire. The companies that manufacture or control them seek a profit. Popular culture commodities are the product not of the individual imagination but of the calculations of the large, ever conglomerating corporations that construct them to appeal to the largest part of their audience. The results are then positioned for the most appropriate segment of that audience; marketed according to age, gender, race, class; and promoted and sold accordingly. The commodities and their audience become part of the cost/price, profit/loss, asset/liability, manufacture/distribution structure that makes up industrial practice.

There are even wider, more profound, and potentially dangerous splits between subcultures who enjoy the products of popular culture itself. Religious and political differences mark divergent interests in radio programs, kinds of music, and films. People who listen to National Public Radio are identified as different both by themselves and by others from those who listen to right-wing talk shows, as are those who watch MSNBC or Fox News. People who watch action movies are seen as different, first of all by the moviemakers themselves, from those who watch adaptations of Jane Austin novels. In such divisions, the resentment and anger felt by one group toward another are marked and sometimes unsettling.

MEDIA AND CULTURES

The roots of all this are complex and indicate how any narrow definitions of culture are insufficient to describe the strong and changing elements of the larger culture we belong to. What follows is a very abbreviated sketch of some complex events and movements that created subcultures within larger cultural groups, but it will give an idea of how culture keeps generating itself, how vital groups within it create its art, and how that art changes and transforms the culture.

In European culture, the "serious" production of music, painting and literature goes back to the Middle Ages, when it belonged to the royal courts. The "lower classes," illiterate peasants mostly, had cultures indigenous to their country and place, based on crafts and oral traditions, a phenomenon that is true of most non-European cultures as well. The formation of a property-owning and goods-trading middle class began in the Italian Renaissance, and it is this new group that brought high culture out of the palaces and into the villas, the homes of wealthy traders and property owners. Owning or sponsoring fine art was part of the movement of the burgeoning middle class toward owning cultural property. Well-to-do Italian merchants became patrons of the arts, commissioning painters, for example, who, in gratitude, would paint an image of their benefactor at the feet of Christ. Ownership was a sign of wealth. Owning or patronizing art was a sign of wealthy good taste. It still is.

During the eighteenth century, the property-owning middle class grew across Europe, small shopkeepers flourished, and an industrial working class began to expand. Each of these classes continued developing its own cultural forms. The novel, for example, was developed in the early eighteenth century and was originally directed at middle-class women, who read or had read to them, for example, the romantic adventures of the heroine of Samuel Richardson's *Pamela; Or, Virtue Rewarded* (1740), and *Clarissa* (1747–1748) with devotion and identification (and, sometimes, a sense of irony) that many contemporary people still devote to romance novels. **Melodrama**, a popular working- and lower-middle-class form, was born of the novel, the theater, and politics, especially in the late eighteenth-century theater of post-revolutionary France. It started as pantomime with music—recall that "melodrama" means drama with music—in response to laws that forbade traditional theatrical performances in which actors spoke their lines. Early melodrama in Europe and in the United States was broad, moral, and political, with exaggerated gestures and simplified structures of good and evil—too broad and "common" for upper-class tastes. It was broadly participatory as well, inviting emotional and even verbal response. Melodrama was a form of satisfaction and gratification, a communal expression of a desire for stability, place, and confirmation of simple moral values. In various forms, it has thrived in many cultures in the West and the East, and its cinematic version was examined in some detail in Chapter 10.

Music hall variety entertainments were, by the mid-nineteenth century, another working-class site of comedy, popular music, parody, and gender lampoon (cross-dressing in British variety shows remains popular and is still accepted without embarrassed innuendo). Music hall was and is performed in a space that encourages lively audience response. (We see remnants of this in television singing and talent competitions like *The Voice* and *America's Got Talent*.) Along with melodrama, the American version of music hall, vaudeville, was to prove an enormous influence on the development of film, as well as an early venue where film was projected.

In order for popular culture to become mass culture, storage and distribution methods had to be developed. Print culture was well advanced by the eighteenth century, and novels and newspapers enjoyed a fairly wide circulation. In the case of the novel, some transmission occurred through people reading aloud to groups. In order for the music, images, and **narratives** that were enjoyed by mainly working- and lower-middle-class audiences to become mass culture, other means had to be developed, which happened by the late nineteenth and early twentieth centuries. The new technologies of photography, telephony, the phonograph, radio, and the movies served everyone well, especially those who did not have the time or the means to contemplate the complexities of high culture. These new technologies quickly became dominant. When this happened, the culture of print, with its demands of education, leisure time, and access to the quiet and solitude that reading fiction or poetry demands, ebbed.

We have examined one form of storage and distribution in some detail: the photographic emulsion on plastic strips, which, when exposed to light and developed into a series of high-resolution images, can be cut together in various ways, put in cans, and sent around the country and the world to be projected on movie screens. Electronic transmission was another important nineteenth-century development. The telephone, phonograph, and radio delivered voice and music, news and entertainment, into the most intimate of spaces, the home. When film began its gain in popularity, people had to go out of the house to see it, with all the planning and expense that entails. By the 1920s, radio was omnipresent in the domestic sphere and became the dominant form of entertainment. When sound came to film in the late 1920s, a vigorous interchange between the two media began. Radio carried film advertising as well as programming based on current films. Radio stars played in films; film stars appeared on radio.

One version of print media expanded along with movies and radio by becoming integral to them. Newspapers advertised and reviewed radio and film. Movie magazines and newspaper gossip columns extended the work of studio publicity by keeping the stars and their personal lives in the public eye. It would be no exaggeration to say that, by the end of the 1920s, an elaborate, integrated network of popular culture had evolved in which listener and viewer had access to an **intertextual** web of radio, movies, magazines, and newspapers. By intertextual, I mean that all of these elements referred to one another, reproduced or represented each other. Radio broadcasts were used as narrative elements in film; films were turned into radio drama; newspapers reviewed both and printed film publicity and scandal; film music and popular music were connected so that a movie theme was available on record and on the radio. By the 1940s, a film might include a title song composed especially so that it could be released as a single. I said earlier that a text has boundaries, but this needs to be amended by the fact that textual boundaries are extremely porous.

The only thing missing was a means of delivering moving images to the home, and that problem was solved after World War II. With the coming of television (which began development in the 1930s), the web of mass-mediated popular culture was ubiquitous, available to anyone who could afford it. By the mid-1950s, almost everyone could. The intertextuality of this cultural web grew as well. Radio ceased being a medium for drama and assumed a major role, first, as a delivery system for popular music and, recently, as a site for the expression of usually right-wing political views. Film and television took immediately to one another, even though television cut deeply into film attendance and moviemakers pretended nothing but scorn for the new form. Today that is changing, as series for cable television and streaming media are drawing top talent and critical acclaim.

Television became the delivery mechanism for old films and for films made specifically for television. Movie studios bought television outlets and assisted them with product. Some producers have added television shows to their roster of productions. With the advent of the videocassette and cable television in the late 1970s, movies and television became, on a very important level, functions of one another. Filmmakers depended upon videocassette and now DVD and Blu-ray sales and rentals to round out the profits of a film. Today, only about 15 percent of a film's profits come from theater tickets. Moviegoers balance viewing at home with going to the movie theater. DVDs, along with their supplementary material, became so popular that at one time their sale accounted for an amazing 58 percent of a film's income to the studios.[2] They are also—and this is certainly even more amazing—giving the studios ideas that films are worth preserving and may have educational value, two ideas that had never occurred to them previously. DVD sales are currently slipping as more and more viewers turn to streaming video on their smart TVs and phones, and so consumption of moving images is changing again.

Meanwhile, the domain of "high" culture shrank. It remains proscribed by class and education and finds a home in museums, concert halls, and bookstores—the few that exist outside of Amazon.com—with some airplay on radio and television. But "high" culture was always marginalized, and its demise always widely predicted. It survives still. The "popular," in particular the American version of the popular, is, with few exceptions, the dominant form around the world. Within it thrive many varieties and subforms, many national and international inflections as we have seen in films from India. In almost all cultures, film is ubiquitous, and the most ubiquitous of all, the dominant of the dominant, is, of course, American film.

THE NEW WEB

I've used the image of a web to define the ways in which popular culture is spread and integrated. I've mentioned as well the various media that grew in the nineteenth century to create this web. "Web" of course has not only taken on new meaning but has also created yet another set of subcultures—although its ubiquity throughout so much of the world would seem to constitute a large culture of its own, with many subcultures branching off. In other words, everyone with access to a computer logs on to the Internet. But everyone uses it in slightly different ways and communities of various kinds have emerged as subcultures.

Film is the product of nineteenth-century technology that emerged from photography. It is, in fact, the first technological art. During the mid-1990s, at the same time that the digital was making its way into film production, computers were becoming a household item, and the Internet and the World Wide Web were creating new "screens" on which new communities were forming, including communities where film is the subject of discussion.

Like almost everything on the computer screen, the Internet and the Web are places of process in which everything happens but little is resolved. One narrative of the Internet is in fact the story of investigation, participation, and outrageous narcissism, an individual's or group's progress through an open-ended system of commentary, blogs, tweets, rants, and sometimes downright bad behavior. The Internet is also a place in which small movies can be made, shown, and discussed. YouTube has become a major site of creativity, from people dancing in their bedrooms to sketch comedy routines, to full-length films. It is an archive, where older films, no longer under copyright, or new ones pirated, are available. Creativity and nastiness exist within the intricacies of the Internet's worldwide architecture.

Culturally and practically, the Web and the Internet that carries it, along with computer games, have created an unusually close integration with film and television, each form interacting with the other, distributing each other's content, and providing some space for participation and interactions with the viewer, as well as more income for producers. In fact, the Internet has embraced and in many instances swallowed up older forms of technological transmission: radio and recorded music can be streamed online; newspapers read online; movies viewed online; life as we would like it online.

The Internet has also raised issues of ownership. Who owns it? Who pays? Many want content to be free because, at its inception, the Internet was a free and open space. Content, especially in the form of music, was traded and downloaded at will. But the artists who made the music and the producers who owned it wanted to be paid. The same happened with online newspapers and, eventually, television shows. There is an ongoing battle over **bandwidth**—the size of the "pipe" that allows content to flow across the Internet—and again, many want equal access to download speeds while Netflix and YouTube (which is owned by Google) want special access at the expense of ordinary users. This "net neutrality" struggle is ongoing, and all of this indicates the dynamism of the Internet, its continuing unsettled state. It confirms as well the dynamism of culture, continually changing and renewing itself.

THEORIES OF CULTURE

Again and again, we need to remind ourselves that culture for profit—in any of its forms—does not excuse us from analyzing it. Owned or free, controlled by the user or the provider, the viewer or the studio, we are still part of it. In order to understand the place of popular culture in general and film in particular within the larger complex of cultural practice, it will be useful for us to look at some theories of cultural studies that discuss mass media and film. **Cultural studies** looks at various kinds of texts within the context of cultural practice, that is, the work, production, and reception of the material stuff of daily life, marked as it is by economics and class, by politics, gender, and race, by need and desire. Cultural studies examines the form and structure of cultural texts as they create meaning or have meaning created by the people who produce them and the people who are entertained by them. Cultural studies thinks about meaning as an ongoing process built out of complex relationships between people in their daily lives and the works of imagination they look to for emotional and intellectual sustenance and release.

THE FRANKFURT SCHOOL

An early wave of cultural criticism that studied mass media found its subject deeply troubling, and for very good reason. The Frankfurt Institute for Social Research was founded in Germany in 1924. Its function was to integrate the study of sociology, psychology, culture, and politics. Among its members and associates, known as the **Frankfurt school**, were some of the most important left-wing thinkers of the twentieth century: Max Horkheimer, Theodor Adorno, Herbert Marcuse, Erich Fromm, Siegfried Kracauer, and Walter Benjamin. Because they were left-wing and many of them Jewish, the Institute was closed down by the Nazis in 1933. Many of its members came to America, where they taught and pursued their work.

A core part of that work was the study of film and mass media. Siegfried Kracauer wrote two major studies of film, *Theory of Film: The Redemption of Physical Reality* (1960) and *From Caligari to Hitler: A Psychological History of the German Film* (1947). The latter was an attempt to describe a cultural mood and its expression in film that would lead to the cultural and political catastrophe of Nazism. Theodor Adorno wrote books and articles on philosophy and music and coauthored with Max Horkheimer *The Dialectic of Enlightenment* (1944). A chapter of this book, "The Culture Industry," along with Walter Benjamin's magisterial essay "The Work of Art in the Age of Mechanical Reproduction," laid the foundation for future studies of media, culture, and politics. It proved to be a difficult foundation to build on. Given the society they observed, the conclusions about mass culture reached by Adorno, Benjamin, Kracauer, and others of the Frankfurt school were either very negative or ambivalent.

Germany in the 1920s was a society going through a massive political upheaval that would lead to the most brutally destructive regime in modern history. The Frankfurt school viewed the rise of popular culture in this society as part of the growing authoritarianism in Germany's political culture. Instead of a web of interrelated texts in which the listener or viewer is part of a complex structure of commercially produced and distributed music, news, images and sound, the Frankfurt school saw a vertical structure where government and industry worked in close collusion with each other, producing mass media that was distributed downward to the people, dominating the masses with films, music, and radio. The audience for popular culture was an undifferentiated and passive mass, robbed of subjectivity and individuality by an authoritarian government, which swayed the people to its needs by manipulating the popular media.

To the Frankfurt school, the audience for the popular was in fact created, given form, made compliant, *composed*, turned into a willing tool of the ruling political party. Again, this view was based in a strong reality. Hitler's Nazi government was the first to use mass media—radio and film especially (they were busily developing television)—as a controlled means of communication, fashioning information, entertainment, and outright propaganda in such a palatable way that its audience could not, did not want to, resist.

The Frankfurt school looked upon the government and its associates in industry, journalism, broadcasting, and film as strong and controlling, the audience as weak, willing, and easily fooled. Horkheimer and Adorno wrote: "Life in the late capitalist era is a constant initiation rite. Everyone must show that he wholly identifies himself with the power which is belaboring him . . . . The miracle of integration, the permanent act of grace by the authority who receives the defenseless person—once he has swallowed his rebelliousness—signifies fascism."[3] Leni Riefenstahl's *Triumph of the Will* (1935) that we discussed in Chapter 9 is an interesting example.

The Frankfurt school understood that mass media did not have to clobber its audience into submission, that people have free will that can be easily, willingly subdued. They understood the comfort that comes with joining a group, swallowing rebelliousness, integrating oneself into the mass, and receiving authority's grace. They saw and noted how easily popular culture accepted anti-Semitism, agreed to mindless calls for sacrifice to the fatherland, to the promises of redemption from a despairing and oppressed life. Totalitarian power—along with the offerings of banal entertainment in the form of musicals, melodramas, and comedies made by the ruling powers—was hard for most Germans to resist.

Under Hitler, cultural difference, individual expression, artistic experimentation were not simply discouraged but destroyed. Serious art, modern and critical art, was declared decadent and was banished. Books were burned. Artists fled the country. Popular art was molded into the narrow spectrum of hatred of Jews and Communists, adulation of Hitler, and celebration of a lower-middle-class life of home, family, and fatherland, driven by exhortations to keep sacrificing in order to perpetuate Nazi ideals. Fascism became a model for the Frankfurt school's analysis of the culture industry as a conspiracy of politics and business to form, out of the most profound and uninformed aspects of a culture's collective fears and desires, superficial entertainments that confirmed and reinforced the basest instincts of that culture. The culture seemed to yield unquestioningly.

THE CRITIQUE OF AMERICAN POPULAR CULTURE

Unsurprisingly, Frankfurt school scholars tended to look down upon popular culture from an elitist perspective. Anything that was part of such an abominable political culture could not have any value. They took this elitist position with them when they came to the United States in the late 1930s. Theodor Adorno particularly disliked the popular and wrote often of the debasement of jazz and popular music. The worst part of Frankfurt school elitism was popularized in the United States during the 1950s and became integrated with the general concern over what some people perceived as a decay of the culture and a rise in adolescent misbehavior. The 1950s were a period of serious cultural instability, during which post-World War II anxieties were heightened by the Cold War with the Soviet Union. A paranoia about being subverted and infiltrated by Communism took over the country during the first half of the decade, and popular culture became a main target of its fears. "Containment" of the Soviet Union, of domestic behavior, of anything that deviated from a largely imaginary norm was the watchword that entangled itself in anticommunist discourse.

The anti-popular culture discourse of the 1950s was carried on by many sides. Attacks by right-wing politicians and journalists were not very sophisticated, though they stirred up many anxieties. They did not present the Frankfurt school's complex portrait of a culture industry that was an interrelated process of the government and the producers of entertainment crafting their products to manipulate the willing masses. Indeed, some Cold War writers and politicians put the argument of the Frankfurt school on its head. Where the Frankfurt school analyzed a top-down control of media and the population, 1950s critics of the media argued that the media—especially film and television—were elitist and left wing (many on the right still do). Rather than controlling the belief system of the people, the media subverted it, destroying their values. This led to the red-baiting witch hunts in Hollywood and the blacklisting of film and media people during the period of investigations by the House Un-American Activities Committee and Joseph McCarthy's senate committee.

Less virulent ideologues, indeed many 1950s intellectuals on the left, argued that popular culture was simply too debased and shallow. If people were entertained by mass media, they were already diminished in intellectual and emotional response by contact with films, pop music, and television, or soon would be. Some critics of popular culture saw it—and some still do—as a promoter of violence and sexuality. Comic books, movies aimed at teenagers and, near the end of the decade of the 1950s, rock and roll music were deemed the worst offenders. Congressional hearings investigated their influence. And, of course, the explosive growth of television in the 1950s was looked on with dismay. While its manufacturers, producers, and promoters saw it as a miracle that would placate bored housewives and keep families together, its detractors saw it as a further degradation of cultural standards. Television was yet another sign that the culture was being reduced to a featureless, homogenized mass.

HIGH CULTURE, MASSCULT, AND MIDCULT

The social and cultural complexities of mass media were not as important to 1950s critics as the pronouncements of decay and corruption. In the 1950s and early 1960s, elitist categories maintained a strict segregation of the arts and their audience based on matters as vague as taste. The film reviewer and cultural critic Dwight MacDonald categorized 1950s culture into three parts. Creating a less ethnically and racially biased metaphor than the old "low-brow, middle-brow, and high-brow" classification, he spoke about High Culture—the complex, resonant art for the elite—but concentrated his attention on what he called Masscult and Midcult: the first being popular culture produced for mass consumption, the second something in between, not high, not low, but peculiarly middle-class. By splitting popular culture into two groups, MacDonald could address a decade that was entertained by a new range of entertainment from Elvis Presley records and movies to plays and films written by Tennessee Williams and live television drama.

These new categories began to introduce an element of complexity into the American discussion of popular culture. They were still derogatory and judgmental: Masscult, MacDonald says, "is bad in a new way: it doesn't even have the theoretical possibility of being good." Midcult only reproduces the bad in a better light: "It pretends to respect the standards of High Culture while in fact it waters them down and vulgarizes them." Midcult gives the impression of seriousness while reproducing the same banalities of Masscult: films made from eighteenth- and nineteenth-century novels, PBS series about early twentieth-century manor houses and their inhabitants, or recent best-sellers might be considered current examples of Midcult.[4]

In a 2014 article in the *New York Times*, film and cultural critic A. O. Scott wrote an interesting variation of MacDonald's theories:

> The natural affinity of the high and low, and their mutual suspicion of the middle, has been a remarkably durable idea, though it has never proven to be anything more than an idea, a nostalgic vision of ideal order. At heart it is a fantasy of aesthetic authenticity secured by static and hierarchical social distinctions. A world of landlords and peasants, of masters and servants, of patrons and workers is one in which art and life harmonize. In such a world, the middle will always be a place of vulgarity and ostentation, (a) kind of money-grubbing, backslapping, self-conscious display . . . .

This presents an interesting complement to MacDonald, noting a conspiracy of high and low toward the middle in order to attain a status quo of economic and cultural class. Scott concludes, reflecting on the current state of income inequality, by saying that "Social inequality may be returning, but that doesn't mean that the masterpieces will follow. The highbrows were co-opted or killed off by the middle, and the elitism they championed has been replaced by another kind, the kind that measures all value, cultural and otherwise, in money. It may be time to build a new ladder."[5]

These complex, often derogatory classifications at least began to recognize or point to the fact that popular culture was not monolithic, that issues of class, economics, and taste could be used to achieve a finer definition, or even a different definition entirely. But, without the Frankfurt school's complex ideological analysis and with the conservative bias so many of them held, the mass media critics of the 1950s and early 1960s, continuing to the present moment, railed and raised alarms. These were the views from above. Meanwhile, the culture of the popular expanded.

By the late 1950s, rock and roll, which began as African American rhythm and blues that was then integrated with country and western formats, became an important component of a revived, activist youth culture that began to have purchasing power to match its desire for a unique entertainment. In cinema, the influence of foreign films began nudging movies in the direction of high culture, the film culture that we examined in Chapter 8. At the same time, because of population shifts to the suburbs, movie attendance began to fall off and television viewing went up. In response, American cinema changed and began targeting specific age groups with specific kinds of movies, trying to pinpoint an ever-changing audience with both Masscult and Midcult films. Popular culture—both its products and its audience—grew more complex and needed new theories to deal with it.

WALTER BENJAMIN AND THE AGE OF MECHANICAL REPRODUCTION

New theories began to converge from many directions. The growth of film studies in the 1960s and the development of feminist theories in the early 1970s laid the ground for a growing interest in serious analysis of popular culture. Many of these theories grew from an essay by an associate of the Frankfurt school, originally written in 1936. It helped form the basis of a nonjudgmental, appropriately political, speculative, and complex meditation on popular art and its relation to the larger matrix of cultural practice. Walter Benjamin's "The Work of Art in the Age of Mechanical Reproduction" takes as its starting point new technologies of reproduction, storage, and distribution that made film and other forms of popular cultural practice possible. For Benjamin, the difference between the old art of the elite classes and the new popular art of the masses is that popular or mass art is readily available outside the usual high-culture sites of museums and libraries. The image (film is Benjamin's main object of study, though his ideas can usefully be applied to recorded music, photography, television, and now to digital media) is not a unique, one-of-a-kind event, kept in one place and viewed with awe and reverence. The image is now infinitely reproducible and available. It has lost that which makes it special, even worthy of cultural reverence, what Benjamin calls its **aura**.

Aura can be thought of as the uniqueness of a work of traditional high art. An original painting has aura. It is one of its kind, visible in its originality only where it is hung, looked at with the privileged relationship of viewer and the work itself. The autographed first edition of a novel might have an aura, as would the live performance of a play or symphony. Aura is the non-reproducible, the authentic, the original production from the hand of an artist or ensemble, viewed from a reverent distance. Popular, mass-produced art is without aura. The music by a rock group that you download is the same as thousands—hundreds of thousands—that were recorded, digitized, and downloaded in turn. The print of a film viewed in a mall multiplex in Cleveland, or on a DVD in your living room, is the same as a print viewed in a multiplex or a DVD in a living room in West Palm Beach or (except perhaps for the redubbing of the soundtrack) in Frankfurt, Germany. There is nothing unique about it, other than the possible uniqueness of the imagination that created it. There is nothing palpable about it. Nothing is there but digital, electronic, or optical data; no human presence but the beholding eyes and ears of the viewer, who the producers hope will respond in the same way as every other viewer anywhere—by paying for access.

Benjamin, unlike most of his Frankfurt school associates, did not look at this development with alarm. He looked at it as historical and technological fact—something going on despite what social and cultural critics might think about it. He thought about the growth of popular culture as something to be understood not as an oppressive reality but as a potentially liberating one. Loss of aura and ease of access meant two things. Everyone could come into contact with works of the imagination, and everyone would be free to make of the auraless work what she could. Curiously, the loss of aura could lead to a greater intimacy with the work. The ritual and awe that surround the creation and reception of original genius might be replaced by the intimate interpretation of each viewer. "The progressive reaction," Benjamin writes, "is characterized by the direct, intimate fusion of visual and emotional enjoyment with the orientation of the expert." Every person becomes a critic, able to make sense and make judgments. Every person's perception becomes enlarged. "By close-ups of the things around us, by focusing on hidden details of familiar objects, by exploring common place milieus under the ingenious guidance of the camera, the film, on the one hand, extends our comprehension of the necessities which rule our lives; on the other hand, it manages to assure us of an immense and unexpected field of action." The camera, he says, is like a surgeon's knife, cutting through reality, bringing the viewer into an intimate connection with the world.

Film and other mass media offer a place of entry and participation in the imaginative representations of the world. They offer them for everyone. Certainly, Benjamin was not out of touch with the realities of mass media and politics, especially in his own country. He knew that the larger an audience, the more difficult it would be for mass art to present progressive ideas. He knew as well what the Nazis were doing with mass media and to the culture as a whole. He experienced it directly. Forced out of his country in 1940, this Jewish, mystic, Marxist intellectual, who wrote about angels as well as the mass media, would take his life while trying to escape. He understood that fascism attempted to introduce a false aura into mass-produced art, turning it into spectacle and putting it into the service of political ritual and, inevitably, of war. Communism, he believed, might work the other way, by liberating the viewer and the work of art into a politics of communal action. While such a view did not quite work out in the course of history, it reflects an understanding that an art of the masses can mean a participation of the masses in the political work of the culture. A Utopian vision!

Benjamin was a prophet of culture, and his words, directed at film, can be applied today to the digital. He wrote in "The Work of Art in the Age of Mechanical Reproduction":

> Every day the urge grows stronger to get hold of an object at very close range by way of its likeness, its reproduction . . . .To pry an object from its shell, to destroy its aura, is the mark of a perception whose 'sense of the universal equality of things' has increased to such a degree that it extracts it even from a unique object by means of reproduction. . . . The adjustment of reality to the masses and of the masses to reality is a process of unlimited scope, as much for thinking as for perception. . . . The (masses are) the matrix from which all traditional behavior toward works of art issues today in a new form.[6]

But what happens when the "new form" is figuratively within its shell? A movie viewed on the 5-inch screen of a smartphone is so far removed from the aura of, for example, one viewed on an Imax screen that it becomes something different. Owned and personalized, reduced to the palm of one's hand, the image becomes both less and more. Less than the detailed, highly resolved image originally created by the filmmaker, but more available, more in line with Benjamin's notions of "the universal equality of things."

THE AURA OF STATE INTERVENTION

There have been important examples of governments working with artists to promote a popular art that involved many people on many levels, including the political. The artistic activity that immediately followed the Russian Revolution—and formed the model for Benjamin's idea of a communal, politicized art—is one successful example. The work of Sergei Eisenstein, Dziga Vertov, and other filmmakers, writers, and visual artists in the 1920s exhibited an energy and a desire to reach their audience and actively engage the audience's intellect and emotions. Stalin put a stop to all that.

Elsewhere, throughout the twentieth century, there were many attempts at state intervention in the arts. Germany revived its film industry in the 1970s through state subsidies to television. Films there were made for television and also exhibited in theaters. Popular response was mixed, but most of the films made under the subsidies were important works, as we pointed out in Chapter 8. By and large, public funding has helped to foster a serious and engaged, personal and political cinema—as we saw in the example in Chapter 7 of *Daughters of the Dust*. Many European productions and some independent American filmmakers receive funding and distribution from a variety of public and private European sources. But public funding has been less successful in forging the large-scale interaction of audience, work, and culture at large that Benjamin hoped might occur in the age of mechanical reproduction, and many governments, our own included, are becoming more and more reluctant to take a financial role in the process.

THE BIRMINGHAM SCHOOL OF CULTURAL STUDIES

Cultural studies is less a movement than a loose affiliation of intellectual agreements and arguments about how to think of culture, its productions, and its audiences. Started by the Germans in the 1920s and 1930s, coalescing around Benjamin's essay, it was developed by the British cultural theorist Raymond Williams, and given its name by the British Birmingham Centre for Contemporary Cultural Studies. It is a wide-ranging discipline, always in process, but with some important foundational principles: that the study of culture be interdisciplinary and broad. All events are seen in the context of cultural practice, and that practice is determined not only by the elite culture industry but by the activities and interventions of many subcultures, which are determined by class, race, and gender. Cultural practice involves both the production of works and their reception by an audience. Culture and all its various components can be understood as coherent, legible, interactive "texts."

These texts can be analyzed for the purpose of study and then placed back in their cultural context. I can analyze Alfred Hitchcock's *Psycho* (1960) or James Cameron's *The Terminator* (1984) as unique texts. I can examine their formal structure, their images and narrative form. But I must also integrate them within the culture of the late 1950s and the economics of the end of the **studio system**, in the case of *Psycho*, or the apocalyptic consciousness in the 1980s and the melding of the superhero and science fiction **genres**, in the case of *The Terminator*. I can read parts of these films as cultural texts: the way the automobile in *Psycho* reflects an ambiguous response to mobility and security and how the old dark house recapitulates familiar images from gothic literature and Hollywood horror movies. I can look at the way robotics in *The Terminator* are a sign of the culture's long-term attraction to and repulsion from the image of the automated human.

Psycho and *The Terminator* can be analyzed as another entry into the popular imagination of Freud's story of Oedipus. *Psycho* talks about a child destroyed by his mother; *The Terminator* and its sequels address the unending and impossible search for patriarchal figures who destroy and are destroyed. *The Terminator* can be figured as a response to the end of the Cold War and the unknown terrors that occur when we discover that the enemy is really us and our technologies and not "them". Both films can be seen as ways in which the culture continues to come to terms with the modern world, with despair, emptiness, and terrors of the unknown, how it deals with issues of the feminine and masculine, with its attraction to and repulsion by sexuality, with its fascination with and fear of otherness and difference.

More recent horror and science fiction (examined in Chapter 9) speak to two different cultural strains. One is the love of the digital **mise-en-scène**, the pleasure in seeing imaginary worlds minutely articulated: videogame art raised to the big (or small) screen, without first person shooter control. The other is a kind of amused fear of destruction, even annihilation in a degraded world where viruses and then their victims get out of control. In all instances these films are culturally determined by a desire for mastery over the unknown, the pleasure of the visible, the fear that all of this and more will come to nothing. Cultural nihilism is not peculiar to our moment and certainly not a universal concern. But expressed in our visual arts, it gives us relief while playing out our fears.

RECEPTION AND NEGOTIATION

Text and context—in their usual senses of the work of art and its cultural and historical surroundings—are reconfigured in cultural studies. The individual work, the work of culture, our acts of looking, understanding, and participating can all be read as interacting texts. The very interaction of viewer and film is a kind of text that can be interpreted. Form and meaning make sense only when we examine their intersections in all their complexity. The key is legibility, the ability to read culture and its work, to understand, dissect, and then reassemble what we have read into a coherent analysis. No one element can be taken for granted. The whole is made of its parts, and each part responds to the other.

Reading Benjamin, we introduced another principle of cultural studies that opposes many of the traditional ideas of mass media studies. Instead of positing a "culture industry"—a conglomeration of governmental, political, and business forces that determines the commodities of popular culture and conforms the culture from the top down—cultural studies sees a complex interaction of production and response and reception. The consumers of popular media are not a dumb, cowed, undifferentiated mass, repressed and oppressed by the banal homogeneity of what they see and hear. People consume in many different ways, and with varying degrees of comprehension and ability to make interpretations. Individuals, as well as small and large groups, determined by their economic and social classes, make up subcultures who negotiate (a key word for the Birmingham school of cultural studies) meanings with popular texts, much as readers of high cultural products do. Negotiation implies a relationship between the work of popular culture and the consumer, with the latter taking what she wants from a song, a television show, or a movie, and possibly not taking it at all seriously—or more seriously than is warranted.

People have different backgrounds and different needs, which they put to use in negotiating with the text meanings that are most useful or pleasurable. People are capable of comprehension and of articulation, of struggling against the desire of the producers of the popular to inundate them with sounds and images. Everyone interprets; everyone responds. What traditional mass media studies saw as a monolith, cultural studies sees as a complex group of class, race, and gender marked individuals, with desires and with intelligence. We don't merely accept what the culture industry hands down: we deal with it and use it.

Along with the process of negotiating with the text comes the work of unpacking. In Chapter 2, I spoke about the economy of the image. Films made in the classical style, as well as television, advertising, the Internet, and other popular forms, pack a great deal of information into a small space (or perhaps more accurately a sprawling space in the case of the Internet). Much narrative detail is stored in a glance, a gesture, a nod, a camera movement, a cut, a link, a tweet. We understand films because we know the conventions, we know how to read and interpret because, exposed to films, we have learned what they are about, at least on the immediate level. Cultural studies holds that we can move through the conventions and unpack more subtle meanings that we decode according to what we want or need to understand about a film or a song or a television program: think, for example, how much information and emotional response about gender is gathered from the television shows *Sex and the City* or *Girls*. We open the text, pick, choose, and interpret. What we interpret might not necessarily be what the producers intended. Women fans of *Star Trek* or *The Lord of the Rings* films, for example, write highly erotic, homosexual stories, called "slash fiction," about the heroes of their favorite programs or movies and publish them on the Web. Freddy Krueger, the evil dream figure of the *Nightmare on Elm Street* films, becomes a figure of fearful admiration for adolescents. Rap music and its lyrics provide the rhythms and narratives of African American street life. *The Terminator* moves, by means of subtle negotiation between filmmaker, audience, and movie star, from destructive monster to substitute father, climaxing in 2003 as the governor of California. Forrest Gump becomes a role model for simple-minded courage. The class-crossed lovers of *Titanic* (James Cameron, 1997) become objects of adoration and a confirmation of teenage despair. The same director's *Avatar* (2009) creates a world in which we are permitted to imagine—and as a result of 3D, inhabit—an alternative life. Boy bands and girl bands provide a sublimation of desire for teenagers and icons of sexual liberation. In Russia, members of the girl band *Pussy Riot* were imprisoned for focusing attention on that country's oppressive politics. In 2014, a fictional figure appeared on the Internet called "Slender Man," who apparently was taken so seriously that murder was committed in his name by young girls. In all these cases, many viewers and listeners respond in different ways and understand with a touch of irony or even violence the intentions such artifacts hold for them.

JUDGMENT AND VALUES

Perhaps not all the negotiations, unpacking of codes, and re-readings of cultural texts are for the good. Popular and high culture can turn out badly or stupidly. Some audiences may not respond wisely. During the horrible wars in the Balkans during the 1990s, Serbian nationalists dressed up like Rambo, the 1980s film icon of individual heroism, and killed people. Killing in the name of a fictional figure who is alive only within the vagaries of the Internet is not ennobling for anyone. Killings shown on the Internet by radical Islamists, using sophisticated production and distribution techniques, create only impotent horror. "Going viral" on the Internet is a common cliché, though viruses virtual or real are often deadly. But the dangers of the Internet may be as much a cultural cliché as is the notion that popular culture is debasing. That some individuals or groups create or use cultural productions badly is not unique or new. The Nazis made Jewish prisoners who were musicians play Mozart in the concentration camps. The point is that cultural studies attempts to be non-judgmental while, we can only hope, maintaining a moral center. Cultural studies first seeks to describe and analyze and broaden. Judgment comes after comprehension.

This is a very complex point, because it places us between common sense, careful analysis, and wholesale dismissal. Some people still dismiss film, television, and rock as worthless and potentially dangerous. They see the Web as a hotbed of pornography or of stealing other people's identity and intellectual property. Conservative politicians blame Hollywood for ruining the culture. Study after study attempts to discover whether violent film, television, or video games provoke violence in children, and each study seems to deliver a different answer.

In the end, some judgment has to be applied. The interplay of perception and analysis, guided by the methodologies that make up critical thought, must lead any critic to abstract what she finds about the culture into broad, general patterns and then analyze those patterns for subtle meaning within the specific texts being studied. The description and evaluation of these patterns will be subjective, based upon the values and moral beliefs held by the critic. Some aspects of popular culture will, indeed, be found wanting, even intellectually or morally degrading, but this judgment ought not then to become an all-embracing condemnation. Perhaps the key element of cultural studies is its ability to analyze broadly and make judgments discerningly.

INTERTEXTUALITY AND POSTMODERNISM

This discernment is difficult, largely because of the simple attractions of the works of popular culture and the desire of one part of the culture to put them down and the other to embrace them and make them their own. The works themselves make discrimination difficult because they tend to feed upon themselves, interact, and absorb one another to a remarkable extent. Films refer to other films; musical styles are filled with quotations from one another—sampling, for example, is a popular formal element of rap; television news indulges in sensationalism and fearmongering; sexuality and violence constitute the major elements of almost all mass media, substituting themselves for more rational explorations of the world. The culture seems to be enthralled with images and sounds rapidly edited together. Fragmentation rules—and not in the way either Eisenstein or the **classical Hollywood style** intended. The influence of MTV rock videos of the 1980s and the desire of filmmakers to make their work appear dynamic, the unifying elements of the classical style in film, are sacrificed to the sensation of rapidity without the analytic and political energy of Eisensteinian **montage**. The classical style made fragments look like wholes, and while that style still predominates in narrative films, the average shot length—the amount of time a shot is held before cutting to another shot—of American film has become shorter. David Bordwell has noticed that the average shot length has shortened from eight to eleven seconds before 1960 to four to six seconds in recent film.[7] In other forms—online videos, television commercials, news reports—fragments are presented only as fragments while at the same time moving in a **flow** that is almost undifferentiated. Commercials occur in film in the form of "**product placement**," brand names that are conspicuously placed within a shot. Commerce, imagination, culture, and news intermingle and move us along in a process that makes analysis difficult.[8]

This is the style of the postmodern, where hierarchies, definitions, and separations are broken down, and the quickly seen is substituted for the deeply understood. Cultural studies discovered the postmodern and, as if by necessity, adopted it. No one can look at popular culture for long and not recognize—with delight or with horror—the often indiscriminate flow of images and undigested ideas. In film and television, images of extraordinary violence become as commonplace as the sentimentality of the characters who are the targets of the violence; images of the poor, the hurt, and the starving appear indiscriminately on television news, call upon our emotions, and as rapidly disappear again. When images disappear, so does sympathy. Everything seems to be occurring on the same plane of comprehension, or willing incomprehension. Popular culture appears to be in a steady state of assertion and denial, of claiming the importance of what is shown and then denying that it really means anything.

This must, of necessity, make media historians and critics of us all. Intertextuality—the interpenetration of various texts, one within the other—keeps reminding us how wise we are to the popular culture we've grown up with. The rapid association of images in film, television, and advertisements forces us to analyze and make sense of image inundation. Staccato shrieks of violins in a television commercial will make us all think about *Psycho.* A commercial for a local car dealer will play the opening of Richard Strauss's *Also Spake Zarathustra*, and we will recall *2001: A Space Odyssey.* An episode of *The Simpsons* will contain references to half a dozen movies. Everyone is wise to the sounds and images of the culture, though, perhaps, no one is the wiser.

If you detect overtones of the Frankfurt school as well as 1950s critiques of the popular in this argument, it is because of the tension between the open embrace offered by cultural studies and a need to maintain some sense of what may be important and what may not be. Cultural studies insists on accepting all aspects of the popular with an understanding that individuals take from it what they feel is important to them. More traditional criticism asks for value judgment, discrimination, and a preservation of hierarchies. Some practitioners of cultural studies may applaud the undifferentiated flow of the postmodern, while other critical schools look in despair at the surrender of judgment and discrimination. As always, an intelligent compromise works best. The concept of negotiation, the recognition that the audience for the popular is not stupid, helps us understand that there may indeed be discrimination at work. A postmodern critic might argue that it is precisely because viewers and listeners are so sophisticated that sounds and images can be used in a rapid-fire, punning, intertextual structure. Perhaps it is because we have seen and heard it all before that no one accepts the old meanings, and the new ones have yet to be invented. At the same time, any critic must be aware of boundaries even as they are being broken down. Making judgments depends upon recognizing boundaries. We may not always want to keep them in place, but we must note their location, their history, and where they might be moved.

Our discussion of the form and content of film to this point has offered tools for comprehension, analysis, and judgment. Understanding the cultural contexts of film and the means at our disposal to read and account for our judgments offers the opportunity to explore another important element, the film narrative and its contexts: we have seen how films tell stories, who does the telling, and what stories are being told. Now, using what we know about the contexts of form and culture, we can attempt to understand a broader context for those stories.

CULTURAL CRITICISM APPLIED TO *VERTIGO* AND *THIS IS 40*

How do we combine a theory of cultural studies with an understanding of the formal structure of film and come up with a reading of cinematic texts that situates them within larger cultural practices and within the culture as a whole? Such a task would involve looking closely at a film and how it is put together, including its form, its narrative structure, the function of the actors and stardom in general. We would need to address the thematic structure of a film, what in fact it is trying to say to us. We would want to place the film in the context of other films of its kind and examine its intertextual structure. We would then need to take all of this and look at the film through the eyes of the period in which it was made as well as the period in which it is being analyzed. In other words, we would try to see the film as its contemporaries did and then see it again as it looks to us now. We would have to place all this information in line with larger social issues: technology, politics, questions of gender, race, and class, of ideology and how the film in question fits or contradicts those general ideas and images we hold about ourselves and our place in the world. We would want to draw some value judgments about the film. This should not be done mechanically, because the best criticism is written in a comfortable, integrated style, in which ideas are set forth and analyzed, grounded by the film being studied. There will be digressions along the way, but they constitute part of the complex weave of a film and its cultural surround.

I would like to attempt such analysis of two films that could not seem more different and distant from one another within the contexts of film, high art, and low comedy. They are *Vertigo*, a film made by Alfred Hitchcock in 1958, and *This is 40*, a film made by Judd Apatow in 2012.

Every ten years, the British Film Institute polls some 846 film critics, academics, and distributors to determine the top films of all time.[9] For fifty years, the number one position was held by Orson Welles's *Citizen Kane* (1941). In the 2012 survey, *Kane* was replaced by *Vertigo*. *Vertigo* is a film of great complexity and high seriousness made by one of the few filmmakers in America whose name is as recognizable as that of a movie star. Hitchcock's popular television program, *Alfred Hitchcock Presents*, started airing in 1955, and that, combined with his cameo appearances in his own films, made his name a household word.

Hitchcock made over fifty films in his lifetime, and *Vertigo* appeared during his most fertile period, right after the popular films *Rear Window* (1954), *To Catch a Thief* (1955), *The Man Who Knew Too Much* (1956), the less popular, darker film *The Wrong Man* (1956), and just before *North by Northwest* (1959) and the enormously successful *Psycho* (1960). *Vertigo* is a careful, deliberatively crafted film by a director who attended to every last detail of his films and his career. A self-conscious artist, Hitchcock tried to gauge public taste and his own imaginative needs, to make the commercial and the subjective work together. Most of his films are accessible to a wide audience while providing fodder for a serious film critic.

This is 40 is a sequel of sorts to Judd Apatow's 2007 hit, *Knocked Up*. It is not serious (it is a comedy, after all), and its complexities are hidden behind its genial, talky, profanity-laced surface. Apatow came to films from stand-up comedy, writing for other comics, and television, where he created the show *Freaks and Geeks* that began its relatively brief run in 1999, and where he began gathering his stock company of man-child actors: Seth Rogen, Jason Segel, and James Franco. More recently, he was an executive producer of the HBO series *Girls*. He started his film career as a producer, his own company producing a long list of films beginning with *Anchorman: The Legend of Ron Burgundy* (Adam McKay, 2004) all the way through *Anchorman 2: The Legend of Ron Burgundy Continues* (Adam McKay, 2013), and including such films as *Superbad* (Greg Mottola, 2007) and *Bridesmaids* (Paul Feig, 2011). He has directed, in addition to *Knocked Up* and *This is 40*, *The 40-Year-Old Virgin* (2005), *Funny People* (2009), and *Trainwreck* (2015). Self-conscious in different ways than Hitchcock, Apatow maintains a recognizable point of view across the films he has produced and directed, and is no less talented than Hitchcock at gauging public taste—despite the fact that some might argue about the level of taste he gauges.

THE CULTURAL–TECHNOLOGICAL MIX: FILM, TELEVISION, DIGITAL

Analyzing films in their cultural contexts leads us into interesting, sometimes unexpected byways: we need to think about the technologies of film and television, about actors and acting styles, about the size of the viewing screen itself, because they all speak to the cultural context of the works in question. Both *This is 40* and *Vertigo* owe a great deal to television. Both Hitchcock's and Judd Apatow's fame had blossomed because of their respective television programs. *Vertigo*'s debt to television, while playing on the audience's recognition of Hitchcock, is more indirect, more technical, and driven by economics. It has to do, interestingly enough, with screen size, which, as discussed in Chapter 3, is an element of shot **composition**, and becomes part of the film's aesthetic.

Hollywood film is made to immerse us in the process of its narrative. Part of that immersion is the consequence of the sheer size of the image. Larger than life, the traditional screen image engulfs the viewer, overwhelms his space. Think of Imax. Television, on the contrary, is overwhelmed by the space around it. Despite the advent of the digital, high definition, wide screen TV, its image is still not comparable to the large, sharp image projected on the movie screen, even though that projection is itself digital in more and more theaters. When television began, its image was small and very low definition, so, during the 1950s, when audiences left theaters by the hundreds of thousands to stay at home and watch TV, Hollywood responded by making movie screens larger and wider. Hollywood pretended not to get what television was all about—namely, visual narratives delivered for free in the comfort of home—and thought their films could conquer the desire for TV by further overwhelming the viewer with the image. Of course, to hedge their bets, they also bought television stations and produced films and series for TV.

The various wide-screen processes that were developed, invented, and reinvented in the early 1950s brought few people back to the theaters, and, as we've seen, it has led to a lack of a coherent compositional **frame** for a filmmaker to use. Paramount Pictures, Hitchcock's studio during much of the 1950s, developed its own wide-screen process called "**VistaVision**" and used it to compete with 20th Century Fox's **CinemaScope**. All of Fox's films from 1954 to the end of the decade were filmed in 'scope. All of Paramount's films during the same period were filmed in VistaVision, *Vertigo* included.

Hitchcock turned necessity to advantage. *Vertigo* is, in part, a film about a man wandering and searching. In the first part of the film, Scottie, the central character played by Jimmy Stewart, tails someone who he believes to be a friend's wife. He falls in love with her, and when she dies, he searches for a replacement for her. Much of the first half of the film is taken up by shots of Scottie in his car, driving through San Francisco, following the woman, Madeleine (Kim Novak), to a restaurant, a flower shop, a museum, Golden Gate Park. While these languid **sequences** of driving, looking, spying constitute a major narrative expression of Scottie's deeply obsessive personality, they are also a kind of travelogue of San Francisco, presented in VistaVision. Hitchcock was a studio director and paid his debt by filming in the studio's proprietary format. At the same

FIGURE 11.1 Scottie (James Stewart) drives around San Francisco trailing a ghost—Madeleine in her green car, who is really Judy (Kim Novak), luring him into a trap that will destroy him

FIGURE 11.2 In typical shot/reverse shot cutting, we see what Scottie does out of the window of his car—even though what he sees is not what he thinks he sees. *Vertigo* (1958)

time, he made the wide-screen part of the film's mise-en-scène and narrative structure, using its horizontal frame to show Scottie's wanderings and also his boundaries. The screen opens **point of view** and limits it as well.[10]

Judd Apatow and the digital

By the 1990s, the screen-size wars were over. Films were, and continue to be, made in a variety of wide-screen formats. *This is 40* was shot in Panavision in the ratio of 1:2.35. But it was shot in digital, making it part of the continuing movement away from celluloid to the cheaper, more efficient process of digital filmmaking. There has been some handwringing about the loss of celluloid, based partly in a concern about the degradation of the image, partly in nostalgia, partly in theoretical concerns about the difference between analogue, where the image on celluloid bears direct, visual relationship to the image in front of the camera, and digital, where the image is translated into numbers and translated back again into light.

In fact, digital cinematography, well made at a high resolution and carefully projected, is all but indistinguishable from celluloid. Nostalgia for celluloid is, alas, like nostalgia for anything else: it feels good but will not change the facts of progress. As to the theoretical concerns, I have argued from the start that the cinematic image is not the real thing but rather a mediation. In digital cinematography, the mediating process is invisible unless viewed on a computer. Unlike a strip of celluloid, you cannot hold a hard disk up to the light and see an image. But, for distribution and archival purposes, the digital format allows for an infinite number of copies without a loss of quality, and a high resolution digital image projected on a screen is, again, all but indistinguishable from the projection of a celluloid strip.

The introduction of wide screen put an end to the knowable, dependable compositional frame. Today, the great variety of screen sizes challenges a director to either compose toward the middle, so that our gaze is concentrated on the characters and their actions, or to cleverly exploit the frame and make composition as eloquent as it was until the early 1950s. The introduction of digital cinematography, on the other hand, reduces challenges, allowing filmmakers to work more cheaply, more efficiently.

THE ACTOR'S PERSONA: JAMES STEWART AND THE APATOW BOYS AND WOMEN

In our discussion of acting in Chapter 6, I pointed out that the personality of movie stars is constructed by a combination of their films and their publicity. Big stars become part of the culture, recognized, identified with, gossiped about in the tabloids, their private lives becoming public affairs. The stars of *Vertigo* and *This is 40* have undergone interesting modifications in this process.

James Stewart

James Stewart, as a movie actor who had been in films since the 1930s, had broad audience recognition. His acting range was somewhat limited, but this was a limitation that allowed him, in the course of his very long career, to become something of a cultural barometer. Stewart's on-screen persona embodied, until the 1950s, variations of a passive, sweet, vaguely embarrassed, and self-effacing character. His public persona was as quiet and reserved as the roles he played. That very passivity and self-effacement seemed to make him into a kind of rubber stamp, onto which could be impressed not only the characterizations demanded by a particular role, but the responses of the audience as well. The illusion of simplicity and gentleness made him something of a mirror for everyone's best intentions. Until the 1950s, he specialized in comedy roles, often assuming a foot-shuffling, head-down, aw-shucks characterization, whose simplicity was irresistible. His characters were non-threatening; a viewer could feel both kindly and superior to him.

The role of George Bailey in Frank Capra's *It's a Wonderful Life* (1946) simultaneously summed up and altered this persona that Stewart, his various directors and the audience, had so carefully nurtured. Stewart and Capra added a measure of anxiety and despair to George. The film's narrative is driven by his attempt to get out of Bedford Falls and his continual frustrations in realizing this dream. The frustrations and anxieties reflect the lack of clarity about how an individual of ordinary means would make it in the new, unfamiliar world that had formed at the end of World War II, a world where old institutions and accepted ways of life were changing. *It's a Wonderful Life* is a rare Hollywood film that refuses to give its hero his life's dream and forces him instead to accept another role—almost literally forced upon him by the film. Indeed, the frustration George feels leads him to attempt suicide because his story refuses to come out the way he wants it to. Only through angelic intervention does he understand that, without him, the town he wants so desperately to leave would be a dark, violent, corrupt place. With this understanding, he takes the more "responsible" path and becomes a family man, a banker, and a protector of his town's interests (see Figures 9.1 and 9.2).

It's a Wonderful Life is one of the great postwar narratives of uncertainty about the present and the future, a statement of the culture's discomfort and yearning for fantasies of simpler times. It still strikes a chord and remains, along with a World War II film, *Casablanca* (Michael Curtiz, 1942), one of the favorites of old, black and white movies. It launched Stewart's career in a different acting direction. His roles became more serious, and that aspect of despair and moral confusion that he manifests in *It's a Wonderful Life* is played out through a succession of roles, most notably in the films he made for Hitchcock and in a series of Westerns he made for Anthony Mann, such as *Bend of the River* (1952) and *The Naked Spur* (1953). Hitchcock began playing on the changes in Stewart's acting persona in *Rope* (1948), *Rear Window* (1954), and *The Man Who Knew Too Much* (1956). In *Rear Window*, a serio-comic film about the unpleasant consequences of being a voyeur, Hitchcock began to elicit from Stewart a worried, somewhat obsessive performance. A photographer confined to a wheelchair because of an accident, the character spies on his neighbors and forces his girlfriend to investigate a murder he believes occurred in an apartment across the way. Beneath its jokey surface, the film raises serious points about the gaze, about the morality of looking and seeing what you are not supposed to see. It is a virtuoso riff on the technique of **shot/reverse shot**. In *Vertigo*, Hitchcock plays up further the obsessive characteristics he gave Stewart in *Rear Window*, and the two of them create one of the most troubling portrayals of psychosis in contemporary film.

The Apatow stock company

Paul Rudd, Leslie Mann, Jason Segel, Seth Rogen, Melissa McCarthy, and the rest of the Apatow community of players are hardly known for their gravitas. They are all relative newcomers to film, but in a short time have become expert comic performers, able to riff with agility on absurd, often vulgar lines of dialogue, and play off of one another's talents with a rhythmic certainty, aided by Apatow's editing that moves the films from laugh to laugh. Like Stewart's characters in Hitchcock's films, they are obsessive. But this obsessiveness does not overflow into psychosis, only into the comedy that results from repetition and exaggeration.

There is a trio of hilarious sequences in the middle of *This is 40*. Debbie (Leslie Mann—Judd Apatow's wife) viciously takes down little Joseph (Ryan Lee), who has insulted her daughter by not putting her on his Internet hot list. The young man withers under her assault: "You look like a miniature Tom Petty . . . . You think that haircut's cool. It's not. It looks like you put your Justin Bieber wig on backwards." She blows in his face. "So next time you think about writing something nasty on my daughter's Facebook page . . . , I will come down here and I will fuck you up . . . ." The kid breaks down. Debbie relents and Joseph says he understands, his mother is going through menopause too. Debbie, who is pregnant (this being the dramatic crux of the film) curses some more and walks off in a rage. Later, Pete (Paul Rudd) confronts Joseph's mother, Catherine (Melissa McCarthy), who accuses him of touching her nipple as part of a big argument as to just where her breasts are, and this little subplot finally plays out in a meeting with the school Vice Principal (Joanne Baron), in which Catherine unwinds a volley of profanity and abuse, played for laughs and, this being comedy, the impression of no one being seriously emotionally threatened.

The dialogue and the acting in these scenes and the rest of the film take on an immediacy and a sense of contemporary life that is missing in *Vertigo*, not only because the film is so distant from us in time, but because Hitchcock is aiming at something more profound and universal than Apatow. Hitchcock was not likely to refer to popular culture in a film that aims at something higher. And even though *Vertigo* is profoundly about sexuality, contemporary censorship kept sexual references in check, something (as we will see) to be alluded to in ways that are more disturbing than direct sexual references.

FIGURE 11.3 "A miniature Tom Petty." Debbie (Leslie Mann) browbeats little Joseph (Ryan Lee), who has refused to put her daughter on his online hot list. Judd Apatow's *This is 40* (2012)

VERTIGO AND THE CULTURE OF THE 1950s

To understand the cultural milieu of *Vertigo* and *This is 40*, we have to understand what happened in the late 1940s and 1950s to bring about the despair in Hitchcock's film. We need to consider the economics of the 2000s as well as the new openness about sexuality and profanity that surrounds and infiltrates Judd Apatow's film.

The end of World War II did not bring a feeling of victory and power to American culture. Instead it created a churning discomfort, an uncertainty about the future and a lack of clarity about the past. The revelations of Germany's extermination of the Jews and the explosion of two atomic bombs over Japan that ended the war shook the culture and confirmed how easily our myths of civility and order could fall. The Communist revolution in China, the expansion of the U.S.S.R. into Eastern Europe, and the testing of a Russian A-bomb in the late 1940s further upset a society that had thought the second great war of the century might settle things down overseas.

At home, major changes in the economy, in race, gender, and class relations began in earnest in the early 1940s, continued throughout the war years, and generated anxiety for years after. Labor expressed its discontent through a number of strikes during the war. A migration of the African American population from South to North responded to economic opportunities for those who had not experienced them before, while disturbing the majority white population. Meanwhile, African American soldiers fought bravely in a segregated army overseas. Attacks against Hispanics resulted in the "zoot suit riots" that spread from southern California to Detroit, Philadelphia, and New York. The outbreaks of violence not only signified the willingness of minorities to express and defend themselves but set the stage for the creation of the myth of the juvenile delinquent after the war.

By the early 1950s, the culture was wracked with change and dislocation it could barely understand: suburbanization and the flight from the central cities, the formation and institutionalization of the multinational corporation, the slow painful progress of civil rights, the continued redefinition of gender roles. However, the United States sublimated these and many other pressing issues into a struggle against a mostly mythologized external enemy (and then a totally mythical internal one), the "Communist threat." Almost every issue was absorbed into the Cold War discourse of anticommunism.

Beginning in the late 1940s and continuing through the 1950s, the House Un-American Activities Committee, the Senate committee run by Joseph McCarthy, newspapers, magazines, and much of the language of political and popular culture condemned as Communist almost anyone who had once held or continued to hold liberal or left-wing views. People informed on friends and colleagues. Government workers, teachers, screen and television writers, directors, and actors lost jobs. Intellectuals were discredited. The blacklist thrived. American culture and politics underwent a purge.

Women were, in an analogous way, also purged from the culture. Their roles changed dramatically during the years of World War II. With most young men fighting abroad, women came flooding into the workforce, did quite well, and enjoyed financial power, many of them for the first time. While few women rose to executive positions, they kept factories and shops operating and discovered a welcome liberation from old domestic routines. The liberation was such that, when the war was over, a massive ideological retooling had to be put into place. Men were returning from battle and wanted their jobs back. Women had to be reinserted into their former passive routines. Movies, magazines, and newspapers once again extolled the importance of motherhood and family, the submissive role of women, the nuclear family in which mother was anchored to home while father was free to move like a satellite out of the home, into the office and back.

Discussions about gender got caught up in the absurd momentum of the anticommunist discourse. The political and the personal, the power of the state, the workplace, the family, the sexual all became confused and self-contradictory. The larger fears of subversion and conformity, of being taken over and changed by enemies from within and without were filtered down into the more immediate concerns of the role of men and women in the culture and the way gender determined the structure of power. 1950s culture was as much obsessed with sexuality and gender roles as our own. It tried to assuage obsession through control. The decade's most conservative desire was to maintain a perfect imbalance of male domination and female subservience, male mobility at work and female stability in the domestic space. Fear of women, fear of difference, fear of Communism, and fear of conformity marked this age of anxiety.

People seemed to find security in sameness, while fearing that too much conformity would be dangerous. For example, while the growth of corporate culture was recognized as the source of secure jobs for men and a secure consumer economy for the country, it was also seen as something that interfered with the image of the free, unfettered male, who should be making his own way in the world. Voices were raised and books were written about men being unmanned by their new subservience to the corporation and the family.

Some popular literature was quite direct about this anguish over conformity, the apparent diminishing of male potency, the growth of corporate culture, and also Communism. Articles in the popular *Look* magazine, gathered in a 1958 book called *The Decline of the American Male*, claimed that women control male behavior, from the early formation of men's psyches, to the kinds of jobs they take, to their competitiveness. Because women now demanded satisfaction that was equal to or greater than the male's, they were beginning to control his sexuality. The subjugation to women and the pressures brought by the culture had produced a broken shell of a man, without individuality, without power, overworked, stressed-out, unable "to love and to make moral decisions as an individual." Men were weakened and regimented, made impotent and recessive. "In the free and democratic United States of America, he had been subtly robbed of a heritage that the Communist countries deny by force." As males went, so went the country. Communism by female control.[11]

The Kinsey Reports

Sexuality, control, anticommunism: the triad of 1950s cultural obsessions. The gender problem was further aggravated by the publication of two scientific reports that became, next to anticommunism, among the most influential and disquieting events of the decade. The Kinsey Reports on male and female sexuality (published in the late 1940s and mid-1950s respectively) were works of scientific, statistical analysis, representing themselves as objective, methodical surveys. They frightened almost everyone by claiming that there was no normative sexual behavior, no controllable, conventional way of defining what people do in the bedroom. In a world where moral, cultural, and political safe harbor was becoming increasingly harder to locate the more it was demanded, the Kinsey Reports seemed to remove yet another anchor. What the Reports seemed to be saying about sex became part of the general concern about subversion—cultural, political, and gender. Nothing seemed secure.

THIS IS 40 AND THE CULTURE OF THE EARLY 2000s

The first part of the new millennium was marked by horrendous events and political confusion: the 9/11 attacks that brought down the World Trade Center towers, the war in Iraq fought because of lies told to people by their elected officials, the economic collapse of 2007, the Boston Marathon bombing in 2013, the escalation of mass shootings in schools and public places, the growing proof of global climate change, the outbreak of disease. The result of all this seems to have been a contradictory mix of withdrawal, denial, a low-level cultural anxiety, extreme right-wing belligerence, and an evasion of reality. In response, there have been films about the Iraq and Afghanistan conflicts, all but a few—*The Hurt Locker* (Kathryn Bigelow, 2008), *Lone Survivor* (Peter Berg, 2013), *American Sniper* (Clint Eastwood, 2014)—commercial failures. There has been an upsurge in superhero films, many of whose characters are conflicted about their roles and purpose, reflecting, perhaps, that even our imaginary saviors are not up to the task of saving a world whose complexity belies digitally enhanced battles between good and evil.

Comedies, romantic or otherwise, tend not to engage directly with the world. By that I mean that they create their own universe, glancingly related to the one we know on a daily basis, located in the cities or suburbs that are familiar to us, but engaged in antics that are integral only to the conventions of comedy. However, even comedy is touched by anxiety. *This is the End* (Evan Goldberg, Seth Rogen, 2013) is a parody of the apocalyptic films we spoke about in Chapter 9, starring, as themselves, the usual gang of contemporary comic actors: Rogen, Jonah Hill, James Franco, Jay Baruchel, Michael Cera, etc. (see Figure 6.11). The film makes fun of the fears of world disaster by (literally and figuratively) exploding the **subgenre's** conventions. One function of comedy is to turn anxiety into hilarity.

The modulations exhibited in Apatow's comedies reflect the continuing loosening of **Production Code** standards, especially in the use of language and sexual references. There was a key event in the late 1990s that allowed comedy to move beyond the already loosening standards of the code: the Monica Lewinsky scandal, in the wake of which President Bill Clinton was almost impeached for lying about having (in his words) "sexual relations with that woman." The seamy details of Clinton's affair became common discussion in the media and in public discourse. Like the Kinsey reports in the 1940s and 1950s, Clinton and Lewinsky opened up sexuality and added to the further erosion of what might and might not be spoken about in television and movies. Added to the uncensored vulgarity found on the Internet, and the freeing up of language and sexuality used and shown on cable television, there are now few restrictions imposed on what characters in a film might say or do.

The economic influences on *This is 40* are more subtle. As a response to the Great Depression of the 1930s, a subgenre called "**screwball comedy**" appeared—*The Awful Truth* (Leo McCarey, 1937) is an excellent example—that depicted usually well-to-do married couples verbally sparring with each other, separating, and inevitably getting back together. Their sophistication amidst the Depression's depths offered escape and even a sense of superiority over the arguing rich folks. *This is 40* is a kind of modern screwball comedy, with hints of the Great Recession that began in 2007 lingering in the background. Pete's record promotion business is failing and he supports his father, Larry (Albert Brooks), and the many children he's had with his young wife Debbie. Larry can't keep track of his children's names, mooches continually off his son, and resolutely refuses to find work. With the exception of Debbie's father, Oliver (John Lithgow), who is aloof and unhelpful, there are no rich people in *This is 40*. But there is also no dwelling on economic distress; it lies deep below the witty exchanges between Pete and Debbie, who, in the spirit of the genre, surmount difficulties in the full bloom of their uninhibited relationship.

One major difference between Apatow's comedies and screwballs lies in the representation of their male characters. Screwball males—so often played by the debonair actor Cary Grant—and their wives are strong willed, witty, and resilient characters. They are a far cry from the overgrown adolescents that people the Apatow universe, and the ways in which male characters are represented in these films bears comparison with Scottie in *Vertigo*. To do this, we need to return to the 1950s.

FIGURE 11.4 The 1930s screwball couple. Upper class, well-to-do, and made for each other. Cary Grant and Irene Dunne in Leo McCarey's *The Awful Truth* (1936)

FIGURE 11.5 The contemporary screwball couple. Middle class, struggling, and made for each other. Pete (Paul Rudd) and Debbie (Leslie Mann) in *This is 40*

THE VULNERABLE MALE IN FILM

Many films of that decade examined questions of gender (as they did with racial issues) with some delicacy and complexity. A few somewhat altered conventional notions and old stereotypes of the rugged male hero. Some of these films, such as *A Place in the Sun* (George Stevens, 1951) and *The Man in the Gray Flannel Suit* (Nunnally Johnson, 1956), presented male characters who in their passivity, sensitivity, and vulnerability took on characteristics and attributes usually associated with female characters.

A number of postwar film actors—Montgomery Clift, James Dean, Marlon Brando, and Paul Newman, in films like *A Place in the Sun*, *Rebel Without a Cause* (Nicholas Ray, 1955), *The Wild One* (Laslo Benedek, 1953), and *The Left-Handed Gun* (Arthur Penn, 1958)—expressed a desire for new ways of expression under the guise of a withdrawn sensitivity. Their acting styles, as we noted in Chapter 6, were a major break with prewar movie conventions; their roles spoke to the repressed anger and sexuality of the culture at large. Even established actors took part in this examination. Humphrey Bogart, in Nicholas Ray's *In a Lonely Place* (1950), plays a film director confused and in contention with his violent tendencies that cost him work and relationships (see Figure 10.4). In *The Wild One*, Marlon Brando plays a biker with a very sensitive soul, who, in one scene, alone with his motorcycle in the night, weeps. Early in the film, a girl asks him, "What are you rebelling against?" "Whaddya got?" he asks. This film, along with *Rebel Without a Cause*, spoke to many people's feelings about the constraints and confusions of the decade. *The Wild One* was considered subversive enough to be banned in England for many years, but its interest is really not in the rebelliousness of the male character but in his ambiguous expression of anger and passivity. Despite the gang brawling, the film's representation of masculinity plays against conventions of heroism and strength; it is, finally, the feminizing of the male that makes this and other films of its kind attractive and curious.

FIGURE 11.6 Johnny (Marlon Brando) breaks down in tears. The 1950s sensitive male in Laslo Benedek's *The Wild One* (1953). Also see Figures 6.4, 6.5, 8.5

Vertigo is not a film about youthful rebellion. Nor is it on any explicit level about fears of conformity or Communist subversion. Quite the contrary, it is about a middle-aged man who implodes under the weight of sexual repression and obsession and despair, bringing about the death of other people in his wake. As such it is of a piece with the decade's concerns with change and betrayal, with power and passivity, domination and servitude, and sexual panic. It quietly addresses all of these concerns and the culture's general sense of incompleteness, its feeling of unfinished, perhaps unfinishable personal business, its pervasive anxiety. It touches, in an oblique way, on the Cold War obsessions of containment. The political culture of the 1950s was obsessed with containment of the "Communist threat." *Vertigo* personalizes the political by creating a deeply repressed man, contained by his fears and driven by his obsessions.

Paul Rudd's Pete in *This is 40* is hardly the tormented and tormenting male equal to James Stewart's Scottie. But in general Judd Apatow's male characters are hardly models of stereotypical movie male heroes. They are either millennial stoners or middle-aged bumblers, self-centered in ways that their 1950s antecedents were not. They seek pleasure—particularly aided by weed and beer—and are often heedless about the pain they cause others, at least until a baby comes along to melt their hearts and trigger a sense of responsibility. But, still, like Scottie in *Vertigo*, they are damaged: not psychotic, but incomplete characters, sexually immature, and, unlike Scottie, quite willing to allow a crude joke to take the place of a serious thought. Scottie's sexual damage is a constant undercurrent throughout *Vertigo*. *This is 40* begins with Pete and Debbie having sex in the shower, cut short by Debbie's annoyance that Pete took Viagra, leading to the inevitable discussion of erections.

Pete is self-indulgent (he can't keep away from a cupcake), failing in business, and in constant contention with his wife. He is evasive and comically thoughtless. At the same time, despite his cupcake fetish and his refusal to seriously consider ways to support his family, he is, unlike Scottie, fairly functional even if somewhat undeveloped emotionally. Despite their constant bickering, he maintains a relationship with his wife, who, in the screwball tradition, gives back as much verbal sparring as she gets. Pete is an average man in a comic universe, entering middle age with his wife and children (and a new child on the way) without equanimity, but with emotional resources on the brink of being developed sufficiently to the task. Squabbling and joking along with often crude sexuality are marks of the Apatow male; not heroic, almost normal.

Scottie is into middle age without emotional resources, without a partner to spar with. He is a man so weakened by physical and emotional vertigo that he can find no footing in a melodramatic universe in which the usual arc of emotions associated with the genre is reversed. In a traditional melodrama, the central character gains more than he or she had at the beginning, or if that is impossible finds oblivion in death. Scottie finds only oblivion. Where Pete and Debbie manage to prevail, Scottie and Madeleine/Judy suffer total loss. Madeleine/Judy dies. Scottie dies as a functional man.

The role of the hero, intimately tied to issues of masculinity in any cultural period, is always under question. It was being questioned in the 1950s, and it is again in the early 2000s. The notion of the strong, moral, righteous, and courageous man of action, who would cleanse the entire culture of corrupt and violent force—by means of greater violence—has never held up very well when tested in reality and is often wobbly in our films. After World War II, the premise of heroism was examined in film across the board. John Ford, as we have seen, was exploring the corruption of the Western hero as far back as *Fort Apache* in 1948. In *The Searchers* (1956), Ford was pressing his and America's favorite heroic figure, John Wayne, to give a performance in a film that explored the proximity of heroism to psychopathic obsession (see Figure 9.17).

Two years later, Alfred Hitchcock was doing the same, this time to the less heroic persona of James Stewart. In our time, superhero films question the rectitude and commitment of our fantasy figures of perfect, selfless heroism. Our comedies reduce masculinity to adolescent innocence posing as sexually aware awkwardness.

FILM, FORM, AND CULTURE

In order to understand more clearly where our two films and their protagonists diverge and converge, we need to consider their narrative approaches and formal structures, which determine the way they speak to their moment and to ours. *Vertigo*, with its dark, ironic structure, is a modernist narrative. Modernity encapsulates the movement of technological advancement, increased urbanization, rapid fragmentation of dependable, cohesive structures such as the family, religion, dominant race or ethnicity, and government, along with the falling away of individual agency and power. The responses to modernity are represented in various ways, including the stories the culture tells itself, its **dominant fictions**. Movies and television bring our fears to our attention, sometimes confirming them, sometimes attempting to assuage them with narratives about mastering our destiny, overcoming great odds, and recuperating our emotional losses. Comedy turns anxiety into absurdity; melodrama turns anxiety into the desire, sometimes hopeless, for release.

In the 1950s, science fiction films spoke to our terrors of vulnerability to alien forces (allegories of the "Communist threat" back then, as we noted in Chapter 9)— stories that are being retold again today only with different enemies—terrorists, Russian mafia, zombies. Melodrama tended to confirm the loss of individual power by insisting that the family, the married couple with children, rather than the individual, was the best bulwark against modernity—all the while confirming the fragility of the family. *Vertigo* is an unusual observation of the disintegration of both the family and the self in modernity. It has romantic elements and touches of fantasy. It is a modernist work in its concern with the coming apart of the modern male, his loss of agency and subjectivity. Hitchcock's expression of this through the carefully crafted formal structures of his medium also marks its modernism.

Scottie is lost, unable to act or to love. His female friend, Midge (Barbara Bel Geddes), has been unable to get him to respond to her sexually. Her simplicity and directness frighten him. So does her sense of humor. She is a designer, currently working on a brassiere ("You know those things. You're a big boy now," she tells him). The brassiere she's designing has "revolutionary uplift," based on the principle of the cantilever bridge, and it parodies the 1950s fetishism of the female breast, the formulating of women's bodies into preconceived male fantasies.

Scottie's own fantasies are so powerfully conceived that women are unattainable for him, and he suffers from either impotence or sexual incompetence or complete gender panic. Immediately following the banter about the brassiere, Scottie and Midge talk about a moment, years ago, when they were engaged for "three whole weeks." Scottie insists that Midge called it off. She doesn't respond. But Hitchcock does. He cuts twice to a **close-up** of her, very tight, and high enough to knock the balance of the frame off center. She simply frowns a bit and looks slightly off into the distance. It's a very typical Hitchcockian gesture, exploiting the standard grammar of the **reaction shot** to expand the viewer's comprehension of the situation. In this case, the reaction shot of Midge indicates to us that Scottie not only is in trouble sexually but is unaware of it. He is unaware of who he is and what he is capable or incapable of doing.

FIGURE 11.7 Scottie teases Midge (Barbara Bel Geddes) about their brief engagement years ago

FIGURE 11.8 Hitchcock cuts to a high angle of Midge, whose look says everything. "Three whole weeks," she says

FIGURE 11.9 "You were the one who called off the engagement," says Scottie

FIGURE 11.10 Again Hitchcock cuts to Midge's eyes and her knowing look. *Vertigo* (1958)

Scottie is an emotional void, into which a rich businessman pours an incredible plot about his wife, who, he says, thinks she is inhabited by the spirit of a nineteenth-century woman who committed suicide. (A major best-seller in the early 1950s was *The Search for Bridey Murphy*, about a woman who, under hypnosis, revealed a past life. In 1956, Paramount, the studio that produced *Vertigo,* made a VistaVision film of the book. Hitchcock may be consciously parodying the Bridey Murphy story in *Vertigo*.) The businessman, Gavin Elster (Tom Helmore) asks Scottie to follow a woman he identifies as his wife, who is actually someone pretending to be her, and report on her actions. She becomes the obsessive core of Scottie's life, which is so lacking a strong center that it barely survives. Scottie is the man of the postwar age, without power, without a sense of self and able only to recreate his desires in other people, who are not who he thinks they are.

Everything is false, a huge ruse created by Elster—and by Hitchcock, who gives nothing away until much later in the film—to cover up the murder of his wife. Though on close examination, he does give something away. The sequence in which Elster spins his plot for the gullible Scottie is played out in Elster's office, with its huge window overlooking his shipbuilding works. It is an image of power, the word itself used by Elster as he speaks about the old San Francisco (the word "power" is repeated a number of times in the film as a kind of rebuke to Scottie's powerlessness). As he talks, he moves to a raised platform behind Scottie, indicating his power, as Scottie himself is seen smaller in the foreground, sitting in a chair. Elster is creating a narrative for his dupe and for us, the viewer, who is, at the moment, as ready to believe the story, despite Scottie's initial reluctance to do so (see Figures 7.9–7.13).

The ruse itself, as is typical in a Hitchcock narrative, is less important than its effects on the characters and the viewer, though formally fascinating. Hitchcock creates a plot within the film's narrative, a fake plot that is nonetheless taken for real by Scottie. We are privy to the results of this willing gullibility: the decay of Scottie Ferguson from someone who is already weak and afflicted to an obsessive-compulsive, to a sadomasochist, to a shell of a man gazing down at the abyss, having finally caused the death of the woman he has tried to re-create into another's image. If this sounds melodramatic, it is. *Vertigo* is in the tradition of 1950s melodramas about repressed desires exploding and then imploding back onto the central character. *Vertigo* makes its figure of melodramatic suffering a man, playing with his perceptions and then ours. We must disentangle ourselves from Scottie. In the first part of the film, we tend to identify with him; in the second, we are asked to pull away and judge. There is no comfortable closure for anyone. Neither the character nor his world is redeemed at the end of the film. Scottie is left utterly, unrecuperably alone and in despair; in short, *Vertigo* has aspects of tragedy about it, a modernist melodramatic tragedy.

Modernity, modernism, the postmodern

Modernity and its narrative expression, modernism, speak to the loss of a center through an ironic voice with a whisper of tragedy. Comedy is not immune to a modernist approach (we see it at work in the plays of Samuel Beckett, for example), though contemporary film comedy is most often postmodern in structure. Postmodernism does not fret over the loss of the binding stories and beliefs of the culture. The dominant fictions no longer work, and the way to acknowledge their loss is to refer to them jokingly, sometimes sentimentally, through superficial irony or downright cynicism. Where modernism references history, postmodernism references the history of popular culture and depends on its audience being in on its joking allusions. So we have the cruel hilarity of Debbie's teasing her daughter's bully by calling him a "miniature Tom Petty." So too the running joke about Pete's attempt to revive the career of the old rocker Graham Parker, and the somewhat soothing effect of having Parker play a gracious version of himself in the film.

Postmodern history is internalized as the history of the moment. Apatow's characters live in immediacy, with little notion of past or future. Where Scottie Ferguson's life is an unrealizable quest to ease the pain of his desire, the people of *This is 40* avoid pain by satisfying desire through action or words. They convince themselves about their lives and take pleasure in their episodes of unhappiness by joking their way through it. Sex—especially talking about it—predominates their lives, but at the same time they are not entirely superficial. They are able to slough things off, whether it is Pete's failing business, or an employee's stealing from Debbie's clothing store, or, ultimately, her mid-life pregnancy. At the film's end, when Pete's fortieth birthday party falls apart, insults fly; Pete takes off on his bicycle and gets hit by a car; Debbie and Pete's mooching father have a serious talk in the hospital (ending with him taking $100 from her); Debbie's estranged father sits with their children watching the end of the TV show *Lost*—gentle and amusing reconciliations occur. There is even hope, as Pete and Debbie go to a concert and she convinces Pete to sign the singer Bryan Adams as a client.

Postmodern or traditional, comedy must end in hope and reconciliation, just as melodrama must end on a note of sacrifice and desire, in some way squelched. I said earlier that comedy exists in a closed universe. It might be said of melodrama that the universe closes in on its protagonists. Comedy's characters rise or remain in steady state; melodrama's fall. Comedy's characters end perhaps just above the level they begin with; melodrama's characters reach for more and fail.

Scottie in *Vertigo* wants to be the hero who saves the heroine in distress, except that the heroine is not in distress, he is. First he pursues the lie that Elster manufactures for him, then he attempts to re-create the lie by searching for a woman who never existed. In the second part of the film, Scottie discovers Judy—who was the woman who "played" Madeleine in Gavin Elster's hoax. Scottie forces her to remake herself as Madeleine. He denies her personality and tries to suck her into his. They return to the Spanish mission, and she falls to her death from the roof of the bell tower. There is no triumph over evil here, or even the triumph of good. Everything, finally, is a manifestation of Scottie's lack of moral center, a lack shared by the decade of the 1950s itself. Where love and reconciliation are offered at the end of *This is 40*, Scottie is left with only his own narcissism and madness. *Vertigo*, like its title, is about an unstoppable downward spiral.

Perhaps both films exist in a fantasy world. The bickering between Pete and Debbie is too fantastic (and fantastically funny) to reflect the realities of day-to-day life. No couples enjoy the equal give and take that this fictional pair does. The film asks us to join in on the joke—on all its jokes. *Vertigo* asks us to observe Scottie with pity, fear, and even tragic awe as he destroys his life. The relationship between viewer and *Vertigo* is as serious as Hollywood ever demands such a relationship to be. We are asked to read this film carefully, to understand its subtleties, to stay with it as it reveals to us the secrets that aren't revealed to its central character. There are no secrets in *This is 40*, only non-stop jokes, momentary bits of relevance, irreverence, irrelevance, and the lightest touch of sentimentality.

Formal structures

Unlike *Vertigo*, it also refuses to seriously consider cinematic form. But, while *This is 40* is shot in the basic **continuity style**, Apatow knows that the rhythm of editing, the exact point to place a reaction shot, how long to allow dialogue to dictate shot length are the formal methods that make comedy work. When little Joseph's mom Catherine goes through her ferocious tirade against Debbie, Pete, and the school Vice Principal, Apatow allows her energy to control his editing. After establishing the three participants and the school Vice Principal, he focuses on Catherine, cutting for reactions from the Vice Principal, cutting to put Catherine in soft focus in the right foreground as Pete and Debbie look on and deny everything, or over Debbie's shoulder looking at Catherine. And so on through the cutting and verbal onslaught—"that's what you look like," Catherine snarls at Pete and Debbie—"like you're a bullshit bank commercial couple"—the scene builds its comic pace, ending with Debbie's disingenuous but triumphant, "now you know what we're dealing with."

The formal structure of *Vertigo* is much more meticulous. Hitchcock is not at the service of comic dialogue and instead creates mood by the way he composes his shots. Using Bernard Herrmann's extraordinary score and the deliberate movement of camera, characters, and editing, *Vertigo* moves slowly toward its almost predetermined fall. As we noted, the first part of the film depends a great deal on how Hitchcock plays on the conventions of shot/reverse shot. He first sees Madeleine/Judy in an upscale restaurant, and as she moves before him, the wall behind her glows red as a sign of his sudden passion (see Figure 3.24). Following her through the streets of San Francisco, Scottie pulls into a dark alley. As he opens a door that Madeleine/Judy just entered,

FIGURES 11.11–11.15 Apatow cuts the sequence in which Catherine (Melissa McCarthy) confronts Debbie, Pete, and the school Vice Principal (Joanne Baron) in a simple editing pattern emphasizing dialogue and reaction. He begins with a master shot of the participants and then does a reverse shot showing facial expressions—Debbie and Pete looking smug, Catherine not amused. In her close-ups, she becomes more and more enraged and outrageous as Debbie and Pete proclaim their innocence

the scene before him glows in the bright colors of a florist's shop. At a museum, where Madeleine/Judy stares at a portrait of Carlotta—the woman who is supposed to be possessing her—Hitchcock and Herrmann's score play a counterpoint of shot/reverse shot as Scottie focuses obsessively on the two figures: the painted image on canvas and the image painted for him by Elster's fantastic story.

CONCLUSION

We could conclude from all this that the Frankfurt school and the 1950s media critics were correct, that there is an unalterable breach between high and low culture and that, at its best, *Vertigo* just manages to escape from Dwight MacDonald's category of Midcult and, at its worst, *This is 40* is irredeemably Masscult. *Vertigo* attempts to be tragedy, though, at bottom, it is a strong romantic melodrama with modernist inflections, incredibly constructed, dark, complex, and resonant. *This is 40* makes no such reach and comfortably accepts its Masscult status as a simple entertainment, acceptable as straightforward coming-of-middle-age comedy. Its refusal to take seriously any of the issues it raises only emphasizes its lack of commitment to serious intellectual inquiry.

FIGURES 11.16–11.20 Hitchcock's cutting is complex, encompassing, as we see in Figures 11.1 and 11.2, the shot/reverse shots of Scottie in pursuit of Madeleine/Judy. As this pursuit continues, this pattern becomes more profound, even hypnotic as Scottie falls for a ghost. A dark alley opens into a colorful florist's shop. At the museum, the cutting pattern turns into a counterpoint of gaze and its object

But our reading suggests another path. By noting the different directions the films take, and recognizing that despite their different intentions, they are very serious about how film communicates within its generic structures, we discover a common base. Then, analyzing their proximity to their cultural contexts and the ways in which, consciously or not, they address those contexts, we see that it is possible to understand both films as serious, imaginative statements that come out of commercial intent. We could argue correctly that *Vertigo* is structurally and thematically more complex and makes more demands upon the attention and the intellectual and emotional responses of the viewer than Judd Apatow's film. Ultimately, this is a difference in address, in the way the filmmakers and their films decide to talk to us, and of course the genres they choose to work in. The address and genre require a difference in response, the ways in which we choose to react to the film.

This brings us back to the cultural studies position. The imagination operates in many different ways and for many different reasons, none of them completely pure or completely corrupt. The imagination of a viewer responds in different ways to different films. I find the irreverence and the delighted give and take between the characters of *This is 40* irresistible. *Vertigo* impresses me with the extraordinary care and detail of its structure and moves me tremendously with the depth of its insight into male vulnerability. Both films are impressive in the ways they deal, subtly but pointedly, with the culture from which they emerge.

On another level, both films, fascinating as they are in their differences, clarify the ways all films tell their stories, no matter how different those stories are. But there are interesting similarities as well. Both films are concerned with gender, with the ways in which men and women interact, with obsessive, near psychotic behavior in Hitchcock's film, with comic back and forth in Apatow's. Race is a more tenuous issue in these films. With the exception of references to the Hispanic Carlotta in *Vertigo*—and she is referenced with stereotypes of the sexually active and ultimately mad handmaiden of powerful white men—the film is strictly concerned with white, middle-class people. Race in Apatow's films is played with the same lightness of touch as everything else. Asians and Indians are played for laughs and for sympathy. In other films of Apatow's, African Americans are treated unexceptionally, as randy and genitally obsessed as their white counterparts.

Vertigo was not a commercial success in its time. It was too dark and complex for contemporary 1950s audiences. Since Hitchcock depended on box office successes to maintain his independence, he followed it with *North by Northwest*, a guaranteed crowd pleaser. *This is 40* did very well, though hardly a blockbuster. *Vertigo* went on to become, years after its appearance, the most important film ever made. *This is 40* will hardly be remembered. But we are remembering it here not because it is a great film, but because, like *Vertigo*, it is a film with all the interesting, formal properties and cultural constructs that go with any film. Like any film, it invites us to look and analyze what we see.

FURTHER READING

The literature on cultural studies is quite large. Here are a few titles: Stuart Hall, ed., *Culture, Media, Language: Working Papers in Cultural Studies, 1972–79* (London: Hutchinson, 1980); Stuart Hall, *Critical Dialogues in Cultural Studies,* ed. David Morley and Kuan-Hsing Chen (London and New York: Routledge, 1996); Richard Hoggart, *On Culture and Communication* (New York: Oxford University Press, 1972); Lawrence Grossberg, Cary Nelson, Paula A. Treichler, eds., *Cultural Studies* (New York: Routledge, 1992); and John Fiske, *Television Culture* (London and New York: Routledge, 1989); Andrew Milner, Jeff Browitt, *Contemporary Cultural Theory, An Introduction*, 3rd ed. (London: Routledge, 2002). Recent books exploring the influence of the digital on the media are Henry Jenkins, *Convergence Culture: Where Old and New Media Collide* (New York and London: New York University Press, 2006) and William Merrin, *Media Studies 2.0* (New York and London: Routledge, 2014).

For a serious discussion of fans and their work, see Henry Jenkins, *Textual Poachers: Television Fans and Participatory Culture*, rev. ed. (New York and London: Routledge, 2012).

A classic work on subcultures is Dick Hebdige, *Subculture: The Meaning of Style* (London: Routledge, 1988).

A book that combines mass media and cultural studies is James W. Carey, *Communication as Culture: Essays on Media and Society*, rev. ed. (New York: Routledge, 2009).

One critic in the early 1950s attempted a somewhat neutral analysis of popular culture, although some of his work is marked by Cold War rhetoric: Robert Warshow wrote some groundbreaking analyses of the Western and gangster film genres, which we have referred to in our discussion of genres. See his book, originally published in 1962, *The Immediate Experience* (Cambridge, MA: Harvard University Press, 2001).

Another critic, Gilbert Seldes, also wrote against the grain in his book *The Seven Lively Arts,* originally published in 1924, the early, formative period of mass culture (Mineola, New York: Dover Publications, 2001).

An excellent analysis of the relationship between Benjamin's essay and film and new media is in Lev Manovich, *The Language of New Media.* A difficult but rewarding book on Benjamin and the Frankfurt school is Miriam Bratu Hansen, *Cinema and Experience: Siegfried Kracauer, Walter Benjamin, and Theodor W. Adorno* (Berkeley: University of California Press, 2012).

A sharp, concise summary of postmodernism can be found in Todd Gitlin's essay, "Postmodernism: Roots and Politics," in *Cultural Politics in Contemporary America,* ed. Ian Angus and Sut Jhally (New York: Routledge, 1989). See also Stuart Hall, ed., *Representation: Cultural Representations and Signifying Practices* (London: Sage, 2000). The classic work on the postmodern is Jean-François Leotard, *The Postmodern Condition, a Report on Knowledge*, trans. Geoff Bennington and Brian Massumi (Minneapolis: Minnesota University Press, 1984).

For a study of Hitchcock's popularity, see Robert E. Kapsis, *Hitchcock: The Making of a Reputation* (Chicago: University of Chicago Press, 1992).

For a good history of the 1950s, see James Gilbert, *Another Chance: Postwar America, 1945–1968* (Homewood, IL: Dorsey Press, 1986). On the zoot-suit riots, see Stuart Cosgrove, "The Zoot-Suit and Style Warfare," in Angela McRobbie, ed., *Zoot Suits and Second-Hand Dresses* (Boston: Unwin-Hyman, 1988), pp. 3–22. There is a large literature on the work of the House Un-American Activities Committee in Hollywood. Two excellent sources are Larry Ceplair and Steven Englund, *The Inquisition in Hollywood: Politics and the Film Community, 1930–1960* (Berkeley and Los Angeles: University of California Press, 1983); and Victor S. Navasky, *Naming Names* (New York: Hill & Wang, 2003). One of the most popular books voicing the fear of conformity in the 1950s was William Whyte's *The Organization Man,* originally published in 1956 (Philadelphia: University of Philadelphia Press, 2002).

One of the best recent studies of the changing ideas of masculinity in the 1950s, by a scholar whose work led me to the *Look* articles, is Steven Cohan, *Masked Men: Masculinity and the Movies in the Fifties* (Bloomington: Indiana University Press, 1997). Susan Jefford's *Hard Bodies: Hollywood Masculinity in the Reagan Era* (New Brunswick, NJ: Rutgers University Press, 1994) offers an interesting political take on contemporary action/adventure films. See also Peter Lehman, ed., *Masculinity: Bodies, Movies, Culture* (New York and London: Routledge, 2011).

Two books on *Vertigo* are Dan Auiler, *Vertigo: The Making of a Hitchcock Classic* (New York: St. Martin's Press Griffin, 2001) and Katalin Makkai, ed., *Vertigo* (London and New York, Routledge, 2013).

SUGGESTIONS FOR FURTHER VIEWING

A few significant Hitchcock films not mentioned in the text: *Shadow of a Doubt* (1943); *Notorious* (1946); *Strangers on a Train* (1951); *The Birds* (1963).

Other films directed by Judd Apatow: *Funny People* (2009); *Trainwreck* (2015).

A brief selection of films produced by Apatow not mentioned in the text: *Talladega Nights: The Ballad of Ricky Bobby* (Adam McKay, 2006), *Forgetting Sarah Marshall* (Nicholas Stoller, 2008), *Pineapple Express* (David Gordon Green, 2008).

NOTES

1 The "target audience" is actually quite complex, with producers and studios segmenting the audience by genre and age appropriateness. Animations are targeted at children; romantic comedies to men and women in their twenties and thirties; adaptations from novels to an older audience.
2 Information on the percentage of profits from ticket sales is from John Thorton Caldwell, *Production Culture Industrial Reflexivity and Critical Practice in Film and Television* (Durham and London: Duke University Press, 2008).
3 The quotation from Max Horkheimer and Theodor W. Adorno comes from *Dialectic of Enlightenment*, trans. John Cumming (New York: Herder & Herder, 1972), pp. 153–154; original publication, 1944.
4 The quotations from Dwight MacDonald, "Masscult and Midcult," are in *Against the American Grain* (New York: Da Capo Press, 1983), pp. 4, 37.
5 The quotations from A. O. Scott come from "The Squeeze on the Middlebrow: A Resurgence in Inequality and Its Effects on Culture," *New York Times* (August 3, 2014), AR1.
6 The Walter Benjamin quotations are from "The Work of Art in the Age of Mechanical Reproduction," in *Illuminations*, trans. Harry Zohn (New York: Schocken Books, 1968), pp. 223, 234, 236, 239. A more exact translation of the title is "The Work of Art in the Age of its Technological Reproducibility."
7 Bordwell's discussion of average shot length can be found at http://www.cinemetrics.lv/bordwell.php (accessed 17 March 2015).
8 Raymond Williams first articulated the concept of "flow" when he noticed how various television events moved together without being differentiated. See his *Television: Technology and Cultural Form* (Middletown, CT: Wesleyan University Press, 1992).
9 Information on the British Film Institute poll is at http://www.bfi.org.uk/news/50-greatest-films-all-time (accessed 17 March 2015).
10 David Parker of the Library of Congress pointed out to me the connections between Scottie's driving around and VistaVision.
11 The quotations about declining masculinity are from J. Robert Moskin, "Why Do Women Dominate Him?" and George B. Leonard, Jr., "Why Is He Afraid to Be Different?" in *The Decline of the American Male*, by the editors of *Look* (New York: Random House, 1958).

Glossary

180-degree rule From one cut to another, the camera may not cross an imaginary line drawn behind the characters.

90-degree rule The camera may never be placed 90 degrees facing the subject, but rather set off the center to give an illusion of depth.

actualités Events filmed as they were happening, events that would be happening even if the camera weren't there.

ambient sound See **room tone** and **world tone** below: the sound added to a sequence to provide aural atmosphere.

anamorphic process The camera lens "squeezes" an image onto the film. When unsqueezed by the projector lens, the ratio of the image is 1:2.35. Panavision was the most common proprietary anamorphic process.

aspect ratio The relationship of screen width to height. There are four ratios. "Standard" ratio existed from the early 1930s through the early 1950s and is 1:1.3. Two wide-screen ratios are 1:1.6 and 1:1.85. Anamorphic wide screen (CinemaScope, Panavision) is 1:2.35.

aura Critic Walter Benjamin's term for the uniqueness of a work of art which is lost when, as in film, it is mechanically reproduced.

auteur Originally French but now a universal term for the film director who realizes a personal style in his or her films.

auteur theory This analyzes film based on the idea that the director is the creative force.

automatic dialogue replacement (ADR) A method, largely digital, of dubbing in dialogue after the film is completed. See also **looping**.

avant-garde Often used to explain works of artists that are personal, experimental, and not aimed at a wide audience.

backlighting Lights behind the characters that set them off from the background.

back story Filling out the plot with a related story or action; filling in a character's background.

bandwidth This measures the amount of information or data that flows across the Internet.

Bollywood Loosely applied to the vast number of films produced yearly, mainly in Mumbai, featuring extravagant production numbers, but also serious drama.

captivity narrative One of the major dominant fictions of the United States, expressing its fear of being dominated. Articulated in film, it is realized by showing women in distress, held by vicious men, and in need of rescue by a strong hero.

CGI (computer-generated imagery) The variety of backgrounds, foregrounds, digital animations, and effects created on the computer and transferred to film.

chiaroscuro A term from art history that refers to the use of deep shadow in the **mise-en-scène**.

CinemaScope Developed in 1926, introduced by 20th Century Fox in 1953, one of the first modern anamorphic processes that squeezed a wide image onto 35-mm film, which was then unsqueezed by the projector to a ratio of 1:2.35.

cinéma vérité A version of documentary developed by the French in the late 1950s and 1960s that attempted to capture the ongoingness of everyday life without narration.

cinematographer See **director of photography**.

Cinerama A wide-screen process that originally used three cameras to capture the enormous width of the image on a curved screen, with a ratio of 1:2.65.

classical Hollywood style or **classical narrative style** The classical Hollywood or narrative style refers to a complex collection of formal and thematic elements that became basic to Hollywood filmmaking by the early 1920s. **Continuity cutting**—including **shot/reverse shot** and **over-the-shoulder** cutting—the **180-degree rule**, happy endings, psychologically motivated characters, villains getting punished, women becoming wives and mothers are all associated with the classical Hollywood style. The **continuity style** or cutting is a subset of the classical Hollywood style.

close-up The actor's face or an object fills the screen. Also, **medium close-up**, where the actor is seen from the shoulders up.

coding Conventions that telegraph a lot of information economically, as in older films where the way a coffee cup was held or a cigarette smoked told the audience much about a character. A storm or the dying embers of a fireplace might indicate sexual intercourse.

compilation film A film made by editing footage from other films.

composition The arrangement of characters and surroundings within the boundaries of the screen frame.

continuity style/continuity editing Smooth, seamless editing that links shots so that the cuts appear invisible to the viewer.

coverage Filming enough variations of a scene to allow the editor to put it together with perfect continuity.

crane An apparatus that can lift the camera into the air and is therefore responsible for a crane shot.

cross cutting Editing shots that represent different places, to give the illusion of simultaneity. Also called **parallel editing**.

cross tracking A variation of **shot/reverse shot** in which what a character in motion sees is also shown in motion. Often used by Alfred Hitchcock.

cultural studies A wide-ranging critical approach to works of imagination that examines them in light of the cultures they are part of and that create them.

culture The sum total of the intricate ways in which we relate to ourselves, our peers, our community, our country, world, and universe.

cut Another word for **edit**, indicating the cutting and splicing together of two shots.

deep focus In deep-focus cinematography, all objects from front to rear of the composition are in sharp focus.

digital colorist He or she works with the director and cinematographer to achieve the desired colors on the **digital intermediate**.

digital intermediate Film is turned into digital files for color correction and editing.

direct cut One shot follows another without any optical transition like a dissolve.

director The individual responsible for translating the script to screen. The director can be the driving imaginative force of the film. See **auteur**.

director of photography or **cinematographer** Working with a film's director, the cinematographer lights the scene, chooses the appropriate lenses and film stock, and therefore carries a large responsibility for determining the look of a film.

dissolve One shot fades out and another fades in. Usually the two occur simultaneously and we see one shot fading out as the other fades in. In this case we have lap dissolve.

docudrama A film that mixes historical truth with a fictional narrative.

documentary A film that records actual events, often creating dramatic impact through editing.

dolly An apparatus that holds the camera but can, itself, move in, out, or from side to side. A dolly-in or dolly-out refers to a movement toward or away from a figure.

dominant fiction The templates or blueprints of the stories a culture wants to hear about itself and that partake of the ideological structure of the culture. They are made concrete in the various genres of film.

edit The cutting of a piece of film or the joining together of two pieces of film.

editing The process of cutting film footage and assembling the pieces into an expressive, narrative structure.

editor The person who assembles the shots of a film into its final shape.

establishing shot Before a cutting pattern can begin, there must be a shot that establishes the whole space. Examples of establishing shots are the initial two-shot of characters in a dialogue sequence, or the image of an entire roomful of people, or of the city in which the film takes place.

eye line match Continuity editing dictates that, if a character is looking in a certain direction in one shot, she should be looking in the same direction in the following shot. This is crucial in the over-the-shoulder pattern, where the characters must seem to be looking at one another (even if both actors are not physically present at the same time when the shots are made).

fill lighting Lights that fill in the scene, creating accents, removing or adding shadow.

film noir A genre of film developed in the 1940s. Noir has a literary heritage in the hard-boiled detective fiction of Raymond Chandler and Dashiell Hammett and the novels of James M. Cain. Its cinematic lineage is German Expressionism, French poetic realism, and Welles's *Citizen Kane*. It is marked by a **mise-en-scène** of heavy shadow and narratives of weak men destroyed by predatory women.

final cut The version of the film released for distribution.

flashback When we see something a character remembers.

flat wide screen A non-anamorphic process in which the film is matted top and bottom to create the illusion of wide screen, usually 1:1.66 or 1:1.88.

flow A notion developed by the British cultural scholar Raymond Williams to define the ways in which disparate and incoherent elements, commercials, promotions, and the shows themselves move together seamlessly on television.

foley Foley design and the foley artist create the sound effects of a film. The name comes from a sound effects pioneer, Jack Foley.

frame The borders of the screen that, along with the composition of the shot, determine the limits of what we see. A single image on an actual strip of film is referred to as the frame.

Frankfurt school Short for the Frankfurt Institute for Social Research, founded in Germany in 1924, devoted in particular to the study of popular culture and its productions.

French New Wave A group of young film critics who turned to filmmaking in the late 1950s and changed the language of cinema. Among the group were François Truffaut, Jean-Luc Godard, Eric Rohmer, Claude Chabrol, and Jacques Rivette.

genre A "kind" of story or narrative, made up of character types, plot lines, and settings common to all its members. Science fiction films and Westerns are genres, for example.

German Expressionism An artistic movement in film, painting, and theater in post-World War I Germany, where the **mise-en-scène** expressed the exaggerated, agitated psychological state of the characters. Now it is used to refer to a mise-en-scène that is dark, distorted, and menacing.

green screen Characters are photographed against a green screen; the background is photographed or digitally rendered separately. The two (or more) parts are then joined digitally or photographically as the green background is dropped out to create the illusion of a complete image.

high-key lighting This creates a bright, evenly lit scene.

image track As opposed to the soundtrack, the series of images that contain the film's visual content.

intertextuality The way in which texts are interwoven or refer to each other in film, music, and the other arts. "Sampling" in rap is a kind of intertextuality.

iris shot Shrinking or expanding the frame by a dynamic, circular black mask. Mostly used in the silent period.

jump cut The result of editing out unnecessary transitions so that continuity is replaced by rapid changes in space.

key light The main overhead light that lights faces and is reflected in the eyes.

location A place filmed outside the studio—such as a city street, the desert, an actual house or apartment.

logline A very short summary of the filmscript.

long take In an average film, shots last six to nine seconds. A long take may last sixty seconds or more and contain rich narrative and visual information.

looping An older term meaning the post-dubbing of dialogue. A section of film was looped over and over again to allow the actors to synchronize their voice to the lip movements in the shot.

master shot The entire scene shot without cutting.

matte painting A detailed, photo-realistic painting of a background over which images of characters in the film are placed.

matte shot A method of shooting characters against a painted or colored—usually blue or green—backdrop. Then, other elements are added to the shot. If a blue or green screen is used, these elements replace the colored background.

mediation All of the events—visual, political, personal, conventional, cultural—that stand between ourselves and the world. We, in fact, do not know the world directly. Every perception is mediated.

medium close-up A character is shown from the shoulders up.

medium shot A character is shown from the waist up.

melodrama With comedy, this is the major genre of film, providing large arcs of emotion, often spilling into the music and **mise-en-scène**, and ending with the death of a beloved character or a closure in redemption.

mise-en-scène The use of space within the frame: the placement of actors and props, the relationship of the camera to the space in front of it, camera movement, the use of color or black and white, lighting, the size of the screen frame itself.

mismatched cut The shots on either side of the cut don't match—the movement may be out of sync, the characters may be in the wrong place, etc.

montage A style of editing that juxtaposes shots to build dramatic tension. Sergei Eisenstein used montage as the basic structure of his films.

Motion Picture Association of America (MPAA) One of the most powerful political lobbyists, it is also responsible for the various ratings—NC17, PG, R, etc.— that are intended to tell audiences what kind of sexual or violent content a film has.

moviola For many years the standard machine for editing, now largely replaced by digital editing.

music cue The short pieces of music written for specific sequences.

narrative The construction of a film's story, the way in which a story is told by the film.

neorealism Developed by Italian directors at the end of World War II, a genre that defied studio conventions by filming on the streets, using nonprofessional or semi-professional actors to define a working class ruined by the war.

one-shot A shot in which a single character is shown, often inserted into the over-the-shoulder cutting pattern.

optical printer A synchronized projector and camera that allows exposed film to be recorded on another piece of unexposed film to create a process shot.

optical soundtrack An "image" of the sound waves that, converted and amplified, reproduces the recorded sound of the film.

over-the-shoulder cutting pattern A major component of the **classical Hollywood style**. A dialogue sequence (two people talking to each other) begins with a two-shot of the participants and then proceeds to cut from over the shoulder of one speaker to over the shoulder of the other. Occasionally a shot of one of the participants talking or listening will be cut into the pattern.

pan The camera pivots on its tripod or dolly, side to side.

panned and scanned The only way to show the entire width of a wide-screen film on pre-flat screen television was to matte the top and bottom of the screen with black bars (the process is called letter-box format). Because many people believe they are seeing less of the film in this format (they are actually seeing more), television broadcasters and videotape distributors blow up the image to a square and move the focus around in that image to find what they think are the important elements.

parallel editing Two scenes occurring at different places shown one after the other, creating the illusion of simultaneity. See also **cross cutting**.

point of view Simply, the representation of what a character sees. But it also refers to the dominant "voice" of the film, the teller of the tale, similar to third-person point of view in fiction.

post-studio period The current state where many films are independent from the major studios or only codependent on them for financing and distribution.

process shot Any shot, some of whose elements are added optically or digitally after the initial shot is made.

producer The individual who administers the making of an entire film and often puts together its financing.

producer system Put in place in the early 1920s, this gave the producer control over the film from inception to release.

product placement Advertising embedded in a film.

Production Code Starting in the early 1930s, a strict set of guidelines that set out for filmmakers what could and could not be shown on screen. The code died in the early 1960s, to be replaced by the MPAA ratings.

production designer The person who conceives and elaborates the film's rooms and exteriors that help give a film its visual texture.

reaction shot A cut is made to the response or reaction of a character to what has just occurred.

rear-screen projection The background of a scene is projected on a screen from the back, while the actors play their roles in front of the screen. Actors and the projection are photographed by a camera in front of them and the screen.

release print A print made by the film distributor to send out to theaters.

reverse shot Cutting to the opposite side of the previous shot. In a dialogue scene, a reverse shot occurs when a cut is made from over the shoulder of one character to over the shoulder of the other character. If a character is seen looking at something and a cut is made to what she is looking at, that is a reverse shot.

room tone A sound effect that creates **ambient sounds** of people talking or just a low volume sound in the background of an enclosed space. See also **world tone**.

rotoscope A method in traditional or digital animation in which live action is drawn over to create an animated effect. Rotoscoping has become a major tool in live action film, as a computer traces the movement of a figure that is then animated.

scene A unit of action or a segment of a film narrative.

scopophilia Literally "love of looking."

screwball comedy A film of the 1930s in which both members of a romantic— often married— couple carry equal weight with dialogue of wit, strength, and self-possession.

second unit A small crew that is sent out to shoot locations that will be intercut with the studio footage or as part of a process shot.

sequence Sometimes used interchangeably with **scene**, it can often mean a related series of scenes and shots.

shallow focus Figures in the foreground are in focus; the background is very soft.

shot An unedited, or uncut, length of film.

shot/reverse shot Any pair of shots in which the second shot reveals what is on the other side of the previous shot. If, for example, the first shot is a character looking at something and the second shot is a hat, the hat constitutes the reverse shot and we assume that the character is looking at the hat.

silent era From the beginning of film to the late 1920s, there was no recorded sound accompanying the image. Nonetheless, films were rarely shown without sound. A piano or, in a big movie palace, an entire symphony orchestra played a score that was often created especially for a particular film.

soft focus This occurs in any shot in which elements—including the figure in close-up—are not in perfect focus.

soundtrack Either an optical or a magnetic strip along the side of the film that contains the recorded sound for the film.

Steadicam A gyroscopic mechanism that allows the camera operator to strap the camera to his body and create steady tracking shots.

stop action The camera is shut off, elements of the scene changed, and the camera restarted, creating trick effects. Stop motion refers to photographing an object one or a few frames at a time, used when creating pre-**CGI** animation.

storyboarding Sketching out the shots before production. These days called previsualization and rendered on the computer.

studio system Beginning in the early 1920s, the film studios developed a production process—with the producer at the head on any given film—and a style of shooting and editing that, despite many variations, remains to this day.

subgenre Films that use major elements of an established genre along with other conventions belong to a subgenre. The heist film is a subgenre of the gangster film, as are many road movies and even some **films noir**.

suture effect A critical theory that addresses the way the viewer is "stitched" into the fabric of a film's narrative.

take A shot made during the production of a film. A scene in a film is the result of editorial choices made from many differing takes.

Technicolor A proprietary color process that used three strips of black and white film, each one exposed to either red, or blue, or green light. These strips were then used to transfer color dye to impart a rich color to film that did not fade with age.

three-point lighting The basic lighting pattern of key light for the face, back light to separate the figure from the background, and fill light to create the appropriate shadow and bright spots in the frame.

track The camera moves on a transport mechanism like a tripod or dolly. This mechanism is put on rails so that the camera will move smoothly. A lateral track moves horizontally. The result is a **tracking shot**.

trailer An industry term for "coming attractions."

two-shot A shot composed of two people.

VistaVision Paramount's response to **CinemaScope**, a non-anamorphic wide-screen process that originates on 70-mm film moving horizontally through the camera and is then printed vertically for the 35-mm **release print**.

voice-over narration Either a character in the film or a voice not associated with a character tells some of the story and fills in some of the blanks. In the hands of some directors, notably Stanley Kubrick, the voice-over narrator is not dependable.

wide shot A shot that takes in a large amount of space, often created with a wide-angle lens.

wipe An editing device, now defunct, in which one shot is removed and a second one introduced by a diagonal line sweeping it off the screen.

world tone A sound effect of traffic and other street sounds to accompany a sequence taking place outside.

zoom Changing the focal length of lenses by moving them while the camera is stationary, creating the impression of movement from near to far or the reverse.

Index

Note: Page numbers in *italics* refer to figures.

abstract painting 20–1, 83–4
Actors Studio 138
Adaptation (2002) 4
Adorno, Theodor 300
Affleck, Ben 4
African Americans and film 7, 9, 15, 172, 173–6
Aguirre: The Wrath of God (1972) 195–7, *197*
Air Force (1943) 127–8
Akerman, Chantal 199–200
Alexander Nevsky (1938) 125, *126*
Ali: Fear Eats the Soul (1974) 278, 280, *285,* 285–6, 287, *287*, *288*, 289
Alice Doesn't Live Here Anymore (1974) 171
Alice in Wonderland (2010) *11*
Alien (1979) 242, 247–9
All is Lost (2013) 42
All That Heaven Allows (1955) 198, 278, 280–5, *281*, *282*, *287*, 288
Altman, Robert 4, 154, 156–7, *157,* 240–2
Alton, John 261–2
ambient sound 123
American popular culture 300–1
American Public Broadcasting 230
anamorphic process 63, *64*
Anderson, Paul Thomas 152, 294
anticommunism 240, 244, 316
Antonioni, Michelangelo 47, 73, 83–4, 187–9
Apatow, Judd 289, 310, 312, 317–18, 320, 323, 324, 326
Apatow stock company 313–14, *314*
Apu trilogy 43, *44*, 203
Argo (2012) 4
Arness, James 245, 246
Aronofsky, Darren 42
Arzner, Dorothy 168, *168*
Arrival of a Train at La Ciotat Station (1896) *31*, 58
Asian cinema 200–3
aura, defined 303, 304–5
Auteuil, Daniel 206, *207*
auteurism: current day 176–8, *177*; overview 178–9; theory 151–6, *153*, *154*, *155*; women auteurs 167–70; *see also* director/directing
automatic dialogue replacement (ADR) 122
Avatar (2009) 10, 307
The Awful Truth (1937) 317, *318*

Bachchan, Amitabh 203
back stories 127
Bale, Christian 177
bandwidth of web 298–9
Baron, Joanne *325*
barrenness in images 83
Barthelmess, Richard 267, *269*
Baruchel, James *141*
Bassett, Angela 171
Batman (1989) 118, 222
Batman Begins (2005) 176
Batra, Ritesh 204
Battleship Potemkin (1925) 104–6, *106*
Bazin, André 19–20, 23
Bel Geddes, Barbara 321, *322*
Belmondo, Jean-Paul 191, *192*
ben Salem, El Hedi 280, *285*
Bénichou, Maurice 207, *207*
Benjamin, Walter 302–4
Bergman, Ingmar 115, 152

Bergman, Ingrid 36, 275
Bertolucci, Bernardo 189–90
Bicycle Thieves (1948) *184,* 184–5
The Big Sleep (1946) 128, 259
The Bigamist (1953) 170
Bigelow, Kathryn 171–2, *172*
binge viewing of Netflix 26
Binoche, Juliette *145*, 206
Birdman (2014) 56
Birmingham Centre for Contemporary Cultural Studies 305–6
The Birth of a Nation (1915) 58, *62,* 113, 229
The Bitter Tears of Petra von Kant (1972) *198*
black and white films 8, 33, 66, 81, *107*, 116; in film noir 265–6; Keaton's use of *69*; Pawlikowski's use of *70*, 116; Payne's use of *83*, 116; in *Psycho* 81, *82*; realism and 265–6; Stone's use of *14*, *107*; Wenders' use of 194, 195, *196*
Blade Runner (1982) 247–9, *248*
Blow-Up (1966) *46,* 46–7
Blum–Byrnes Accords (1946) 2
Blu-ray discs 297–8
Bogart, Humphrey 36, *38*, *86*, 220, 235, 258, *262*, 271, 319
Bollywood 203–4
Bracco, Lorraine *56*
Brando, Marlon 138–9, *138*, 138–9, *189*, 189–90, 319, *319*
Breathless (1960) 191, *192*
Brecht, Bertolt 193, 286–7
The Bride of Frankenstein (1935) *74*
British documentary movement 229–30
British Film Institute 205, 310
Brokeback Mountain (2005) 276–7, *277*
Broken Blossoms (1919) 267–71, *269*
Brunelleschi, Filippo (1377–1446) 17
Burton, Tim *11,* 118, 126, 176

The Cabinet of Dr. Caligari (1920) 73–4, *74*, 81
Caché (2005) 206–7, *207*
Cagney, James *68*, *221*, 235
camera obscura in painting 18, *19*
Cameron, James 10, 42, 305
Cape Fear (1991) 75, 160
Capra, Frank 182, 213–14, *214,* 230, 313
captivity narrative 89, 240
Casablanca (1923) 36–7, *38*, *40*, 40, 41, *86*, 272, 275
celebrity fame 146
censorship 130, 216–17, 252, 258, 259, 314
Chaplin, Charlie 33–6, 113, *141*, 181–2
chiaroscuro lighting 258
cinéma vérité 231–4
CinemaScope 63, 311
cinematographer/cinematography: collaboration with 113; composition in 58; film noir and 258; overview 114–16, *116*; photographic *vs.* 23; screen actors and 136
Cinerama 62–3
Citizen Kane (1941): cinematographer for 115; deep focus 76–81, *78, 79, 80*; as film noir 257, 258; introduction 3, 8; mise-en-scène 75–6, *76*; popularity of 310; producer role in 130
Clarke, Arthur C. 9
classical Hollywood style: based on character and action 30; break from conventions 104, 108; in *Casablanca* 36–7, *38*; dominant fictions in 215; editing in 85–9, *86, 88*; foundations of 89; ideology in 99–102; narrative of 107–8; neorealism *vs.* 183; 180-degree rule 80, *96*, 96–7, *97*; unconsciousness of form and structure 50–1
classical narrative style 30
A Clockwork Orange (1971) 57, *57,* 164
close-up shots 40, 57, 61, 93–4, 237, 240
Closed Circuit (2013) *59*
closure in popular films 214
Cobb, Lee J. *144*
coding in filmmaking 102–3
Cohen, Leonard 125
Cold War 301
collaboration as creativity 113–14
color *14*, 30, 64, 66, 69–70, *69*, 71–3, *73*, *88*, *107*, 195, 265–6; Bertolucci's use of 189; Fassbinder's use of 198; Kubrick's use of 151–2, 163; Scorsese's use of 161; Sirk's use of 280–2; Wong Kar-wai's use of 202
Columbia Pictures 25
Comcast 2
comedy: musical 203; romantic 4, 120, *145*, 223, 274; screwball 258–9, 317–18, *318*; slapstick 182; structure of 323–4
Communism 263, 301, 304, 316
composers 123–6, *126*
composition: in early cinema 58; experimental 65–6; in filmmaking 57–62; framing considerations 37, 57, 61–5; overview 57, 85; two-dimensional compositional space 81–4, *82, 83*
computer-generated imagery (CGI) 44–5, 119–20, *121*, 289
The Conformist (1977) 189
continuity styles: cinéma vérité and 231; cutting 87, 89–90, 100–1; editing 117; neorealism *vs.* 183
conventional cutting 103–4
Coppola, Francis Ford 220–1
copyright concerns 1–2, 298
corporate filmmaking 35–6
Costner, Kevin *14*
Cotton, Joseph 76, *76*, *80*
coverage, of scene 101
crane up 55
creativity and collaboration 113–14
Crisp, Donald 268, *269*
cross cutting 89, 102, 267
Cuarón, Alfonso 44
culture and film: American popular culture 300–1; aura of state intervention 303, 304–5; formal structures in 324–5, *325*; Frankfurt school 299–300;

in international cinema 208–9; intertextuality and postmodernism 308–9; introduction 6–7; judgement and values 307–8; mass media, complexities of 301–2; mechanical reproduction age 302–4; media culture 295–8; modernity, modernism, the postmodern 323–4; narrative approaches/formal structures 321–3; in new millennium 317–18; new web of 298–9; overview 293–4; reception and negotiation 306–7; studies on 299; subcultures 295; technological impact on 310–12; as text 294–5; theories of 299; the vulnerable male *319*, 319–21
cutting techniques: continuity cutting 87, 89–90, 100–1; conventional cutting 103–4; cross cutting 89, 102, 267; direct cut 86; final cut 113, 130, 136, 149; by Griffith 90–2, *91*; jump cut 191, *192*
cycloramas 23

Dance, Girl, Dance (1940) 168, *168*
Daniels, William H. 115
Dardenne, Jean-Pierre and Luc 205
Dark City (1998) 248–9
The Dark Knight (2008) *66*, 176, *177*
Dash, Julie 174–6, *175*
Dassin, Jules 186
Daughters of the Dust (1991) 174–5, *175*
Davis, Bette 271, *273*
The Day the Earth Stood Still (1951) *244*, 244–5
De Niro, Robert *44*, 95, *112*, 158–9, *159*, 160, 162
Dean, James 138,*138*
Death of a Salesman (1949) 231
deep focus: as compositional imperative 75; in film noir 258; long take in 76–81, *78, 79, 80*
Delsarte, François 136–7, *137*
Dench, Judi *144*
Depp, Johnny 5
Despicable Me (2010) 120
The Devil Wears Prada (2006) *140*
Di Sica, Vittorio *184*, 184–5, 186
Dickson, William K.L. 24, 30, 32, 113, 122
Dietrich, Marlene *68*
digital cinematography 312
digital colorists 114, 115
digital intermediate 10, 73, 116
digital mise-en-scène 114
direct cut 86
director/directing: African American directors 173–6; auteur theory 151–6, *153, 154, 155*; auteurism today 176–8, *177*; defined 178–9; European origins of 150–1; overview 149; producer as 149–50; screen actors and 136; women auteurs 167–70; women filmmakers, today 171–2; *see also* auteurism
director of photography (DP) 10, 61, 67, 73, 114, 167, 208, 265
dissolve shot 86, *86*
dissolving shot 37
Django Unchained (2012) 9, *116*, *140*
docudrama 32
documentary films: British documentary movement 229–30; cinéma vérité 231–4; early masters of 224–9; genres of 234; history of 30; introduction 8; neorealists and 183; newsreels and television 223–4; overview 223; during World War II 230
Dogme 95 198
La Dolce Vita (1960) 188
dollying 89
dominant fiction 89, 214–15, 217, 219, 220, 223, 235, 236, 240, 250, 260, 270, 321, 323
D'Onofrio, Vincent *145*
The Double (2013) *145*
Double Indemnity (1944) 259–61, *260*
Dullea, Kier *164*, *250*
Dunne, Irene *318*
DVDs 297–8
Eastman Kodak 70
economics of image 32–3
Edison, Thomas Alva 24, 25, 30–2, *31*
editor/editing: in classical Hollywood style 85–9, *86, 88*; continuity styles in 117; in filmmaking 85–9, *86, 88*; mise-en-scène and 117; montage in 104–7, *106*, *107*; parallel editing 89; in *Psycho 165*, 165–6; screen actors and 136; of shots 45–7, 114; storytelling by 116–17
8 1/2 (1963) 188, *188*
Eisenberg, Jesse *145*
Eisenstein, Sergei: Eisensteinian montage 104–7, *106*, *107*, 182; influence of 181–2; state intervention against 304; working with composers 125, *126*
elegiac films 242
elements of a shot *40*, 40–3
Elephant (2003) 85
Eliot, T.S. 156
L'enfant (2005) 205
entertainment and invisibility 39
European cinema 182–200, 205–7; *see also specific countries*
European origins of the auteur 150–1
experimental cinema 4
experimental composition 65–6
Eyes Wide Shut (1999) 72, *72*, 142–3, *143*

fabricating the image 39–45, *40, 41, 42, 45*
Fahrenheit 9/11 (2004) 232
Fairbanks, Douglas 35, 113
The Fall of the Romanov Dynasty (1927) *225*
Far From Heaven (2002) 198, 278, *279*, 280–4, *288*
Fassbinder, Rainer Werner 152, 197–8, *198*, 278, 285–9
Faulkner, William 127–8
The Fault in Our Stars (2014) 276
Fellini, Federico 187–9, *187*, *188*
feminist movement 274

Fiennes, Ralph 171
film/filmmaking: as artificial 3; coding in 102–3; color 69–73; composition 57–62; continuity cutting 87, 89–90; culture of 3–4; deep focus 76–81, *78*, *79*, *80*; editing 85–9, *86*, *88*; experimental composition 65–6; framing composition 37, 57, 61–5; gender in 102, 283–9; history of 4, 8; image importance 29; invention of film 24–6; lighting 67–8, *68*; long take 53–7; mise-en-scène 33–4, 66; montage in editing 104–7, *106*, *107*; 180-degree rule 80, *96*, 96–7, *97*; point of view shot 92, 95; shot/reverse shot 48, 92–5, *94*, 97–9, *98*; sight lines 95–6; two-dimensional compositional space 81–4, *82*, *83*; *see also* mise-en-scène; story structure of film; storytelling in film
film noir: climax of 262–5; darkness as theme in 80–1, 161; expressionist roots 65, 258; hard-boiled fiction 258–61; overview 257–8; rebirth 265–6
final cut 113, 130, 136, 149
Fincher, David 72, 152, 294
Fitzgerald, F. Scott 127
Flaherty, Robert 225–6, *226*
Flaherty Film Seminar 225
flashback 86, *86*, 167, 170, 175, 260, 272
"flat" wide screen 63
Flight (2012) 276
The Fog of War: Eleven Lessons from the Life of Robert S. McNamara (2003) *233*, 234
foley artist/design 123
Fonda, Henry 263
Forbidden Planet (1956) 245–7, *247*
Ford, Harrison 247
Ford, John 152–4, *154*, 237–40
Fort Apache (1948) 238, *238*
The 400 Blows (1959) 191, *191*
frame: composition of 37, 57, 61–5; freeze frame 162, 191, *191*; loss of standards 64–5; two-shot framing 93; wide screen 62–4, *66*
Franco, James *141*
Frankfurt school 299–300, 303, 325
freeze frame 162, 191, *191*
French New Wave 2, 43, 150–1, 190–3
Full Metal Jacket (1987) *145*, 163, 165
Funny Games (1997/2007) 205–6

Garbo, Greta *65*, 115
Gavin, John *98*
the gaze 17–18, 37, 48, *49*, *79*, 92, 95, 97, *98*, 135, 136, 137, 177, *177*, 207, 215, *239*; acting and 142–3, *143–5* ; gender and 102, 168, *168*, 171, 199–200; in Hitchcock 165, 313, *326*; in melodrama 271, *273*, 285–6, 287, *287*, *288*
gender in filmmaking 102, 168, 170, 218, 235, 236, 316, 319; in film noir 257, 262, 283–9; in *Broken Blossoms* 267, *269*, 271 in *Short Cuts* 156–7; in *Vertigo* 321
The General (1926) 141
genre films: defined 215, 217; of documentary films 234; horror films 6, 7, 75, 242–3, 305; narrative economy and 222–3; origins of 218–19; patterns in films 220–2, *221*; post-apocalyptic world and zombies 250–2; resilience of 289–90; *see also* comedy; film noir; science fiction; Westerns
German Expressionism: directing and 161; film noir and 65, 258; international cinema and 181; mise-en-scène in 73–5, *74*
Gimme Shelter (1970) 231, *232*
The Girl and Her Trust (1910) *143*
Gish, Lillian 268, *269*
Godard, Jean-Luc: documentaries and 30–1; film noir and 257; image of the world 34; influences on 286; overview 191–3, *193*
Godfather films *138*, 220–1, *221*
The Gold Rush (1925) *141*
Goldwyn, Samuel 126
Good Will Hunting (1997) 85
Goodfellas (1990) *56*, 56–7, 87, *88*, 161–3, 221
Grand Hotel (1932) *65*
The Grandmaster (2013) *202*, 202–3
Grant, Cary *94*, *318*
Gravity (2013) 44, *45*
The Great Gatsby (1974, 2013) *119*
The Great Train Robbery (1903) 87–9, *88*
green screen 10, 42, 44
Grierson, John 229–30
Griffith, D.W.: cutting techniques 90, *91*; economics of filmmaking 113; experimental undertakings of 50; impact of 229; melodrama and 267–71, *269*; narrative strands in 104; overview 58–61, *60*; screenwriters 136; *see also* classical Hollywood style
The Group Theater 138
Guardians of the Galaxy (2014) *42*, 42, 120, *121*
Guy-Blaché, Alice 167–8
Gyllenhaal, Jake 276

Haneke, Michael 152, 205–7, *207*
Hanks, Tom *144*
happiness in melodrama 289
hard-boiled fiction 258–61
Harlow, Jean *68*
Harrelson, Woody 15, *144*
Hauer, Rutger 248
Haynes, Todd *279*, 279–80, 286
Hays, Will 113
Haysbert, Dennis 280, *288*
Heckerling, Amy 171
Helmore, Tom *166*
Henreid, Paul 272, *273*, 275
Hepburn, Katharine 168
Herrmann, Bernard 124, 324
Herzog, Werner 195–7, *197*
Heston, Charlton 55, *55*, 265
high angle shot 80

high-key lighting 101
Hill, Jonah *141*
hip-hop music 7, 294
Hitchcock, Alfred: cultural analysis of 305, 315–16; as director *48,* 71, *71,*108, 115, 152, 162, *165,* 165–7, *166*, 263, 268, 309–13; documentaries and 230; filming without cutting 55; the gaze 142, *143, 145*; genre in film 252; high angle shot 80, 152 ; mise-en-scène in 81, *82,* 311–12; music in films 48, 124; opposition to widescreen 63; power of the image 187; shot/reverse shot *94*, 97–9, *98*, 151, 159–60, *311*, 324–5, *326*; sexuality in films 321–3, *322;* television fame 310–11; two-dimensional compositional space *82*; use of color 70, 72
The Hitch-Hiker (1953) *169*, 169–70
Hoffman, Philip Seymour *142*
Holt, Tim 54, *54*
homosexuality in films 276–7, *277*, 283–9
Hong Kong filmmaking *202*, 202–3
Hopkins, Anthony *107*
horror films 6, 7, 75, 242–3, 305
House Un-American Activities Committee (HUAC) 186, 243, 263, 301
Houseman, John 130
How the West Was Won (1962) 63
Hudson, Rock 284
Hunger Games series *141*, 218, *218*
The Hurt Locker (2008) 172, *172*, 317
Huston, John 36
Hyams, Peter 10

I Am a Fugitive from a Chain Gang (1932) *68*
Ida (2013) *70*
ideology in film 7, 99–102
image/images: barrenness in 83, *83*; bits and pieces of image 45–7; economics of 32–3; editing track 122; etymology of 13; evolution of 29; fabricating the image 39–45, *40*, *41*, *42*, *45*; manipulation of 21–2; moving images 23–6, *25*; to narrative 29–32, *31*; objectivity of 15–16, *16*; overview 9–10, *10*; photographic *vs.* cinematic 23; photography and 19–21; power of 187–90; reality as image 22–3; tricking the eye 17–19, *18*, *19*; truth of 10–15, *11*, *12*, *14*; urge to represent reality 17
In a Lonely Place (1950) 262, *262*
In the Mood for Love (2000) 202
Iñárritu, Alejandro González 56, 104
Inception (2010) 178
Indiana Jones films 222
Inglourious Basterds (2009) 9, *10*
Insomnia (2002) 176
international cinema: Asia 200–3; Bollywood 203–4; early influences 181–2; in Europe 205–7; film culture 208–9; French New Wave 190–3; Italian cinema after neorealism 187–90; New German Cinema 194–8; overview 181; women filmmakers 199–200; *see also* neorealism; *specific countries*
intertextuality in culture and film 297, 308–9
The Interview (2014) 2
Intolerance (1916) 58, 104, 113
Italian cinema 43, 187–90
It's a Wonderful Life (1946) 213–15, *214*, 313
Ivanir, Mark *142*

Jackson, Samuel L. 103, *140*
Jagger, Mick 231, *232*
Japanese cinema 200–2, *201*
Jaws (1975) 48, *49*, 50, *50*, 101, 126
The Jazz Singer (1927) 36, 122
Jeanne Dielman, 23 Quai du Commerce, 1080 Bruxelles (1975) 199–200, *200*
JFK (1991) 13–14, *14*, 16
Jha, Prakash 203
Jonze, Spike 4
jump cut 191, *192*

Karloff, Boris 242
Kazan, Elia 138
Keaton, Buster 33–6, *34*, *69*, *141*
Keener, Catherine *142*
The Kid with a Bike (2011) 205
Kidman, Nicole 142–3, *143*
Kim Jong-un 2
Kinetoscope 24, 58
King, Rodney 15–16
Kings of the Road (1976) 194, *195*
Kinski, Klaus 196, *197*
The Kiss (1896) *31*
Kiss Me Deadly (1955) *263*, 263–4
Koepp, David 129
Kubrick, Stanley: cutting techniques 92, *92*; as director 57, 163–5, *164*; image and reality 9–10; music for films 125; 180-degree rule *97*; photographic effects by 120; three-strip process 63; tracking shots 108; two-dimensional compositional space 81, *83*; use of color 72, *72*
Kurosawa, Akira 200

Lang, Fritz 74, 243
Langlois, Henri 257
The Last Days on Mars (2013) 205
Last Tango in Paris (1972) 189–90, *189*
The Last Temptation of Christ (1988) 160–1
Lawrence, Jennifer 218, *218*
A Late Quartet (2012) *142*
layered shots 75
Léaud, Jean-Pierre 191, *191*
Ledger, Heath *66*, 176, 276, *277*
Lee, Ryan 314, *314*
Lee, Spike 173–4, *173*
Leigh, Janet 55, *55*, 97, 265
Let There Be Light (1946) 230
Leung, Tony 202
Lewis, Juliette 15
lighting: chiaroscuro lighting 258; by cinematographers *116*; darkness as theme in film noir 80–1, 161; in filmmaking 67–8, *68*; high-key lighting 101; light and shadow effects 203
Liotta, Ray *56*, 161

Little Big Man (1970) 240–2
Little Caesar (1931) *221*
Livingston, Margaret *41*
logline 127
The Lone Ranger (2013) 5, 128
The Lonedale Operator (1911) 90, *91*
long take/shot 53–7, 76–81, *78, 79, 80*
looping technique 122
The Lord of the Rings Trilogy (2001, 2002, 2003) 44
Lorentz, Pare 226–7, *227*
Lorrain, Claude 18
Lucas, George 229, *229*
Lumière, Auguste and Louis 30, *31*, 34, 76
The Lunchbox (2013) *145*, 204
Lupino, Ida *169*, 169–70

McBride, Danny *141*
McCabe and Mrs. Miller (1971) *155*, 240–2
McCarthy, Joseph 301
McCarthy, Melissa 313–14, *325*
MacDonald, Dwight 301–2, 325
McDowell, Malcolm *57*
MacMurray, Fred 259, *260*
Magnani, Anna *185*
The Magnificent Ambersons (1942) 54, *54*, 56, 130
Magritte, René 11, *12*
The Maltese Falcon (1941) 36, 259
Man with a Movie Camera (1929) *225*
Mankiewicz, Joseph 282
Mann, Anthony *261*, 261–2
Mann, Leslie 313–14, *314*
Marey, Etienne-Jules 24, 30
Marshall, Penny 171
Masina, Giulietta 187, *187*
master shot 101, *325*
Maysles, David and Albert 231–2
Mean Streets (1973) *41*
media culture 295–8
mediation 11–13, 19, 22, 31, 312
Méliès, Georges 30, 31, *31*
melodrama: in contemporary film 276–7; conventions 278; culture of 296; driving force 280–2; emotions generated by 219; examples of 267–75; the gaze 287, *287, 288*; gender in films 283–9; happiness in 289; overview 266–7; race in films 282–3; structure of 323–4
Memento (2000) 103, 176
The Method 137–9, *138*
Metropolis (1927) 243, *248*
MGM 25, 67
mid-story plot 127
Miles, Vera 97, *98*
Miller, Arthur 231
Mira, Brigitte 280, *285*
mise-en-scène: Ackerman and 200; defined 33–4, 66; color and 69–73, 114; digital *42*, 305; editing and 117; expression of image in 190; Fassbinder and Sirk and 197–8, 278, 280; film noir 258, 262; German Expressionism 73–5, *74*; Hitchcock and 81, 165–7, *166*; 311–12; international cinema 181, 208; Kubrick and 164; light and shadow in 203; melodrama 268, 271, 275, 280; music and 124; narrative and 101, 183; neorealism and 185; Nolan and 178; Ozu and 201–2; production designer 118; science fiction and horror 75, 305; Scorsese and 160, 161; screen acting and 135-9; sound and 123, *264*, 265; Welles and 75–6, *76*
Modern Times (1936) 34
modernism in culture and film 20, 321, 323–4
modernity in culture and film 20, 249, 321, 323–4
Modine, Matthew *157*
Monroe, Marilyn 139, *140*
montage in editing 104–7, *106, 107*
Montgomery, Robert 95
Moore, Julianne *279*, 280
Moore, Michael 232–3
Moorehead, Agnes 54, *54*, 77
Morris, Errol *233*, 233–4
Moscow Art Theater 138
Motion Picture Association of America (MPAA) 113, 129
moving images 23–6, *25*
Müller, Robby 194
Muni, Paul 67, *68*
Murder, My Sweet (1944) 259–61, *260*
Murnau, F.W. 41, 74, *75*
music in films 7, 48, 124–6, 203, 294; *see also* soundtrack
musical comedy 203
The Musketeers of Pig Alley (1912) *60*, 61
Muybridge, Eadweard 24, *25*, 30

Nanook of the North (1922) 225, *226*
narration: story structure of 48–50; voice-over narration 161, 164, 231, 259, 260; in World War II films 230
narrative: classical narrative style 30; constraints 215–16; defined 48, 87; from still image to 29–32; in neorealism 183
National Broadcasting Company (NBC) 2, 131
Native American stereotypes 241
Natural Born Killers (1994) 15–16, *16*
Nebraska (2013) 81, *83*, 83–4
neorealism 182–90
Netflix 26
New German Cinema 194–8
Nicholson, Jack 189, 252
90-degree rule 80
Nixon (1995) 107, *107*
No Way Out (1950) 282
Noah (2014) 42
Nolan, Christopher 103, 176–8, *177*, 266
Nolte, Nick 160
North by Northwest (1959) *94*
Novak, Kim 71, *71*, 142–3, *143*, *311*
Now, Voyager (1942) 271–5, *273*
Nykvist, Sven 115

objectivity of image 15–16, *16*
O'Brien, Edmond 170
Office of War Information 230
O'Hara, Maureen *168*

Oldman, Gary 177, *177*
On the Waterfront (1952) *138*
180-degree rule 80, *96*, 96–7, *97*
optical printer 86
optical soundtrack 122
Out of the Furnace (2013) *144*
over-the-shoulder shot 93, *94*, 193
Owen, Clive *145*
Ozu, Yasujiro 200–2, *201*

pan (panning of camera) 37, 64
Panavision 63, 312
Panic Room (2002) 129
parallel editing 89
Paramount Pictures 25, 36, 63, 106, 118, 311
Paris, Texas (1984) 195
Paris Cinémathèque 257
Payne, Alexander 81, *83*, 83–4
Peckinpah, Sam 240–2
Penn, Arthur 240–2
performance methods 135–9, *137*, *138*
Perkins, Anthony 97, *145*, *165*
Perry, Tyler 174
perspective in early painting 17–18, *18*
Pesci, Joe *88*, 163
Philomena (2013) *144*
photography and reality 19–21, 23
Pickford, Mary 35, 113
Pidgeon, Walter *247*
piracy issues 1–2
The Player (1992) 4
plot: of avant-garde film 21; development of 206; film narrative and 280, 323; introduction 1–3; mid-story plot 127; mystery revealed in 166; structure of film 48–50; subplot 314; visual form *vs.* 191
The Plow that Broke the Plains (1936) 227, *227*
point-of-view shot 92–3, 101, 108, 159, 249, 268
popular films: censorship 216–17; closure in 214; documentary films 223–9; dominant fictions 214–15; generic origins of films 218–19; generic patterns in films 220–2, *221*; genre, defined 215, 217; narrative constraints 215–16; overview 213–14; subgenres 217–18
post-apocalyptic world and zombies 250–2
postmodernism in culture and film 308–9, 323–4
post-studio period 115
Powell, Dick 259, *260*
"primitive" cinema 58
process shot 43
producer: as director 149–50; influence on filmmaking 101, 117; introduction 4; prime male audience and 294; role of 115, 129–31; screen actors and 136
producer system 35, 129–30, 149
product placement 308
Production Code 113, 216, 274
production designer 116–19, *119*, 208, 258
Psycho (1960): acting in *145*; composition and editing sequence *165*, 165–6; cultural analysis of 305; overview 81, *82*, 252; shot/reverse shot 97–9, *98*
The Public Enemy (1931) *68*
Pulp Fiction (1994) 103, *263*

Quaid, Dennis *279*, 280, 284
Quinn, Anthony 187

race in films 282–3
Radio Corporation of America (RCA) 2
Raging Bull (1980) 158–9, *159*, 161
The Railway Man (2013) *64*
Rains, Claude 37, *38*, 272, 275
rap music 7
Ray, Man 21
Ray, Nicholas 138, 194
Ray, Satyajit 203
rear-screen projection 42, 43–4
Rear Window (1954) 313
Rebel Without a Cause (1955) 138, *138*
Red Desert (1964) 73, *73*
Red Hook Summer (2012) 173–4, *173*
Rennie, Michael 244, *244*
Renoir, Jean 152, 182
Riefenstahl, Leni 228, 229
RKO Pictures 25, 129–30
Robinson, Craig *141*
Rogen, Seth *141*
romantic comedy 4, 120, *145*, 223, 274
Rome, Open City (1945) *185*, 185–6
room tone 123
Rope (1948) 55–6
Rossellini, Roberto *185*, 185–6
rotoscoping 44, 120
Rudd, Paul 313–14, *318*
runaway productions 114
Russian Ark (2002) 56
Russian Revolution 304

Saint, Eva Marie *94*
Salesman (1969) 231
Sarris, Andrew 151–6, *153*, *154*, *155*
Satyagraha (2013) 203–4, *204*
Saving Mr. Banks (2013) *144*
Scarlet Street (1944) 259–61, *260*, 263
Schenck, Joseph 35
science fiction: conventions of 192; introduction 4–6, 9–10; noir detective genre inside 191; origins of 32; overview 30, 242–3; production decisions over 130; space travel in 119; special effects in 43
scopophilia 13
Scorsese, Martin: as director 87, 157–63, *159*, 171; faked depth of field 75; film noir and 266; film processing 70; genre of films 221; long take by 56; music for films 125; point-of-view shots 95
Scott, Ridley 242, 247, *248*
Scream (1996) *144*
screen acting: celebrity and 146; cultures of 139–42, *140–2*; the gaze and gesture in 142–3, *143*, *144–5*; The Method 137–9, *138*; overview 135; performance methods 135

Screen Writers Guild (SWG) 128
screenwriters 114, 126–9, 208, 216
screwball comedies 258–9, 317–18, *318*
The Searchers (1956) 154, *239*, 239–40
Seberg, Jean *192*
Segel, Jason 313–14
sequence shot 46
Seven (1995) 72, *72*
Seven Chances (1925) *69*
The Seven Year Itch (1955) *140*
sexuality in film 314
Seyrig, Delphine 199, *200*
shallow focus 65, *65*
Shanghai Express (1932) *68*
Shankar, Ravi 203
Sherlock, Jr. (1924) 35
The Shining (1980) *97*, 251–2, *269*
Short Cuts (1993) 156–7, *157*
shot/shots: bits and pieces of image 45–7; in building blocks of film 53; close-up shots 40, 57, 61, 93–4, 237, 240; defined 40, 85, 87; dissolve shot 86, *86*; editing of 114; Eisensteinian montage 104–7, *106*, *107*; elements of *40*, 40–3; forced perspective of 74; fragmentation of sequence 101; high angle shot 80; in history of filmmaking 30, 31; layering of 75; long take/shot 53–7, 76–81, *78*, *79*, *80*; manipulating components of 35, 50; master shot 101, *325*; over-the-shoulder shot 93, *94*, 193; point-of-view shot 90–3, 101, 108, 159, 249, 268; process shot 43; sequence in 46; sketching on storyboards 40; tracking shot 37, 161, 162; trick shots 30–1, *31*, 34; wide shot *91*, 93, 115, 240; zoom shot 48, *50*, 97, 154, 156, 162; *see also* composition
shot/reverse shot 108; Hitchcock and 151–2, 160, *311*; imaginative use of 159–60, 324, *326*; overview 92–5, *94*; in *Psycho* 97–9, *98*; tension from 48; variation of 151–2; in *Vertigo* 324, 326
"show runner" 208
Shub, Esther 224, *225*
sight lines 95–6
silent era films 30, 181–2
Sirk, Douglas 197–8, 278–84
slapstick comedy 182
soft focus 57, 65, *65*, *68*, 324
Sokurov, Alexander 56
Sony Pictures 2
sound designers 122–3, *123*
soundtrack 37, 57, 61, 172, 174, 188
special effects and CGI 119–20, *121*
Spheeris, Penelope 171
Spielberg, Steven 48, 101, 126, 162, 250
Stagecoach (1939) 237–8, *238*
standards, loss of 64–5
Stanford, Leland 24
Stanislavski, Konstantin 138
Stanton, Harry Dean 195
Stanwyck, Barbara 259, *260*
Star Wars (1977) 229, *229*
The State of Things (1982) 194–5, *196*
Steamboat Bill, Jr. (1928) 33–4, *34*
stereotypes in films: by American filmmakers 150; character changes in 222; cultural stereotypes 272, 295; foreigners 225; gender-specific stereotypes 102, 257, 319, 327; of heroism 216; of human behavior 215; introduction 5; Mammy stereotype 174; melodrama 266; 1950s stereotype 170; Westerns 235, 236, 237, 241
Stewart, James 71, *166*, 213, *214*, *311*, 312–13
Stone, Oliver 14, *14*, 15, 107, *107*, 152, 182
stop action photography 32, 119
story structure of film: bits and pieces of image 45–7; convention and consciousness 50–1; corporate filmmaking 35–6; development of 33–5; economics of image 32–3; entertainment and invisibility 39; evolution of image 29; fabricating the image 39–45, *40*, *41*, *42*, *45*; image to narrative 29–32, *31*; invisible form of 47–8; story, plot, and narration 48–50
storyboarding 40, 115
storytelling in film: cinematographer 114–16, *116*; collaboration as creativity 113–14; composers 123–6, *126*; craftspeople in 114; editor 116–17; overview 111–12; producer, role in 129–31; production designer 117–19, *119*; screenwriters 126–9; sound designers 122–3, *123*; special effects and CGI 119–20, *121*
La Strada (1954) 187, *187*
Strange Days (1995) 171–2
Strangers on a Train (1951) 160
Strasberg, Lee 138
Stravinsky, Igor 126
streaming movies 26
Streep, Meryl *140*
Stroheim, Erich von 136
studio system 33
subcultures in film 295
subgenres 217–18, 223
Sublime, defined 22
subplot 314
Sunrise (1927) 41, *41*, *75*
suture effect 92, 270

Talbott, Gloria *281*
Tarantino, Quentin 9, *10*, 103, 157
Tarr, Bela 85
Taxi Driver (1976) 95, 112, *112*, 159–60, 266
Technicolor *69*, 69–70, 265
The Terminator (1984) 305
Terms of Endearment (1983) 274
Thalberg, Irving 129
The Thing from Another World (1951) 245, *246*
This is the End (2013) *141*
This is 40 (2012): cultural criticism of 309–10; formal structure 323–4, *324*, 327; overview *314*, 314–18, *318*

Tim's Vermeer (2013) 19
Time Warner 2, 131
Titanic (1997) 42, 307
T-Men (1947) *261*
Tokyo Story (1953) 201, *201*
Toland, Gregg 258
Too Wise Wives (1921) 167–8
Touch of Evil (1958) 55, *55*, *153*, *264*, 264–5
tracking shot 37, 161, 162
Travolta, John 103
The Treachery of Images (Magritte) 11, *12*
trick shots 30–1, *31*, 34
tricking the eye 17–19, *18*, *19*
A Trip to the Moon (1902) *31*
Triumph of the Will (1935) *228*, 228–9
Truffaut, François 191, *191*, 257
Trumbull, Douglas 120
truth of image 10–15, *11*, *12*, *14*
12 Angry Men (1957) *144*
Two Days, One Night (2014) 205
two-dimensional compositional space 81–4, *82*, *83*
two-shot framing 93
2001: A Space Odyssey (1968): cutting techniques in 92, *92*; influences on 246; introduction 3, 9–10; irony in 164, *164*; music for 125; overview 249–50, *250*; shooting techniques in 63

The Unchanging Sea (1910) 58, *60*
United Artists 35, 113
Universal Pictures 2, 25, 131, 242
Universal Studios 75, 197

Vermeer, Jan (1632–1675) 19
Vertigo (1958): cultural criticism applied to 309–11, 314; cultural milieu of 315–18, 320; formal structure 321–6, *322*, 323, 324, *326*; mise-en-scène in *166*, 166–7, *311*; overview 71, *71*; screen acting in 142, *143*; shots used in 48
Vertov, Dziga 224, *225*, 304
Vietnam War 4–5
VistaVision 63, 311
Vogler, Rüdiger 194, *195*
voice-over narration 161, 164, 231, 259
Vorkapich, Slavko 182
voyeurism 13, 313
the vulnerable male *319*, 319–21

Walken, Christopher *142*
War of the Worlds (1898) 243
Warner Bros. 25, 36, 67
Washington, Denzel 276
Wayne, John 139, 237, 238, *238*, 239, *239*
Weber, Lois 167–8
Weekend (1967) 193, *193*
Welles, Orson: as actor *80*, *153*; collaboration with cinematographer 115; as director 152, *153*, 258, 264; long take by *54*, 54–5, *55*, 56; mise-en-scène 75–6, *76*; power of the image 187; producer role and 129–30; tracking shots 108
Wells, H.G. 243
Wenders, Wim 152, 194–5, *196*
Westerns: after 1950s 240–2; classical nature of 236–7; gender/racial bias in 236; introduction 4–5; landscape in 235–6; overview 235
White Heat (1949) *221*
wide screen 62–4, *66*
wide shot *91*, 93, 115, 240
The Wild Bunch (1969) 240–2, *241*
The Wild One (1953) *319*
Williams, John 126
wipe device 86
Wollen, Peter 154–5
women auteurs 167–70
women filmmakers 171–2, 199–200
women screenwriters 127
Wong Kar-wai *202*, 202–3
Words and Pictures (2013) *145*
The World of Apu (1959) *44*
world tone 123
World War II 2, 182, 230, 297
World War Z (2013) 251, *251*
World Wide Web 298
The Wrong Man (1956) 263
Wyman, Jane *281*

Zero Dark Thirty (2012) 172
Zischler, Hanns 194, *195*
zoom shot 48, *50*, 97, 154, 156, 162
Zoopraxiscope 23, *25*